GUNBOAT JUSTICE

British and American Courts in China and Japan
(1842 to 1943)

Volume I
White Man, White Law, White Gun (1842-1900)

Douglas Clark

Gunboat Justice

By Douglas Clark

Volume 1 - ISBN-13: 978-988-82730-8-9
Volume 2 - ISBN-13: 978-988-82730-9-6
Volume 3 - ISBN-13: 978-988-82731-9-5

This book has been reset in 10pt Book Antiqua. Spellings and punctuations are left as in the original edition.

HISTORY / Asia / General

EB054

Published by Earnshaw Books Ltd. (Hong Kong)

In memory of my maternal grandfather

The Honourable Mr Justice Russell Skerman

Supreme Court of Queensland

Foreign Office Map Of The Main

MAP Nº 8.

PARTS OF

SIA & THE PACIFIC

Scale of English Miles.

Treaty Ports In East Asia, 1925

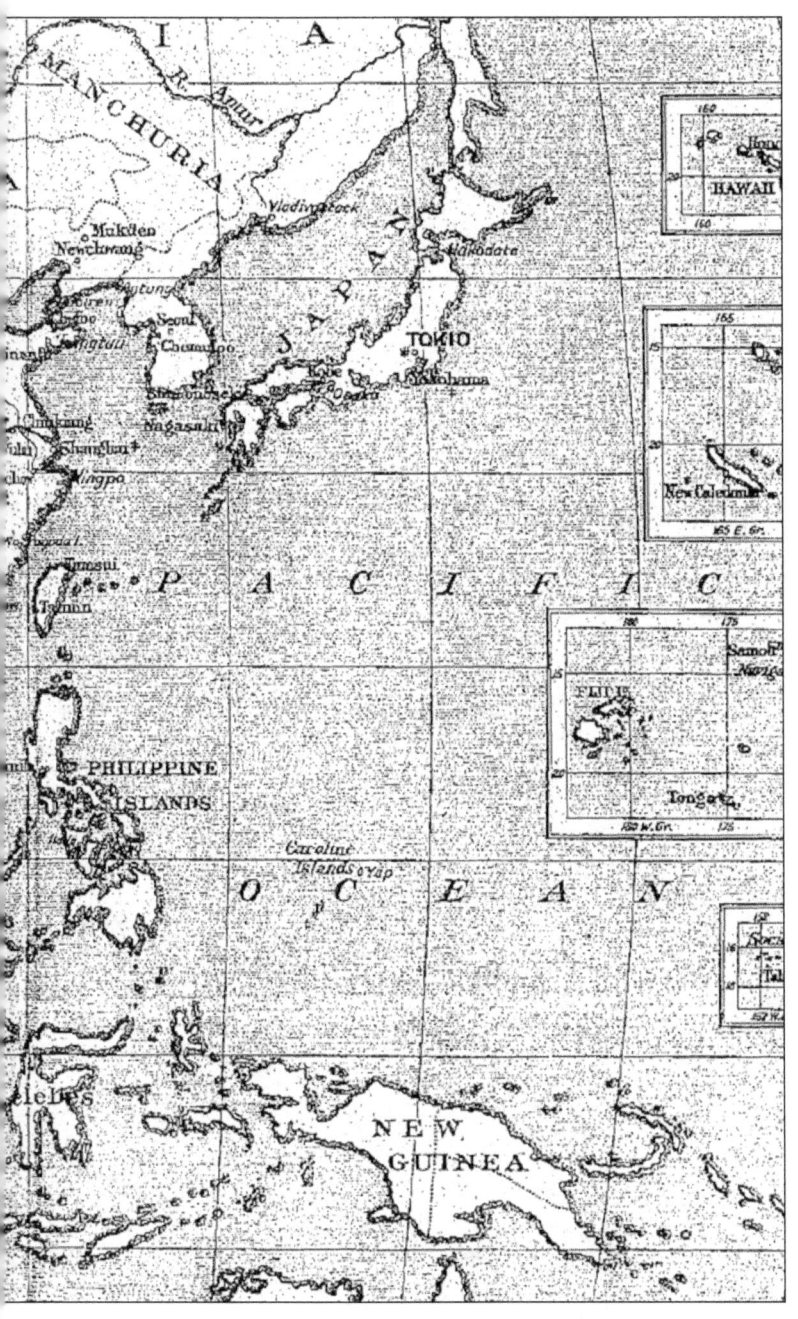

Contents

Volume I White Man, White Law, White Gun (1842-1900)

AUTHOR'S NOTES	1
Foreword	3

Introduction – Extraterritoriality: An Extraordinary System   7

Part One: The Beginning (1842 to 1865)   19
     Chapter 1 – White Man, White Law, White Gun   21
     Chapter 2 – Courting the Law: Consuls as Judges   39

Part Two: Establishing British Justice (1865 to 1878)   49
     Chapter 3 – The Founder: Sir Edmund Hornby   51
     Chapter 4 – Establishing the Court   59
     Chapter 5 – Opening the Court: The First Cases   73
     Chapter 6 – The Younger Generation: Learning the Ropes   83
     Chapter 7 – Order Out of Legal Chaos   99
     Chapter 8 – Bricks and Mortar: A Home for the Court   111
     Chapter 9 – Reforming the British Courts in Japan   129
     Chapter 10 – Building the New Japanese Legal System   147
     Chapter 11 – Mixed Justice in China   159
     Chapter 12 – The End of an Era: Hornby retires –
           Goodwin dies   177

Part Three: Reorganisation (1878 to 1881)   187
     Chapter 13 – Reorganising the Courts   189
     Chapter 14 – The Bullion Dollar Question:
           The Ross Case   219
     Chapter 15 – The Chinese Challenge   229
     Chapter 16 – Some Corner of a Foreign Field:
           The Death of George French   249

Part Four: Consolidation (1881 to 1891)   253
    Chapter 17 – Jockeying for Promotion   255
    Chapter 18 – Chinese Demand Justice   263
    Chapter 19 – Enlarging Jurisdiction   277
    Chapter 20 – Japan Demands Change   283
    Chapter 21 – A New Arrival And A Fond Farewell   291

Part Five: Japan Rises – China Falls (1891 to 1900)   301
    Chapter 22 – The Amalgamation   303
    Chapter 23 – Japan Asserts Itself   319
    Chapter 24 – Infidelity and Murder in Yokohama   337
    Chapter 25 – Endings and New Beginnings   367
    Chapter 26 – A Time for Rejoicing not Revenge   391
    Chapter 27 – The Full Stop in the Wrong Place:
                     Vale Sir Nicholas   401

Conclusion to Volume I   412

Index   414

Volume II Destruction, Disorder and Defiance (1900-1927)

Introduction to Volume II   3

Part Six: China Boxed In (1900 to 1905)   7
    Chapter 28 – The Boxer Rebellion   9
    Chapter 29 – The High Court of Weihaiwei   23
    Chapter 30 – Ambition Achieved: Wilkinson CJ   31
    Chapter 31 – 1905: A Year of Change   53

Part Seven: The United States Court for China   71
    Chapter 32 – Taming the Wild East   73
    Chapter 33 – The Wild East Fights Back   97

Part Eight: Dying Dynasties (1906 to 1911)   119
    Chapter 34 – Korea's Hero: Ernest Bethell   121
    Chapter 35 – The Ricshaw Coolie and the Sampan Man   135
    Chapter 36 – For Better or Worse   145
    Chapter 37 – The Law of the Land   157

Part Nine: Revolution and War (1911 to 1920)   169
    Chapter 38 – The Republican Revolution   171
    Chapter 39 – New Roles and New Faces   179
    Chapter 40 – World War I   195
    Chapter 41 – Farewells and Promotions   213

Part Ten: The Roaring Twenties (1920 to 1927)   223
    Chapter 42 – Bad Behaviour at the Bar   225
    Chapter 43 – Gun Runners   249
    Chapter 44 – A Sad Farewell: Lobingier Retires   263
    Chapter 45 – Rebel with a Cause: Lawrence Kentwell   273
    Chapter 46 – The Rise of Nationalism   305
    Chapter 47 – Intermingled Jurisdictions   327
    Chapter 48 – Recognition, Retirements and Advances   337
    Chapter 49 – The Dirty DA   349

Conclusion to Volume II   363

Appendix: Introduction to Vol I   366

Index   378

Volume III Revolution, Resistance and Resurrection (1927-1943)

Introduction to Volume III   3

Part Eleven: A New Hope (1927 to 1931)   7
    Chapter 50 – The Rise of China   9

Chapter 51 – The Work of Two Men   35
Chapter 52 – Extraterritoriality to End   43

Part Twelve: The Japanese Empire Strikes Back (1932 to 1941)   55
Chapter 53 – Major Battles   57
Chapter 54 – The Last Judges   73
Chapter 55 – Predators   87
Chapter 56 – In the Shadow of the Gallows   105
Chapter 57 – The Badlands of North China   123
Chapter 58 – Dark Days   131
Chapter 59 – Live by the Gunboat…   159

Part Thirteen: The End (1937 to 1943)   183
Chapter 60 – The End of Extraterritoriality   185
Chapter 61 – Summing Up   195

Postscript - Life After Death   199

A note on the writing of this book   209

Acknowledgements   215

Further Reading and Places of Interest   221

Table of Appointments (British courts)   227

Judges and District Attorneys of the US Court for China   232

Appendix: Introduction to Vol I   233

Index   245

Table of Cases   280

Table of Jury Members   291

Tables of Illustrations   296

Photographs   302

Romanisation And Place Names

I have used transliterations of Chinese personal and place names in accordance with the transliterations used during the period covered by this book. Where someone is now much better known by a different transliteration, I have used this.

For place names in China, for any reference prior to the Communist Revolution in 1949, I have generally used the contemporaneous English names, such as Canton and Amoy. Beijing is referred to as Peking for the most part but also as Peiping for the period that was its official name. This is the way the names appear in the documents of the time and would have been spoken in English.

For street names in Shanghai, I have used the pre-World War II street names. Where appropriate I give the current street name in parentheses.

For references to places and personal names in China after the Communist Revolution, I have used Hanyu Pinyin, except where a person is much better known by a different transliteration.

For Japanese names, I have used modern romanisations. For Korean names I have used contemporaneous transliterations.

For all quotations or names of publications I have kept the original spelling.

Currencies in Shanghai

There were four major currencies in use in Shanghai during the period covered by this book. For almost the entire period, the Pound Sterling to United States Dollar exchange rate was £1 = US$5. For a time, the US dollar was also referred to as the Gold Dollar (G$). The other two currencies in use were Mexican silver dollars and the Chinese Tael (based on the price of silver). The value of these currencies fluctuated wildly. In 1930, US$1 was equal to about 3 taels and $3.5 Mex. However, at other times the Mexican dollar was equivalent to or worth more than the US$.

I have not attempted to give any conversions of currency in the book.

File References

Unless indicated otherwise, all files references are to the UK National Archive file reference for a document. PRONI files refers to the Wilkinson Papers kept at the Public Records office of Northern Ireland. Where possible full file references have been given for the PRONI papers. However, these were not always available.

Cartoons and Illustrations

All cartoons and illustrations accompanying the text, with two exceptions, are contemporaneous drawings published at the time. The exceptions are the sketches of the Supreme Court and George French's grave which have been made from photographs.

FOREWORD

By Rt. Hon. Sir Robin Jacob
Former Lord Justice of Appeal

DOUGLAS CLARK ASKED ME to write this by an email. It ended with this: "If you are interested, I will send you through the page proofs so you can see if you would be happy to be associated with my work. Please do not feel any obligation at all to say yes." I am so glad I did. For this is a riveting work – almost novel-like with its rich content of quotations from the seemingly larger than life characters who set up and administered the outposts of law – mainly the English Common Law - in the Far East.

Yet this book is not a novel, and the characters were real. Living people. To today's eyes the notion of the "Supreme Court of China and Japan" or, a little later in time, the "Supreme Court of China and Corea" seem surreal. But real they were, created and manned by men (had to be all men) of vision coupled with both energy and, largely a fierce sense of justice. Their jurisdiction was over the British men (and women) out in the Empire (and beyond). Although it was a jurisdiction taken from the countries concerned by the power of the gunboat it was frequently fair. Take for example this quotation from a direction of Sir Edmund Hornby to a jury hearing a case where an Englishman was accused of the manslaughter of a Chinese man: "A Chinaman's life is as precious as that of our own countrymen." The defendant had taken a pistol to confront a group of men who were protesting about the building of a lighthouse. In a scuffle the pistol had gone off, killing its victim." Sir Edmund clearly thought that taking a pistol to the confrontation was much more than was warranted. He directed the jury to convict, was deeply sorry when it refused, and said so. Or consider how the English Judge in Japan protected Chinese coolies from being transported as slaves from Macao (Portuguese) to South America.

Of course it was not perfect justice. Nor without its racism. Take an acquittal in 1898 Korea of a Briton accused of murder or manslaughter of a gardener in the British Legation. After the Judge described the death as follows:

> "The defence was borne out in court by competent medical evidence that this was one of those interesting cases where an Oriental injured in his feelings will turn his face to the wall and die."

And the force of the all-powerful Royal Navy lay behind these courts – hence Douglas Clark's vivid title. Yet another quote makes this come alive. This was when there were anti-missionary riots in the Yangtze Valley in 1891 (not perhaps all that surprising since the missionaries, like many zealots often rather aggressively ignored Chinese laws and customs). When the riots were threatened the telegram seeking help simply read:

> "Riot Wuhu, catholic premises being destroyed; send gunboat immediately"

This book is full of such tales and of such gem quotes. The tales are not only told well but are full of these gems from the sources of the day, the newspapers in Shanghai and Japan, the reports of cases, letters from and to the participants, civil service records and so on. The original research has obviously been extensive, even though the style is easy and tends to disguise the erudition behind it. You are made to feel close to these people, almost as if you knew them.

The inquisitive might ask why Doug Clark asked me of all people to write the foreword. The reason is my connection with the world of which he writes. My father was what was known in Shanghai as a Baghdad Jew. He was the third of ten children of Iraqi Sephardic Jewish parents who had come to Shanghai because of trade. My grandfather worked for Sir Victor Sassoon in Sassoon House (now the Bank of China) on the Bund, hard by the junction with the Nanking Road (now Nanjing Road West). From 1917 to 1923 Dad went to the Shanghai Public School for Boys, a sort of grammar school manned entirely by Oxbridge teachers – not as upmarket as the Cathedral School, a sort of public school. Little England in Shanghai! It was through his school that Dad learned about the law – he played the Attorney-General in a mock murder trial. And in Shanghai he first saw an English Court – the same one described in this book, with judge and counsel in the standard wig and gown. He said "I want to do that, but in London, home of Empire". That is what he did. And I followed.

My interest in the Shanghai court is therefore in part personal. I have tried to imagine how someone without such a connection might react. I think I can fairly judge – they will be riveted. This will particularly be so for those concerned today with the Far East. From these vivid stories and Douglas Clark's insight, they will have much to learn, not only about the past but how that past must inevitably influence the dealings between East and West today.

The Rt. Hon. Professor Sir Robin Jacob
University College London,
July 2014

INTRODUCTION

Extraterritoriality – an Extraordinary System

IN 1874, SIR EDMUND HORNBY, Chief Judge of the British Supreme Court for China and Japan, entered a court room in the northern Chinese seaport of Chefoo in the full red robes of a British criminal judge. All those in court rose and bowed to him. As he took his seat, behind him was the British coat of arms bearing the words "Dieu et Mon Droit" ("God and my Right"). Before him in the dock was Thomas Fawcett, a British foreman accused of killing a Chinese man. After a trial in which Chinese witnesses were brought to court in chains to give evidence, Fawcett was acquitted by the British jury. For the next three days and two nights, the local Chinese population besieged Hornby's house demanding proper justice. He wrote later: "Of course, I never tried another British subject accused of killing a Chinaman at an outlying port, unless there was a gun-boat at hand."

What was a British judge, bewigged and fully robed in red, doing trying a criminal case against a British subject in northern China? Why was there a British jury? Why the gun-boat? The simple answer is: extraterritoriality.

In China, for almost a century, Britain, America and other foreign countries ran their own civil and criminal justice systems. These legal systems were, as far as possible, entirely separate from the Chinese system. They had their own courts, judges, lawyers and, even, prisons. In Japan, almost identical foreign legal systems to those in China also existed for just over forty years.

These justice systems were created as part of the forced opening of China and Japan in the 1840s and 1850s. Until then, for more than 200 years, both China and Japan had been closed to Westerners and in both countries, only limited foreign trade had been allowed at a single port far away from the capital.

Britain and America changed this. In 1842, following the two-year Opium War, a British Navy flotilla led by Captain Henry Pottinger forced China to sign - at the point of their gunboat barrels - the Treaty of Nanking which opened five ports to Western trade. In 1854, an American naval squadron, led by Commodore Matthew Perry, forced Japan – also at the point of their gunboat barrels – to open to Western trade and sign a Treaty of Amity and Commerce. Other Western countries were quick to follow Britain and America's lead and signed similar treaties with both countries.

The Chinese and Japanese, not surprisingly, hated the "unequal treaties" that had brought foreigners to their shores. They, however, had no choice but to accept them. The treaties allowed the treaty powers to base army and naval forces in China and Japan, and on numerous occasions, British, American and other treaty powers' gunboats and armies were brought in to enforce "treaty rights." Peking was attacked and the Summer Palace burnt to the ground by the British and French in 1860. Kagoshima in southern Japan was shelled and all but destroyed by the British in 1863. Shimonoseki was held to ransom by the British, American, French and Dutch navies in 1864. China fought and lost numerous wars with foreign powers in the late 19th century. Right up to the 1940s, foreign navy boats, exercising treaty rights, patrolled the coast of China and the Yangtze River to protect foreign interests. Foreign troops were stationed in Peking and all along the railway line between Peking and Tientsin.

China and Japan's reaction to their forced opening to the

West continues to this day to have a strong impact on how they both view and treat each other and the rest of the world. Each country faced an almost identical challenge, but the results were diametrically opposite. Japan was the big winner from the unequal treaties while China was the big loser. Neither country has forgotten this – and neither country will. Ever.

This history explains the deep enmity that exists to this day between the two countries and why the 21st century tensions between the newly-strong China and still-strong Japan are so dangerous. If pushed, neither side will back down to the other.

For Japan, its forced opening is, now, a matter for celebration. All over Japan can be found memorials to the arrival of the foreigners and their contribution to the development of Japan. Museums commemorating the foreign settlements and the foreigners who helped build them can be found in all treaty ports. In a country where land is scarce, and despite having fought the British and Americans in World War II, foreign cemeteries from the 19th century have been preserved and are well maintained. On the 150th anniversary of the British and Japanese Treaty of Amity and Commerce, the Japanese Foreign Minster, at the Foreign Office in London, launched a "Japan-UK 150" celebration.[1] In Yokohama, you can enjoy lunch at "Le Jardin de Perry" near where Matthew Perry landed.

For China, its forced opening and the 100 years that followed are now described as "the Century of Humiliation." Anti-foreign sentiment is taught in schools, fills China's history books and is on display in all its museums. Foreign cemeteries have all been destroyed. You could never imagine any Chinese Foreign Minister celebrating an anniversary of the

---

1 Speech by Mr Shintaro Ito, State Secretary for Foreign Affairs, at a Reception to celebrate 150 Years of Diplomatic Relations between the United Kingdom and Japan at the Foreign & Commonwealth Office, London, September 16, 2008.

Treaty of Nanking anywhere, let alone at the Foreign Office in London. There is no "Le Jardin de Pottinger" in modern-day Nanjing.[2]

How can two countries which faced almost identical challenges have travelled such different roads?

In Japan, the opening of the country led to a civil war between reformers and those who wanted to retain the old feudal government under the Shogunate. The reformers won. From the late 1860s, the basic policy of the Japanese government was "reform or die."

Japan launched headlong into a program of rapid and large scale Westernisation. The Shogunate and old feudal system was abolished; foreign laws were studied and adopted; and, democracy was steadily introduced. The results were amazing. Japan went through a period of massive industrialization and economic growth and year after year became, politically, economically and militarily stronger. In less than 40 years, by 1894, Japan was strong enough to be able to reach agreements with all foreign countries to abolish all the unequal treaties. The following year, it defeated China in war and imposed its own unequal treaty on China. It continued to go from strength to strength, defeating Russia, annexing Korea and, over time, taking over large parts of China. Ultimately, during World War II, Japan occupied almost half of Asia.

China, on the other hand, was at the time of its forced opening already ruled by foreigners, the Manchus from Manchuria in what is now northeast China. The basic policy of the Manchu-run Qing Dynasty can be summarized as "if we reform we will die." Any change in China's system of governance, they believed, would weaken Manchu rule. One large-scale revolt in the 1850s and 1860s, the Taiping Rebellion, did threaten the government (and the Foreign Settle-

---

2   There is a Pottinger Street in Hong Kong, but that is another story.

ment in Shanghai), but was put down. The Qing Dynasty fu-
tilely resisted reform, relying instead on "self-strengthening,"
modernization in certain limited areas. This response, which
led to further wars with foreign powers which China almost
invariably lost, allowed China's sovereignty to be chipped
away by more and more unequal treaties.

The Republican Revolution in 1911 offered hope, but collapsed into civil war. Germany's defeat in World War I and the
Russian Revolution brought the end of extraterritorial rights
for Germans and Russians, but saw Japan take over most of
Germany's interests in China. Unification under the militarily powerful Nationalists in 1927 offered even more hope; the
European powers and America were willing to give up some
rights. But by this time Japan was too strong for China to resist alone. By the time World War II started, Japan occupied
more than half of China.

To this day, anti-foreign and particularly anti-Japanese
propaganda is a fundamental part of the Chinese Communist Party's hold on power. Regular anti-Japanese protests are
encouraged (and then, when they get too big, discouraged)
by the government. In the 2010s, Sino-Japanese tensions have
been upped by the Chinese by the use of military threats to
assert China's claims over the Diaoyutai/Senkaku Islands. In
March 2014, almost eighty years after World War II finished,
the Secretary General of the Chinese Communist Party and
President of China Xi Jinping said on a visit to Europe that the
"war of aggression committed by Japanese militarism alone
inflicted 35 million Chinese military and civilian casualties.
These atrocities are still fresh in our memory."[3]

How Japan which until the mid-1840s had co-existed relatively peacefully with China has became China's sworn enemy is a story that for most Westerners has long been forgotten.
But given modern-day tensions between the two countries,

....

3 "Japan's wartime atrocities 'still fresh in memory'", *South China Morning Post* March
30, 2014, p3.

it is well worth remembering. The story is not just Chinese
Communist Party propaganda: China was treated appall-
ingly by foreign powers, including Britain and to a lesser extent, the United States, for over 100 years. Japan's treatment
of China, after it threw off the unequal treaties that had been
imposed on it, was even worse.

Extraterritoriality - foreign justice in foreign lands - was a
fundamental part of this humiliation. Extraterritoriality un-
derpinned the foreign presence in China. It served day to day
to remind Chinese they were not sovereign in their own land
and the assertion of "treaty rights" often resulted in military
force being used against China.

Extraterritoriality meant that the governments of China
and, while the treaties were in force there, Japan had almost
no power to control foreigners enjoying treaty rights. Foreigners were allowed to freely enter the treaty ports, they were
not subject to local laws and, could not be punished by local
authorities. The most local officials could do was to arrest foreigners and hand them over to their own consular authorities
for trial. They could not even deport them. Any threat by the
Chinese or Japanese to breach these rights resulted in the dispatch of gunboats to enforce them.

Extraterritoriality created a remarkable system. Each
treaty power established courts staffed by consular officers
to try cases against their nationals. At its peak, in Shanghai,
there were at least 23 different courts operating in the city: 19
foreign courts, three Chinese courts, and a Court of Consuls
for bringing cases against the foreign-run Municipal Council.
Close to twenty courts operated in the main Japanese treaty
port, Yokohama. The consular courts were an alphabet soup
of jurisdictions including German, Italian, Austro-Hungarian, Russian, Belgian, Danish, Dutch, French, Hungarian,
Spanish, Mexican, Chilean, Norwegian, Swedish, Russian
and Spanish courts.

While they hated the unequal treaties that allowed for-

A scene from the Italian consular court in Shanghai in 1920s. Italian and British witness give evidence before an Italian judge and assessors.

eigners freely to enter and trade with their countries, Chinese and Japanese attitudes towards extraterritoriality, at least at the beginning, were equivocal. Despite later protestations and propaganda, neither China nor Japan were against extraterritoriality in the early years. Extraterritoriality had been demanded to protect treaty foreigners from the "barbaric" Chinese and Japanese legal systems which, to be fair to the foreign powers, did regularly torture parties before the courts. For both the Chinese and the Japanese, foreigners handling disputes between other foreigners seemed like a good idea.

Indeed, perhaps most telling of their early attitudes to extraterritoriality is that in the 1870s, China and Japan agreed to provide for mutual extraterritoriality for their citizens in each other's countries. In the 1880s, when foreign countries entered into unequal treaties with Korea, both China and Japan also imposed extraterritoriality on Korea.

The real problems with extraterritoriality came as more and more foreigners arrived in China and Japan and interacted with the locals. Particularly in China, foreigners in the form of missionaries, traders and officers of the foreign-run Imperial Maritime Customs spread across the country. Everywhere they went they mixed with local Chinese, creating friction that lead to disputes and, in the worst cases, to a number of killings. The Japanese managed, for the most part, to restrict foreigners to treaty ports but even in these ports, just as in China, disputes would arise with and crimes be committed against Japanese. Local Chinese and Japanese could only seek justice – in their own country - by going to a foreign court using a foreign language and applying foreign law. They often felt that justice was not done when foreigner judged foreigner. This could lead to violence. The first British Chief Judge, Sir Edmund Hornby, quoted above, had had to call in the gunboat in Chefoo because a mob had besieged his bungalow for three days, angry at the acquittal of the British foreman.

The problems were exacerbated by the fact that most

countries did not appoint trained lawyers to handle legal cases. Cases were instead handled by consuls, often with no legal training. For many countries, consuls were not even professional consular officers, but merely local merchants appointed to handle their country's interests. Cases could be, and often were, very poorly handled and decided.

In order to deal with some of the problems with consular courts, the British, by far the largest Western power in East Asia, were the first to establish a formal court system in China and Japan staffed by professional judges. In 1865, the British Supreme Court for China and Japan was established in Shanghai. It was run from the British Foreign Office in London. The British Court for Japan, under the Shanghai Supreme Court, was established in Yokohama 14 years later. America, as its economic and political interests grew in China, established the United States Court for China in 1906 in Shanghai. This was for most of its life run by the Department of State from Washington DC.

These three courts tried in China, Japan, and, for a period, Korea (or Corea as it was then known), cases of every type imaginable: murder, sedition, rape, contract disputes, divorces, mass fights on board merchant ships, assault, battery, theft, fraud, ship collisions, and even, patent, copyright and trade mark infringement cases.

The courts were in almost all respects fully functioning British and American courts. They were staffed by professional judges. Qualified lawyers appeared before the courts. British or American law was applied and British and American rules of evidence and procedure were used. In the case of the British courts, juries were empaneled for all major civil and criminal cases. British judges and barristers all wore the traditional wigs and gowns, even in the oppressive heat of summer. Case reports were published and full records kept. Every quote from a judge, lawyer or witness in this book is from a contemporaneous report or record.

The only major anomaly was that there were no juries in the American courts. The United States Supreme Court had, in 1891, ruled that the constitutional right to a jury did not apply in extraterritorial courts. This was challenged on a number of occasions with Americans making comparisons to the much-preferred practice in the British courts of trial by jury. Even American judges would from time to time lament not having a jury to assist them in trying cases.

The following chapters tell the story of these British and American judges, their courts, and the lawyers and the parties that appeared before them. The story is told in 13 parts in chronological order beginning from the treaties that established extraterritoriality and continuing through to the end of extraterritoriality in, first, Japan and then China.

At a much higher level, this book also tells the story of China and Japan's forced opening to the world and how extraterritoriality influenced and guided the development the legal and political systems of both countries, so much so that the history of extraterritoriality still has a strong impact on how both countries view the world today.

The men who came to the Far East as judges and lawyers of these court were all adventurers; being willing to travel far away from home to be a judge or practice law in what in the early days were primitive conditions. For the British all, perhaps bar one or two lawyers, were men of Empire. They all believed in extraterritoriality and the benefits it brought to British interests.

The British judges of the 19th century were truly remarkable. The founder of the court, Hornby, was a force of nature who by his own personal will established a fully functioning legal system. His assistant, Charles Goodwin, was a genius, a world famous Egyptologist and Bible scholar. Many other judges had come to China and Japan as British consular officers, committing themselves to spend their entire career in the Far East. They all learnt Chinese or Japanese and could read, write and speak their chosen language fluently. As consular officers they were required to conduct official business with the Chinese or Japanese in the local language. Others were barristers from England who had come to China at a young age seeking their fortunes; one, Nicholas Hannen, achieving the rare honour of becoming both Chief Justice and Consul-General in Shanghai.

The 20th century brought many more changes. Extraterritoriality had been abolished in Japan. The United States Court for China was established to oversee the US consular courts. China was starting to reform its government and legal system, spurring further changes. Shanghai had also grown to be a cosmopolitan city and was no longer the hardship posting it had once been considered to be. These developments brought a new type of judge and lawyer to the courts. For the most part, in both the British and American courts judges were brought in from outside China, not always successfully - the first two American judges were forced to resign. The American legal profession also improved, helped in no small part by the overzealous efforts of the first judge of the US Court to clean up the quality and standards of the bar.

Change also brought new challenges to the courts. They had to deal with two Chinese revolutions, civil war, warlords and rising Chinese (and, in the British courts, Indian) nationalism. World War I brought cases of sedition to both courts as well as tricky questions of how to deal with enemy nationals who lived side by side with Americans and British in China. The entire existence of the US Court was challenged by one American lawyer who launched a large-scale attack on the court in Washington DC. One half-Chinese British barrister denounced the British court for practicing "gunboat diplomacy."

The Japanese incursions into and ultimate occupation of most of China in the 1930s and World War II brought its own difficulties. There were numerous cases before the courts involving spies; murders of, and by, Japanese soldiers; *habeas corpus* applications for the release of Chinese prisoners wanted by the Japanese; and, even whether it was necessary to pay rent when Chinese and Japanese troops were fighting pitched battles outside your front door.

Milton Helmick the last judge of the United States Court for China, who served right up to the commencement of the Pacific War, described the job of an extraterritorial judge:

"For ordinary every day judging he ought to have known ... all about extraterritoriality, a little international law, a smattering of the laws of other countries, something of Chinese law, a great deal about China, a lot about international politics, considerable about diplomatic usages, a bit of anthropology and a modicum about bomb dodging."[4]

So, where did extraterritoriality come from?

4   M. Helmick, "United States Court for China", Far Eastern Survey, Vol. 14, No. 18 (Sep. 12, 1945), p252.

PART ONE

THE BEGINNING
(1842 TO 1865)

Chapter I

White Man, White Law, White Gun

The Foundations

CALEB CUSHING, A NOTED American diplomat, politician and lawyer, drafted the wording that would be the foundation of almost 100 years of extraterritoriality in China. Cushing, who had been sent by the US President to negotiate a treaty, said that he:

> "entered China with the formed general conviction that the United States ought not to concede to any foreign state, under any circumstances, jurisdiction over the life and liberty of a citizen of the United States, unless that foreign state be of our own family of nations, in a word, a Christian state."[1]

Surprisingly, perhaps, given how long extraterritoriality lasted, it took only two short paragraphs to create the system. The paragraphs were Articles 21 and 25 of the Treaty of Wanghsia signed between the United States and China in 1844 to "establish firm, lasting, and sincere friendship between the two nations."

The articles provided that Chinese who committed crimes against Americans in China would be tried in Chinese courts

---

1 Note from Cushing to Calhoun, C. Lobingier, *Extraterritorial Cases*, Vol I, p4.

but Americans who committed crimes in China against anyone would be tried by American consuls. All civil claims
against Americans would be dealt with by American consuls. Almost identical wording was used in every later treaty
signed by China, Japan and Korea granting extraterritorial
rights.

Article 21, as far as it dealt with criminal offences by
Americans, the treaty provided that:

> "citizens of the United States who may commit any
> crime in China shall be subject to be tried and punished
> only by the Consul or other public functionary of the
> United States thereto authorised according to the laws
> of the United States."

Article 25, dealing with civil claims, read in part:

> "All questions in regard to rights, whether of property
> or person, arising between citizens of the United States
> in China shall be subject to the jurisdiction of and regu-
> lated by the authorities of
> their own Government."

Cushing had been appoint-
ed by United States President
John Tyler to go to China to
negotiate a treaty. In his subsequent report to the Secretary
of State, John Calhoun, Cushing said that he had insisted
these articles be included in the
treaty because he wanted "the
laws of the Union to follow its
citizens and its banner protect
them, even within the domain

*Caleb Cushing, American jurist who
negotiated America's first treaty
with China*

of the Chinese Empire."

The protection of the American flag was necessary, he explained, because China was not a Christian country. "States of Christendom are bound together by treaties" which oblige them to treat nationals of each country equally. On the other hand, he said, "Mohammadem or Pagan States" do not recognize these obligations. Western countries could not deal with the governments of non-Christian countries "except by force, and at the head of fleets and armies."
Cushing continued:

> "… it is only during the present generation that treaties, most of them imposed by force of arms or by terror, have begun to bring down the great Mohammedan and Pagan governments into a state of inchoate peaceful association with Christendom."

Cushing, however, had not needed to lead an American fleet or army to China to get the Chinese to sign the Treaty of Wanghsia. The British, two years previously, had already done that for him by convincingly defeating China in the first Opium War of 1839-1842.

China until the 1840s had been a hermit empire. Since the 17th Century, the country had been ruled by the Manchus from Manchuria in the northeast of today's China. The Manchus were foreign rulers of China. They spoke and wrote their own language, wore their own clothes and garrisoned Manchu soldiers in the major cities of China in separate quarters. Chinese men were forced by the Manchus to wear their hair in a long braided ponytail, called a queue. The penalty for not doing so was death.

The Manchus had closed China off to foreign contact. They believed they had no particular need for foreign goods and, in particular, had no desire for the Chinese people to be infected by Western religions or thoughts. They did, however,

Chinese boats blockade the Canton factories

allow for some limited trade in Canton (Guangzhou) in the
far south of China. Foreign traders were restricted to the Canton factory - so-called because factors, or agents, were based
there. These were warehouses on the Pearl River in Canton.
Foreign traders were permitted to deal with a select number
of local merchants.

The trigger for Britain's attack on China was a war on
drugs. China said "No." Britain had other ideas. Britain was
running a huge trade deficit with China and started importing opium from India to even things up. The Chinese, not surprisingly, in 1836, banned its import. Two years later, in 1838,
an Imperial Commissioner Lin Zexu started to aggressively
suppress the domestic consumption of opium as well as the
import of opium by foreigners. British merchants in Canton
were blockaded in their factories until they agreed to hand
over their opium stocks.

In March 1839, Captain Charles Elliot, the British Superintendent of China Trade, the most senior British official in
China, agreed to the Chinese demands. He ordered the merchants to hand over more than 20,000 chests of opium. Elliot
told the merchants that the British government would compensate them for their loss. Lin arranged for the opium to be

destroyed by being released into ponds near the sea in the town of Humen in southern Guangdong province.[2]

The reaction in Britain was one of outrage. The British government determined that the Chinese must be taught a lesson and dispatched an expeditionary force under the command of Captain Elliot. Elliot first headed north to Tientsin (Tianjin) where he was convinced to return to Macao for negotiations. When he realized the Chinese were prevaricating, he attacked Canton, taking it in May 1841.

Despite this success, when he returned to Macao from Canton, Elliot was dismissed for failing to prosecute the war with China properly. He was replaced by Henry Pottinger. China at the time had no major cities on the coast. Peking was located inland from Tientsin and was impossible to attack without land troops. Pottinger decided instead to attack Nanking, a major inland trading port on the Yangtze River, which controlled the supply of grain to northern China. The British forces, under the command of Pottinger, sailed up the coast of China, first bombarding and briefly taking Amoy (Xiamen) before moving on to Ningpo (Ningbo). They wintered in Ningpo and brought in reinforcements from India. After easily repelling Chinese counter attacks, they arrived at the walls of Nanking in August 1842 and threatened to bombard the city unless the Chinese agreed to their demands.

The Chinese Emperor in Peking finally realized the British forces were vastly superior to China's. He authorized his officials to negotiate whatever settlement they could. On August 29th 1842 a treaty was signed aboard HMS *Cornwallis* between Britain and China.[3]

The treaty was the historic Treaty of Nanking.

The main terms of the Treaty of Nanking allowed for Brit-

---

2 The ponds have been preserved and can be seen at Lin Zexu Memorial Hall and Opium War Museum in Humen, Guangdong Province.

3 This summary of the war is principally taken from *The Opium War*, by Julia Lovell which describes the first Opium War in detail.

ish merchants to trade with China. It opened five cities, Canton, Amoy, Foochow, Ningpo and Shanghai to foreign trade and allowed British merchants to live in these cities. The cities became known, along with all ports opened under later treaties, as "treaty ports." Hong Kong Island was also ceded to the United Kingdom in perpetuity to serve as a British base in China. China was also required to pay a total of $21 million, a massive sum at the time, as reparations for the war.

The Treaty of Nanking made no specific reference to extraterritorial rights or consular jurisdiction. The closest it came was to say that the British government would appoint "Superintendents, or Consular officers, to reside at each of the above-named cities or towns, to be the medium of communication between the Chinese authorities and the said merchants." The British may have considered this sufficient to exercise extraterritorial rights. In the Canton Factory, the Chinese had allowed British authorities to handle any legal disputes involving British subjects. A "Court for China" had been established to do so.

Even when a supplemental treaty, the Treaty of Bogue, was signed the following year, no specific mention was made of extraterritoriality. The Treaty of Bogue, did however, include a "Most Favoured Nation Clause" which provided that if the Emperor granted "additional privileges or immunities to any of the subjects or Citizens of Foreign Countries, the same privileges and immunities will be extended to and enjoyed by British Subjects."

It was therefore the signing of the American Treaty of Wanghsia in 1844 together with the Treaty of Bogue's Most Favoured Nation clause that gave Britain full extraterritorial rights in China.

The Treaties of Nanking and Wanghsia only opened the treaty ports to trade. They did not give free access to China for British or Americans. Foreigners could only travel short distances inland. Most importantly, foreigners were banned

Henry Pottiinger forcing opium on Lin Zexu

from the Chinese capital, Peking, and were not treated as equals by the Chinese government or officials. Also, in a strange historical anomaly, despite the fact that it brought an end to an "opium war," the Treaty of Nanking did not allow for opium trading. The British had been told that the Emperor would never accept a term allowing for legal trade in opium.

Not satisfied with the limitations in the Treaty of Nanking, the British over the years sought to reach a new agreement with China. China consistently rebuffed them.

In 1856, an opportunity came along to force the issue when the Chinese Governor of Canton seized what he believed to be a pirate ship, the *Arrow*. The British claimed that the *Arrow* was registered in Hong Kong and had been sailing under a British flag. In fact, its registration had expired. Nevertheless, Harry Parkes, the British Consul in Canton, was determined to teach the Chinese a lesson. Although Canton had been opened to foreign trade the local authorities refused access to the Chinese city. Using the seizure of the *Arrow* as an excuse, at Parkes' instigation, the British seized a Chinese warship and then attacked Canton. In December 1857, Canton was occupied by a joint British and French force. Early the next year, the fleet sailed to Tientsin where they negotiated and signed treaties with China. America also signed a treaty at the same time. All of these treaties were called the "Treaty of Tientsin" and had similar terms. They were much more de-tailed than the earlier treaties and gave foreigners far more rights in China.

The treaties loosened the restrictions on travel around treaty ports allowing residents to travel up to 100 li (about 50 kilometres) for a five-day period without restriction and to travel further in the interior with internal passports. The Yangtze River was opened to trade and five more ports were opened to trade. Christian missionaries were allowed to enter China to proselytize.

The Chinese government took responsibility for protect-ing foreign citizens and their property. Until 1860, no Chinese official or ministry had been directly responsible for foreign affairs. The treaty required the Chinese to nominate a senior official to deal with diplomatic affairs. This resulted in the cre-ation of China's first Ministry of Foreign Affairs the "Tsung Li Kekuo Shiwu Yamen" (Zongli Geguo Shiwu Yamen) or "Gen-eral Office for Handling Affairs of Foreign Countries" - usual-ly shortened in English and Chinese as the "Tsungli Yamen."

Foreign countries were given permission to establish legations (one rank below an embassy and headed by a minister) in Peking. China was required to treat foreign representatives on an equal footing. A specific provision stated that the term "barbarian" was not to be used to describe foreigners in official documents.

The second Opium War did end with the legalization of the importation of opium. The actual provision, which indirectly legalized opium imports by making them subject to a tariff, was hidden in trade regulations enacted under a Supplemental Agreement to the treaty. Foreigners were still prohibited from internal trade in opium and could only import opium into treaty ports.[4]

The British formalized their extraterritorial rights by including in Articles 15 and 16 of the treaty provisions for the handling of civil and criminal cases in similar terms to the Treaty of Wanghsia.

These provisions did not, however, make it clear how to deal with crimes or disputes between foreigners and Chinese. A new article (Article 17) was included in the Treaty of Tientsin to deal with so-called "mixed disputes." The new rules were that where a British or Chinese had a claim against a person of the other nationality, they should bring them to the consul to resolve them amicably. If the disputes could not be resolved amicably, then the consul "shall request the assistance of the Chinese authorities, that they may together decide on the merits of the case, and decide it equitably." This, as we shall see, did not prove to be a satisfactory formula.

The signing of the treaties was not, however, to be the end of the matter. In 1859, the British and French returned to exchange ratifications of the treaties in Peking. They attempted to enter the Hai River leading to the city of Tientsin so as to sail as close as they could to Peking. The entry to the river at

4 Rule 5, Agreement made pursuant to Article 26 of British Treaty of Tientsin.

Taku (Dagu) was heavily fortified with large forts built on either side of the river. Cannon were mounted on the forts and any boat attempting to enter the river could be fired on from either side.[5] In a rare victory, the Chinese successfully repulsed the British and French with substantial British and French casualties. American ships, breaking neutrality, provided firepower to assist in the retreat.

On the other hand, the Americans accepted a Chinese offer to allow their Minister, John Ward, to travel to Peking without troops and exchange ratifications. Upon reaching Peking, Ward was housed in a small temple. After several days, he was informed he would not be allowed to meet the Emperor and instead the exchange of ratifications would be done at Peh-tang (Beitang). Ward and the Governor General of Chi-hli Province exchanged ratifications there. Strictly speaking, upon ratification of the American Treaty, Britain, France and other treaty powers could take advantage of the Most Favoured Nation clause in their early treaties to enjoy rights under the American Treaty of Tientsin.

However, to the British and French it was clear that, to ensure the rights granted under their treaties were fully respected, greater force would be needed. As Lord Loch, a member of the British forces, put it at the time:

"The treatment to which Mr. Ward was subjected

British and French forces prepare to attack Tientsin and Peking

5   A museum has been built at Dagu (as it is now known). A small part of the forts have been rebuilt. The narrow river entrance can be seen from the top of the re-built fort.

showed the evident intention of the Emperor not to admit any of the Treaty Powers on a footing of equality with the Emperor of China, unless compelled by force to do so."[6]

The British and French governments decided that they must enter Peking on equal terms and dispatched more gunboats from Europe. The British commanded by Lord Elgin, brought a large number of army troops from India. These troops captured the Taku forts from the land side. With the forts neutralized, they sailed up river as far as they could and then marched on Peking. A number of British officials, including Harry Parkes and Lord Loch, went forward under a flag of truce to negotiate, but while they were returning to their lines they were seized. They were treated badly as prisoners and at least 20 of them died. Some had their hands tied tightly behind themselves for nine days with water being poured on the ropes to make the rope shrink. The blood vessels in their hands burst and they became infected, leading to dementia and death. Their bodies were then thrown in the moats around the prison. Parkes and Loch were at first put in a normal Chinese prison and tortured. They were later moved to a small temple.

During their stay in the temple, Parkes and Loch found a chair marked with Chinese characters stating that it had been supplied for the use of the "American tribute-bearer," John Ward, the previous year. This confirmed to Loch that the British and French had been right to insist, by force, on coming to Peking as equals rather than allowing the Chinese to view them as "tributaries."[7]

Parkes was asked to assist in negotiations between the Chinese and British but refused until he was released. The

6 H. Loch, *Personal Narrative of Occurrences during Lord Elgin's Second Embassy to China*, p16. Loch also describes the capture of the Taku forts.

7 H. Loch, *Personal Narrative of Occurrences during Lord Elgin's Second Embassy to China*, p138

Emperor issued an order for the execution of Parkes and Loch, but they were released just before it was received. The British and French forces then attacked Peking and took it after heavy fighting. In reprisal for the capture and killing of those travelling under a flag of truce, the British and French looted and burnt to the ground the Summer Palace, or Yuanmingyuan, a massive collection of palaces to the northwest of Peking.[8]

The British and French Treaties of Tientsin were ratified and a Convention of Peking was signed at the cessation of hostilities. The Convention of Peking provided for payment of indemnities, the ceding of the Kowloon peninsula in Hong Kong to Britain and the opening of Tientsin to foreign trade. The British selected a site for their legation in a Chinese palace and established it immediately.

In remarkable diplomatese, the Convention of Peking referred to the battles leading to the capture of Peking and the burning of the Summer Palace as a "misunderstanding" for which "the Emperor expressed his deep regret." The Convention blamed the "breach of friendly relations" on "the act of the garrison of Ta-ku."[9]

For the next 50 years until the collapse of the Qing Dynasty, the Chinese continued to resist foreign encroachments. This led to wars that China almost always lost and to further unequal treaties.

Japan: The Black Ships
Just like China, Japan had been closed to foreigners since the 17th century. Dutch traders were allowed to trade in Nagasaki at the far western end of Japan in the small fan-shaped man-

---

8   See *Personal Narrative of Occurrences during Lord Elgin's Second Embassy to China*, 1860 by Henry Loch, 1869 for a detailed on the ground account of the war, his and Parkes' capture and the burning of the Summer Palace. The ruins of the Yuanmingyuan can be seen to this day just north of Peking University.

9   Article 1 of the Convention of Peking. The Convention was published in the London Gazette Extraordinary, December 28, 1860, p5303.

Commodore Perry of the US Navy arrives to force Japan open to trade

made island of Dejima.[10]

The Americans took the lead to open up Japan. The negotiations were much easier, assisted in no small part by the clear military successes that the British and French had had in China. The Japanese were, by the 1850s, well aware of the China's defeat in the first Opium War and the overwhelming firepower of foreign ships.[11]

In 1853, Commodore Matthew Perry of the United States Navy sailed into Tokyo Bay leading four ships, the *Mississippi, Plymouth, Saratoga,* and *Susquehanna.* He demanded the opening of Japan to foreign trade. Perry left a letter for the Shogun and said he would return in a year's time for the answer. In 1854 he returned with eight ships. The Japanese,

10 For further details of the Seclusion Policy and the opening to trade in Japan, see Akagi, *Japan's Foreign Relations 1542-1936: A Short History,* Chapter 1. Dejima still exists today, but it is landlocked due to reclamation in Nagasaki Harbour. A museum has been built on the former island showing the way in which the Dutch lived there. In Japan, certain locals were also allowed to study Western science.

11 In 1849, a book *Kaigai Shinwa* (New Stories from Overseas) by Mineta Fuko had described the first opium war in detail with maps and drawings of battles and pictures of the foreign troops. The book made it clear that the wars were a warning to Japan. See also T Brook, and T Wakabayashi, *Opium Regimes: China, Britain and Japan, 1839-1952,* p62 for details of other books in Japan that discussed the Opium Wars, many advocating Japanese support for China.

knowing they did not have the power to fight the Americans and with the defeat of China in the Opium War in mind, capitulated. The Shogunate, without obtaining the consent of the Emperor, signed the Convention of Kanagawa with the United States opening the ports of Hakodate, in Hokkaido, and Shimoda, in Tokyo Bay, to foreign trade.

From 1856, the US Consul in Japan, Townsend Harris, sought to sign an expanded treaty. In 1858, he was able to get a treaty signed first by literally telling the Japanese "The British are Coming" as the British and French sent a fleet to Japan following the Second Opium War to negotiate treaty rights in Japan. Harris told the Japanese they had better sign up to the "favourable" terms he was offering (which included a ban on importing opium) rather than have the British and French impose their own. The British and French were more than happy to sign treaties along the lines agreed with the United States without the need for war.

The Japanese treaties with America and Britain progressively opened up a total of eight cities between 1859 and 1863. American and British subjects were limited to travelling only certain distances from each town, generally a distance of 10 ri (approximately 40 kms).[12] The treaties provided for the opening of Kanagawa and Hiogo, both of which were to become major ports. However, Japanese officials in both areas only provided land in nearby towns, Yokohama and Kobe. The treaty ports were therefore built in these locations, leading to them being referred to officially as Kanagawa and Hiogo to comply with the treaties even though in fact they were a few kilometres away.

The terms in the British and American treaties regarding extraterritoriality were very similar to the Treaty of Tientsin. The treaties provided that "all questions in regards to rights, whether of property or person" arising between British or

---

12 See Article III of the Treaty.

American subjects shall be subject to the jurisdiction of their own authorities.

In criminal cases, Japanese subjects who committed crimes towards Americans or Britons were to be "arrested and punished by the Japanese authorities according to the laws of Japan." American or British subjects who "commit any crime against Japanese subjects, or the subjects or citizens of any other country, shall be tried and punished by the Consul or other public functionary authorized thereto," according to the laws of their own country.[13]

The treaties were signed with the Tokugawa Shogunate which had ruled Japan since the early 1600s. The Shogun as the head of the Shogunate was the senior military and political leader in Japan. Above the Shogun was the Emperor, but the Emperor held no true political power. Below the Shogunate, feudal lords, or Daimyo, ruled over their own domains. They were required to show allegiance to the Shogunate, but had substantial power in their own domains.

Not all Japanese or feudal Daimyos accepted the arrival of the foreigners and there was, initially, strong resistance to the treaties based in part on the fact that the Shogunate had signed the treaties without the approval of the Emperor. Two major battles, which the Japanese lost decisively, triggered rapid change in Japan. In 1863, a British citizen, Charles Richardson, was killed near Yokohama by a samurai who was a member of the Satsuma clan from Kagoshima in far Western Japan. When the Satsuma clan refused to punish the offender, seven British naval gunboats were sent to Kagoshima. When

13 Jones, *Extraterritoriality in Japan*, Yale University Press, 1931, p27. These terms were not entirely clear. For example, it was not clear whether a claim against a British subject by another foreigner should be brought in Japanese or British Courts. This was clarified in the treaty entered into by the Austro-Hungarian Empire and Japan, which America and Britain were able to take advantage of under most favoured nation clauses in the treaties. In the Austro-Hungarian Treaty the following sentence was added to the provision dealing with civil claims: "In like manner the Japanese shall not interfere in any question which may arise between Austro-Hungarian citizens and the subjects of any other Treaty Power." Similarly with regard to crimes, the Austro-Hungarian Treaty added that if crimes were committed by Austro-Hungarians against "subjects of any other nation" they were subject to Austro-Hungarian jurisdiction.

The British fleet bombards Kagoshima in retribution for the killing of Charles Richardson

negotiations failed, the British ships bombarded the city, all but destroying it.

In 1864, the Choshu clan also from Western Japan, on orders of the Emperor who had directed the foreigners be expelled, closed the Straits of Shimonoseki by shelling any foreign ships seeking to sail through them. The narrow straits are the main routes for ships sailing from Japan through to China. The British, American, French and Dutch navies set out for Shimonoseki and after a short battle landed troops who destroyed the cannon. They then held Shimonoseki to ransom, telling the Choshu that, as under the rules of war, they could have destroyed Shimonoseki but had not; the Choshu now had to pay a ransom for the city.

Following these defeats, the Choshu and Satsuma clans applied the maxim "if you can't beat them, join them." They sent a number of young men overseas to study, including Hirobumi Ito, who later became one of Japan's leading reformers and statesmen. The Choshu and Satsuma also pushed for a program of opening and westernization. This led to a civil war where the Choshu and Satsuma defeated the Shogunate. The Koumei Emperor who had ordered the expulsion of foreigners died in 1867. In February 1868, in what is now known as the Meiji Restoration, the very young and newly-installed Meiji Emperor issued a proclamation that the Shogun had been given permission to return the governing power to the Emperor. The Emperor then allowed the reformers to establish a new government.

Anti-foreign sentiment in Japan did not die out immediately. At almost the exact time the Shogunate was giving up power, Japanese troops passing near Kobe shot and killed an American sailor who had crossed the street in front of them, a mortal insult to the samurai class. They then attacked other foreigners. Foreign troops and artillery were landed to defend Kobe and a group of foreigners chased after the Japanese troops. The samurai responsible was ordered to commit harakiri, witnessed by foreign officials. Ernest Satow, a junior British consular official who later became the British Minister in Japan and China, described in great detail the ceremony by which the samurai sliced open his stomach followed by his second chopping his head off so:

> "the head dropped down onto the matted floor, and the
> body lurching forward fell prostrate over it, the blood
> from the arteries pouring out and forming a pool.
> When the blood vessels had spent themselves all was
> over."[14]

Attacks continued on foreigners that included the murder of eleven French sailors in Sakai. Twenty Japanese troops were ordered to commit harakiri; but after the bloodbath of eleven deaths the French Captain pardoned the others. Harry Parkes, who had been appointed British Minister in Japan in 1865, and Satow were also attacked in Kyoto when in a procession to visit the Emperor.[15]

The goal of the new Japanese government was to reform Japan's society, economy and legal system. The old feudal system and classes were abolished. The focus was on reform and the government adopted a hands-off attitude to the treaty ports. By 1875, reform was well under way. All foreign troops left Japan and gunboats were no longer needed to protect for-

14 E. Satow, *A Diplomat in Japan*, Chapter XXVI (killing and battle) and p378 (Harakiri).
15 E. Satow, *A Diplomat in Japan*, Chapter XXIX (French sailors) and p394 (Kyoto).

eigners.

These treaties with China and Japan created the rules for extraterritoriality.

How did these rules work in practice?

CHAPTER 2

Courting the Law: Consuls as Judges

The Early Years

IN PRACTICE, IN ITS EARLY YEARS, extraterritoriality was a mess.

At the beginning there were the teething problems one would expect in setting up a new system. Consuls had to be appointed and consulate buildings leased. That was the easy part.

Once appointed, the new consuls had none of the tools of state to run a legal system.[1] They had no court rooms, no policemen and no prisons. The lack of court rooms could be easily solved. Any room will serve as a court if necessary. The lack of policemen and prisons was a far greater problem. When the treaty ports first opened, by far the greater part of the judicial work of a consul was dealing with seaman from foreign ships in port. Seamen in those days were tough guys. They were subject to harsh discipline on board their ships and looked to any shore leave to relieve tension. In 1847, Rutherford Alcock, the consul in Shanghai described the vessels in Shanghai "as manned by the lowest class of London and Liverpool seafaring men or by Lascars [Indian seamen] and Manilamen whose knives were always ready for service." Six years later, he said it was "not uncommon for a whole suburb of Shanghai to be put in terror by the drunken violence of some of Sydney and San Francisco's most dissolute men

---

1 In 1842 the British Parliament passed the Foreign Jurisdiction Act. This provided rules for exercising jurisdiction over British Subjects in foreign countries including China. The American Congress also authorised the establishment of consular courts in Asia by an act of 16 May 1848.

armed with bowie knives and revolvers." At one point in 1857, the British and United States consuls in Shanghai were inundated with work trying to keep order amongst some 2,000 hard partying seamen in port.[2]

At least in Shanghai there were foreign police to assist. When Ningpo was first opened, the British consul, who had no constable to assist him, admitted to tailoring his sentences to his expectation of how compliant the prisoners would be. A quiet person could be sentenced to a fine and imprisonment whereas a "troublesome fellow likely to cause a disturbance might escape punishment."[3] In many treaty ports, initially, Chinese prisons were used to house prisoners. One consul in Amoy, took six prisoners to a Chinese prison in 1845. He found "a state of misery and filth almost too shocking for him to behold and far too horrid for him to narrate."[4] Eventually, most consulates also built their own jails. These were often, however, just rooms attached to the consulate from which escape was easy. The Amoy consular gaol was so easy to break out of that imprisonment was "mere form." Even in Shanghai, prisoners were able to escape from the consular jails with apparent ease. In 1863 a prisoner under sentence of death escaped from the US consular jail.

Over time, these problems were resolved as communities and consulates grew. Most consulates were able to employ at least one constable. In the major treaty ports such as Shanghai, Tientsin and Amoy, foreign police forces for the settlements were established and better and larger jails built.

Even after the initial teething periods, the exercise of consular jurisdiction remained a mess. The reality was that consuls untrained in law were being asked to act as judges in sometimes complex matters. The early consuls, in particular, had to be chosen from a very small pool of people. Many

2 P.D. Coates, *The China Consuls*, p47-8.

3 P.D. Coates, *The China Consuls*, p22.

4 P.D. Coates, *The China Consuls*, p48-49.

countries, but not Britain, for many years appointed merchants living in the treaty ports as consuls. America appointed merchant consuls for the first 10 years but then shifted to political appointments. Tyler Dennet, an American historian, is scathing in his criticism of the system:

"The American consular service throughout the [19th] century presents a picture over which one would wish to draw the veil. The system of merchant consuls continued in China without change until 1854 when they were replaced at the five ports by others whose only legitimate emoluments were $1,000 a year for judicial services under extraterritoriality, and part of all of the fees of their office ... The men who displaced them [the merchant consuls] were often appointed from the lower ranks of political "hangers-on" in the United States where the costs of respectable living ranged upwards from three or four thousand dollars a year."[5]

American consuls were expected to pay themselves from fees they collected. Most importantly, a "consul was never selected for his legal training." A later government report on the United States consular services in Asia and South America found that "almost every consulate has some defect in history, owing to the endless rounds of evils incident to official rotation. Abuses have been committed in the collection of fees; in the exercise of judicial powers; in the adjustment of the business affairs of American citizens."[6]

It was not until the late 19th century that the United States sought to professionalize its consular service leading in 1906 to the passing of a consular reorganization law.

Britain from the outset avoided the worst of the merchant consul system by establishing a China Consular Service al-

5   R. Chang, *Justice of Western Consular Courts in Nineteenth Century Japan*, p13.
6   R. Chang, *Justice of Western Consular Courts in Nineteenth Century Japan*, p12.

most immediately. Half the first consuls were appointed in 1843 by Henry Pottinger, now the Superintendent of Trade based in Hong Kong, from men who had some experience of China. Others were appointed directly by the Foreign Secretary and some Foreign Office staff were re-assigned to China. Very few of the first senior appointees spoke Chinese. They were a mixture of ex-army officers, seamen and doctors. These included Harry Parkes who had been on Pottinger's staff since 1841 in Macau and Rutherford Alcock, a doctor in Foreign Office service. Both Parkes and Alcock later became British Minister in both Japan and China. For interpreters, Pottinger looked to anyone who had made an effort to study Chinese. W.H. Medhurst, the son of a missionary was one of the first interpreters appointed and later became consul in Shanghai. Thomas Wade was also appointed but had to return to England due to poor health. He was re-appointed in 1847 after having spent time as an interpreter for the Hong Kong Supreme Court. He later rose to the very top of the British hierarchy in China becoming the Minister in Peking. He also developed, with another consular officer, H. A. Giles, the Wade-Giles system of Romanizing Chinese.[7]

Most of the first recruits performed admirably. However, in 1860 the Civil Service Commission, recommended appointment by open competition. A parliamentary select committee agreed with this recommendation. The next year, Britain introduced competitive examinations for the China consular service as well as the newly-created Japan and Siamese consular services. Those selected were expected to serve their entire careers in China, Japan or Siam and to learn the local language. At first, the Foreign Office asked for nominations from selected universities. By the late 1860s, this had been abandoned and from 1872 until 1907 the appointment system for China, Japan and Siam, was opened to all by competitive

---

7 See P.D. Coates, *The China Consuls*, Chapter 1 for full details of early appointments and pp76-77 on the introduction of competitive exams.

examination. After 1907, this was considered too egalitarian and nominations were once more required.

Consuls as Judges

Greater professionalism improved the quality of consular officials, but the fact remains that most consuls who tried cases were not lawyers and had no legal training. Justice in the consular courts could be rough. The problem was exacerbated where a young consular officer could be called upon to act as a vice-consul.

Ernest Satow, when he first acted as a vice-consul in the 1870s, wrote:

> "Fancy me an acting Vice Consul. Such is the truth. It is quite absurd. I did not know how to register a birth till the constable showed me. Now I live in daily terror lest a case should be brought into my court and I am compelled to sit in judgement. Not having the faintest idea of how to preside. To say nothing of complete ignorance of the law."[8]

Sir Edmund Hornby, the first Chief Judge of the British Supreme Court wrote to the then British Foreign Minister, Earl Clarendon, of the consular court system he found in Japan:

> "[A]s the whole judicial business has to be done by Her Majesty's Consular Officers who have no legal education, and who are besides very young and inexperienced, the hearing of cases occupies a great deal of time, and the result is often most unsatisfactory. I do not think however, it would be fair to attribute any blame to the officers themselves, they conscientiously endeavor to do the work before them, but as they have

8 Quoted in Allyson Honjo Yuki, *Japan's Early Experience of Contract Management in Treaty Ports*, p101.

neither the necessary education or experience the result is as unsatisfactory to themselves as to the public. Indeed, their position is very like mine would be if your Lordship insisted on appointing me to the post of Chief Surgeon to a London hospital."[9]

One remedy for this situation was to encourage consular officials to study for the bar. All of the British consular officials who became judges of the Supreme Court had studied for the bar during long leave at Home.

Even before professionalization of the American consular service, some American consular officials were also lawyers. Thomas van Buren, the consul-general in Yokohama in the 1870s and 1880s was a former Civil War general and qualified lawyer. George Seward, the consul-general in Shanghai in the

The Chaos of a Consular Court - A hearing in Kanagawa

9　FO 881/1749. Memoramdum from Edmund Hornby to Lord Clarendon from Yokohama dated October 23, 1869.

1860s and later American Minister in Peking, was also a lawyer. This was a good thing because American consular courts in China and Japan had very broad powers, much broader than the British consular courts. They could and did try serious cases including death penalty cases.

In 1864, in Shanghai, Seward, imposed the death penalty on three prisoners.[10] Only one was executed: one escaped and the other committed suicide. In Yokohama in the early 1880s, van Buren also sentenced a murderer, John Ross, to death, although he was later reprieved. Consular justice could be particularly harsh justice. Initially appeals from the decisions of American Consular Courts could be made to the Ninth Circuit in San Francisco. This was abolished in the late 19th century with appeals only being allowed to the American minister in China or Japan. A system for judicial appeals was re-introduced in 1906 with the creation of the United States Court for China.

In the first 20 years of extraterritoriality, British consular courts had much more limited powers than the American consular courts. Hong Kong had, under the Treaty of Nanking, become a British colony in 1842. The Supreme Court of Hong Kong was established in 1844 (taking over the jurisdiction of the Court for China that had been established in Canton). In addition to having full jurisdiction in Hong Kong, the Hong Kong Supreme Court was given extraterritorial jurisdiction over China and, later, Japan. Death penalty and other serious cases had to be tried in Hong Kong before a jury. This created the serious problem that it was very difficult to gather necessary evidence of a crime in China or Japan that would satisfy a jury in Hong Kong that the accused was guilty. Consuls would prefer to try British prisoners in the consular courts even for serious offences rather than see them acquitted in Hong Kong.

---

10 E Scully, *Bargaining with the State from Afar*, pp68-69.

Appeals from decisions of British consular courts in China could also be brought to the Supreme Court of Hong Kong.[11] From 1847, appeals in criminal cases were limited to cases where the sentence of imprisonment or fine was greater than 12 months or $500. Appeals could also be brought in civil cases where the amount in dispute was greater than $500.[12] This increase in thresholds for bringing an appeal was introduced because the Hong Kong Supreme Court had in 1846 overturned a decision of the Consul in Canton imposing a fine on a Mr Compton for instigating a large-scale riot by Chinese against foreigners. Chief Justice John Hulme had been highly critical of the way in which the case was handled. Sir John Davis, the Governor of Hong Kong wrote to Lord Palmerston, the Prime Minister, stating: "Some fresh ordinance will inevitably be required to prevent such mischievous interference in international cases."[13]

After the opening of Japan, the Hong Kong Supreme Court was also given appellate jurisdiction in Japan. This led to one case where Rutherford Alcock, then the British Minister in Japan, was sued in the Hong Kong Supreme Court for false imprisonment and lost because he had added a term of imprisonment to a fine imposed by a consular court.[14]

Dissatisfaction with the Hong Kong Supreme Court continued for many years. *The Times* of London in July 1863 was scathing:

"This Supreme Court of Hong Kong is the greatest nuisance in the East. Any Consul or Custom-House office who dares to take any measures against any of the 'scum of Europe' found running goods, or levying

---

11 G. Keeton, in Chapter V of *The Development of Extraterritoriality in China*, discusses the position of the Supreme Court of Hong Kong in detail.

12 G. Keeton, *The Development of Extraterritoriality in China*, p230 and 232.

13 G. Keeton, *The Development of Extraterritoriality in China*, p220-223 and p 230.

14 D. Botsman, *Punishment and Power in the Making of Modern Japan*, p133.

blackmail or shooting natives in China or Japan is immediately sued in the Supreme Court."[15]

In early 1865, a question was asked in the British Parliament about whether it was proposed to take any steps to "remedy the evils arising from the Consular Courts in China being the only accessible Courts for the trial of Civil and Criminal as well as the ordinary Police cases; the Consuls not being lawyers by education, and the amount of business having become very large?"[16]

The answer was "yes." To favourable comment from the *Times* and others, it was decided to relieve the Hong Kong Supreme Court of "most troublesome and burdensome work for which it never gained credit,"[17] and to establish in Shanghai Her Britannic Majesty's Supreme Court for China and Japan.

To do so, the Foreign Office turned to a man who had already set up one extraterritorial legal system and had earned a reputation for getting things done: Sir Edmund Hornby.

15 Cited in G. Keeton, *The Development of Extraterritoriality in China*, p240-241.

16 Hansard, HC Deb 23 March 1865 vol 178 c81.

17 J. Norton-Kyshe, *History of the Laws and Courts of Hong Kong*, vol 1, p80.

Part Two

Establishing British Justice
(1865 to 1878)

CHAPTER 3

The Founder: Sir Edmund Hornby

SIR EDMUND HORNBY, the founder of the British Supreme Court for China and Japan, was one of those larger-than-life characters that populated the British Empire. He was by his own and others' accounts a "man's man," not only willing to face down a crowd of Chinese in a remote port angry at the acquittal of a British defendant with a shotgun in his hand, but as the *Times* said in a review of his autobiography to "berate a Secretary of State, rebuke an Ambassador, and bluff or bully for their own ultimate benefit any number of high foreign officials."[1] He had his eccentricities. He kept as his "constant companion in all climes" for more than 40 years a parrot which a judge from the Gold Coast in Africa had given him in lieu of payment for helping him gain his appointment.[2] He also wrote a long account of meeting a ghost in Shanghai, an account that to this day, given the position of the author, is still cited by many as clear proof of paranormal activity.

Despite his eccentricities and probably because of his strong personality, Sir Edmund, then Judge of the British Court at Constantinople was more than likely to have been the Foreign Office's first choice as the first Chief Judge in Shanghai. Hornby knew how to get things done and nothing and nobody scared him.

Hornby had originally been sent to Constantinople in 1855 as Commissioner of the Turkish Loan, money lent by

1 The *Times,* January 18, 1929.
2 Hornby, *An Autobiography,* p54.

*Sir Edmund Hornby, founder and Chief Judge of the
British Supreme Court for China and Japan*

England and France to finance Turkey in its war with Russia. Hornby's job was to monitor the disbursement of the money and make sure it went to the war effort and not into the pockets of Turkish officials. Britain also had extraterritorial rights in the Ottoman Empire. Hornby was asked by the Foreign Office to write a report on the exercise of judicial powers in Turkey by consuls who had no legal training or background. Hornby recommended setting up a court with dedicated staff to handle judicial work. This was accepted and on August 27, 1857, at the age of 32, Hornby was appointed Judge in Constantinople.[3] He was knighted five years later in 1862 at the remarkably early age of 37.

Hornby had been born in 1825 in Yorkshire where his father was from. His mother was one of the Venetian Grimani's with a Palazzo on the Grand Canal. In 1841, at the age of 16, he commenced worked as private secretary to his uncle, Henry Southern, who was then British Minister in Lisbon and later followed him to Spain.

He was called to the bar of the Middle Temple in 1848 after a pupillage with Knight and then James Shaw Willes (later Mr Justice Willes), whom he very much admired. After being called to the bar, he describes having "little or no business for two or three years." His fortune changed when one of his father's clients asked for his opinion in a dispute involving a claim by some merchants against the Spanish Government. Four Queen's Counsel, relying on a notarized translation from Spain, had advised that he did not have a good claim. Hornby, who spoke fluent Spanish, disagreed with the translation. With the assistance of one of the QCs he wrote an opinion that was seen by the Foreign Secretary, Lord Clarendon. Clarendon was an exceptional Spanish scholar and asked to meet Hornby, a young barrister prepared to disagree with the advice of four Queen's Counsel.

---

3 Raymond A. Jones , *The British Diplomatic Service, 1815-1914*, p87.

Hornby recounted his interview:

"Whatever qualms I had were soon dissipated by Lord
Clarendon's kind and genial manner. 'Where did you
learn Spanish?' he asked. I told him in Spain whilst I
was private secretary to my uncle Southern. 'What', he
cried out, 'my old Cambridge chum – why he was my
private secretary whilst I was minister in Madrid. You
have learned to some purpose. Your view is the right
one and the Notary's wrong.' He then asked what I was
doing and if I cared to do some work for the Office, as
he was not satisfied at all with the way the cases from
the Office were sent to the Law Officers for their opinions – adding that it was hardly work for a barrister." [4]

Hornby accepted. He later wrote that he "speedily reduced
chaos to order." Within a month he was asked if he would be the
British Commissioner on a Mixed British and American Commission settling outstanding individual claims between Britain
and the USA. The Commission was due to sit for 15 months
from September 1853 till January 1855 at a salary of £600 per
year. He was told that the work would not interfere with his
private practice and should not reduce it too much. Hornby
was not so concerned about the effect on his practice as he was
only making £25 per year as a barrister. The position led to his
appointment as Commissioner to monitor the Turkish loans.

Hornby was only 41 when he took up his post in Shanghai. He initially left his family in Europe and spent his early
years in Shanghai as a single man. His first wife, the former
Elizabeth Maceroni, died suddenly in Dieppe, France in 1866.
He remarried to Mary Hudson in 1868, who did live with him
in Shanghai.

When he was single in Shanghai his Chinese maid tried to

---

4   Hornby, *An Autobiography*, pp58-59.

set him up with a concubine because "Master work all day, wanchee play at night. More better Master take one piecy girl." He declined the offer, despite an interview with the girl and numerous entreaties from his maid. In some ways, Hornby had been keeping to a half promise he had given before leaving England to establish the court. He wrote:

> "I was invited also the day before I left England to meet Lord Shaftesbury at the house of a China magnate, to discuss no less a subject than a means to put a stop to the practice of English clerks in mercantile houses in China keeping Chinese mistresses. At least no other subject was discussed, and as I did not see how I could in my judicial capacity prevent the habit, I simply promised to set a good example in not keeping one myself, which I am afraid was looked on as a sign of levity." [5]

As a man, he was described as having a "cordial and manly personal character" and being "a resolute foe of pretension or unreality" but also being "curiously deficient in the gifts that secure the applause of the multitude." Perhaps because of this "as an adviser he was sagacious, as ready to give his counsel and help to those who had opposed him as to those who were personally friendly to him."[6]

One newspaper said on his death that he was a "man of extraordinary energy and varied experiences, and that as a raconteur he had few rivals." In particular, he had a sufficient sense of self-awareness that "he was never more amusing than when telling stories against himself." One story that the

---

5 Hornby, *An Autobiography*, pp193-194. Hornby also wrote in his autobiography that English clerks were eventually banned by their employers from keeping Chinese mistresses leading, directly, as he saw it to an increase in embezzlement cases before him as the clerks were then forced to seek the favours of the limited numbers of foreign ladies in Shanghai. See pp288 – 290.

6 Article on Hornby's retirement in the *Japan Weekly Mail*. Reproduced in the *North China Herald*, June 17, 1876, p603.

writer particularly remembered was when Hornby met with the British Attorney-General before heading out to Constantinople as the new Judge. The Attorney-General asked him how he intended to travel. Hornby told him he planned to go via Venice and take a steamer from Venice to Constantinople. The Attorney-General then said "Ah then, perhaps in the solitude of your cabin in the Adriatic you will employ your leisure in reading up a little – a very little criminal law."[7]

It was true that as a judge, Hornby was not in the habit of writing long judgments or engaging in deep analysis of the law.

He also suffered from a particular virulent form of judgitis, "the smartest man in the room" syndrome.[8] Every article on Hornby as a judge, and many of his judgments made it clear that Hornby was one of those judges whom lawyers hate to appear before. Hornby had no time for arguments by lawyers. In most cases, he would have already made up his mind before hearing counsel and would tell them so. As the *North China Herald* in an editorial half way through his term in office commented:

> "Argument of legal questions by trained and educated
> advocates, though expensive, may often throw light
> upon the points at issue and even Chief Judges may
> sometimes be brought by it to see that their first im-
> pressions are wrong."[9]

Hornby was proud of the way he handled cases. Before a trip to Japan in 1870, he wrote:

> "I can dispose of all pending cases – and the mere fact

7   Obituary from a Cairo paper, re-printed in the *North China Herald*, 29 January 1897, p152.

8   In modern times, this should be called the "smartest person in the room syndrome." Female judges are just as susceptible to it as men.

9   *North China Herald* August 11, 1870, p101.

of my being there will precipitate all those that are hatching. There is always a lull in litigation after I have been in place, because I talk people out of their absurd grounds and settle those amicably which really have any points in them without fighting – and in criminal matters, I generally manage to inspire a wholesome respect for the law, that the Rowdy chaps keep in order for at least three months after I leave."[10]

Another article published in Japan on his retirement saw some silver linings in Hornby's attitude to judging:

"of course the faults in his judicial character were severely commented on, for they were only too obvious but really flowed from the most admirable quality of his mind, his keen insight, and almost intuitive power of discerning where the difficulty of a case lay. He strove to strip every case of needless technicalities, and to administer the Law according to the dictates of common sense."[11]

Continuing, the article said, "it frequently happened that his decisions offended the Bar," but "a Judge who is popular with the Bar will generally be one who is fertile in discovering difficulties. A Judge who is popular with the laity will be a Judge who is fertile in finding solutions. Sir Edmund Hornby acted up to the spirit of the Order in Council, and strove to stop litigation." The article concluded that he would be missed by many despite his "many faults of manner and an impulsive temper."

Perhaps not the sort of man you would look to become a

10 Hornby to Foreign Office, March 21, 1870, F017/557, cited in C. Roberts, *The British Courts and Extraterritoriality in Japan, 1859 to 1899*, p50.

11 *Japan Weekly Mail*, May 27, 1876, p464; Reproduced in the *North China Herald*, June 17, 1876, p603.

judge of an established court but, as the Foreign Office clearly decided twice, the exact type of man you want to set up a court in a remote foreign land where there are many opponents to that court's authority.

There is no doubt that Sir Edmund Hornby was the right man for the job.

CHAPTER 4

Establishing the Court

HAVING BEEN APPOINTED to set up the British Supreme Court for China and Japan in Shanghai, Sir Edmund Hornby travelled back to London from Constantinople in late 1864. He recalled:

> "I presented myself at the Foreign Office and set to work with my old friend FS Reilly (afterwards Sir Francis Savage Reilly, KCB) to draw an Order in Council defining the jurisdiction of the new Court to be established in China, and in hard work found occupation."[1]

An Order in Council is a regulation made theoretically by the King or Queen, but in reality drafted by the government. The Orders in Council governing the British Courts in China and Japan were all made under the Foreign Jurisdiction Act, which provided the legal foundation for extraterritoriality.

One of the goals of the British in setting up the British Supreme Court in China and Japan as well as in Constantinople was to set an example to the governments of all three places as to how a legal system should function. In particular, Hornby wanted to show the importance of judicial independence and "how necessary it was to separate entirely the judicial from executive and administrative authority."[2]

---

1 Hornby, *An Autobiography*, p 193.

2 This and following quotes come from: Hornby, *An Autobiography*, pp94-95n. Hornby in his book refers to the Ambassador rather than the Minister. However, during Hornby's time the highest British official in China or Japan was the Minister. I have changed the references in the text to Minister.

In order to do this, the Chief Judge was given full authority over judicial matters without reference to his nominal chief, the British Minister in Peking.[3]

Some years later, Prince Kung, the Emperor's uncle, asked Hornby about his powers. Did he have to obey an order of the Queen in relation to a particular case? Hornby said "certainly not." Prince Kung then asked if he meant that if the Minister gave him an order he would not have to obey it. Hornby said that the Minister would never give him such an order and that if he did he would not take any notice of it. Prince Kung said this made Hornby all-powerful:

"Then you are, in your capacity of Judge, above not only the Minister but also above the Sovereign."

Hornby replied with an explanation of the Rule of Law, which even to this day would not be understood by most Mainland Chinese leaders:

"Not so, I am simply the mouth-piece of the law which, according to our system, rules alike Sovereigns and Ministers."

Prince Kung evidently did not appreciate this lesson. As we shall see, some years later, he would personally ask the British Minister to re-try a British defendant, who had already been acquitted of murder; and then, execute him.[4]

Ordering the system
Hornby and Reilly's work in drafting an Order in Council

---

3 A minister is, in diplomacy, one rank below an ambassador and is usually in charge of a legation. Prior to World War II most countries only established embassies, headed by an ambassador, in major countries. In other countries legations were established, headed by a minister. Until the 1930s, Britain and the United States only had legations in China. The highest diplomatic official in China was therefore, until then, the Minister.

4 See Logan Case in Chapter 18

ended with the issue of the China and Japan Order in Council, 1865 on March 9 of that year. The Order in Council provided that the Supreme Court for China and Japan be presided over by a Judge, who had to be a barrister with a minimum of seven years experience, as well as an Assistant Judge. The existing Consular Courts were renamed Provincial Courts and given very broad powers in relation to civil actions. They were also given a very broad criminal jurisdiction, except that the Supreme Court was given the sole authority to try death penalty cases. Capital cases were either to be tried in Shanghai or when the judges of the Supreme Court travelled around China and Japan on circuit.[5]

In the Shanghai Consular District, the Shanghai Consular Court was abolished and the Supreme Court at Shanghai was given complete jurisdiction to handle all cases. Outside the Shanghai area, the Supreme Court was given concurrent jurisdiction with the Provincial Courts. This meant that parties in consular districts outside Shanghai could choose to bring their case either to their local Provincial Court or directly to the Supreme Court. Appeals could be brought to the Supreme Court in civil cases from Provincial Courts. In criminal cases, appeals were allowed only on points of law (by way of a case stated).

The Supreme Court and Provincial Courts were required to apply English Common Law, Rules of Equity and Statutes, as were from time to time in force in England. Where the Order in Council did not make specific provision, the procedures of courts in England were to be used.

The Deputy – Charles Goodwin
Hornby chose Charles Wycliffe Goodwin, a barrister practicing in London, as his assistant judge. Goodwin was much more famous (then and now) as an Egyptologist, but was also recognized as an expert on the Bible as well as being a music

---

5   The full China and Japan Order in Council 1865 was published in the London Gazette, May 5, 1865, p557.

and art critic.[6]

Goodwin had been a child prodigy and continued to be considered a genius for the rest of his life. Of his prodigious talent, his brother, the Reverend Harvey Goodwin recalled how at the age of nine, Goodwin had found an error in the interpretation of Hieroglyphics by Champollion, one of the early European discoverers of ancient Egypt and said:

Charles Wycliffe Goodwin, Egyptologist, Bible scholar and genius – Hornby's Assistant Judge

"He was much excited by having, as he believed, detected an error into which he averred that Champollion had fallen with respect to the name of one of the kings..."[7]

"An earnest Egyptologist of nine year's old may be regarded as a somewhat interesting specimen of precocity. But my brother's mind, like that of many a remarkable man, flowered and bore fruit early in many departments without injury to the mature crop. As a boy he made himself a fair botanist, a fair geologist, a fair Hebraist; he was well up in the mysteries of Gothic architecture, having studied Rickman before the days of the Cambridge Camden Society; he read German in his play hours, and afterwards made himself a good German scholar by a residence in Berlin; he played the flute with real skill, the violoncello and pianoforte a little, and studied the theory of harmony so as to

6   See for example Review of "The Letters of Peter le Renouf" published in 2004 which makes reference to Goodwin as a renowned Egyptologist. http://www.thebritishmuseum.ac.uk/bmsaes/issue5/renouf.html.

7   Letter by Harvey Goodwin to the *Athenaeum*, reproduced in *North China Herald*, May 18, 1878, p519.

be capable of composing; and all this while pursuing
the ordinary routine of mathematics and classics, in
the latter of which he obtained high honours in a year
remarkable for the names of Vaughan and Lyttelton."

Goodwin was despite his brilliance (or perhaps because of
it) very absent-minded. Harvey Goodwin recalled:

"My brother's powers had many of the attributes of
genius, and he was not free from the eccentricities by
which genius is frequently accompanied. He was as
different from the common run of men in his power
of dealing with the ordinary affairs of life as he was
different from them in high mental gifts. Seldom did he
travel without losing his luggage, or getting into some
difficulty such as ordinary men do not encounter. Upon
one notable occasion, in order to secure himself against
his proverbial ill luck, he determined to sit upon his
portmanteau till the train arrived at the station at which
he was to embark. He did so, or thought that he did so,
but when the train came he found to his dismay that all
his care had been bestowed upon another passenger's
portmanteau, and that his was nowhere to be found."

Goodwin had, like his brother, originally intended to become a priest, but had given up theological studies in the late
1830s. He first travelled in Europe and then studied for the
Bar at Lincoln's Inn. According to his brother, he found the
study of law uncongenial:

"Oh, how he groaned under it. How often he demon-
strated that the system of English jurisprudence was
without philosophical foundation, and with what
delight would he turn from law papers to hieratic
papyri!"

Perhaps not surprisingly, after being called to the bar, Goodwin decided to give up the law and become a teacher. He became a fellow at St Catharine's Hall in 1840 and in 1843 returned to St Catharine's to teach. He, however, lost his fellowship four years later in very strange circumstances. The constitution of St Catharine's required that at least two fellows be priests and one a deacon. When Goodwin became a fellow in 1840, four fellows were priests. By 1847, following first a retirement and then a death, only two priests remained as fellows. St Catharine's therefore voted to forfeit Goodwin's fellowship. Goodwin appealed the decision to Queen Victoria who referred the matter to the Lord Chancellor. The Lord Chancellor upheld the decision of the Hall.[8]

What the true reason was for Goodwin losing his fellowship is a mystery. If St Catharine's had wished to keep him, they could have appointed a new fellow who was a priest or a deacon. In his petition to the Queen, Goodwin stated that he "was not then in deacons' orders, nor in a condition to become one in so limited period." What he meant by this is unclear. He does not appear to be ruling out becoming a deacon or priest, just that for some reason he was not able to do so.

Three years later, Goodwin had what appears to be an illegitimate daughter, Agnes, with an unknown mother. Perhaps the two incidents are connected.

Having lost his fellowship, in 1847, Goodwin returned to London to practice as a barrister. His practice was principally in the probate courts although his work as a barrister did not keep him particularly busy. He did, however, keep himself occupied publishing three legal books on probate, succession duty and copyhold entitlement.

Egyptology remained his great love but he also dabbled in almost every other area of intellectual pursuit. Stephen Glanville, one of the world's most famous Egyptologists, in giving

8 *In Re St Catharine's Hall, Cambridge, Ex Parte Goodwin, London Standard,* December 8, 1849, p4.

a speech on the growth and nature of Egyptology, described Goodwin's life in England:

"By the time Goodwin left Cambridge, he was a first-class Greek scholar, an accomplished Hebraist, and an authority on Anglo-Saxon with valuable editions of new texts to his credit. He also had a considerable knowledge of natural history, especially geology. In London, where his practice was not large, he wrote music and art criticism; was for a time editor of the Literary Gazette; was the only layman among the seven contributors to the much talked of Essays and Reviews (1860); and, because of his Greek and Hebrew scholarship, was frequently consulted by the Revisers of the New Testament. But throughout his life, his main interest, begun when he was at school, was in the elucidation of Ancient Egyptian and Coptic texts, more especially those Egyptian texts written in the cursive script called hieratic."

"In London, he spent much of his time in the British Museum, copying papyri, a material prepared in Egypt from a water plant. He was in close touch with Samuel Burch, then Keeper of the Oriental Department and was constantly exchanging information by correspondence with other leading Egyptologists of his day."[9]

Goodwin had until the 1860s been able to live off income that his father had generated from a very successful solicitor's practice. But his father died in 1859 and his estate got caught up in a probate battle. Goodwin, desiring a more stable income, in 1861, made an application for a position as a judge through Sir Henry Layard, the Parliamentary Under-Secretary to Earl Russell, then Foreign Secretary. Layard,

9 "The growth and nature of Egyptology: an inaugural lecture By Stephen Ranulph Kingdon Glanville", Cambridge University Press.

Foreign Office, March 31, 1865.

The Queen has been graciously pleased to appoint Sir Edmund Hornby, Knt., late Judge of the Supreme Consular Court at Constantinople, to be Judge of the Supreme Court for China and Japan.

The Queen has also been graciously pleased to appoint Charles Wycliffe Goodwin, Esq., to be Assistant Judge of the Supreme Court for China and Japan.

The Queen has also been graciously pleased to appoint John Fraser, Esq., to be Law Secretary and Registrar of the Supreme Court for China and Japan.

Appointment of Hornby, Goodwin and Fraser in the London Gazette

when forwarding Goodwin's application, said he had only met Goodwin once but that he had struck him as "a hard-headed, able man." His letter made no reference to Goodwin's legal qualifications but supported the application on the basis of Goodwin's theological scholarship and especially of his study of hieratic papyri.[10]

Earl Russell was a little more practical and wrote on the note from Layard that what was required was "legal and not theological orthodoxy." He asked that enquiries be made as to "Goodwin's standing and proficiency as a lawyer." These enquiries must have proved satisfactory because on 13 March 1865, four days after the Order in Council was issued, Goodwin received a letter from the Foreign Office on behalf of Earl Russell informing him he had been appointed Assistant Judge of Her Britannic Majesty's Supreme Court for China and Japan.

10 W. Dawson, *Charles Wycliffe Goodwin, a Pioneer in Egyptology*, p38 and generally for biographical information.

Two weeks after this, on 1 April 1865, Goodwin, at the age of 47, married – or, as he put it in a letter to a friend "committed matrimony" - to Augustine Anne Rutherford. Anne, as she preferred to be called, then aged 22, was the daughter of a long-term friend of Goodwin's, Edward Rudderforth, a London surgeon. This appears to have been Goodwin's first marriage. Despite this, as briefly mentioned above, Goodwin had a daughter, Agnes, who had been born in 1850 in an unknown place to an unknown mother.[11] The Rudderforths must have been very good friends, because in 1861, Agnes was living with the Rudderforths as a boarder. Anne, Goodwin's new wife, who was eight years older, must have been like a big sister to Agnes.

The marriage ceremony was conducted at St James' Church, Piccadilly by Goodwin's brother, the Reverend Harvey Goodwin.

Travelling to Shanghai

In June 1865, Hornby and John Fraser left England for Shanghai to set up the court. Fraser, whom Hornby had first met in a Vice-Consulate in Asia Minor, had been appointed Law Secretary. In this position, Fraser was responsible for administration of the court, trying as a magistrate minor criminal cases and prosecuting more serious cases before the court. Hornby and Fraser first stopped in Malta and then went on to Egypt.

Goodwin and Anne, after a brief honeymoon, left a little earlier planning to meet up with Hornby and Fraser in Egypt. They went to France so Goodwin could meet another famous Egyptologist, Francois Chabas, in person in Marseilles. They

---

11 Agnes' origins are a mystery. On her tombstone in the Foreigners' Cemetery in Yokohama, her birthdate is given as April 10th 1850. Goodwin's biographer, Warren Dawson, makes no mention of her, even though he must have known of her. He interviewed Goodwin's surviving children for the biography. Agnes lived with Goodwin and his other children for 6 years in Shanghai and Yokohama so there is no question they knew her. I can find no birth record for her, the only record in England being the 1861 census record showing her living with the Rudderforths. An 1851 census form completed one year after Agnes' birth, Goodwin recorded himself as living alone at Lincolns' Inn and being unmarried. Goodwin's descendants do not know any more of her origins.

then went on to Egypt because, as Hornby put it, Goodwin "longed to take a last fond look at some Papaqui and hiero-glyphic slabs."

Goodwin had arranged to join Hornby and Fraser at Cairo to take the train to Suez. Hornby gave a delightful description of the scene that met him at Cairo station:

"I was surprised to find a guard of honour – several Pashas and Beys and the Corps Consulaire in full rig, cocked hats, etc. A saloon carriage was attached to the train, at the door of which stood an English guard. I asked him what swell was going by the train, to which he replied 'The English Judge'. Feeling certain that I was not that distinguished individual, I patiently waited until the guard saluted. All the cocked hats were raised and an immense hand-shaking took place --- the object being my little fat friend Goodwin in a pith helmet and green veil, his newly-married wife on his arm. Of course I stood by whilst he was escorted to the carriage, and when good-byes were said I humbly asked if I might get in also."[12]

After their train trip, Hornby, Goodwin and Fraser sailed from Suez to Singapore and on to Hong Kong on board the P&O Steamer, the *Carnatic*. They arrived in Shanghai on July 16, 1865.[13] Hornby described landing in Shanghai:

"On landing I was agreeably disappointed to find, instead of a second Wapping, as it had been described to me in London, a handsome quay or bund, along the

12 Hornby, *An Autobiography*, p.198.

13 Hornby, *An Autobiography*, p193 to 203; the *North China Herald* reported on July 1, 1865 (p102) that the arrival of Hornby and his judicial staff was expected by the next Mail but as far as they could "ascertain no preparations had been made for their reception." For their ship and arrival in Hong Kong, see Norton Kyshe, *History of the Laws and Courts of Hong Kong*, Vol 2, p80. W. Dawson, *Charles Wycliffe Goodwin: A Pioneer of Egyptology*, p43.

Shanghai as it was when Hornby and Goodwin arrived

length of which were visible a line of very handsome buildings – indeed it would require but little stretch of the imagination, and hardly then be an exaggeration, to call some of them palaces. Fine roomy house they undoubtedly are, and as convenient and comfortable inside as they are architecturally tasteful and fair to look upon outside …. Several of the streets were paved, but they were indifferently lighted but badly drained. "I was much struck by the completeness of everything in Shanghai. There were no shams in it. There is a beautiful English Church, now converted into a Cathedral; a Roman Catholic Church, and American Episcopal Church, and two Dissenting Chapels. There is an excellent hospital for foreigners under the care of an able physician and six sisters of Charity."[14]

Goodwin was not as enamoured of Shanghai as Hornby. In a letter to his sister, he described Shanghai as "very like England - green and flat … Everything here is in a state of disorganization – People rob one another – and submit to be robbed by their Chinese servants." In a later letter to a friend

14 Hornby, *An Autobiography*, p204 to 206. Hornby may have been describing some things that were built between when he arrived in 1865 and left in 1876.

he wrote: "Shanghai certainly is not the most interesting place to come to – The City is a second or third rate one, & the country around it is very dreary, flat and damp."[15]

No proper preparations had been made for the arrival of the officers of the court. Goodwin and his wife were invited by Reverend Butcher, the Chaplain of Settlement, to stay at the Chaplaincy.

The day after their arrival, Hornby was invited to a farewell dinner for Her Majesty's 67th Regiment. After a number of toasts, Mr Keswick proposed a toast to the health of Hornby, "who had for the first time appeared amongst them, but from whom much is expected." The toast was then drunk with acclamation. Hornby responded, saying he "regretted that his first speech in Shanghai necessarily commenced with an apology, but really the heat of the weather and the lateness of the hour compelled him to content himself with expressing his warm thanks for the hospitable manner in which he had been received."[16]

Very soon after this, Hornby was elected Commandant of the Shanghai Volunteer Corps, a paramilitary force made up of foreign volunteers that had been established to defend Shanghai during the Taiping rebellion in the 1850s. He was elected despite a brave suggestion – subsequently withdrawn - by Mr Lawrance, that "toadyism" in the appointment of Commandants was not appropriate.[17]

Hornby also sat, at the invitation of the Consul and with the consent of the parties, as an assessor in one of the last cases before the Shanghai Consular Court before it was subsumed into the Supreme Court, *Gilfillan v Glover & Co.* Gilfillan was claiming for losses arising from the failure of Glover & Co. to sell a steamer, the *Chusan*, at Nagasaki. The case report mere-

15 Letter dated March 8, 1866 to Renouf, cited in W. Dawson, *Charles Wycliffe Goodwin: A Pioneer of Egyptology* p44.

16 *North China Herald*, July 22, 1865, p116.

17 *North China Herald*, July 29, 1865, p119.

ly states: "Judgment entered for the defendants with costs."[18] However, from a letter written to the *North China Herald* by Gilfillan, it appears, not surprisingly, that Hornby effectively took over the case and delivered the judgment.[19]

With that taste of judicial power, Hornby was now ready to open his new court.

---

18 *Gilfillan v Glover & Co, North China Herald*, August 12, 1865 p126-127. Glover & Co was the large Western trading house based in Nagasaki. Glover became very successful and his house is still preserved in Nagasaki.

19 Letter from Mr Gilfillan, *North China Herald*, August 19, 1865, p131.

CHAPTER 5

Opening the Court: The First Cases

HER BRITANNIC MAJESTY'S Supreme Court for China and Japan was formally opened on September 4, 1865. The *North China Herald* in a summary of the week in which they said that the "Shanghai is again flooded by rain and the streets are buried in mud" and that the "incidents of the week have been few and uninteresting," reported:

> "On Monday, the Supreme Court of China and Japan was formally opened by Sir Edmund Hornby. The Royal Warrants appointing the Judge, Assistant Judge and Law Secretary were read, and Sir Edmund Hornby then proceeded to swear himself into office, after which the oath was administered to Messrs. Goodwin (Assistant Judge) and Fraser (Law Secretary). Messrs. Myburgh, Eames and Robinson signed the roll of practitioners in the Court, and the ceremony ended."[1]

Goodwin was installed as Judge of Civil Cases and Fraser, the Law Secretary, as magistrate. Hornby reserved for himself all "heavy and appeal cases – civil and criminal."[2]

The legal practitioners of the court were either barristers or solicitors admitted in England. Unlike most other English common law jurisdictions, from the start and for the lifetime of the court, there was no distinction drawn in the court be-

1 *North China Herald*, September 9, 1865, p142.
2 Hornby, *An Autobiography*, p214.

tween a solicitor and a barrister. Solicitors could appear as advocates in the court and barristers could practice in partnership with other barristers or solicitors and handle work traditionally within the realm of solicitors, such as conveyancing and drawing up wills. Many firms that would subsequently be set up in Shanghai would be partnerships between barristers or between barristers and solicitors. The legality of this was challenged some 50 years later in the Privy Council.[3]

The court almost immediately started work. John Fraser created Judge's Notebooks for use by the judges and himself to record the cases that were heard. For many cases, the judge's notebooks remain the only record of the case. The first notebook for evidence in criminal cases dated September 4, 1865 covers cases from September to December 1865. It is partially scorched and looks like it has been rescued from a fire, presumably the fire of 1870 that burnt down the Consulate building.[4]

The book is headed:

"Her Majesty's Supreme Court, Shanghai:
Notes of Evidence in Criminal Cases.
John Fraser, Clerk."[5]

The first three cases before the court were on September 5, 1865. Unlike the rest of the notebooks, which contain very detailed notes of the evidence given in each case, the first three cases are very short. The notes for the first three cases were:

R vs John Frerar – Drunk incapable.
Brought up by Policeman Ulls No.999. Cautioned and sent to the Consulate to be tested on board.

---

3 See *Home v Douglas* in Chapter 37.
4 Almost all of the judge's notebooks have survived and are now kept in the National Archives in London. The Consulate fire is discussed in Chapter 8.
5 FO 1092/158

R vs John Procter – Vagrant.
Procter said that he worked his passage here from
Hong Kong and has been without means during the
last 6 weeks which he passed in hospital. Got a week's
support from Brothers and gave himself up to Policeman.
Sentence 15 days imprisonment

R vs Sali – Native of Bangkok.
Accused of wounding with intent. Taken by the [illeg-
ible] and brought to the Consulate yesterday morning.
Remanded to this day. Mahomet boatswain of the [
illegible].
No Jurisdiction

The Sali case thus became the first case where the Court
had to decline jurisdiction because the Defendant was not
British.

The cases heard two days later show what a rough place
early Shanghai could be. First up was *R v J Bigg*. Bigg was accused of making a disturbance at a hotel. He was on bail and
appeared to be either drunk or suffering from the tremors. He
was remanded to prison for the Doctor of the Police to certify
when he would be in a fit state to defend himself. There were
numerous other vagrancy charges as well as a charge of dis-
obeying a lawful command, (*R v James Reeves, William Box and
James Keell*) stealing money (*R v JG Wilson*) and begging (*R v
Ali*) as well as numerous charges of being drunk and incapable.

At the end of September, and then six weeks later in November, the first three "heavy" cases came before Hornby.
The first case challenged the right of the British to prosecute
on behalf of the Chinese Emperor. The next challenged the
entire foundation of the government of Shanghai and other
treaty ports. The third was the first death penalty case to
come before the court.

The right to prosecute

Messrs. Reynolds and Holt were the owners of a block of land on the Putong (Pudong) side of the river, opposite the International Settlement. They had extended the river bank to reclaim land and build a jetty. The Chinese Harbour Master of the Whangpoo River and the Conservator or the Yangtze River had complained about the works to the British Consulate because they were affecting the flow of, and navigation on, the river. The consulate issued a summons in the Supreme Court for Reynolds and Holt to show cause why they should not be punished for, and prohibited from, blocking the river.[6]

Reynolds and Holt had a number of defences, including that their lease entitled them to conduct the works. Of greater importance, they alleged that the British Consul had no power to bring a prosecution on behalf of the Chinese Emperor. Hornby made short work of this argument. He said that he was surprised the argument had been made because if it was allowed to succeed the result would be absurd. Either, the Government of China would have no remedy in cases in which British subjects were wrong-doers, or the "Emperor would be bound to appear as a suitor in a Foreign court on his own soil." Hornby ruled that by obtaining extraterritorial rights, Her Majesty had "implicitly undertaken that she will compel Her subjects to respect the laws of China, as well as the laws of their own country" and would not "subject the sovereign power the indignity of appearing on its own soil in the character of a suitor in a Foreign Court."

The Municipal Council's power to tax

In the next case, Hornby needed to decide if the Shanghai Municipal Council could impose and collect rates.[7] Mr and

6   *R v Reynolds & Holt, North China Herald*, October 21, 1865, p167.

7   *W Keswick, J Hose, T Hanbury, JC Coutts, G Nye and W Probst v the estate of G Wills and S Wills, North China Herald*, November 18, 1865, p182. The case at the time had to be brought in the name of council members. The Land Regulations were amended in 1869 to allow the Municipal Council to sue and be sued in name of the Council. (See the new Article 27).

Mrs Wills had died leaving an infant son. Rates were owed to the council on various pieces of land in what had been the British settlement as well as what had been the American Settlement, called Hongque, before the two settlements were merged. The council sued the Wills' estate for back rates.

This was a very important case that would confirm the legality of the management and financing of Shanghai International Settlement for its entire existence. The legal foundation of the International Settlement was the Land Regulations that had been agreed between the British Consul and Shanghai Taotai in 1853. Formally, the British Superintendent of Trade had issued them under power granted to him by an Order in Council. The Land Regulations provided the basic rules under which Shanghai was to be governed. They established a municipal council elected by ratepayers. The Shanghai Municipal Council could issue by-laws made under the Land Regulations.

The main question in the Wills case was whether the Land Regulations gave the Council the power to charge rates. Other residents of Shanghai had also questioned whether there was proper legal authority for the Municipal Council to levy rates. But without money the Council could not operate, and there would be no money to provide services such as roads and policing. The residents, despite misgivings, paid the rates. The trustees of the Wills estate, however, told the court they had an obligation to maintain the estate and only make payments that they were legally liable for. If they paid money they were not obliged to do so, they could face claims against them for breach of trust. The trustees argued that the Land Regulations were a private agreement between land renters in Shanghai and were thus not binding on those who chose not to participate.

The British Superintendent of Trade had been given power to make regulations for the "peace, order and good government" of British subjects in Shanghai. This was the phrase used in all British colonies to give the colonial governments broad powers to pass laws. The trustees, however, argued that the making of land regulations that gave the power of government to private individuals, that is the Municipal Council, were not regulations for the "peace, order and good government" of the British subjects.

Hornby made short work of this argument saying that there was no reason why the Superintendent of Trade should not have as broad powers as a colonial government to control British subjects. Taking into account the special circumstances of extraterritoriality, the Superintendent had to have that authority:

> "Indeed I am inclined to go further and say it is incumbent on Her Majesty, by virtue of an obligation to be implied from the very privilege of exclusive jurisdiction granted to Her, to provide for the peace, good order and government of those of Her subjects who are within the Empire of China and removed by the consent of the Sovereign power of that country from the operation of its laws and the jurisdiction of its native Magistrates."

He found that the council could charge rates. The courts of almost all the other treaty powers in Shanghai at the time made similar decisions. The previous year the Prussian and Danish consular courts had upheld the Council's taxing power. The same year the French and American consular courts also issued similar decisions. The American Consul-General, George Seward, however, held that the power to charge rates came not from treaty rights but from a delegation of power from the Chinese government. He appreciated that he "was treading on delicate ground" because if this was the case, China could withdraw its consent at any time.[8] But in a mixture of subtle diplomatese and legalese, he concluded by pointing out that the foreign military that was backing the treaties would make that difficult:

> "We are, moreover, so situated in virtue of the extraterritorializing provisions of the Treaties, that it would not be easy to enforce any regulations without our consent, and we are thus able to assert a certain pressure upon the authorities to uphold such Regulations as we deem right."

The first murder

Two days after hearing the Wills case, Hornby tried, with a jury, the first murder trial in the Supreme Court. Mohamed, a Malay seaman who lived in Bamboo Town in the northeastern corner of Hongque, had killed his Chinese wife, Leemah. Leemah was an opium addict who also worked as a prostitute when Mohamed was at sea. Mohamed and Leemah had adopted two Chinese girls aged nine and twelve. Mohamed doted on the girls.[9]

Mohamed had heard rumours that Leemah was prostituting herself. Things came to a head when Leemah pawned his clothes and refused to allow him to see their daughters. After a quarrel, he stabbed Leemah seven times, twice in the kidney. She died quickly. Mr. York, the runner for the Ghaut Serang - the senior supervisor of the Malay community - had found Mohamed at his door. Mohamed told York that he had killed his wife. York did not find any knife. Mohamed said that he had thrown it away.

It appeared a very simple case. However, when Mr. York

---

8 G. Keeton, *The Development of Extraterritoriality in China*, p346-7 and for the quote from Seward below.

9 *R v Mohamed*, North China Herald, November 18, 1865, p183. The names of the jury members was not given in the report.

found him, there was no blood at all on Mohamed's clothes. Dr Johnston who gave medical evidence said that Leemah's clothing was very thin and there should have been some blood splatter.

Phillip Myburgh, a British barrister, prosecuted. Given that Mohamed was facing a death sentence, Mr Lawrance, the British lawyer who had objected to toadyism in appointing Hornby as Commandant of the SVC, volunteered to appear for the defence free of charge. All those present in the court were very aware that this was the first death penalty case to be tried by a British court in China. Myburgh and Lawrence both mentioned this in their arguments. After all the evidence was heard, Hornby summed up for the jury. He very properly cautioned the jury that they might feel sympathy for Mohamed who was facing the death penalty. However, referring to Leemah, he said there was "another being whom you have not seen for whom the same consideration is due."

Hornby said that the only possible defence Mohamed had was that of provocation. This could reduce his crime from murder to manslaughter. In order for provocation to be proved, it would be necessary for the jury to be convinced that Leemah's actions had been so bad as to cause Mohamed to kill her out of passion. Hornby made it clear that he did not consider this to be the case. He told the jury that "society should not be exposed to the consequences of a man losing his temper and surrendering himself to the dominion of his passions, until he is so overcome as to lose all power of regulating his actions."

The jury retired for 45 minutes. Upon returning, they convicted Mohamed of murder but with a strong recommendation for mercy. Before passing sentence Hornby asked if Mohamed had anything to say. He begged for mercy recounting Leemah's terrible behavior. Hornby put on the black cap and sentenced Mohamed to death. He said he would pass on the recommendation of mercy to the minister in Peking, saying it was "possible he might regard it favourably inasmuch as this was the first case of the kind brought before the Court."

Mohamed's sentence was commuted to 20 years in prison and he was sent to Hong Kong the next year to serve his sentence.

The court had now been established. Three of the men who would serve on it in the future were also just beginning their careers in East Asia. Another two were soon to follow.

CHAPTER 6

The Younger Generation: Learning the Ropes

JUST BEFORE OR SOON after the opening of the British Supreme Court for China and Japan, almost all the men who would play important roles in the court in the 19th century - three young consular officers and two young barristers - commenced their careers in China and Japan.

One, Robert Mowat, very soon after the Supreme Court was established, took over as Acting Law Secretary when John Fraser fell ill in 1866. Fraser died in Marseille, France on 18 April 1867.[1]

Mowat had joined the China Consular Service in 1864. He had been born in 1843 in Edinburgh, Scotland making him 21 when he came to China. He was educated in Edinburgh before attending London University, which nominated him for the Foreign Office exam. In his early years, Mowat was an avid cricketer, being a handy wicketkeeper/batsman. He was also a very good chess player solving the newspaper's chess problems quickly and with ease.[2]

Mowat joined the consular service at almost exactly the same time as two other men who would be long standing

---

1 Fraser's death: Foreign Office List July 1867. Due to Fraser's illness, Hornby at one point apologised to the Shanghai Volunteers for failure to attend meetings and offered to resign. *North China Herald*, March 9, 1867, p39.

2 Obituary, The *Times*, June 9, 1925; Cricket match reports *North China Herald*, October 17, 1868 - Mowat scored 82; not out and took a number of catches; November 2, 1876 Mowat keeping and stumping opening batsman. For his chess prowess, see Chapter 24 on the Carew case.

colleagues and rivals for promotion: Hiram Shaw Wilkinson and George Jamieson. In 1864, all three of them took the Foreign Office examination for admission to the consular service made up of papers in Arithmetic, Compound Addition, Orthography, Handwriting, Intelligence, Geography, Precis, Latin, French and English. Mowat came second and Wilkinson third. Jamieson was placed either fourth or fifth.[3]

H.S. Wilkinson (as he generally described himself) left behind his personal papers including the documents he used to apply to join the consular service. These give some idea of the type of recruit the Foreign Office was looking for to send to China and Japan and the long journey they needed to make to take up their posts in East Asia.

At the time of his application, Wilkinson was just completing a Bachelor of Arts at the Queen's University Belfast. He was recommended by Lord Lurgan and received a glowing reference from his professor, George Craick, who described him as a student of the "first rank." Presciently, Professor Craick described Wilkinson's character:

"For regularity in attendance, diligence in preparation and perfect propriety of demeanour I have never had a more exemplary student. And he is distinguished by unusual clearness of understanding, soundness of judgements, readiness in exercise of his faculties, nerve and self-possession; - so that he is not apt to break down in new circumstances, but may rather be counted on as likely to rise with the occasion to be invigorated by the presence of difficulties, and to do more than fulfill expectations."[4]

---

3   C. Roberts, "Hiram Shaw Wilkinson (1840-1926)", *Britain and Japan Biographical Portraits*, Vol VIII, p165 and n3. This article provides a good biography of Wilkinson's career in Japan.

4   Letter of reference from George Lillie Graick, Professor of English Literature and History, Queen's College Belfast PRONI D1292/C/1 (Wilkinson Papers).

The Danish, Belgian, Norwegian and Swedish Consul-Generals all gave Wilkinson personal recommendations attesting to his good character. Wilkinson had worked for the firm of Colvil Auldt for four years before going to university. His former employer wrote that "he conducted himself to the entire satisfaction of said firm."[5]

Wilkinson had just scraped into the service. At the time he took the examination he was 24 - over the age limit for student interpreters. However, as he had been nominated before he turned 24, Earl Russell, the Foreign Secretary, decided he could take the exam. Wilkinson was offered a position in early August 1864. Student interpreters were allowed to select which country they wished to serve in. On 18 August 1864, Wilkinson wrote to Earl Russell saying that his preference would be for an appointment in Japan. He asked that he be allowed to leave for Asia in October so that he could complete his B.A.[6]

Unlike other student interpreters, Wilkinson was married. In his letter to Earl Russell, he asked that the passage for his wife, Prudie, be paid saying he wished to "call to Your Lordship's attention to the case of the wives of officers and soldiers proceeding to distant countries; who are always, I believe, allowed to accompany their husbands at public cost." This was the first the Foreign Office had heard that Wilkinson was married. One junior official wrote in an internal memo that "we do not encourage these early marriages as the Foreign Office does not provide married quarters for Assistants and, a fortiori, would not for Student Interpreters." The official suggested that one-third of Prudie's passage be paid adding a warning to his superiors that Wilkinson was Lurgan's protégé. Edmund Hammond, the Permanent Undersecretary, took a harsher view and said the fact Wilkinson was married

....

5   PRONI D1292/D/2 (Wilkinson Papers).

6   PRONI D1292/C/1 (Wilkinson Papers) Letter from Wilkinson to Russell 18 August 1894

would have been a bar to his appointment, but conceded the offer could not now be withdrawn. Hammond, however, said that Wilkinson should be discouraged from taking his wife to Japan. Earl Russell took a simpler view and decided that Wilkinson must pay Prudie's travelling costs. Wilkinson did pay the extra costs - £102, about half his first year's salary - out of his own pocket.[7]

Wilkinson and Prudie set out for their new life in the Far East on October 27, 1864 sailing from Southampton on board the P&O ship, *Delta*. In those days it was a long journey to Japan of at least two months. It must have felt as if they were leaving Ireland for good. They first sailed to Cairo where they changed for a train to take them to Suez. From Suez they boarded the P&O ship, *Massilia*, for Shanghai via Bombay. From Shanghai they sailed for Yokohama.[8]

Robert Mowat and George Jamieson, both Scotsmen, had sailed for China two months earlier. Mowat had, it appears, an uneventful trip. Jamieson, on the other hand, had probably the most interesting introduction to the East Asia of any new appointee. Jamieson, who was also 21, had graduated from Aberdeen University. He arrived in Shanghai after Tientsin had already iced up for the winter. He was put on a gunboat to Chefoo. There, the British Consul, M.C. Morrison, placed him in a mule litter telling him it would take 16 days to reach Peking overland. A missionary, presumably taking pity on the young man, lent him a sheepskin coat to keep warm. Due to heavy snow it took close to a month to make it to Peking. After 20 days Jamieson had run out of money. He found his way to the Chinese intendant's yamen at the provincial capital where after initially being refused entry he was allowed to meet the magistrate. The magistrate lent him 30 taels and he

7   C. Roberts, "Hiram Shaw Wilkinson (1840-1926)", *Britain and Japan Biographical Portraits*, Vol VIII, p165 for the internal Foreign Office correspondence. Costs: PRONI D1292/C/1 (Wilkinson Papers)

8   PRONI D1292/C/1 (Wilkinson Papers) for the tickets and information on the voyage.

reached Peking a week later.[9]

Wilkinson, Mowat and Jamieson all joined the Foreign Office as student interpreters, the entry level position.[10] The main role of a student interpreter, as the title suggests, was to study Chinese or Japanese and to act as an interpreter. The language training was very tough and all those who made it through the courses could speak, read and write Chinese or Japanese fluently.

By the time Mowat and Jamieson started learning Chinese, the courses were well organized. One student interpreter William Henry Wilkinson (no relation to Hiram Shaw), wrote a book *Where Chinese Drive*, describing the life of a student interpreter in Peking.[11] Wilkinson's experience was summarized in a talk to the Royal Asiatic Society:

"He explained that soon after his arrival a student was provided with a Chinese teacher, and provided himself with a copy of Wade's *Yu-yen Tzu-erh Chi* better known under the title 'A Progressive Course of Colloquial Chinese', which was the only orthodox introduction to the study of Mandarin. The Assistant Chinese Secretary directed his studies. "Working hours are theoretically from 9 to 12, and 1 to 4, but custom has altered these to 10 to 12, and 2 to 4. The four hours thus left will be divided up . . . much in this way: 10 to 10.30 Tone Exercises/10.30 to 11 Reading with Teacher/11 to 11.30 New work/11.30 to 11.45 Writing/11.45 to 12 Character Slips/the Afternoon Scheme being much the same. "Only those who have studied Chinese will appreciate the toil and brain-teasing implied in this simple-looking course of study. As Wilkinson remarks after

9 P.D. Coates, *The China Consuls*, p347

10 I. Nish, *Britain and Japan, Biographical Portraits.*

11 No relation to H.S. and H.P. Wilkinson. The book was published anonymously but is now attributed to Wilkinson.

explaining the 'drill' for acquiring the correct tone in
which to pronounce each character: 'It was dreadful
work. The poor teacher would get hoarse, and have
to imbibe an enormous quantity of tea'. There was an
examination in colloquial Chinese at the end of the first
year and another, in which written work was generally supposed to hold more weight, at the end of the
second year. Besides studying Wade's course, they were
encouraged to dip into the daily *Peking Gazette* in which
they sometimes found a good murder case to read."[12]

Many years later, Norwood Allman, an American student
interpreter, described his language training:

"The first workday each one of us was given an individual Chinese teacher. These gentlemen, well versed
in the Chinese language, were just as ignorant of teach-
ing methods as we were of their language. Their method was to read these strange sounds to us, hand us the
book and tell us to read the sounds back to them. This
would go on for hours. We soon got this method down
to a point where the teacher read while the student
slept and vice versa. By perseverance and countless
repetition we managed to grasp and hold on to a few of
these weird sounds. It was a red-letter day for me when
I overheard one Chinese say to another, 'Listen to what
that foreigner is saying. Sounds almost like Chinese.'
Little did he realize how hard I had worked, between
naps, to make those sounds."[13]

For Wilkinson, in Japan, the training was not so organized,

---

12 Glynn Jones, "The British Legation at Peking 1860 to 1959", a lecture delivered on
August 20, 1962 to the Royal Asiatic Society, published in the Journal of the Royal Asiatic Society, Vol (3), 1963, p.76.

13 N. Allman, *Shanghai Lawyer*, p26 to 27.

but equally intensive. Two of the earliest student interpreters in Japan were Ernest Satow and Russell Robertson who arrived in Japan in 1860, only four years before Wilkinson. Both Satow and Robertson were first sent to Peking to learn Chinese. This was thought a good introduction to Chinese characters which would help them with studying Japanese. The experiment was stopped after eight months when it was found that a letter sent from Japan in Japanese could be not be read by anyone in Peking.[14]

When Satow and Robertson arrived in Japan they found that no arrangements had been made to teach them. There were no textbooks and no teachers. At first they studied by themselves but later were given funds to employ an American missionary for two hours a week. They employed another teacher with their own money. They learnt the language the hard way, "puzzling out the language with books and a Japanese teacher." Satow was a quick learner and in one year could provide passable translation of documents. In 1865 he was appointed as the first "Interpreter for the Japanese language." All future student interpreters in Japan, including Wilkinson, were required to study in the same way but did not learn Chinese first.[15]

Wilkinson's arrival in Yokohama with Prudie was a surprise to the British consular authorities in Japan who had not expected any of the student interpreters to be married. Indeed, Wilkinson had the honour of being the reason the rules were changed to provide that student interpreters could not be married or get married. While still a student interpreter, in 1866, Wilkinson had one more surprise for his superiors. The birth of his first son, Hiram Parkes Wilkinson, called Harrie. In an act of sycophancy that certainly did not hurt Wilkinson's career, Harrie had been named after Harry Parkes who had been promoted from China to be the British Minister in

14 E. Satow, A Diplomat in Japan, p3 and for their learning experience in Japan below.
15 I. Nish, *Britain and Japan, Biographical Portraits*, p99

Tokyo. Three years later, Prudie gave birth to a second son, Thomas Gaffikin Wilkinson. Tragically, she died soon after in March 1870 leaving Wilkinson the widowed father of two young boys. Harrie also almost died as a child in Yokohama, when his Japanese amah let his pram roll down the hill, being saved only by it hitting the wall of the French Consulate. Wilkinson took long leave soon after Prudie's death and took the boys home to Belfast. He never remarried.[16]

After completing their language training Wilkinson and Jamieson were both appointed consular officers. On January 1, 1868 Wilkinson was appointed to the rank of Third Assistant. In that position he acted as the accountant in the legation in Tokyo. In 1870, he was appointed a First Assistant, backdated to April 1, 1868. Jamieson was appointed a 2nd Class Assistant in 1867 and in 1868 appointed, despite his very junior rank at the time, Acting Consul in Tainan, Taiwan.

Wilkinson during his long leave studied for a Bachelor of Laws at Queen's College in Belfast as well as pursuing a pupillage at the Middle Temple. In order to gain experience in the courts he also worked for the County Antrium Prosecutor. He qualified as a barrister of the Middle Temple after completing only seven of the required eight terms after the personal intervention of the Foreign Secretary, Lord Granville, with the bencher's of the Middle Temple.[17]

Unlike Wilkinson and Jamieson, Mowat appears never to have entered full time consular service. As soon as John Fraser became ill in 1866, he was appointed Acting Law Sec-

16 Position as student interpreter: *London and China Telegraph*, February 28, 1867; Birth of Harrie, Harrie's near death and return to Belfast: HP Wilkinson Reminiscences: *North China Herald* of October 31, 1925 pp200-201; Birth of Thomas and Wilkinson's position: Baptism Certificate of TG Wilkinson, PRONI, D1292. Change in regulations: P.D. Coates, *The China Consuls*, p.346. A number of consular officers in Japan entered long term relations with Japanese women. Ernest Satow publicly acknowledged, but never married, his common law Japanese wife. As shall be seen in Chapter 26, JJ Enslie another senior consular official, left a substantial sum of money to Japanese housekeeper, Ms Kozawa, out of "love and affection." Perhaps (and I have not been able to find any evidence of this) Wilkinson entered a similar relationship.

17 C. Roberts, "Hiram Shaw Wilkinson (1840-1926)", *Britain and Japan Biographical Portraits*, Vol VIII, p166.

retary of the Supreme Court and then to the subtantive position in 1868. Perhaps Mowat had not been as successful in his language studies as Wilkinson and Jamieson and the position in the court, which did not require Chinese language skills, suggested to him.

Mowat also applied to study for the bar during his long leave in 1869 "in order to qualify himself for his duties." Jamieson was appointed Acting Law Secretary of the Supreme Court while Mowat was away. After Mowat returned, Jamieson took his long leave and also studied for the bar.[18]

Mowat was the Law Secretary when Robert George, an Indian foreman at Farnham and Co at Collier's dock, was tried for the murder of a Chinese co-worker, Wang Aran. The shooting had occurred some hours after a violent confrontation between them, which had started when Wang "broke wind" in front of George. Wang had also committed a "revolting act" over their food. George then insulted a carpenter and yelled "I'll have my revenge before 6 o'clock tonight." He returned later with a gun and shot and killed Wang and seriously injured another carpenter. After being arrested by a British co-worker, George told him, "I am not sorry for the Chinaman."

George was charged with the crime of willful murder. The Chinese authorities viewed the case very seriously and sent a Chee Seen or deputy magistrate to assist in the trial of the case.[19] The bench in the old consular court was packed. Sir Edmund Hornby and Charles Goodwin were there in their scarlet robes and white wigs together with the Chee Seen, also dressed in his official robes. The British Consul in Shanghai, Walter Medhurst, also sat on the bench in his full dress consular uniform of dark blue with gold buttons.

---

18 Letter from Mowat to Hornby January 15, 1869, FO17/530 cited in C. Roberts, The British Courts and Extraterritoriality in Japan 1859-1899, p54.

19 *R v Robert George*, *North China Herald*, July 22, 1869 p389 and August 5, 1869, p421. *Supreme Court and Consular Gazette*, July-Dec, 1869.

The very tall Richard Rennie lights a cigar on a street lamp

Normally, Mowat, as the Law Secretary, would have prosecuted the case. However, probably given the seriousness of the charge and the Chinese authorities' interest in the case, a barrister, Richard Rennie was briefed for the prosecution. A young barrister, newly arrived in town, Nicholas Hannen, defended George. Rennie and Hannen were both destined to become judges and this case pitched them against each other for the first time in a major case.

Rennie, who had been born in 1839, was the fourth son of George Rennie who had been a well-known sculptor, Liberal Member of Parliament and Governor of the Falkland Islands. His great uncle, John Rennie, was a famous Scottish engineer who, amongst other things, designed the new London Bridge. Rennie was called to the bar of the Inner Temple in 1860, having qualified by commencing a pupilage straight out of school. His father died the same year leaving a relatively modest estate of £3,000. Rennie practiced before the Western Circuit for five years before moving to Hong Kong, where his brother, William Hepburn Rennie, had been serving as Auditor-General since 1858. As he put it himself, he had come to the Far East to "seek his fortune." He stayed in Hong Kong for two months before he moved to Shanghai in 1866, at the age of 27, and "fell in love with the place." The year after moving to Shanghai, in November 1867, Rennie married very well to Marie de la Rue, the young Swedish widow of Thomas De la Rue at St John's

Church, Paddington.[20] Rennie was very tall. All cartoons from the time show him towering over everyone else.

Nicholas Hannen who had been born in 1842 was three years younger than Richard Rennie. He was the sixth son (and thirteenth child) of James Hannen, a wine merchant, of Kingswood, Dulwich. Because of a "reversal of family fortune" that seems to have been caused by a clerk embezzling from his father's business, he was raised on the Continent in Koblenz, Ostend and Liege. One of his sisters was responsible for his schooling. The family returned from the Continent when he was around 15 and they lived at 1 Kildare St Bayswater. Hannen traveled from there daily to City of London School, according to his sister's journal, walking one way.[21]

He then attended University College London where he obtained a BA in 1862 with honours in logic and moral philosophy. He was called to the Bar at the Inner Temple in 1866. He arrived in Shanghai, via Hong Kong, in 1868, at the age of 26, and was admitted to the Supreme Court for China and Japan in that year. Like Rennie, he had a relative in China. His brother, Charles Hannen, was with the Imperial Maritime Customs. Another brother, James Hannen, was a judge in England and a good friend of Edmund Hornby. No doubt Hornby had told James Hannen that there were good opportunities as a barrister for his younger brother in China. Hannen married Jessie Woodhouse, the daughter of James Woodhouse of Henley-on-Thames in 1869, the year after he moved to Shanghai. He had met and become engaged to Jessie while at university.[22]

....

20 George Rennie: Oxford Dictionary of National Biography; Richard Rennie: *London and China Telegraph* December 9, 1878, p1045; *North China Herald*, April 3, 1891, p408-9; *Cork Examiner Morning*, November 12, 1867 (Marriage); William Hepburn Rennie: Hong Kong Audit Commission History (www.aud.gov.hk).

21 Email from Sarah Collins, keeper of the Hannen family records, 15 May 2004.

22 Biographical information: Obituary, Times, 28 April, 1900; Obituary, North China Herald, May 2, 1900, p766; Hannen was admitted as a barrister in Hong Kong on 2 March 1868. See: Norton Kyshe, *History of the Laws of Hong Kong*, Vol 2, p141; Re James Hannen: Hornby, An Autobiography, p54. Hornby, despite mentioning Nicholas Hannen, makes no mention of the fact that Nicholas Hannen was the brother of James Han-

For George's trial, a jury of five Englishmen was empaneled. Rennie, for the prosecution, called three English and five Chinese witnesses to give evidence. The Chinese magistrate assisted with the examination of the Chinese witnesses. There was no doubt that George had killed the co-worker. The only question for the jury to decide was whether he was to be convicted of murder or manslaughter.

Hannen had a tough case. George had promised to get his revenge and had come back and done so. Hannen did the best he could. He objected to there being a jury of only five, arguing there should be 12 members, as in England. He also argued that the evidence of the Chinese witnesses as non-Christians could not be relied upon. Hornby overruled these objections.

In his closing speech, Hannen sought to convince the jury that the various attacks that had been made on George were sufficient for the jury to consider manslaughter the appropriate verdict. He said that it is "well known how easily people from his country can be roused to anger, and, how long it is before their blood cools." The jury should weigh all the provocations "with the known excitability of Indian men and take a favorable view of them."

In his summing up Hornby reminded the jury of their solemn duty to themselves and the public not to allow feelings or weakness to affect their verdict. The jury then retired. They returned twenty-five minutes later. Mowat, as Law Secretary, asked them for their verdict. "Guilty" said the foreman, but with a strong recommendation for mercy. English law at the time did not allow judges to show mercy for convicted murderers. There was only one sentence that could be passed. Hornby hated this aspect of being a judge. He put on the black cap and pressed a book between his left side and the bench to prevent his violently beating heart from bursting.[23]

nen in his autobiography.

23 Hornby, *An Autobiography*, p256. Hornby describes how much he hated passing a death sentence.

Doing all he could to control his voice, he said:

"You have been found guilty. The sentence is Death."

Hornby told George that he had no hope of mercy and earnestly exhorted him to:

"spend the rest of your short time on earth in making peace with your God."

The sentence was not yet the end of George. The case raised three important issues concerning the conduct of trials in extraterritorial China. First and probably most importantly for Hornby, he did not want ever again to sit with a Chinese judge. Soon after the trial was completed, Hornby wrote to the British Foreign Secretary, George Villiers, to "urgently entreat" Villiers to spare him "from being compelled to sit on the bench with a Chinese mandarin whose language I do not know, as he is ignorant of mine", but more importantly, "who cannot by any possible amount of interpretation be made to understand the principles of law and form of procedure which I am bound to follow." Hornby finished:

"the presence of such an official on the bench of an English court must be an empty form and a farce, or – if it be supposed to give a guarantee for truth being vindicated or right being done – it is an insult to English justice."[24]

Hannen also raised again his legal challenges. He argued that having a jury made up of only five jurors instead of 12 as was required in England, was unconstitutional. The Order in Council, as sub-legislation, could not take away a fundamen-

24 Letter of July 27, 1869, FO228/484 cited in P. Cassel, *Grounds for Judgment*, p76.

tal constitutional right such as trial by jury. Only Parliament could by enactment of a law amend the Constitution.[25]

Hannen also argued again that the evidence of the Chinese witnesses, as non-Christians, could not be relied upon. During the trial, the Chinese witnesses had been asked if they believed in a God who would punish them if they told a lie. The witnesses said that they believed in a God of Thunder who was able to punish them. They did not believe he would certainly punish them. Hannen argued that for pagans, the law should only accept their evidence if they believed they "would be assuredly punished." He concluded, "the God of Thunder is not an all seeing Being, and any rate, not that Being that the law of England requires in its oath."

Rennie tried to keep his argument in response simple, pointing out that the British Parliament had recently passed an act that allowed for unsworn testimony in certain cases. The Chinese witnesses had given sworn testimony even if to a non-Christian god. This had to be better than unsworn evidence.

But with judges like Hornby and, in particular, Goodwin, a leading bible scholar, on the bench, it was never going to be kept simple. Hornby and Goodwin both pondered as to what were the motives that restrained a man from doing wrong. Hornby considered that "it is an innate consciousness that it is wrong." Goodwin asserted, "it was a conception of punishment in the background, inexpressible, but which was the deterring power."

Hornby gave a ruling four days later. He gave short shrift to the argument that a trial with five jurors was unconstitutional. He held that the Foreign Jurisdiction Act, which established the court and empowered the making of Orders in Council, gave more than sufficient authority for the Orders in Council to limit the size of a jury to five jurors. He gave more consideration to the question of whether a non-Chris-

---

25 *R v. George North China Herald and Market Report*, August 5, 1869, p429.

tian witness could give evidence and ruled that "the object is to know whether the witness believed in the existence of any superhuman Being, who take cognizance of his action and to whom lying is offensive," and that the law of England "is ready to recognise any variety of this belief." He said that he and Goodwin were satisfied the Chinese witnesses had the appropriate fear of God and dismissed the applications.

Nothing now stood between George and the gallows. He was hanged at the British Consular Gaol, just southwest of the consulate, six weeks later at 5.30am on August 31, 1869. Robert Mowat, along with the British Consul, Mr Medhurst, the British Chaplain, the Chee Seen and the Chinese Magistrate of the Mixed Court, had the unpleasant duty of witnessing the execution.[26] The machinery of death, even in those days, was expensive. Consul Medhurst charged to the consulate's accounts the cost of erecting and dismantling the gallows, a coffin, extra food and beer for 44 days for George and a cash bonus and new suit for the executioner.[27]

26 *North China Herald*, July 22, 1869 p389 and August 5, 1869, p421. *Supreme Court and Consular Gazette*, July-Dec 1869, Vol VI, p46-48 and p164 P. Cassell, *Grounds of Judgment*, pp73 to 74; Hornby, *An Autobiography*, p255-257.

27 P.D. Coates, *The China Consuls*, p218.

CHAPTER 7

Order Out of Legal Chaos

EDMUND HORNBY WAS CLEARLY a bundle of energy. He had been chosen for the position of Chief Judge because in the Ottoman Empire he had "showed his special fitness for dealing with an imperfectly developed legal system, and for eliciting order out of legal chaos." There was no greater legal chaos in the British legal world than the consular courts in China and Japan and:

> "once more he set to work drilling junior members of the Consular service into police magistrates, establishing precedents and 'organising' in the fullest sense of the word a system of legal and judicial coherency out of a confused and random entanglement."[1]

One of his first steps was within a year and a half of arrival to publish a detailed set of Guidelines to Consuls on handling legal cases in China and Japan and to arrange for the establishment of the *Supreme Court and Consular Gazette*. The Guidelines, based on guidelines he had prepared when in Constantinople, were written for non-lawyer consuls who had to act as judges. They gave practical guidance on the policy behind laws as well as actual legal guidance on how to decide cases.[2]

1 *Japan Weekly Mail*, May 27, 1876, p464; Reproduced in the *North China Herald*, June 17, 1876, p603.
2 The Chinese Supreme Court to this day will issue certain guidelines in a very similar

SUPREME COURT

AND CONSULAR GAZETTE,

AND

LAW REPORTER F R H. B. M SUPREME AND PROVINCIAL COURTS,
AND THE CONSULAR COURTS OF CHINA AND JAPAN,

VOLUME 1
January 5th to June 29th, 186

SHANGHAI
PRINTED AND PUBLISHED AT 8 KIANGSE ROAD

The first volume of the Supreme Court and Consular Gazette

The *Supreme Court and Consular Gazette* was a collection of case reports from the courts. Hornby said of the *Gazette* that his "object was to induce uniformity of action, decision and sentences throughout the English Consulates of China and Japan," and, then perhaps a bit immodestly, "I succeeded beyond my expectations."

The first edition of the *Gazette* was published on January 5, 1867. In its first editorial, the publishers said they had started the *Gazette* to "supply a want which has long been felt; and that accurate reports of cases and of decisions of the Supreme Court on questions of Mercantile Law cannot fail to be interesting to a community whose whole prosperity is bound up in Commerce and Trade." Criminal reports were to be published to remind readers of what an infraction of the law is. The reports were prepared from the judge's notes, not only of the evidence, but of the arguments of counsel and the judgments delivered. The publishers added that "the Proprietors have obtained the promise of such assistance as the Officers of the Courts are alone enabled to give, to secure correct versions of what takes place." Hornby, in his autobiography, said that this assistance was that the notes were actually written by either himself or Goodwin.

The editorial added that there were two further goals in publishing the reports. First, to bring a uniformity of practice to all courts and to allow all merchants in China to know what the law was. The second was to publicise the workings of the court, "the publicity of Courts [being] an important feature of our legal system."

The first issue of the *Gazette* also published records of prisoners sent to Hong Kong for imprisonment from all the treaty ports. From September 1865, five prisoners were sent to Hong Kong; the most serious offence being robbery with violence

way that set out both policy and law. See for example, the Opinions of the Supreme People's Court on the handling of Intellectual Property Cases under the Current Economic Situation issued in 2009.

committed by James Reeves, William Box and James Kelly. In 1866, 14 prisoners were sent to Hong Kong, the most serious offence being murder, committed by Mohamed. Two others were deported from Shanghai in 1866 and three were deported from Hakodate in Japan for desecration of Ainu graves.[3]

The Supreme Court and Consular Gazette only survived three years. In 1870, it was merged into the *North China Herald*, which became the *North China Herald and Supreme Court and Consular Gazette*. The *North China Herald* promised on the incorporation that "in no respect shall the new paper derogate from its former standard."[4] It continued to publish detailed reports of all major cases including full transcripts up until the 1930s. One reason for this, in addition to public service, was almost certainly that the case reports provided an endless supply of free content. In the days before modern communications, newspapers did not have easy access to news from around the globe. The court cases provided a very simple and cheap way to entertain readers with true crime dramas and the dirty underside of other people's business and personal lives. Even divorce cases were reported in detail, providing readers with prurient thrills. Norwood Allman, an American lawyer in Shanghai in the 20th century, noted that the United States Court for China "was an unfailing source of front page newspaper material in the days when the local scene was barren of sensational copy … even a ordinary breach of contract suit was written up fully in the local newspapers."[5] In short, the court reports were the 19th century and early 20th century equivalent of reality TV.

Hornby and the ghost
Hornby not only lived and breathed case reporting, but per-

3 *Supreme Court and Consular Gazette*, 1867, Vol 1, p11. These case reports were a treasure trove of information for me in writing this book and Hornby must be saluted for bringing the Gazette to life and allowing us through the cases that are reported to look back in time.

4 *London and China Telegraph*, February 21, 1870, p114.

5 N. Allman, *Shanghai Lawyer*, p98.

haps also dreamed of it. In order to allow journalists to report cases the same day a judgment was handed down, Hornby allowed them to pick up the case the night before from his home. This practice led to one of the strangest events recorded in Hornby's life, where, towards the end of his time in Shanghai, he claimed to have met the ghost of Dr Lang, the editor of the *Shanghai Courier*. Hornby wrote at the time that he had given his butler an envelope with a report inside to give to Dr Lang. He then woke in the middle of the night to find Lang at the end of the bed and tried to send him away. The man refused to leave. Hornby continued:

"I was losing my temper, but something in the man's manner disinclined me to jump out of bed to evict him by force. So I said, simply, 'This is too bad, really; pray leave the room at once.' Instead of doing so he put his hand on the foot-rail and gently, and as if in pain, sat down on the foot of the bed. I glanced at the clock and saw that it was about twenty minutes past one. I said, 'The butler has had the judgment since half-past eleven; go and get it!' He said, 'Pray forgive me; if you knew the circumstances you would. Time presses. Pray give me a precis of your judgment, and I will make a note in my book of it,' drawing his reporter's book out of his breast pocket. I said, 'I will do nothing of the kind. Go downstairs, find the butler, and don't disturb me—you will wake my wife; otherwise I shall have to put you out.' He slightly moved his hand, I said, 'Who let you in?' He answered, 'No one.' 'Confound it,' I said, 'What the devil do you mean? Are you drunk?' He replied quickly, 'No, and never shall be again; but I pray your lordship give me your decision, for my time is short.' I said, 'You don't seem to care about my time, and this is the last time I will ever allow a reporter in my house.' He stopped me short, saying, 'This is the last time I shall ever see you anywhere.

"Well, fearful that this commotion might arouse and frighten my wife, I shortly gave him the gist of my judgment . . . . He seemed to be taking it down in shorthand; it might have taken two or three minutes. When I finished, he rose, thanked me for excusing his intrusion and for the consideration I had always shown him and his colleagues, opened the door, and went away. I looked at the clock; it was on the stroke of one."[6]

The next morning, Hornby was told that Dr Lang had died the previous night. After questioning all involved, it appeared that his premises had been securely locked.

Visits to Provincial Courts

Hornby had been instructed by the Foreign Office to visit each port in China and Japan in turn "so as to form some idea of the mode in which judicial and magisterial work was done and how it might be improved."[7] Hornby first set off on a trip to the North that took him to Chefoo (now part of Yantai), Tientsin, Peking and Newchang (Niuzhuang) in Manchuria.[8] At Newchang, Hornby heard a number of cases, including a homicide case where an Englishman had killed a Chinese carman (carriage driver). The jury returned a verdict of manslaughter and the accused was sent to prison. Soon after Christmas 1865 Hornby then went on a southern tour

---

6   The ghost was meant to have appeared in January 1875, after Hornby's second wife had died, but he had not married his third wife, yet he mentioned being in bed with his wife. The original source given for this quote is: E. Gurney and F.W.H Meyers, "Visible Apparitions," Nineteenth Century, 16 (July 1884): 89 -91; An article debunking the story appeared later that year in many papers. See for example, The North China Herald, August 15, 1884, p179 and The West Australian, November 29, 1884, p3.; Hornby defended the story in the November 1884 Issue of the Nineteenth Century saying the ghost may have appeared some time later after he re-married. See: North China Herald, December 17, 1884, p677.

7   Hornby, An Autobiography, p214.

8   Hornby, An Autobiography, Chapters, III to VI. The case in Yingtsu is at pp248-249.

to Hong Kong, Canton, Swatow (Shantou), Foochow, Amoy, and a group of islands, presumably Pagoda Island. Later, he went to Formosa (Taiwan) and also visited Ningpo, Hankow and Yichang.[9] He also visited Japan but, it appears, did not try cases on his first visit. He did return on circuit in 1867.[10]

In Peking, Hornby recalled, "the only European who did not condescend to call on me ... was Mr Robert Hart (now Sir Robert Hart) the Chief Inspector of Chinese Customs." The Chinese Maritime Customs Administration had been established in 1842 with the opening to foreign trade. From 1855, the service began to employ foreigners to assist with collecting customs duties from foreigners. In 1865, Robert Hart had just been appointed the Inspector General of the Customs Service. He remained in that position until 1910. Throughout China, the Customs Service employed numerous foreigners, and used English as its official language.[11] The Service was structured like the British Customs service and included below the Inspector General, a Commissioner in each port. Other positions included watchers, whose job it was to watch for smugglers, a tide-waiter who would board ships as they entered harbour to ensure they tied up at a controlled dock and a tide-surveyor whose job it was to supervise tide-waiters. Until 1912, the Customs service did not directly collect duties. They were paid directly to the Chinese government based on assessments made by Customs.

Hornby either with great prescience or 20/20 hindsight set out the reason why Hart did not want to meet him:

"His object was to ignore the fact that he himself and the other English officials --- Commissioners, Clerks, Revenue Officers, Tidewaiters etc, etc, -- in the employment of the Foreign Customs Department were under

9 Hornby, *An Autobiography*, p267.

10 C. Roberts, *The British Courts and Extraterritoriality in Japan 1859-1899*, p20n.

11 Memorandum for British Cabinet from the Foreign Office, July 30, 1926 Annex II Maritime Customs Administration, p20, CAB-24-181-CP-308.

the jurisdiction of the Supreme Court."[12]

Hornby said that if they were not subject to the authority of the Supreme Court they could become corrupt, or as Hornby put it: "revenue officers and men have opportunities for doing things not only hurtful to their own countrymen but to natives." On the other hand, if they were subject to local Chinese jurisdiction, they could be unfairly punished as foreign scapegoats.

Some years later, Hart did in fact seek to avoid liability in the British court regarding statements that he had made about Baron von Gumpach to the Tsungli Yamen. Hart had employed von Gumpach on behalf of the Tsungli Yamen as a professor of mathematics and astronomy at a new college they had set up to teach Western languages and science.

Von Gumpach sued Hart personally in the Supreme Court. The case was heard by Hornby and Goodwin with Richard Rennie appearing for von Gumpach and Nicholas Hannen for Hart. Hart in his defence pleaded that as an employee of the Chinese government, he could not be held liable in the British courts for making defamatory statements. Von Gumpach applied to strike this part of the defence out. The effect of striking out parts of a defence is that the court is deciding that the defence will not succeed as a matter of law. Hornby and Goodwin agreed with von Gumpach and struck out the paragraphs. In giving judgment, Hornby stated:

"The Order in Council expressly gives jurisdiction to this court in all cases between British subjects (and these parties are British subjects). To say that this plea is a good answer in law would be to say that anything Mr Hart might do or say against another British subject who happened to be in service of the Chinese govern-

12 Hornby, *An Autobiography*, p239-240.

ment, however false or malicious, he might do with impunity. For all acts done, within the sphere of duty, persons in Mr Hart's position are protected, but they are not protected from the consequence of false statements or misrepresentations, because it can never be an act of duty to make false statements or misrepresent facts."[13]

The case was tried some time later by Goodwin with a jury. The jury found in von Gumpach's favour on two out of three claims. Hannen made an application to set aside the jury verdict on the grounds it was not supported by the evidence. Hornby refused to do so. Hart appealed to the Privy Council in 1873. The Privy Council dodged the question of whether the Supreme Court had jurisdiction over Hart by holding that Hart had not properly raised the point. The Privy Council then found in Hart's favour on the ground that Hart should have been allowed to plead that his communications with the Chinese government were privileged and sent the case back to the Supreme Court for a new trial. The Privy Council said it did not expect there would be a new trial. There was not.[14]

As we shall see, in a later murder case Hart employed two of the top British lawyers in China to argue that employees of the Customs service were not subject to the jurisdiction of the Supreme Court.[15]

After five years in office, in August 1870 Hornby left Shanghai for England on long leave. He travelled via Yokohama where he heard some cases. There were rumours that he might not return. Hornby had himself in his 1869 memo regarding the court in Japan suggested that he might retire. It was clear on his departure that the Brithish community either

13 Reported in *North China Herald*, April 21, 1870 pp282-283.

14 *von Gumpach v Hart*, *North China Herald* April 21, 1870 pp283-289 (jury trial).. The Privy Council decision which is still cited to this day is reported at *Hart v Gumpach*, L.R. 4 P.C. 439; [1873] UKPC 9.

15 See the Edward Page case in Chapter 15.

loved him or hated him. It was also clear everyone respected him. A large number of the foreign community in Shanghai prepared and signed a public address to Hornby to "give expression to the feelings of esteem and respect with which you have inspired us, during your five years tenure of office." It thanked Hornby not only for his service as Judge but for his help in drafting the Code of Regulations for the Municipal Council and for his "genial character and the active interest [he had] displayed in the social pursuits of the Community."[16]

The address was glowing in its praise. It stated first that in establishing the Supreme Court:

> "It was essential that the first Chief Judge appointed should not only be a good and sound lawyer, but still more a man whose mature experience, power of organization, courteous demeanour and general ability, would render the Court not only a respectable channel for legal proceedings, but also a tribunal for reconciling differences, smoothing over difficulties, and promoting harmony. "These requirements you have satisfied in an eminent degree. You have organized an efficient Court, you have checked litigation, promoted good feeling, encouraged the ready settlement of difficulties, and in those cases where resort has been had to the final arbitrament of the law, you have pronounced decisions with which few people (if any) have had cause to be dissatisfied."

The editor of the *North China Herald* was one of those who was dissatisfied. In a front page editorial of the same edition the address was published in, he first acknowledged that Hornby had been the right man for the job, saying:

> "The previous judicial experience of Sir Edmund

---

16 *North China Herald*, August 11, 1870, p110.

Hornby in the Levant, his clear and vigorous brain, his strong sense of justice, and his courteous demeanour, pointed him out as the man who was fitted for the important and responsible office of Chief Judge; and even of those, in Shanghai and elsewhere, who may have been disposed to cavil at the way in which he discharged his functions there are very few who will say that a better selection could have been made."[17]

Referring to the "highly eulogistic" address, the editorial acknowledged that this reflected the views of many in the community. But then came the big but. The position of Chief Judge in China and Japan involved not just the handling of litigation, but the supervision of the Provincial Courts and the giving of advice and counsel, even on cases that may come before him in a judicial capacity. "The position is one of delicacy and difficulty; and perhaps the worst that can be charged against Sir Edmund Hornby is that, in the excess of his zeal, he has sometimes overrun the limits thus indicated."

Then aiming directly at Hornby's "smartest man in the room" syndrome, the editorial, while acknowledging that "litigation is undoubtedly a great evil", questioned whether settlements based on the judge letting the parties know his opinion up front were really satisfactory.

Turning back to the system, the editorial said too much power was vested in the Chief Judge who, without a local appeal court above him, could tend to do justice based on his personal view of the case rather than deciding the case according to the law. It suggested that the establishment of a Court of Appeal in Hong Kong with the judges from Shanghai, Hong Kong and Singapore sitting on it would be a solution.

---

17 *North China Herald*, August 11, 1870, p101. The editor of the *Japan Weekly Mail* was on the other hand, very impressed by Hornby. The *JWM* also published a reply by Hornby to the address. See *Japan Weekly Mail*, 1870, p409 and 414.

Then, perhaps realizing the personal criticisms had gone too far, the editorial finished:

"We have been led into these reflections, not from any wish to detract from Sir E. Hornby's great qualities, but rather now that we are about to lose his services we feel that, should his successor not prove to be a man of like calibre, or equal to the position, it is not unlikely, with the Court constituted as it is now is, evils may result to British residents in China and Japan."

Hornby did not retire. He had not yet finished the work he had started.

CHAPTER 8

Bricks and Mortar: A Home for the Court

SIR EDMUND HORNBY was a visionary. He had a vision not only for the operations of the British courts in China and Japan but also for the home of the court in Shanghai. All higher courts are housed in grand buildings. In London, the High Court is an imposing, ornately designed building on the Strand. In Washington DC, the Supreme Court is a large white marble building directly opposite the Capitol. Hornby wanted the same for his court.

When the Supreme Court for China and Japan was established in 1865, it took over the small and unsatisfactory consular court in the British consulate on the northern end of Shanghai's Bund.[1] Hornby lost no time in trying to get a permanent building for the court erected. There was considerable correspondence between Hornby and the Foreign Office about the need to have a proper court building and whether the court and the consulate should be in the same building. Hornby wrote a long letter in November 1866 setting out his requirements, which included "a Civil Court and a Police Court, the former should be capable of accommodating a couple of hundred people with ease."[2]

---

1 *North China Herald*, June 19, 1868, p284. Some alterations were made in 1868 which "greatly improved the accommodation for both the Judges and Officers or the Court; and for spectators," there was however "still much to desire, especially in the matter or space."

2 WORK 10/432, Document 11.

He suggested the Vice-Chancellor's court within the old gate at Lincoln's Inn in London would be a good model. The Police Court could be simple and much smaller. He requested "a room for the Chief Judge, another for the Assistant Judge and a third for the Police Magistrate all of whom perform different functions and have to receive a variety of people." He also said the Chief Clerk, Civil Clerk and Police Clerk, financial department, English Interpreter and Chief Usher would all need rooms. He added that given the climate, a verandah around the building would be essential.

By late December 1866, Hornby had found an alternative. He spent New Year's Day 1867 writing to the Foreign Office with a proposal to take over two floors of the New Commercial Bank Buildings.[3] Hornby had full designs drawn up for making use of two floors of this building for courtrooms and offices for the judges, clerks, interpreters and court staff.[4] These plans were, presumably, considered too grand and the renovation did not go ahead.

Finally, a decision was made that a new court building would be built next to the Consulate, but the judges' offices and Magistrate's Court would remain in the Consulate. Hornby wrote on January 6, 1868 that he would be "equally satisfied with this arrangement" but added "I do beg and beseech everyone connected with the suggested buildings to stand not upon the order of the same but go and build at once."[5]

Hornby then wrote a memo which made reference to "simple plans and elucidations" to show the accommodation required. Hornby proposed that "the building be erected at the south end of the house at present occupied as court offices. The entrance to the Police Court would be from the Verandah of the Law Secretary's office, on each side of this entrance would be one room for the prisoners and one for witnesses.

3   WORK 10/432, Document 12.
4   MPD 1/210.
5   WORK 10/432, Documents 13 and 14.

The Public could enter from the South end."

Turning to the court room for the Supreme Court, Hornby wrote:

"Above the Police Court and the two rooms alluded to would be the Civil Court – say 50 ft. by 30 ft. The Judge's entrance would be from his present room immediately onto the Dais, the public would enter from two sets of stairs to the Verandah at the South end of the building ... the roof of the police court would be flat, about 15 ft. from the ground. The roof of the civil court would be something like this, [Hornby drew in a diagram looking like the letter A] about 22 or 24 ft. from the floor. Windows would be all round the Court capable of being opened into the verandah for fresh air when required..."

Plans were finalized for the building on a much less grand scale than envisaged by Hornby. The building was a simple two-storey structure with offices for servants and messengers on the ground floor and one large court above it. There was no Police Court and the office accommodation was rather simple. At the same time the decision was made to build a new Consular Gaol on Soochow Creek. This was to be a very large building that could accommodate up to 100 prisoners.

Construction of both the Supreme Court and Consular Gaol commenced in 1869. The Hiogo News, in February 1870 carried an article by a Shanghai correspondent, whom I suspect strongly to be Hornby, describing both buildings. Referring first to the new Supreme Court, the correspondent wrote:

"The New Consular 'works' (as they are called) seem to be in a perpetual state of building. It was the custom for a long time to see men driving piles, then for another very long time, they clipped stones; they are still endea-

vouring to bring order out of chaos, but there is nothing to write about it yet. I suppose when it is finished it
will look, as all government buildings look, respectable,
heavy and costly, but unattractive to the eye, gloomy,
uninteresting and sad, and above all a lawful excuse for
the British taxpayer to indulge in his habitual pastime of
growling."[6]

The same correspondent wrote that a new jail was also being built on Soochow Creek that was large enough to hold half
the British residents of Shanghai. He suggested that, perhaps,
it was being built as a castle for protection (with Hornby as
commander in chief) of the British if there was not sufficient
room on gunboats in the event of disturbances.[7]

As we have seen, Hornby wrote of the time he was in the
Foreign Office that he "reduced order to chaos." This seems
to be a particular Hornbyism. Hornby, certainly, cannot have
been satisfied by the small size of the Supreme Court given
his original grand plans, particularly when the prisoners he
was sending to gaol would be going to a much larger building than the court.

Opening the new Supreme Court

The new Supreme Court building was opened on June 1, 1871
on Yuenmingyuen Road.[8] Hornby was on leave at home at the
time. Contrary to the expectations of the Hiogo News' correspondent, the building was, at least to some extent, attractive

6   *The Hiogo News*, February 19, 1870, p58-59.

7   According to Foreign Office records, the gaol would, at the time, house up to 100
prisoners per day, mainly made up of crews of British ships in port. By the 1880s, this
number dropped substantially as sailing ships were replaced by steamers which remain
only a few days in port and "are manned by Asiatics." The North China Herald carried
a full description of the new jail in an article on March 1, 1871, p141-143. The article said
that at one time up to 95 prisoners had been in the old consular jail. See also: FO656/58
Letter dated February 13, 1883 re proposed sale of Municipal Gaol to SMC.

8   Now Yuanmingyuan Road. While, no doubt not intentional, it is ironic that the Supreme Court for China and Japan was located on a street named after the Summer Palace looted and burnt down by British and other foreign troops in 1860.

to the eye. The *North China Herald* described the building in glowing prose:

> "The design, free Ionic, is carefully carried out in So-ochow granite, and for grace, elegance of design and careful workmanship is surpassed by few buildings of its kind at Home and certainly by none in the East with which we are acquainted.
> "The Courtroom is lighted by ten large windows, five on each side; and the walls are panneled in oak, finely polished. The domed and deeply coffered ceiling with its cornices is also of the same material, and the dais and canopy above is a beautiful specimen of workmanship."[9]

And indeed it was. The only surviving photo of the original court that I have found shows a beautiful, if somewhat small building that is a fine specimen of workmanship. The

The original courthouse of
Her Britannic Majesty's Supreme Court for China and Japan

9   *North China Herald,* June 2, 1871, P430.

courthouse ran parallel with Yuenmingyuen Road. The court room was about 50 feet (16 metres) long by 30 feet (10 metres) wide. It had a spacious verandah on the front side. Access to the court was provided from the front by two large flights of stone steps immediately inside the entrance door leading up to a front verandah. One set of windows opened out onto the verandah. The other set of windows faced onto what was planned to be a courtyard between the court building and Consulate office building. The windows were essential in providing good lighting in those pre-electric days. For the most part, the court relied on natural lighting. When trials went on after nightfall, the judges and counsel had to rely upon paraffin lamps and candles for light.[10] Immediately below the courtroom was a large room the same size as the courtroom for the servants and messengers of the court.

An American observer sometime later described the inside of the courtroom as follows:

> "His Britannic Majesty's Supreme Court at Shanghai is holden in the Consulate Building. A spacious lofty chamber, with a high seat for the Chief Justice, a low seat for the Registrar, a bench for the bewigged and begowned Advocates, another for the Press corps, a raised rostrum for the witness, and adequate accommodation for the public, it is something like a court of law. The aged-looking woodwork, the green baize, the tall windows, the churchy atmosphere all seem in keeping."[11]

He then recounted the commencement of a hearing, the practice of which remains to this day in British and former

---

10 *North China Herald*, December 14, 1878, p563.

11 Re-printed in the *North China Herald*, February 5, 1904, p264. The judge referred to is most likely to be the Chief Justice of the time, H.S. Wilkinson. Sir Robin Jacob suggests the usher most likely would have said "Court Rise"

A cartoon showing the inside of the Supreme Court in 1908. The case related to the quality of sherry. No alcohol was imbibed during the actual hearing.

British courts:

"At the most the voice of those who wait rise to a sibilant whisper. Suddenly, a hush, and the warning announcement by the Usher: 'The Court!' All rise, as a nice old gentleman proceeds to the throne to incarnate justice. He bows, seats himself, and the others do likewise. 'Somebody v Another!' 'My Lord! I appear for the Plaintiff.' 'And I for the Defendant, my Lord!' All this is done subduedly, quietly, and one has the feeling that a sneeze or a cough would almost be considered contempt of Court, and entail some serious penalty."

The first case tried in the new courtroom, on its opening day, was the prosecution before Charles Goodwin as Acting Chief Judge of William Williams for murder. Williams had killed the mate of his ship in a drunken quarrel. George Jamieson, who was acting as Law Secretary while Robert Mowat was on long leave, prosecuted. Williams defended himself.

The jury returned a verdict of guilty and Goodwin, putting on a black hat passed the sentence that most judges detested:

"The sentence is that you be to be taken to the place whence you came, and that in due course of time you be taken thence and hung by the neck until you are dead, and that your body be buried in the precincts of the prison. And God have mercy on your soul."

Williams was not going to take this lying down and vehemently denounced the verdict: "Then I am an ill-used man. I am wronged; before God and man I am wronged." He was, however, a God fearing man. He finished his outburst by saying "but God be thanked I am going home and every one will have fair play there." He then calmly left the courtroom with the gaoler.

The new consular gaol on Suzhou Creek was opened on exactly the same day as the new court, on June 1, 1871. Fifteen prisoners were transferred to the new gaol that day, including Williams now under sentence of death. The British Minister in Peking confirmed Williams' sentence. When told of this, Williams replied that he deserved it and did not want to live a day more. There was, however, "considerable difficulty" in finding someone willing to conduct the execution. Williams finally "went home" on July 4, 1871, when he was hanged in the courtyard of the new prison. The Acting Consul at the time reported that he went through the ordeal admirably with a prayer on his lips as the bolt was drawn.[12]

The *North China Herald* regretted that the first case for trial in the new court "was that of ... wilful murder, ... but as such cases are happily of rare occurrence in this place, notwithstanding the bad name which has been attached to the Settlement as a 'sink of iniquity.'" The *Herald* added the hope "that the edifice may be venerable with age before it again becomes the painful duty of a Shanghai jury to adjudicate upon the life of a fellow man."

New consulate building and Supreme Court offices

The new Supreme Court building was complete, but not everything had gone according to plan. There was no Consulate building for it to be connected to. Two days before Christmas 1870, on a freezing cold night, the original consulate building burnt down.[13] The fire started in the Chief Judge's private secretary's office, it is thought by ashes being carelessly raked from a fireplace. Originally, the fire smouldered in one room, water was poured on it and it was thought that the fire had been put out. However, according to reports there was a lack of water to be found near the building and the fire then took hold. It is hard to understand why there was a lack of water as the consulate was beside the Soochow Creek and Whangpoo River. Perhaps there was a lack of buckets to carry it.

Fire crews were late to arrive, although in the end, six crews, including two from the French Concession, were on the scene. The Shanghai Municipal Police also attended, led by an Inspector Stripling. The *North China Herald* saluted all who attended on such a bitterly cold night when water froze into the clothes of the firemen fighting the fire. At around 3.30am the roof of the consulate collapsed. Many papers of

---

12 P.D. Coates, *The China Consuls*, p218 and *North China Herald*, July 7, 1871, p496; A formal inquest was held after Williams was hanged and determined that his death was caused by hanging in pursuance of the sentence.

13 The following account is taken from the *North China Herald* December 28, 1871 pp462-463 (except for the loss of Hornby's wig and gown).

the consulate were lost, partly because it was thought the fire would not spread beyond the offices of the court so that papers other than the court papers had not been moved when the fire first broke out.

Fortunately for the Supreme Court, the majority of its property and papers, including, the most important documents, the Judges' notebooks, judgments, and originals of pleadings were saved. Some books from the Law Library were burnt but most were recovered. Current bankruptcy accounts were saved. However, the bankruptcy accounts and private papers of deceased people where the court was waiting for instructions as to how to dispose of them were destroyed. The Supreme Court supply of stationery was also burnt.

Unfortunately for Goodwin, almost everything in his room, which was next to the room in which the fire broke out, was destroyed. This included his dispatch box, "which was once rescued almost at the risk of his life by Mr Stripling, and handed to a member of the Consulate, who handed it to a constable, who appears to have put it down again in a passage and left it to be burned." Goodwin also lost his wig, although his gown "turned up safe, though not altogether sound." "Several specimens of natural history" which were standing in Goodwin's office were also lost. An unnamed member of the bar also lost his official toga and perruque. Hornby's wig and gown were burnt and Hornby later claimed six guineas and nine guineas to replace them.[14]

An official enquiry to ascertain the cause of the fire was held by Goodwin, Consul Medhurst and Mr Boyce of the Public Works office but the report was inconclusive. *The London and China Telegraph* reported "nothing transpired as to the origin of the catastrophe; on the contrary, the evidence went to show that the compradore had not omitted his everyday practice of visiting the rooms after office hours, that the office

14 C. Roberts, The British Courts and Extra-Territoriality in Japan, 1859 to 1899, p39n (re Hornby's wig and gown).

coolie had carefully raked out all traces of fire from the grates before retiring for the night, and that the watchman had twice gone the rounds." The full conclusions of the enquiry were not made public.[15]

The insurance on the building had expired 13 days before the fire, because the treasury had decided to no longer insure government property in China.[16]

The consulate building that stands to this day on the Bund was built to replace the old consulate. The building was specifically designed, in addition to housing consular staff, to house the judges, court staff and a police court.

At the time of planning for the re-building, Mr Medhurst, the Consul, advocated that the offices of the court and the consulate be in separate buildings because of the inconvenience of having two sets of offices under the same roof.[17] One suspects that Medhurst was also sick of having two other officials, and particularly Hornby, in his consulate who outranked him. Hornby and Goodwin, on the other hand advocated strongly that both sets of offices should be in the same building because of the convenience of being able to call upon consular officers and staff when handling cases.[18] Hornby, somewhat hypocritically given his earlier strong push to move the court to the New Commercial Bank Buildings, said in a letter to the Foreign Secretary, Earl Granville:

"Not a day passes but that in the ordinary transaction of business, continual communication is necessary between the Judge and the Consul. I can answer for myself that I am constantly and continuously obliged to refer, not only to the Chief Consular Officer, but to

15 *London and China Telegraph*, March 6, 1871, p166.

16 Hansard, March 2, 1871, p1168.

17 WORK 10/33/8 Letter from Rutherford Alcock to Lord Granville dated March 15, 1871.

18 WORK 10/33/8 Letter from Rutherford Alcock to Lord Granville dated March 15, 1871.

his Subordinate Officers, and in the same way these officers are always coming to me with questions to answer, or for advice. I look upon this intimate intercommunication as of the greatest importance, to the service and to the public. It prevent errors and mistakes, and I do not think either branch of the service can dispense with it."[19]

Hornby described the inconvenience of communication if the offices were apart and the "immense value" he found of the assistance of consular officers. He "did not hesitate therefore to commend that the new Consulate should be rebuilt on the same site and pretty much on the same plan." He also asked that all rooms be shaded and have a verandah to deal with the heat.

The final decision was to re-build the consulate on the foundations of the old building, but with the consular offices on the north side and the Court offices to the south. As the new consulate was being completed, the *North China Herald* reported on a foundation stone laying ceremony.[20] The plan was that the new consulate would be built with the outline of the original building being maintained with an architectural style to harmonise with the new Supreme Court. The *North China Herald* reported:

"The rooms will of course be also rearranged, so that the Court offices may adjoin that building, and the Consulate offices will be concentrated in the opposite wing. Thus, on the lower floor, south side, will be the public Court offices, and at the S. E. corner the Police Court; The Magistrate's office will be in the centre with a fireproof room adjoining, for the safe custody of the

19 WORK 10/33/8 Letter dated March 31, 1871.
20 *North China Herald* June 1, 1872, pp425-426. This includes details of the foundation stones described below.

legal records. And on the north side will be the Consular Shipping offices with another fire-proof room for the custody of the Consular records.

"On the upper floor, south side, will be the Judge's offices, immediately above those of the Clerks; in the middle, immediately above the Magistrate will be the Consul's office, and on the north side, above the Shipping offices, those of the Vice-Consul and the Consular staff."

The main entrance to the consulate was on the southeast side. At the back of the building, a stone staircase with circular branches to the right and left led up to the second floor. In the middle, between the consulate and the court building, a courtyard was created which allowed light to enter the windows of the staircase and the court room.

The original foundation stone of the consulate laid in 1852 had read:

The Foundation Stone
of the British Consulate
Was Laid
On the 29th Day of February, A.D., 1852,
In the XV and XVI Year of the reign of
QUEEN VICTORIA,
by
Henrietta Alcock
Rutherford Alcock, Consul
Brook Roberts, Vice-Consul.
George Strachan, Architect

At the ceremony to lay the new foundation stone, this plate was relaid, under the foundation stone of the new building, with the following inscription on the reverse side:

The building alluded to on the

other side was destroyed by fire on
the 23rd December 1870, and the
present building was commenced
on the old foundations, 28th Feby.
1872.

The new foundation stone was laid by Agnes Goodwin,
Judge Goodwin's now 21-year-old daughter, who had moved
to Shanghai in 1870. The inscription on the stone read:

Foundation stone laid by Agnes Goodwin.

Sir Edmund Hornby	Walther H Medhurst,
Kt, Chief Judge	*Consul*
Charles W Goodwin	Chaloner Albaster,
Asst. Judge	*Vice-Consul*

Robt. A Mowat
Law Secretary
Robert H. Boyce, *Surveyor*, H. M. Office of
Works, London, *Architect*

When the new consulate building was completed, a further ceremony was held at exactly noon on March 31, 1873.[21]
The flags of all nations in Shanghai and the Union Jack were
flown to proclaim "a gala day in the annals of the Consulate."
The *Shanghai Courier* reported that the opening of the new
Consulate and Supreme Court offices would allow the judges, court staff and consular officers to leave their temporary
"wretched accommodation" for the "handsome and commo-
dious premises of the new consulate." A party of about 20,
made up of Hornby, Medhurst and others, assembled in the
gardens of the Consulate on the eastern front of the building facing to the Bund. At the time, Goodwin was on home

---

21 *London and China Telegraph*, May 19, 1873 p315-6 carrying a report from the *Shanghai Courier*.

leave. Two black marble tablets had been inscribed to record the opening of the building. The southern tablet read:

The British Consulate first erected here in 1852, by Consul,
now Sir Rutherford Alcock, K.C.B.,
was destroyed by fire on 23rd Dec., 1870.
The present building
was erected on the old site in 1872, under the direction of
Her Majesty's Office of Works, London.
ROBERT H. BOYCE, Assistant Surveyor (Architect).

The northern tablet read:

This stone was laid on the 24th May, 1872, by
Agnes Goodwin;
and the building was opened for use
on the 1st April, 1873.
Sir EDMUND HORNBY, Knt., Chief Judge.
Chas. W. GOODWIN, Assistant Judge.
W. H. MEDHURST, Consul.
CHALONER ALABASTER, Vice-Consul.
R. A. MOWAT, Law Secretary.

Standing between the two black tablets, Mr Medhurst drank to the success of the new building and then, "according to a custom which prevailed in China under the Chow dynasty," one of those present poured a drink (or libation as Medhurst called it) over one of the tablets. After that, a toast was drunk to Miss Agnes Goodwin who had laid the foundation stone.

An early 20th century short story about an Englishman needing to obtain an internal passport described the consulate buildings as a welcome piece of old England after the cacophony of the Shanghai streets. The Englishman had first

The cacophony of Shanghai streets at the turn of the century

walked from Nanking Road (Nanjing East Road) up the Bund which "was full of Japanese and Russian people, that is, there were certainly some tall, fair English, a few broad-faced Germans, and the right number of blue and mauve-robed Chinese, but quite a pepper and salting of little toddling figures in kimonos … and some dazed looking Russians in round fur caps walking very quietly along."[22] "Just then out came a group of Sikh policemen from a well-kept lawn."

Recalling that he needed to get a passport:

"Towards the lawn he turned, up a gravel walk into a large imposing building. Over the door was the Lion and the Unicorn, a-fighting for the crown, brilliant in gold and scarlet, and the doormat was marked "E.R." – Edward Rex. It seemed like stepping into a bit of real old England again. The corridor was of stone, the wide staircase to the left had white pilasters dentated in classic style; the corridor passage was lighted up with a flickering green light from the waving palms behind the glass

22 "The Master Gets his Hair Cut", *North China Herald*, March 18, 1904, p561.

door. Two Chinamen were playing draughts behind the glass door. Except for them, and the palms, one might be in England. 'Supreme Court', 'Consul-General.' How pleasant these even such words seemed after the tangle of crosses and strokes of the Chinese words along the streets."

In 1912, just after the Chinese republican revolution, it was decided to expand the court by building two new courtrooms. The courts had seen a substantial increase in cases, and it had often been necessary for one of the Judge's Chambers, to be used for hearings "to the inconvenience of everybody."[23] A new law library and extra rooms for the Consular shipping office were included in the plan. A total of £3,000 was the estimated cost for the renovations. This was queried in a supply debate in the House of Commons. Mr Sandys, while reviewing worldwide spending on Consular buildings, questioned the "riot of expenditure." With regard to China, he suggested that "seeing the present fluid condition of everything in China, seeing that nobody knows what will happen there, what will be the future situation of Shanghai, or what will be our future position in Shanghai, that the Government might well consider whether this is a moment to spend £3,000 on a Supreme Court, when the very jurisdiction of that Supreme Court may possibly disappear as soon as those additions are completed!"[24]

The two new court rooms were built on to the south side of the main court. To balance these extensions out, new rooms of the same size were built on the north side for the Consular shipping offices. The Police Court was built on the ground floor and a second court for the Supreme Court on the first floor. The Police Court had a door opening directly into the gardens of the Consulate for the public to enter. Both courts measured about 35 feet (10 metres) by 20 feet (6.5 metres). The second

23 *North China Herald*, July 27, 1912, p280.
24 Hansard, HC Debate 4 June 1912, Vol 39, cc 19-41.

court had a raised dais and teak panelling with a seat for one judge. There was a section fenced off from the main public area in the front for counsel and witnesses. Electric lighting and fans were installed in the court from the beginning and were presumably added to the main courtroom at the same time.[25]

The extensions were completed in June 1913 and a small ceremony was held at the court attended by a number of local luminaries from the Church, the Navy and the Army as well as 25 members of the Bar. Judge Thayer of the United States Court for China was also invited as a special guest. The Assistant Judge, Frederick Bourne, gave a small speech at the opening. He recalled that in 1883 when Queen Victoria had opened the London Courts of Justice on the Strand, he was a pupil at Lincoln's Inn. He had attended the opening in his capacity as a private in the Inns of Court Rifles. After the ceremony they had then been fed a sumptuous dinner with excellent wine. In Shanghai, the best he could do was to invite members of the Navy, Army and Church and to provide for "libations." To applause, he asked that all in attendance "drink that these Courts may be serviceable to the administration of justice in this community."

This was the final stage of the construction of the court and the building served as the home of the British Supreme Court in Shanghai until December 1941 when the Japanese occupied the International Settlement at the start of the Pacific War.

By late 1869 Hornby had laid the foundations of British justice in China and work on the new court building was well under way. Unstoppable as he was, he now turned to his next project.

---

25 *North China Herald*, June 14, 1918, pp785-6. Photograph of Court at WORK (55) 17

CHAPTER 9

Reforming the British Courts in Japan

Establishing the Court in Japan

HAVING SORTED OUT THE major issues with the British Justice system in China, Edmund Hornby's next task as Chief Judge was to get the British court system in Japan working properly.

By 1869, Hornby decided that it would be better that one judge of the Supreme Court be based in Shanghai and the other in Yokohama. Hornby had hinted at this in his decision in the *von Gumpach v Hart* defamation case when Hart had tried to overturn the jury verdict on the basis it had gone against the weight of evidence. Goodwin said there was sufficient evidence to support the verdict even though "he might not have arrived at the same result." Hornby added: "nor perhaps should I, if I had heard the case." Hornby, however, said that he and Goodwin both thought that, "it is most important, *especially out here,* for judges not to interfere with the province of the Jury except a verdict is evidently perverse." Judges should not run the risk of overturning jury decisions, even though the justice "they administer is often rough and ready." He added that "in all probability there will in the future be only one judge at Shanghai." That one judge should not have the power to revise jury verdicts.[1]

In 1869, Hornby visited Yokohama to investigate the workings of the consular courts in Japan. As we have seen in Chapter 2, he was not impressed commenting that the young

---

1   *von Gumpach v R Hart, North China Herald,* May 5, 1870, p326-327 at 327. See Chapter 7 for more on this case.

consular officers were particularly unsuited for handing legal cases. On his departure, he gave a charge to the Grand Jury of local British residents. Hornby said that it was usual for judges on circuit in England to remark on the state of the calendar and it was important for him to comment on the state of litigation before the court. He then covered a wide number of topics which took up three pages of one of the local English newspapers, the *Japan Herald*. Most importantly, Hornby said it was necessary to "avoid litigation" but that if arbitration was chosen, one arbitrator should be chosen rather than two friends who could make a decision "for which no reason could be given." He encouraged parties to lighten the legal workload on consuls by writing down their grievances so that they could be more easily understood. Then, straying somewhat from his duties as Chief Judge, he commented on the sanitary condition of Yokohama and that the government appeared to be one of "stagnation, passive obstruction and lethargy." He emphasized the need to get rid of low-end "grog shops" as it was almost impossible to perform judicial duties "whilst such plague shops were suffered to exist."[2]

After returning from Yokohama, Hornby wrote to the Foreign Secretary, Earl Clarendon, that the consular staff in Yokohama were for a number of reasons "unable to cope" with judicial work due to the complexity of cases as well as their youth and inexperience. Hornby, acknowledging that there may not be a budget for an extra judge in China and Japan, proposed that the Assistant Judge, Charles Goodwin, be transferred to Yokohama.[3]

The plan may not have just been about improving the quality of judicial decision making in Japan. Hornby may have also decided that distance was the best way to maintain a good relationship with Goodwin. Goodwin as a judge was

2   *Hiogo News*, November 13, 1869, p330.

3   FO881/1749 Memo from Hornby to Earl Clarendon dated October 23, 1869. See Chapter 2.

the complete opposite of Hornby. After Goodwin's death, all obituaries, which were absolutely glowing in all other respects, were remarkably silent on his judicial abilities. The *North China Herald*, in a heartfelt obituary, merely mentioned that "a more congenial field than a Judgeship in Shanghai" may have been "more adapted to his taste and adapted to his powers."[4] The *London and China Telegraph* was faint with its praise: "Mr. Goodwin was universally respected as a thoroughly upright and conscientious judge, who would spare no pains to arrive at the true merits of the cases before him."[5]

As a genius, Goodwin was, like Hornby, the smartest man in the room. Compared to Hornby, this produced a completely different type of judge. Goodwin was so smart that he knew there were things he did not know (or as it has been put, that there are "unknown unknowns.") Goodwin, who it should be recalled had spent his life deciphering hieroglyphics, wanted to investigate everything and get everything right. This meant he took a long time to deal with his cases. A one-hour hearing could turn into a one-day hearing. A short trial could become a marathon. Hornby on the other hand, dealt only with known knowns. He just decided the cases on the facts presented to him. A long trial became a short sprint.

Before Hornby's plan to have one judge in China and one in Japan could be put into effect, Hornby then Goodwin were scheduled to take 18 months long leave each; Hornby from late 1870 to 1872, and Goodwin from 1872 to 1873. Someone would need to be appointed to Japan in the interim.

Hornby considered that Robert Mowat was too young and inexperienced to be sent to Japan. He proposed instead "a barrister practicing at Shanghae who appears well fitted for such a post, a Mr Hannen, brother to Mr Justice Hannen of the Queen's Bench. He is well educated in his profession, firm and well calculated to maintain his position in a mixed

4 *North China Herald*, January 24, 1878, p82.
5 *London and China Telegraph*, January 28, 1878, p90.

community like that of Yokohama."[6]

Hornby's proposal was accepted and Hannen was appointed as Acting Assistant Judge of the Supreme Court for China and Japan to be based in Yokohama. The Japan Herald reported this decision had been taken "when the judicial business at Yokohama attained large dimensions while that of Shanghai decreased, it was (with good reason) thought desirable to transfer the Assistant Judge to Yokokama and thus give the chief court of Japan the advantage of a Court presided over by a professional judge."[7]

In a letter to Hannen dated January 10, 1871, Goodwin, as Acting Chief Judge, confirmed the appointment. Hannen was to reside in Yokohama while Goodwin was Acting Chief Judge in Shanghai. As to Hannen's powers, Goodwin wrote:

"Under Order 38 of the China and Japan Order in Council you are empowered to ... hear and determine any cases civil and criminal arising in the district of Yokohama, but this authorization does not include the trial of capital crimes."[8]

Order 38 of the Order in Council provided that the Judges of the Supreme Court could visit any Provincial Court and hear any civil or criminal cases pending in the district at the time.

The Court in Kanagawa styled itself as the Supreme Court and from early 1871 to mid-1872 judgments and case reports were headed "In HBM's Supreme Court for China and Japan."[9] Hannen requested that he be provided with a seal for the Supreme Court for China and Japan for use in Yokohama rather than the seal of the Kanagawa Consulate. Goodwin re-

---

6 FO881/1749, Memo from Hornby to Earl Clarendon dated October 23, 1869.

7 Reprinted in *Japan Weekly Mail*, January 31, 1874, p78.

8 FO656/39 (p1), Letter from Goodwin to Hannen dated January 10, 1871.

9 See, for example, *Japan Weekly Mail* July 6, 1872, p416.

plied that "in the present state of things, it does not matter one fig what the Yokohama seal is."[10] As we shall see later in this chapter, Hannen decided many years hence that, in fact, it did matter what the Yokohama seal was.

The *North China Herald* was happy with the establishment of a branch of the Supreme Court in Japan and the appointment of Hannen, stating that "the institution itself and the personal appointment is regarded as advantageous and satisfactory."[11] Hornby returned from leave in May 1872, and Goodwin then went on leave. Hornby sent Hannen a formal letter extending his appointment.[12]

Although at the time of his appointment as an acting judge he only had four years of practice experience, he had by this time already been involved in some major cases including the George murder case and the Hart defamation case. He also had one further advantage which had, as Hornby's memo-

Nicholas Hannen arrives as Acting Assistant Judge in Japan

10 FO656/39 (p2) Letter from Goodwin to Hannen dated April 11, 1871.
11 *North China Herald*, February 22, 1872, p134.
12 FO656/39 Letter from Hornby to Hannen dated May 27, 1872.

randum specifically stated, helped his selection. This was that his elder brother James Hannen was a noted British judge. What Hornby had left out is that James Hannen was a good friend of Hornby's.[13]

Despite the nepotism implicit in his appointment, everyone loved Nicholas Hannen. They loved him as a judge and as a person. Other than one accusation of bias in an extremely heated mixed case,[14] I have found not one bad word being said or hinted about Hannen. He was one of those exceptional individuals who rose above politics, was friendly to all and multi-talented, also being a good musician and amateur actor. Unlike Goodwin, his calling was clearly the law. Also, unlike Hornby, he had the patience to listen to all but to still make firm rulings. Perhaps because he had spent his formative years appearing before Hornby and Goodwin, he purposefully avoided the worst of each of their traits. In a bar eulogy, the Crown Advocate said of him as a judge:

> "Counsel on either side were listened to with kindliness in whatever they might wish to say. Whatever law they might quote, whatever witnesses they might call, were all carefully dealt with, and that strong mind waited until the last word had been said before - I feel it, and I know we all feel it - before deciding one way or the other. That in itself is one of the most valuable gifts that any judge can have. To some extent it can be improved by training, but I think I may say that, a judge, as regards his frame of mind, is born not made, and that judicial gift of calmness, and patient strength of' mind, was one of Sir Nicholas Hannen's brightest qualities."[15]

13 Hornby, *An Autobiography*, p54. Hornby, despite mentioning Nicholas Hannen, makes no mention of the fact that Nicholas Hannen was the brother of James Hannen in his autobiography.

14 See the Bennertz case, Chapter 25

15 *North China Herald*, May 2, 1900, p786.

The first reported case to be tried by Hannen in Japan dealt directly with one of the major problems of extraterritoriality, the appointment of merchants without legal training as honourary consuls. The issue was exacerbated if someone had a claim against a consul. The consul would either be the one to try the case or there would be no judge to hear the case.

Mr Strauss the Belgian Consul, was one such person. In February 1871, the *Japan Weekly Herald* published an article headed "The Belgium Consulate." The article strongly criticized the fact that Strauss was allowed to engage in trading activities through his company, Comptoir Belge, in addition to his consular duties.[16] The *Herald* claimed that he abused his position as consul to be hard on Japanese traders and that he "has disgraced the civil service of his nation and prostituted the uniform which he wears." Harsh words. Not surprisingly, Mr Strauss brought a libel case against the publisher of the *Herald*, Mr Howell. English defamation law is very pro-plaintiff. Howell was going to have a hard time proving his case, even if what he had written was true. Hannen had no trouble finding that the article was clearly defamatory and awarded damages, inclusive of costs, of $600.[17] Hannen added: "so long as a newspaper proprietor confines himself to attacking a system he will be protected; when he descends to specific and personal charges, he must run the risk and bear the penalty of being unable to fully substantiate the accusations which he brings."

A withered branch
One year after its establishment, in July 1872, in the case of *Findlay Richardson & Co v Pitman & Co*, the nature of the court in Japan was questioned. The unsuccessful defendant, Pitman, made an application to appeal to the Supreme Court in

16 *Japan Weekly Mail*, April15, 1871, p189.
17 *Japan Weekly Mail*, April 22, 1871, p193; 197 to 198 and 206 to 207.

Shanghai, rather than to the Privy Council. Pitman's counsel argued that the Court in Japan was not a branch of the Supreme Court for China and Japan but remained the Provincial Court at Kanagawa. The point was important because appeals could be made from provincial courts to the Supreme Court, whereas if the court was a branch of the Supreme Court, the only appeal lay to the Privy Council in London.[18]

Hannen gave an oral judgment that he was sitting as a judge of the Supreme Court "visiting" Japan under Order 38 and that accordingly there could be no appeal from his decisions to the Supreme Court, but only to the Privy Council. But, he said the parties could apply directly to the Chief Judge for a rehearing and "he hoped the Chief Judge would take such a view as would enable the rehearing to be, in reality, an appeal from his (the speaker's) decision – a view which would be manifestly for everybody's benefit, and also a personal relief to himself." He went on that he fully appreciated the absurdity of appeals only being allowed to the Privy Council. But, he added, it was not appropriate to seek to patch up the jurisdiction of the court by "twisting the words of the Order in Council to the present circumstances." Accordingly, he had to dismiss the motion for leave to appeal.

The *Japan Weekly Mail* in an editorial, agreed that Hannen's judgment was correct, but deplored the loss of the right to appeal, saying that an:

> "inalienable right has been alienated from us. We have been thrown into a pit and sold into bondage. We are lesser Englishmen than our brethren over the world; shorter by a whole right; weaker by a whole invaluable privilege."

The *Mail* congratulated Hannen for boldly facing the de-

---

18 *Findlay Richardson & Co v Pitman & Co , Japan Weekly Mail*, July 20, 1872, p445-447.

fect in the rules so the "legislature may deal with it."[19]

Pitman then applied to Hornby for a re-hearing. Hornby gave an extremely practical, but perhaps not legally correct, judgment. He held that because the parties had brought the case to the Supreme Court for China and Japan, they could not now say this was not the court they had sued in. The judgment should be treated as a judgment of the Supreme Court and the only appeal was to the Privy Council. Then doing a complete about-face, he also found that the Court should in fact be a Provincial Court and ordered that henceforth the court would be treated a Provincial Court under the presidency of Her Majesty's Assistant Judge. Hornby added, for good measure, that from reading the court documents and Hannen's judgment, he agreed with Hannen's original finding.[20]

Hornby's judgment was a fudge. The parties had no choice but to bring the case to the Supreme Court for China and Japan. This was the only court available. If the plaintiff had tried to file his case in the Provincial Court of Kanagawa it would have been rejected because such a court did not, in the eyes of the officials administering it at the time, exist. Hornby, however, realizing that the argument that the Orders in Council did not allow for a branch of the Supreme Court for China and Japan was correct, used a judicial sleight of hand to cover up his own mistake.

The *Japan Weekly Mail* welcomed Hornby's decision in an almost histrionic editorial headed "Our Right of Appeal" which started out: "Everyone must know the welcome sensation of waking from a dreadful dream and finding all its terrors dispelled." Hornby's decision removed a great loss – the loss of the right of appeal, which it compared to making British subjects in Yokohama like Chinese coolies who had recently arrived in Yokohama aboard a Peruvian ship the *Ma-*

---

19 *Japan Weekly Mail*, July 20, 1872, pp438-439.
20 *Findlay Richardson & Co v Pitman & Co ,Japan Weekly Mail*, August 17, 1872, p513-515.

ria Luz.[21] It regretted that the restoration of the right of appeal necessarily brought down the Supreme Court in Yokohama, but the right of appeal was far more important than having a branch of the Supreme Court in Japan.[22]

From then on, Hannen was treated as a judge of a Provincial Court when trying cases. This was formalized in a letter from Hornby to Hannen dated September 13, 1872 where Hornby stated, "you will in future consider yourself presiding over the Provincial Court of Kanagawa and you will not exercise the powers of the Supreme Court except in admiralty cases."[23] Despite losing its status as a branch of the Supreme Court, the court at Kanagawa remained the key British Court in Japan and from 1873 jury trials were extended to the court.[24]

Nine years later, in 1881, when Hannen was acting as Chief Justice in Shanghai, he was able to have the last word on the nature of his appointment in 1871. The case of *Langfeldt & Mayer v Green* came on appeal to the Supreme Court in Shanghai before Hannen and Robert Mowat (who by then had been promoted to Assistant Judge).[25] The Defendant challenged again the legality of the establishment of the branch of the Supreme Court in Kanagawa in 1871. The case involved the enforcement of a judgment given by Hannen, himself, when he was Acting Assistant Judge in Japan in 1871. Hannen had ordered that Green pay the plaintiff $300. The parties had agreed, however, that the judgment should not be enforced for some time. Eight years later, in 1879 the plaintiff applied to the British Court for Japan for enforcement. The defendant opposed the application on the basis that while purporting to be a judgment of the Supreme Court for China and Japan, it was sealed with the seal of the Consulate for Kanagawa – the very issue which Goodwin

21 See the following chapter for the story of the *Maria Luz*.

22 *Japan Weekly Mail*, August 17, 1872, p508.

23 FO656/39 Letter from Hornby to Hannen dated September 13, 1872.

24 FO 17/660. Letter from Granville dated February 7, 1873 under S62 of the 1865 Order in Council sent in response to a dispatch from Hornby of September 17, 1872.

25 FO656/39 *Langfeldt & Mayer v Green*.

had told Hannen "did not matter one fig." In the British Court for Japan, the court declined to enforce the judgment because there was nothing to establish which court had given the judgment.

Langfeldt & Mayer appealed to the Supreme Court in Shanghai. Nowhere in the appeal judgment does Hannen mention that he was the original trial judge, but it is clear from reading the judgment that he had a strong personal interest in the case. Hannen and Mowat dismissed an argument by the Defendant that the court that had made the decree was not the Supreme Court for China and Japan by applying the same logic that Hornby had used nine years before. That is, that the Supreme Court for China and Japan was the court in which the parties filed the case. If they had an objection they should have raised it when filing the case. Hannen and Mowat added that, in any event, they would be bound by Hornby's decision in the *Pitman* case.

As to whether the judgment had been properly sealed by using the seal of the Kanagawa consulate seal, Hannen and Mowat agreed with the defendant. They ruled that it had not been properly sealed and therefore could not be enforced. As to why the wrong seal had been used, Hannen, obviously still smarting from Goodwin's refusal of his request for a proper seal, said:

"The seal affixed to the decree is not the seal of the Court in which in our opinion the decree is pronounced. That it was the only seal ever used in the Court – that there was no other seal available – that it was used, moreover, as the archives of this court show, in deference only to the instructions from his official chief (the then Acting Judge, the late Mr Goodwin) to the Acting Assistant Judge [that is, Hannen] who had requested to be furnished with a seal of the Supreme

Court for use at Kanagawa – none of this can avail against the respondent who relies upon the irregularity, purely technical though it is."

This was not the end of the matter. On the basis that this decision would cause a "grave miscarriage of justice", they gave the Langfeldt & Mayer leave to amend their complaint to plead the court the judgment was given in was the Supreme Court and apply for the judgment to be re-sealed with the seal of the Supreme Court. Once correctly sealed they could then enforce it.

Wilkinson returns to Japan

1872 also saw the return to Japan of H.S. Wiliknson from Home leave. Wilkinson had completed his LLB and qualified as a barrister becoming the first consular officer in Japan to be legally qualified. He was appointed a Vice-Consul in Kobe. This gave him responsibility as one of the British judges in Kobe and Osaka and marked the beginning of his career in law in the British Courts in China and Japan.

Wilkinson as a newly qualified barrister was able to bring some judicial majesty to the Kobe Consular Court. John Carey Hall, who had arrived as a student interpreter in Kobe in 1868, recalled being called upon to carry out the "unpleasant duty" of prosecuting in Kobe two British for assault and battery on the complaint of some Chinese. The British together with an American had seen the Chinese gambling late at night, had broken into their residence and sought to disperse them. One of the Chinese lost his queue during the scuffle. Hall recalled:

"The case was tried by the Vice-Consul, Mr (now Sir) H.S. Wilkinson, afterwards Chief Justice of the British Court at Shanghai. The court-room was crowded and the scene was very impressive. The judge wore his bar-

rister's wig and gown and looked the very imperson-
ation of judicial dignity."[26]

Wilkinson imposed a heavy fine with the alternative of imprisonment. The American ringleader was tried in the American Consular Court and got off with a light fine. Hall recalled
that the penalty imposed by Wilkinson greatly enhanced the
respect of the Chinese in Kobe for British Justice.[27]

Wilkinson was also to show that he was more than willing
to take matters in his own hands. A few months later, he personally apprehended a hot-tempered English merchant. The
merchant, Mr Cousens, had hit the Japanese boatman of the
British Consulate whaleboat when the sampan Cousens was
on had come in close contact with the boat. Cousens had then
boarded an American ship for Yokohama. Wilkinson obtained
a warrant from the American consulate to take Cousens off the
ship. He then boarded with the British consular constable and
had him arrested. Cousens was convicted by the Consul, Mr
Gower, and ordered to be imprisoned for 48 hours. The consular doctor certified that the Japanese jail where he was to be take
was unfit for a Westerner. This may have been true: another
prisoner Wilkinson had sentenced to a Japanese jail in Osaka
had died there. Cousens was, instead, held in a room at the
consulate. Wilkinson and Gower were strongly condemned by
many members of the British community who filed petitions
to both the British Charge d'Affaires, R.G Watson and Hornby complaining about their actions. Watson and Hornby both
passed the buck to each other. Watson said he could do nothing
about any thing they had done in a judicial capacity. Hornby
said he could only hear a formal appeal.[28]

---

26 John Carey Hall, "My Early Kobe Reminiscences", Published in *Japan Chronicle*, Jubi-
lee Number, p46.

27 Hall, himself, was to qualify as a barrister and later to sit on occasions as an acting
judge of the Supreme Court for China and Japan and Court for Japan.

28 *London and China Telegraph*, November 11, 1872, p793; *North China Herald*, September
14, 1872, p217, September 28, 1872, p266 and December 5, 1872, p493

Sir Edmund Hornby and Charge d'Affaires, R.G. Watson deal with petition complaining about Gower and Wilkinsons' handling of the Kobe assault case

H.S. Wilkinson transferred from Kobe to Yokohama in late 1872 as a Vice-Consul. In this role, he handled the prosecution of all the major criminal cases before juries, including one major case before Hannen when a Mr Smyth was accused of raping a lighthouse keeper's wife. Both the British Minister, Harry Parkes, and Ernest Satow attended the hearing. When the Consul, Russell Robertson, was on leave, he acted as a judge in his position as acting-Consul.[29]

Goodwin replaces Hannen

Charles Goodwin returned from long leave in late 1873. He was now ready to take up the role of British judge in Japan replacing Nicholas Hannen who would return to private prac-

---

29 For Wilkinson sitting as an acting consul, see *R v Robert Bingham and Thomas Ducker*, *Japan Gazette*, June 5, 1876, p2. C. Roberts, "Hiram Shaw Wilkinson (1840-1926)", *Britain and Japan Biographical Portraits*, Vol VIII, p169 for details of the *Smyth* case. See also, *R v Alfred Edwin Line*, *Japan Daily Herald*, 2 July 1874 for Wilkinson as a prosecutor. John Carey Hall acted as the Court Clerk in this case.

tice in Shanghai. After spending two months in Shanghai, Goodwin, his wife, and his now large family of four young children, plus his older daughter Agnes, headed south for Hong Kong before then travelling to Yokohama.[30] They arrived in Yokohama in early April 1874 aboard the *Volga*.

On Wednesday April 8, 1874, Goodwin took his seat on the bench at a special ceremony to welcome him. The British Minister, Sir Harry Parkes, and the Consul in Yokohama, Russell Robertson, joined Goodwin on the bench. Hannen, the now retired Acting Assistant Judge, chose not to join them and sat with the other members of the bar attending the ceremony in the special seating that had been arranged in the court. The small size of the court room meant that, in order to accommodate them, all the bar tables and the witness box had had to be removed. As well as Hannen, H.S. Wilkinson, John Lowder a former consular officer but now with the Japanese Customs service and six other lawyers were in attendance.[31]

Mr JF Davidson of the Public Works Department spoke on behalf of the bar to welcome Goodwin to Japan. He then expressed in "highly lengthy and highly eulogistic terms, the great respect and regard in which Mr Hannen was held by the members of the legal profession in the community and the regret at his approaching departure from among them." Hannen had probably chosen to sit with the bar rather than face the embarrassment of sitting next to Goodwin while Davidson praised him so fulsomely. Goodwin thanked the bar for their welcome and said, perhaps with a hint of jealousy, he hoped that when his turn came to vacate the bench, "the same feelings might exist which had just been expressed for Mr Hannen."

It was not just the legal community that were going to miss

---

30 The *North China Herald* of Feb 11, 1874 records Mr and Mrs Goodwin and family leaving for Yokohama.

31 *Japan Gazette*, April 1874, p.9. The other lawyers in attendance were JF Davidson of the Public Works Department, Gavin P Ness, F.W. Marks, G. W. Hill (Legal Adviser to the Japanese court), W. W. Cargill (Japanese Government Railways and Telegraphs) and Mr Duncan.

the Hannens. The *Japan Gazette* and the *Japan Weekly Mail* both published heartfelt farewells praising Hannen as both a judge and as an upstanding and fine member of the community. Hannen and his wife were farewelled by a large crowd and then rowed to their steamer by six members of the Amateur Rowing Club. The *Japan Gazette* expressed the hope that Hannen would be promoted in Shanghai, "as may reasonably be expected" so that they could "see our excellent and much appreciated friends back again."[32]

Goodwin was not as universally liked in Yokohama as Hannen had been. Soon after Goodwin transferred to Japan, the *Japan Punch* published a cartoon headed "the prodigal's return" showing Goodwin returning to Yokohama from a trip with all the lawyers in the city spinning cartwheels of joy. A few months later the *Japan Punch* published a spoof writ headed "In the Supreme Court of Injustice" and addressed to "C. W. Badwine Esq, Supreme Judge."[33] The *Japan Punch* clearly took the view that Goodwin wasted time and worked to make

Charles Goodwin returns to Yokohama to the joy of local lawyers

32 *Japan Gazette*, April 1874, p7. See also Japan Weekly Mail April 11, 1874, p290.

33 "The Prodigal's Return" *Japan Punch*, December 1874, British Library reprint, p 202; Spoof Writ, *Japan Punch*, April 1875, p33.

lawyers rich and happy. This seems to be supported by some of the case reports from the period. One case report in the *Japan Daily Herald* made specific mention of Goodwin "hearing a great deal of argument between the contending counsel" and allowing the plaintiff to open the case "with a long statement." The case itself, which involved the refusal of the defendant to take delivery of some blankets, went on for two full days with Goodwin allowing the lawyers to cite a large amount of case law; so much so that he said he needed time before he could give his judgment.[34]

Another case heard by Goodwin showed the difficulties of extraterritoriality in practice. Mr Benson had let his property, Lot 123 of the Yokohama International Settlement to Jaffray who had, in turn, allowed Japanese individuals to live in tenements on the site. Japanese were prohibited from living in the International Settlement and Benson's title deed specifically provided that the premises could not be used by Japanese for residential purposes. Goodwin was not particularly sympathetic to Benson and said that if keeping Japanese out was a genuine concern then Benson should have included a term in his lease prohibiting Japanese from living on the site. Nevertheless, Jaffray's defence was that the Japanese who were living on the site were employees of foreigners running shops on the site and were not tenants. Some of the Japanese were called as witnesses, and they all stated that they were employees of a foreigner. Eventually, in face of this evidence, Goodwin allowed Benson to withdraw his case but stated specifically he could bring it again if he had evidence to support a case that Japanese had been allowed to rent space in the lot.[35]

Goodwin enjoyed his time in Japan. He was Vice-President of the Asiatic Society, studied Japanese and published a booklet "On Some Japanese Legends" comparing Japanese

34 *Walsh, Hall & Co v John Pitman, Japan Daily Herald*, July 4 to 8 1874. The Judgment can be found in the *Japan Daily Herald* of July 14, 1874.

35 *ES Benson v A Jaffray, Japan Daily Herald* February 4 and 5, 1875.

legends with European legends. He had been helped in this endeavor by his friend and future son-in law, John Carey Hall, then a consular officer in Yokohama who translated the Japanese legends for them. (Hall and Agnes Goodwin married in 1876). Goodwin even managed a visit to the Emperor's palace in Kyoto.

It was not only the British who were reforming their system of justice in Japan. The Japanese themselves were actively working to improve their system.

CHAPTER 10

Building the New Japanese Legal System

By THE EARLY 1870s, Japan, with its civil war having just finished, was now fully committed to reform. The Japanese wanted to change and would use change to bring an end to extraterritoriality rather than fight it.

Japan wants equality

The British-Japan treaty of 1858 provided that revisions could be made after 14 years, namely July 1, 1872. Accordingly in 1871, Count Terashima, Minister of Foreign Affairs, wrote to Sir Harry Parkes, the British Minister, a private memorandum requesting reciprocity in the treaties. Terashima wrote:

"The Treaties are made entirely for foreigners coming to Japan and the only stipulation for Japanese going abroad is that a diplomatic agent may reside in the capital. In these things the same power ought to be inherent in both, and after the question has been examined, equal and concurrent powers should be the phraseology of the Treaties."[1]

Nevertheless, the Japanese knew that in order to bring an end to extraterritoriality, they had to reform their own legal

1   Cited in F. Jones, *Extraterritoriality in Japan*, p79.

system. To achieve this, in December 1871, a mission of 50 of some of Japan's ablest politicians and lawyers, led by Tomomi Iwakura, went on a study tour of the US, Britain and Continental Europe to study their legal systems and at the same time seek an end to extraterritoriality. In a letter to the President of the United States, presented on arrival in the US, they stated:

> "We expect and intend to reform and improve the Treaties so as to stand upon a similar footing with the most enlightened nations and to attain the full development of public right and interest. The civilization and institutions of Japan are so different from those of other countries that we cannot expect to reach the desired end at once. It is our purpose to select, from the various institutions prevailing among enlightened nations, such as are best suited to our present condition, and adapt them, in gradual reforms and amendments of our policy and customs so as to be an equality with them."[2]

Cooling the coolie trade

Six months after the Iwakura Mission left Japan, a major test of the developing Japanese legal system sailed into Yokohama Harbour. The case resulted in a rare display of diplomatic amity between Japan and China, and even rarer praise from China for the work of foreign consular officers.

In July 1872, a Peruvian Ship, the *Maria Luz*, heading from Macao to Peru lost her topmasts in a storm and limped into Yokohama port for repairs.[3] Macao at that time played a key role in China's human slave trade. Although it was illegal to do so, Chinese coolies would be sold into bondage under

2　Cited in F. Jones, *Extraterritoriality in Japan*, p77.

3　I am grateful to Prof Dani Botsman of Yale University for sharing with me his paper "Freedom without Slavery? 'Coolies,' Prostitutes, and Outcastes in Meiji Japan's 'Emancipation Moment'" American Historical Review, December 2011, upon which much of the background material concerning the Maria Luz is based.

China Punch shows the "Embarking of 'Free and Independent' Emigrants at Macao"

alleged contracts of employment. Sir Edmund Hornby described in his autobiography covertly watching a hearing in a Macao court when a judge was meant to confirm that the contracts had been entered into voluntarily:

"The Court is supposed to be a Public Court but no one ever knows, except those interested, when it sits. The almighty dollar, however, can do wonders, and we found our way one morning at 5am into a court where a Judge was presiding, attended by a lot of subordinate officials. A lane formed by barriers and crowded with so called 'Free Emigrants' two deep led to a dock in front of the Bench. As they filed or rather were pushed through this dock, names were called out, answers were given, not by the 'Free Labourers' but by some Chinamen who stood in a kind of witness box, documents were handed in and stamped, and the file of men moved on."[4]

Hornby observed, "every one of the emigrants was under the influence of some drug, they rolled their eyes and staggered forward, some being actually supported to the place in front of the Judge." Questions were asked and no answer was given but the judge would then approve the contract. After he lit a cigar, Hornby's presence was noted. The judge then started to ask questions of the coolies and refused to approve further contracts.

By this time, the British and American governments and courts had already begun to act against the coolie trade. In 1841, the US Supreme Court had ruled in the Amistad case that slaves on board a Spanish ship the *Amistad* were entitled to do whatever was necessary to free themselves including killing the captain and the crew. In 1862, the US Congress passed a law prohibiting the coolie trade. In 1869, a ship, the *Cayalti*, had sailed into Hakodate harbour in Japan flying a US flag. The captain and crew had been killed by the coolies on board. The US State Department investigated and concluded that the ship was not an American ship. However, in their correspondence the State Department made it clear that if it had been an

In the U. S. Consular General Court at Kanagawa, Japan.

J. M. BATCHELDER,
Against

THE PROCEEDS OF THE SALE OF THE BARQUE
"CAYALTI."

To THE FORMER OWNER OR OWNERS OF THE SAID BARQUE AND ALL OTHERS WHOM IT MAY CONCERN. GREETING.

WHEREAS an action has been brought in this Court by the above-named Plaintiff against the proceeds of the sale of the Barque "CAYALTI," now in the hands of the UNITED STATES CONSUL-GENERAL for Japan, praying that the said proceeds may be paid to him on account of monies advanced and transportation and supplies furnished to the crew and coolies belonging to the said Barque "CAYALTI."
Now therefore take notice, that unless answer be filed therein within three months from the date hereof, judgment will be taken by the said Plaintiff according to the prayer of his Petition.
Given under my hand with the Seal of said Court affixed, this 28th day of May, A.D. 1877.

(Signed)   THOS. B. VAN BUREN,
[Seal.]   U. S. Consul-General.
                                              J. 1. 3ms.

The US Consular Court exercises jurisdiction over the Cayalti to sell her

4 Hornby, *An Autobiography*, p299.

American ship based on the decision in the *Amistad* case, the coolies would have been perfectly entitled to kill the captain and crew to obtain their freedom. Despite this, some years later, the US Consular Court in Kanagawa did entertain an action to sell the Cayalti.

In 1871, Kwok A Sing, a coolie was on board a French ship, *the Nouvelle Penelope*, which had sailed from Macao. Kwok and other coolies took over the ship and killed the master landing it in Pakha, China. They abandoned the ship there. At the request of the Chinese authorities, Kwok was arrested in Hong Kong to be extradited to China. Kwok made a *habeas corpus* application seeking his release. Chief Justice John Smale ordered his release on

Sir John Smale and Julian Pauncefote Chief Justice and Attorney General of Hong Kong who battled over the rights of coolies

the basis that the *Nouvelle Penelope* was a slave ship and Kwok was entitled to take any necessary steps to secure his freedom. Julian Pauncefote, the Attorney General of Hong Kong, then had Kwok re-arrested to be tried in Hong Kong for piracy. Piracy is a crime where courts exercise universal jurisdiction, a person can be prosecuted in any court for an act of piracy committed anywhere. Smale again ordered Kwok's release on the basis that the second arrest breached the first *habeas corpus* order. Kwok then sued Pauncefote for damages in the Hong Kong Supreme Court for false imprisonment under the Habeas Corpus Act. He almost won, with the British jury finding 4-3 in Kwok's favour. But because a majority of five was needed to find in Kwok's favour, the verdict was treated as a verdict for

Pauncefote.[5]

When the *Maria Luz* arrived in Yokohama, one of the Chinese coolies on board escaped over the rails and was picked up by the British Man-Of-War, the *Iron Duke*. The coolie, Mo Hing, was handed over to the British consular authorities, who then handed him to the Japanese authorities. After receiving assurances that Mo would not be mistreated, he was returned to Captain Hereira of the *Maria Luz*. The captain of the *Iron Duke* reported to the acting British Consul in Yokohama, R.G. Watson, that they could hear moans and cries coming from the *Maria Luz*. Watson then decided to intervene and inspected the ship.

The *China and London Telegraph* carried a report later of the conditions aboard ship, quoting an unidentified source, possibly Watson:

> "We found them (the coolies) sitting or lying closely together in their numbered berths, reeking and sweltering in an atmosphere which would extinguish the life of an American or European in half a day. Though not confined, except in a few instances, they were not allowed to stir from their cramped quarters. An imaginary ventilation was afforded by a few small holes in the side of the ship, which from their position could only be opened in a quiet sea. To attempt to depict the agony of despair in which the countenances of most of these unhappy creatures were fixed would be a hopeless task .... When we were about to return to the deck, as if by common impulse, they all sprang from their ranks and, clustering about us as closely as they could,

5   *North China Herald*, December 28, 1871, p1003-4 for details of the case against Pauncefote and the US correspondence regarding *Cayalti*. The Kwok A Sing *habeas corpus* cases are reported at *Re Kwok A Sing (No.1)* and *Re Kwok A Sing (No.2)* [2001] HKC 710 and 737. Smale's first decision was upheld by the Privy Council. See *Attorney-General of Hong Kong v Kwok A Sing* (1873) LR 5 PC 179, 42 LJ, PC 64. Special thanks to Dr Gerard McCoy QC SC, who reported the Hong Kong Kwok cases, for bringing them to my attention.

fell upon their knees, lifted their clasped hands, and
with piteous cries implored our intercession."[6]

Edmund Hornby, who was in Japan on circuit when the
Maria Luz arrived, claims in his autobiography to have been
deeply involved in the case including that it was he who first
interviewed the coolie who had made it to the *Iron Duke* when
he was brought ashore. He also claims that with the British
Charge d'Affaires, he convinced the Japanese Government,
through their foreign minister Taneomi Soejima, to take action against the ship. Subsequently, he also claims to have
supported the Japanese government in an arbitration brought
against Japan by Peru for illegal seizure of the vessel heard by
the Tsar of Russia.

Hornby's "grandiose claim to have orchestrated Japanese
policy" has been questioned.[7] Hornby does in his autobiography make other unverifiable claims. Nevertheless, the British
Consul, Watson, and Nicholas Hannen, the acting British judge
in Japan, would certainly have consulted with Hornby as to the
legality of any actions. And the Japanese would certainly have
consulted with the British, at the time the strongest foreign
power in Japan, about any steps they planned to take.

Watson, wrote a strongly worded plea to the Japanese foreign minister Soejima to intervene saying:

"The coolie trade between Macao and the western ports
of South America, particularly the Peruvian, has been
characterized by such barbarity and such disregard to
the rights of the Chinese government, that it has most
justly excited the strongest feeling in Europe and all
civilized countries ... Hitherto the shores of Japan have

6   The *London and China Telegraph*, October 28, 1872, pp748-749.
7   D. Botsman, "Freedom without Slavery? 'Coolies', Prostitutes and Outcastes in Meiji
Japan's 'Emancipation Movement'", American Historical Review, December 2011, footnote 28.

been free from the scandal of this abominable traffic ...
but in the present case there is grave reason to believe
that more than one person on board has been treated in
a manner, which no law could sanction."[8]

Watson was stretching the truth when he said that feeling had been excited in all civilized countries. Many of the
other foreign consuls in Yokohama opposed any action by the
Japanese as an undue interference in international commerce.

The American position was mixed. America was at the
time the representative of Peru in Japan. When the matter first
blew up, Captain Hereira contacted the American Consul,
C.O. Shephard, who was also at the time Charge d'Affaires of
the US Mission. Shephard, who supported the Japanese taking action to help the coolies, declined to assist Hereira. But
soon after this, the US Minister, Charles De Long returned
from leave and tried to help Hereira. This resulted in him being strongly rebuked by the US Secretary of State, Hamilton
Fish, who wrote to him that "it is regretted that you deemed it
proper to take any steps which might wear the aspect of giving the support and countenance of the United States to a vessel suspected by the Japanese Government, not without reason, of complicity in a nefarious traffic, of a character particularly
odious to the Government and people of the United States."[9]

The Japanese Foreign Minister, Soejima, ordered an investigation. Japan had abolished slavery during Tokugawa
Shogunate, ironically, partly to stop the export of Japanese
as slaves to Europe. The Japanese removed the coolies from
the *Maria Luz* and formed a court of inquiry into what had
occurred. This was presided over by the Governor of Kanagawa, Oe Taku, a young man of only 25 years of age. Oe was

8   Cited in D. Botsman, "Freedom without slavery? The Case of the *Maria Luz* and the
Question of Emancipation in Nineteenth Century Japan", Presentation at the conference
on Trans-Pacific Relations, Princeton University, September 2006.

9   J. Hammersmith, *Spoilsmen in a "Flowery Fairyland": The Development of the U.S. Legation in Japan*, pp97-98.

Magistrate Chen of Shanghai chases Capt. Hereira

advised by an American legal adviser, G.S. Hill. Nicholas Hannen also sat on the bench with Oe. Consuls of other nations and Magistrate Chen of the Shanghai Mixed Court, who had been invited to Japan by the Japanese government, observed the trial.

Hereira was represented by a British barrister, Frederick Dickins. The Court of Inquiry, even though it was not a criminal court, as Dickins had pointed out in a formal protest, found that Hereira was guilty of abusing his passengers and said that under Japanese law he should be sentenced to 100 lashes or 100 days house imprisonment. But because the court had decided to "judge him leniently," it had been decided that the Captain should in this case "be pardoned his offence and permitted to depart with his vessel."[10]

This was not to be the end of the matter. Hereira wanted his valuable cargo, the coolies, back and he brought a civil claim for their return. Hannen again sat on the bench with Oe. Given that Japan had only just started to develop a modern legal sys-

10 *Japan Weekly Mail*, August 24, 1872, pp530-531.

tem, Oe stated at the beginning of his judgment that he had relied on international precedents to guide him. He said:

> "In consideration of these actions, I have been very much assisted by the books and authorities produced by the Counsel both for the plaintiff and defendant; for it has been my desire to be guided by the generally approved maxims of international law and the practice of Courts of other States, whenever such maxims and practice have been found to apply; as well as by the somewhat broader principles of natural justice and equity which are of universal application."[11]

After their release, the coolies were returned to Shanghai by the Japanese Government accompanied by Magistrate Chen. China in return, at its own expense, repatriated 45 Japanese sailors who had been shipwrecked near Chefoo. The *London and China Telegraph* in an editorial said that "both nations are to be congratulated on the result of this first post-treaty international communication, and it leads us to hope that the civilising example set by Japan will not be without its conservative instincts of the Chinese."[12]

The Chinese were very pleased with the result of the case. The Chinese Minister of Foreign Affairs wrote an effusive note to the American Minister in Peking thanking them for Mr Shephard's assistance in the case:

> "This action on the part of American officials is satisfactory in the extreme; it is a new and complete manifestation of the sincere friendship and goodwill now happily existing between the two nations and is quite in accord with your express desire to rescue and save our people from harm. To acknowledge our obligation and

11 *North China Herald*, October 17, 1872, pp331-333.
12 *London and China Telegraph*, December 23, 1872, p908.

express our thanks is the object of this note."[13]

Peru made a formal claim for damages against Japan, which was referred to arbitration by the Czar of Russia, Alexander. Czar Alexander found in favour of Japan finding in perfect diplomatese:

"The Government of Japan is not responsible for the consequences brought about by the stay of the Peruvian vessel *Maria Luz* in the port of Kanagawa."[14]

Reform in Japan

While the *Maria Luz* case had made its way through the Japanese courts, the Iwakura Mission had continued its overseas study trip. While not successful in getting the foreign powers to end extraterritoriality, the mission was extremely successful in its main goal of studying foreign legal systems and beginning the process of reforming the Japanese legal system. Upon their return to Japan, the mission made recommendations for changes that were in part influenced by a "burning desire to secure the abolition of extraterritoriality."[15]

In 1873 Japan revised its Penal Code, abolishing the use of torture to extract confessions, reducing the number of crimes where the death penalty would be imposed and almost abolishing corporal punishment. At the end of 1873, with assistance of French experts, work was begun on a comprehensive criminal code. In 1875, drafting commenced on a Civil Code to be based on the French Civil Code. Japanese commentators, however, encouraged caution in changing the system too fast so that Japanese customs and traditions would not conflict too much with the new codes.[16] By 1876 the Japanese

---

13 *London and China Telegraph*, July 8, 1873, p439.

14 *North China Herald*, November 11, 1875, p266.

15 F. Jones, *Extraterritoriality in Japan*, p77.

16 F. Jones, *Extraterritoriality in Japan*, p.79 et seq.

had developed full procedures for handling first instance and appeal cases in their courts.

H.S. Wilkinson had by then become the key British legal adviser in Japan. Sir Harry Parkes, the British Minister, considered him one of his most "trusted officers" and "consulted him on almost every point of law and procedure that came up for consideration."[17] Wilkinson was therefore entrusted with drafting and agreeing with the Japanese authorities procedures for British subjects to bring complaints and appeals to the Japanese courts. The procedures drafted by Wilkinson provided that British subjects could either file their cases or appeals through the consul or could handle them directly if they preferred. Appeals by Japanese against decisions favourable to British subjects would be transmitted to the consul for onward transmission to the British party. The formal rules were issued in both Charles Goodwin's and Wilkinson's names.[18]

Wilkinson received high praise from London for his work. The rules were reviewed by the Treasury Counsel who wrote to the Secretary of State to "express their appreciation of the completeness and ability with which Mr Wilkinson has discharged the duty entrusted to him. The Draft Regulations indeed were drawn up with so much care and are so calculated to meet their object that my Lords have found it necessary to make but a few alterations."[19]

The situation in China was starkly different to Japan. In China, there were no Chinese lawyers, no independent Chinese courts and no system for appeals. The handling of mixed cases, in particular, remained a serious area of dispute between the foreign powers and China.

---

17 F.V. Dickins, *Life of Sir Harry Parkes*, Vol II. p170 and in particular footnote 2.

18 FO 656/237 Notification by British Legation dated June 9, 1877, Guidelines for bringing cases signed by H.S. Wilkinson April 13, 1876 and Correspondence from Japanese Minister of Foreign Affairs regarding appeals attaching new rules, February 23, 1877.

19 PRONI D1292, Extract of letter dated August 21, 1875 from William Law of Treasury Chambers.

CHAPTER 11

Mixed Justice in China

IN CHINA, UNLIKE JAPAN, the question of how to handle mixed cases involving Chinese and foreigners remained a vexed issue. Three cases in the mid 1870s brought the issue to the fore. In two of the cases Chinese had been killed by Britons. In the third, Sir Edmund Hornby made himself very unpopular with all the foreign powers when he confirmed the right of the Chinese government to be involved in mixed trials - a right soon taken away by another treaty signed at the point of gunboat barrels.

The Shantung lighthouse
In the first case, in 1874, Hornby sailed to Chefoo for the trial of Thomas Fawcett for manslaughter. Fawcett was the supervisor of the construction of a lighthouse by Chinese Customs in Shantung (Shandong). Fawcett was acquitted, resulting in the British Minister, Thomas Wade, questioning why Hornby had allowed Fawcett to go free. Wade's reproof greatly angered Hornby. In his autobiography, he described it as "still an open wound", adding that the case "might have ended badly for me as well as have become an awkward precedent for his successors."

Hornby gives a long account of the case in his autobiography, which must have been written a long time after the event when his memory was failing. In his autobiography, he says he thought Fawcett was innocent and should have been acquitted, whereas in the case report at the time, he clearly considered Fawcett to have been guilty of manslaughter but that if the jury had convicted Fawcett, he may have imposed a light sentence.[1]

The British-run Imperial Maritime Customs had decided to build a lighthouse on the Shantung Promontory, a dangerous headland on which many Chinese and foreign vessels had been wrecked. According to Hornby, the local people did not like the idea of the loss of income they would suffer from ships no longer being wrecked off the coast whether by accident of by the use of false beacons to lure ships to destruction. Regardless of the reason, it is clear that there was significant local opposition to the building of the lighthouse. The local people regularly attacked workers on the site, seeking to stop the work. Ultimately, Hornby wrote "finding that northern men would not or could not show fight and protect themselves and the works, some Canton men were sent for and placed under the charge of an Englishman, a species of stockade was erected around the works, the labourers were armed and sentries patrolled the place during the night." The workers brought in were from the South, but not as far south as Canton, in fact coming from Ningpo.

Though outsiders were forbidden from coming within a mile of the site, fights continued with the locals attacking the site at night and trying to destroy the work that had been done.

Fawcett patrolled the site at night and one evening around sunset, according to Hornby, "seeing some men approaching from several points within the limits, he went to meet them – the two nearest him had the usual heavy pronged hoe used to break up the ground. He ordered them back, drawing his revolver; they refused and one of them raised his hoe. On this, the Englishman, seizing his revolver by the barrel, jumped on one side and struck the man over the arm and caused him to

---

1 Hornby, *An Autobiography* pp240-245; *R v Fawcett, North China Herald*, September 26,1874, pp320-321.

drop his hoe; but the blow caused the revolver to go off."

The bullet killed another man standing nearby and Fawcett was detained by the local Chinese magistrate. Hornby, upon hearing of the case, requested Fawcett be handed over to the British authorities for trial. The Mandarin in charge of the district refused. Hornby sent a couple of officers to collect Fawcett and he was handed over. While he was in detention by the Chinese, a confession was obtained from Fawcett that he intended to kill one of the men, but mistakenly killed the other. At his committal hearing in the British Provincial Court, Fawcett asked the Magistrate who had detained him, Keng Tien-ken:

"Was I not put in irons in your city, and my life threatened, if I would not say that there was a man shot and that I had shot him?"

Keng replied:

"I was afraid you would run away, and I ordered you to be handcuffed because you expressed a dislike to being chained by your neck. I did not threaten you; you made your confession yourself that it was your intention to shoot Wang-chih but that by mistake you shot the other man."[2]

Fawcett was ordered to stand trial before the Supreme Court. Hornby sent, Robert Mowat, the Law Secretary, a lawyer and a Chinese translator to help assist preparation of the case. The case was tried by Hornby with a jury of five at Chefoo with two Mandarins in attendance.[3] Mr W.M. Cooper of the Yantai consulate prosecuted. Nicholas Hannen, now back in

---

2   *R v Thomas Fawcett*. *North China Herald*, September 19, 1874, p278-279 at 279.

3   The jury members were W.J. Clarke, H. Consterdine, W.A. Cornabe, J.M. Farmer and W.R. Fuller. The mandarins were not named in the case report.

private practice in China, came from Shanghai to defend Fawcett. The Chinese prosecution witnesses were brought to court in chains. When Hornby asked why, the answer was given that they refused to give evidence otherwise. Hornby ordered the chains be removed and they were examined by the Chinese officials. The two Chinese who had met with Fawcett gave evidence. They denied trying to hit him and claimed that Fawcett had turned around and deliberately shot the victim.

It was clear that not all the Chinese witnesses were there voluntarily. One witness, after being pressured by the Mandarins, finally exclaimed: "How can you expect I can recollect all you have told me to say, you half starved me, and look here [showing his wrists] see how I have been treated, locked up in a beastly hole, taken away from my family and work for the last moon. I have forgot all, I wasn't there, and I know nothing about the affair, nor do any of them except the two," referring to the men who had met Fawcett. Another Chinese witness said that he had received 150 blows at the Yamen before giving evidence.

An American doctor said that from the drawing of the wounds it appeared that the victim was shot from behind because the wound at the front was larger. A number of the Ningpo workmen also gave evidence that supported Fawcett.

Hornby summed up and made it clear that he thought Fawcett should be convicted. He said that illegal use of a weapon that causes death is manslaughter. A weapon should only be used when absolutely necessary. There was no evidence the use of the revolver had been necessary. Hornby completed his summing up all but directing the jury to convict:

"And then you can, under my direction, have no difficulty in finding the prisoner guilty of the offence with which he is charged ... I tell you distinctly that in my judgment the use of a loaded pistol was unlawful and unnecessary. I trust you will view the case as if it happened between two Englishmen. A Chinaman's life is as precious as that of one of our own countrymen, and you are called upon to do justice."[4]

Hannen objected to the way the law had been explained. Hornby gave leave to argue this later if necessary. The jury then retired, returning in a few minutes, with a verdict of Not Guilty. Hornby then said:

"Gentlemen, I must record your verdict, but I regret it; you have not taken the Law as I laid it down to you, which you ought to have done; it is a most mischievous verdict."

Hannen also protested against this, to which Hornby said:

"I consider it my duty to do so, and most emphatically I say in this case that the jury have ignored the Law as I laid it down to them, and which they were bound to take from me, and they have come to a conclusion not warranted by the evidence. I greatly regret the course they have pursued, and although I have no right to, and do not, interfere in any way with their verdict, which is final and conclusive; but I do claim the right, and shall always exercise it, when I think necessary, to express my disapproval and regret."

The acquittal caused much indignation to the local Chinese, perhaps more than normal given Hornby's comments about the verdict. But, what upset Hornby more was that Sir Thomas Wade, the British Minister considered Hornby should have done more. Hornby recounted in his autobiography that Wade:

4   This and following quotes are all from the case report *R v Thomas Fawcett*, *North China Herald*, September 26, 1874, pp320-321.

"coolly wrote to me that he did not agree with the verdict, and that I ought to have retained the accused in custody, for, I suppose, an investigation or trial by the Chinese or some amateur tribunal."

Hornby felt that Wade was more concerned with not upsetting the Chinese government than whether the Englishman had been properly tried.

The next evening, Hornby's bungalow on the beachfront in Chefoo was surrounded by a mob of villagers headed by the supposed widow, demanding that Hornby hand Fawcett over. Fawcett had in fact already, and wisely it seems, left Chefoo. Hornby's house was besieged for three days and two nights. Hornby sought assistance from the Chinese authorities who sent an officer who told Hornby to give the crowd a dollar or two each and 50 dollars for the widow, which Hornby refused. Instead:

"I closed all my windows, loaded a couple of doublebarreled guns and a couple of revolvers, and walked up and down my verandah."

Eventually, his Chinese servant, or "boy" as Hornby called him, learned that there was a British gunboat down the coast and the boy and a boatman went to find it. The next morning, to Hornby's "intense delight," the gunboat HMS *Hornet* steamed into port and landed a party of Marines and Jacks.[5] Having controlled the crowd by the presence of the British military, Hornby went to see the Mandarin, who said he "was very sorry, but he really had no control over the villagers," but offered a guard. Hornby declined; he now had his own. Hornby remained in Chefoo for a further three weeks, to try

5   Hornby's recollection as to gunboat arriving to protect him from a crowd surrounding his bungalow is supported by contemporaneous reports, see eg, a letter to the *North China Herald* from their Chefoo correspondent dated October 1, published on October 8, 1874, p335.

other cases, with a guard of six Jacks. Complaints were made to the Chinese authorities in Peking, but according to Hornby, he never received "the slightest expression of regret."

Having now had a practical lesson as to where the power supporting extraterritorial jurisdiction really came from, Hornby wrote:

"Of course I never tried another British subject accused of killing a Chinaman at an outlying port, unless there was a gun-boat at hand."

Railroaded

The Fawcett case arose due to problems resulting from the Maritime Customs' desire to build lighthouses, a very welcome modernization. A case in Shanghai two years later involving the death of a Chinese, on the other hand, showed just how strong official and local objections to most forms of modernization were.

The case involved an accident on the Woosung Railway between Shanghai and the port of Woosung, 30 kilometres to the north, where the Huangpu River meets the Yangtze. Planning for construction of the line had commenced in 1865 and a company was formed to build it. But the plan met strong opposition from the Chinese authorities. Eventually, the British promoters received permission to build a road rather than a railway, which they did. They later announced the intention to build a tramway along the road. When the rails were landed, it was clear that they were for a railway. The Taotai objected and requested the promoters stop construction until he could refer the matter to Peking. Construction nevertheless went ahead and the line as far as Kiangwan (Jiangwan), halfway between the International Settlement and Woosung, was completed and opened on June 30, 1876. The train consisted of a small steam engine, like that now seen in amusement parks, and two carriages.

Less than five weeks after the line was opened, on August

The opening of the Woosong Railway. After a Chinese was killed by the train, the tracks were ripped up and dumped on a beach in Taiwan.

3, 1876, a Chinese man walking along the tracks was hit by the train and killed under circumstances, which one contemporary English commentator "suggested either extremely dense stupidity or a malicious intent to commit suicide, and thereby create a prejudice against railways."[6]

Following the accident, the Chinese population became so hostile to the railway that the British Minister, Sir Thomas Wade, who was in Shanghai at the time, ordered the trains stop running temporarily.

The Chinese carried out an inquest into the man's death, at which the driver of the train, Edward Banks, was called as a witness. The Chinese demanded that a mixed court be convened to try Banks for the killing. The British Consulate refused, but instituted a prosecution for manslaughter against Banks in the Supreme Court.[7] At the preliminary hearing before Robert Mowat, sitting as Police Magistrate, Richard Ren-

6   H.B. Morse, *International Relations of the Chinese Empire*, Vol III, p.76 cited in *FL Hawks-Pott, A Short History of Shanghai*, p104. Hawks-Pott introduces the background on pp103-104.

7   *R v Banks, North China Herald*, September 16, 1876, pp282-285.

nie appeared for the Crown and Nicholas Hannen appeared for Banks. Rennie started by asking Mowat to immediately transfer the case to the Supreme Court for trial. He said the Chinese authorities were "deeply interested" in the case but that the Consulate had been unable to convince them that the Supreme Court had authority to try the case, rather than there being a mixed trial. Because of this, no Chinese official was present in the court and that as a matter of "political expediency" a Chinese official should be present at a Supreme Court hearing. Hannen objected saying that the "question of political expediency had nothing whatever to do with the Police Court." Mowat agreed, adding that the court was an open court and that anyone could attend. Mowat ordered that the case should continue.

Mr Cooper, Acting Vice-Consul who had attended the Chinese enquiry and acted as an interpreter, the fireman of the train and an employee of Jardine Matheson who was a passenger on the train all gave evidence. Criminal defendants at the time could not give evidence in their own defence. But Cooper repeated the evidence that Banks had given at the Chinese inquest. This was that he had seen a man on the rails about 100 yards away and had sounded his whistle. The man had got off the tracks. When the train was about 15 yards away, the man had then walked back on the tracks and the train hit him. The fireman, who was Chinese, corroborated this story saying:

> "When I first saw the deceased, he was in danger, but after he crossed the rails he was in a place of safety. If he had remained there he would have been safe. He made no signs that he intended to re-cross the rails; he merely stood looking on."

Mowat found that there clearly was no evidence of culpable negligence to support a charge of manslaughter.

Hannen then made a strange application. He said that he was not applying for costs but wanted an indication of whether, if a similar case was to arise in the future, the accused should be entitled to their costs. He said there was no evidence of any culpability and the Crown should not have brought the proceedings at all. Rennie responded that the defendant should not in the circumstances be entitled to costs because "it was in the interests of all concerned that an investigation should take place." After some discussion with Mowat, Rennie said that the problem was that the British authorities could not hold an inquest into the death of a Chinese and the Chinese could not bring manslaughter charges against a British subject in a Chinese court. The only step that the Crown could take was to bring the case before the court for the court to consider.

Mowat said that this was the type of case where he considered costs should be allowed. If there was no evidence of culpability, it was not proper for the Crown to proceed, even if there were political considerations.

Following the case, during 1876 and 1877, the Chinese authorities negotiated to purchase the railway line from the promoters. A deal was done and the local authorities bought it for 285,000 taels, the actual costs incurred by the promoters. Then, in an act of what can only be described as official Ludditism, they had the rails ripped up. The track and rolling stock were dumped on a beach in Taiwan. A railway line was not seen again in Shanghai for another 20 years.[8]

By contrast, in Japan, by the late 1870s plans were moving ahead to build a national railway system. The first line had opened in 1872 at a ceremony attended by the Meiji Emperor and lines were springing up all over the country.

---

8   F.L. Hawks-Pott, *A Short History of Shanghai*, pp103-4.

Joint trials or sole trials

The Woosong Railway case came before the British and Chinese courts in Shanghai in the same month that Britain and China were finalizing a new treaty that would settle for many years to come how mixed trials were to be handled.

The right of Chinese officials to be involved in trials of foreigners under the Treaty of Tientsin, had been brought to a head by a decision of Hornby the year before in 1875. The British steamship, the *Kwangtung*, registered in Hong Kong, had collided with a Chinese junk, *Kui-tsai-fay*.[9] The junk and her cargo were lost but the crew was saved by the steamer. The owner of the junk brought a complaint to the British Consul General at Foochow, Charles Sinclair, who along with the local Taotai, Mr Pao, established a Mixed Court to try the case. The court found in favour of the junk owners ordering the *Kwangtung* to pay damages. The owners of the *Kwangtung* made an application to the Supreme Court in Shanghai for the judgment of the Mixed Court to be set aside. A solicitor, Mr R.E. Wainewright, appeared on behalf of the owners.

Surprisingly, perhaps, given Hornby's clear disapproval of the Chinese legal system, Hornby found that the creation of a mixed court by the British Consul-General in Foochow sitting with the local Taotai was fully compliant with the Treaty of Tientsin. Hornby also held that no right of appeal lay to the Supreme Court from such cases. The Treaty of Tientsin did not make clear provision for Chinese to make claims against British subjects. Article 17 provided that if a Chinese had a complaint against a British subject, they should seek the assistance of the Consul. If this could not resolve the matter then the Consul "shall request the assistance of the Chinese authorities, that they may together examine into the merits of the case, and decide it equitably."

....

9 *In the matter of a suit heard in HBM's Consulate at Foochow before a Mixed Court composed of HM's Consul Charles A Sinclair Esq, in conjunction with Pan Tautai, North China Herald,* February 11, 1875, p129. The case is also referred to as the *"Kwantung* Case."

Hornby said:

> "I must refuse this rule. I do not entertain, and never
> have entertained, the slightest doubt on the subject
> of the right of Chinese litigants to invoke 17th clause
> of the Treaty of Tientsin, and insist on any matters of
> difference between them and British subjects being
> decided in accordance with such clause."

He explained that the treaty was clear and even if the Orders
in Councils may be interpreted otherwise, no legislation could
override treaty rights. He went on to state that if he was to consider the British defendant's protest "or attach any weight to
it, the result would be to send the Chinaman whose junk had
been run down, as he reports, in the China Seas, to a British
Colony, [that is, Hong Kong] - to a place, the law of which he is
ignorant of, and of the language of which he is also ignorant."

With regard to the role of the Supreme Court in Shanghai,
he said that "it was true that Chinese were willing to sue in
the Supreme Court," but that he had "often seen them and
explained to them that they can go and lay their case before
the Consul, who will call on the Tautai to decide it under the
Treaty. Chinese parties had, however, often refused, and expressed themselves contented to abide by the decision of the
Supreme Court."

Hornby did not say so, but the reason for this is, most
likely, that there was no mechanism to enforce a judgment
of a mixed court, whereas the Supreme Court had numerous methods to enforce judgments against British subjects,
including seizing assets or freezing bank accounts. As any
lawyer knows, most judgments only have value if you can
enforce them.[10]

The *London and China Telegraph* published a long editorial

10 In a small number of cases, parties are happy to have unenforceable judgments if
they establish a principle that can be applied to other cases.

denouncing Hornby's decision as "a sudden and unexpected reversal of the established order of procedure" which had "the effect of entirely overthrowing the order of things." The *Telegraph* beseeched the Crown Law Officers in London to look at the case and put things right.[11]

Hornby's decision caused great consternation amongst all the treaty powers. The Americans were particularly dismayed by the decision coming from the British Supreme Court. George Seward, who had been promoted from Shanghai Consul-General to American Minister in Peking, as part of a joint statement issued by the treaty powers regarding the *Kwangtung* decision stated categorically, "the treaties concluded between the United States and China give, in effect, full jurisdiction in civil matters to the court of the defendant in all cases between Americans and Chinese arising within the territory of China." He added that "this principle has been rigidly adhered to since the date of the first Treaty." Interestingly, the representatives of Russia, Germany, France and Spain all considered that their treaties provided for mixed tribunals although they admitted that, in practice, "the state of affairs is different."[12]

The joint statement was highly critical of the Chinese legal system saying "no codes of procedure worthy to be called such exist. The magistrates, secretaries and constables are often corrupt," adding that it was often difficult to find a court with jurisdiction and no appellate court existed. The statement finished with a the strong comment on the weakness of the Chinese legal system:

"for the latter reasons, questions which should be decided by appeal can only be treated by political

---

11 *London and China Telegraph* April 5,1875, p276.

12 P.H. Clyde, "Attitudes and Policies of George F Seward, American Minister and Peking, 1876-1880", Pacific Historical Review, Vol 2, No. 4, (Dec 1993), p395-397. Citations for the statement of the diplomatic body also come from this source.

View of Chefoo from Consulate Hill

recourse through Diplomatic agents, and become the subject of long and annoying negotiations."

Gunboats resolve the issue: The Chefoo Convention

From a distance of more than a century and a half, it is clear that Hornby's decision was right. Hornby was not the type to worry about the "established order" of things. If the established order was wrong, he would make a decision to that effect. The only way to return to the "established order" was to reach a new agreement with the Chinese. This is exactly what Sir Thomas Wade, the British Minister, did the following year when he forced a treaty upon China that reversed Hornby's decision and established the principle that would apply for the remainder of the life of extraterritorial courts in China. The treaty, the Chefoo Convention, was a "catch-all" treaty that was intended to clarify issues that had remained open from the Sino-British treaties before it.

The genesis of the treaty was that in 1875, locals had attacked a British exploration party in Yunnan in western China, and the British interpreter, Augustus Margary, had been killed. Wade opened negotiations to resolve this issue and put a number of other issues including taxation as well as trade and intercourse on the table. The Chinese initially resisted, pointing out, correctly, that Margary's party had been in Yunnan on false pretences. They had claimed to be in transit to Burma, when they were in fact carrying out surveys. Wade overcame this intransigence by ordering a squadron of gunboats to Tientsin. Eventually, in August 1876, Wade met with Li Hongzhang, who had become the Chinese official primarily responsible for negotiating with foreigners, in Chefoo and signed the Chefoo Convention to resolve the Margary dispute and numerous other issues.[13] The Chefoo Convention was one of many unequal treaties Li negotiated, making him a very unpopular figure in Chinese history.

With regard to the handling of legal cases, the Convention set out that in order to fulfill its Treaty obligations, "the British Government has established a Supreme Court at Shanghai, with a special code of rules." Further, "the Chinese Government has established at Shanghai a Mixed Court." The Convention added, however, that "the officer presiding over it, either from lack of power, or dread of unpopularity, constantly fails to enforce his judgments." It was agreed that the Tsungli Yamen would consult with the legations on ways to improve the Mixed Court.[14]

The Convention then dealt with how Mixed Cases were to be heard by providing that the each side would try their own nationals with the other side attending to observe proceedings. Article 2(3) provided:

---

13 J. Cooley, *T.F. Wade in China: Pioneer in Global Diplomacy 1842-1882*, p119 et seq gives details of the negotiation of the Chefoo Convention and Wade's battle to get it ratified by Britain.

14 Article 2(2) of the Chefoo Convention.

"It is farther understood that so long as the laws of the
two countries differ from each other, there can be but one
principle to guide judicial proceedings in mixed cases
in China, namely, that the case is tried by the official of
the defendant's nationality, the official of the plaintiff's
nationality merely attending to watch the proceedings
in the interests of justice. If the officer so attending were
dissatisfied with the proceedings, it will be in his power
to protest against them in detail. The law administered
will be the law of the nationality of the officer trying the
case."

In the Shanghai International Settlement, this principle
was extended by a consular assessor sitting with a Chinese
magistrate to hear all cases in the International Mixed Court.
A similar court was established in the French Concession.

The Chinese soon ratified the Chefoo Convention, but
in Britain there was much opposition to its terms relating to
trade. It was not until 1885, after much lobbying by Wade,
that the Chefoo Convention was finally ratified by Britain.

The United States also signed a short treaty on Commercial Relations and Judicial Procedure in 1880 to implement directly between the United States and China some of the provisions that had been agreed in the Chefoo Convention. With
regards to judicial procedure, the treaty provided that cases
would be tried by the officials of the defendant's country under that country's laws. An official of the plaintiff's nationality was permitted to attend the trial and was to be "granted
all proper facilities for watching the trial," and the right to
"examine and cross-examine witnesses."[15]

As a bonus for China, the United States, which had never
been heavily involved in the opium trade, agreed to a provision that banned Americans from importing opium into

15 US China Treaty on Commercial Relations and Judicial Procedure, signed at Peking
on November 17, 1880, ratified by China and the US in 1881.

China.

The Chefoo Convention and the US-China treaty of 1880 completed negotiation of treaties underpinning the British and American extraterritorial legal systems in China and formed the bedrock of the exercise of extraterritorial jurisdiction for the next 60 years. From then on, cases against British and Americans were tried in British and American courts and cases against Chinese were tried in Chinese courts. The Shanghai Mixed Court also continued to function and, up until 1911, the Chinese judge was, for the most part, in charge.

The Chefoo Convention was signed just as the British courts in China were about to see great changes.

CHAPTER 12

The End of an Era:
Hornby retires - Goodwin dies

Farewell Sir Edmund

A LITTLE MORE THAN a decade after its establishment, the British Supreme Court suddenly lost its two founding judges. Sir Edmund Hornby retired on a generous pension in 1876 and Charles Goodwin died at a relatively young age in early 1878.

Hornby's decision to retire appears to have been quite sudden. There were no rumours of his retirement published in the *North China Herald* or *London and China Telegraph*, both of which kept a close ear to the ground on judicial movements. Rather, Hornby appears to have been preparing to sit on the bench in Shanghai for years to come. He had been working on a new voluminous Order in Council for some time, the draft of which was circulated on May 13, 1876 with a long explanatory memorandum. The draft contained 600 sections and sought to comprehensively deal with the many problems that had occurred in the exercise of extraterritoriality. Hornby proposed the formal establishment of a Court for Japan, admitting that the current arrangements in Japan were unsatisfactory and required a "forced construction" of the Order in Council. Most startlingly, he proposed some major revisions to criminal laws and procedures that would make it easier to ensure convictions. He justified this on the basis that "the truth is that English criminal jurisprudence has long been marked by an over-tender consideration for the guilty, and has in consequence been in a measure unfair to the innocent." Perhaps with the Shantung lighthouse case in mind, he proposed a rule that where the trial was for offences against native Japanese or Chinese, the court could sit without a jury even in death penalty cases.[1]

In Japan, H.S. Wilkinson was asked by Harry Parkes, the British Minister, to comment on the proposals. Wilkinson wrote a long report that was highly critical of a number of aspects of Hornby's proposal, but in particular the suggestion that trial by jury for death penalty cases be abolished. He wrote:

> "To justify such a departure from the spirit of British jurisprudence a very strong case would require to be shown, if there is a reluctance in British juries to convict where the case rests wholly on native testimony, it is founded on a very justifiable skepticism as to the value of such testimony, and if the reluctance is carried sometimes further than circumstances warrant, the remedy is altogether disproportionate to the evil."[2]

Why Hornby decided to retire is unclear. Hornby had only the year before published and publicly defended his story of meeting the ghost of Dr Lang. Perhaps, it was this or his "lack of judicial qualities" or, perhaps, his decision in the *Kwantung* case had caught up with him. Julian Pauncefote, the former Attorney-General of Hong Kong, had just transferred from the Colonial Office to the Foreign Office as Legal Assistant as Under-Secretary for Foreign Affairs. Pauncefote was well placed to know Hornby's reputation and could well have encouraged Hornby to resign.

On the other hand, it may have been a personal decision.

1 PRONI D1292/M/5 (Wilkinson Papers).

2 Wilkinson Papers, PRONI, D1292/M/5A Memorandum: China and Japan Order in Council 1876, August 8, 1876, para 36.

Hornby, whose second wife, had died in 1873, had just remarried at the age of 51 to the 20-year-old Emily Roberts. They had first met when she was a child on a trip from Shanghai to Japan. He often told one of his daughters of this marriage, Constance, "how much he admired her when she used to fly round the Race Course in Shanghai on her pony in a long riding habit and red turban."[3] Perhaps with a much younger wife, he decided it was time to enjoy life rather than running around China and Japan trying cases. The fact that he had married a lady 30 years his junior may have also been the subject of some adverse comment from the small British community in Shanghai. (But not from Charles Goodwin who had married a wife 25 years younger.)

In any event, Hornby was given a very generous pension of £2,300 per annum. By way of comparison, at the time, Goodwin was making £1,200 per annum as assistant judge.[4] There does not appear to have been a farewell ceremony for Hornby in the court although Goodwin came over to Shanghai from Yokohama presumably to farewell his chief of 11 years.

We have already seen the article from the *Japan Mail* published on Hornby's retirement that described his interesting personality and lack of judicial qualities. The *North China Herald* also published a short farewell editorial just after Hornby left Shanghai in May 1876.[5] It noted the many responsibilities he shouldered, not just as the Chief Judge but as administrator of all the Provincial Courts as well as "to some extent" being the confidential legal adviser of the British Minister, all of which "must be certain to enhance the difficulties of his position, and entail upon him some disagreeable responsibility."

"From responsibility, however, Sir Edmund Hornby never shrunk; and he has brought much quick penetra-

---

3 Hornby, An Autobiography, introduction by Constance Drummond (nee Hornby).

4 *London and China Telegraph*, May 22, 1876, p429.

5 *North China Herald*, May 27, 1876, p501.

tion to bear upon the many delicate and difficult matters which have come before him."

The *Japan Gazette* published a short but very warm farewell taken from the *North China Daily News* saying:

"Sir Edmund has made many friends during his twelve
years' residence in Shanghai who regret his loss, and
not readily forget his deeds of hearty and disinterested
kindness which he has performed for them. Privately
our retiring Judge was a sincere and amiable man and
a sterling friend; in his public capacity he was remarkable for the constant endeavor to prevent litigation to
the utmost of his powers. We need only to express our
best wishes for the future happiness and welfare of
Lady Hornby and himself."[6]

A newspaper in Egypt commenting on his time in Constantinople and the Far East said: "he was admirably adapted for the posts he filled, where gifts of administration and
organization were urgently required." The best farewell for
Hornby was published in the *Times* on his death:

"The building up of the Consular Court system in
[China and Japan], as well as in the Levant, was, to a
very large extent, Sir Edmund Hornby's work, and in
many ways it continues to show evident traces of his
influence and discretion."[7]

Whatever his faults, the Supreme Court for China and Japan would have been a different institution had it been established by anyone other than Hornby.

After retirement, Hornby first tried his hand at farming

6   *Japan Gazette*, June 1, 1876, p3.
7   Obituary for Hornby, *Times*, November 20, 1896.

and insisted on employing ex-prisoners to give them a second chance in life. The results were disastrous and he finally moved to Devon. He maintained an interest in international law and helped to work out a scheme that led to the establishment of the Hague Tribunal. He wrote a pamphlet for the Peace Preservation Society, advocating the establishment in Switzerland of a school or faculty of international law to be kept up jointly by the Powers. He also dabbled in local politics. He returned to Shanghai on a visit in late 1886 and early 1887 with his wife and young children.[8]

Sir Edmund lived 20 years after his retirement, dying in his sleep in 1896 after a long mountain climb in Rapallo, Italy, at the age of 71. Six years after his death, he made a brief cameo appearance in what had become the Supreme Court for China and Corea. In his will, he left his daughters by his third wife, Emily Hornby and Constance Hornby, shares in the Shanghai Real Property Association. Emily Hornby had already become an adult and had sold her shares back to the promoter of the SRPA who held the majority of the shares in the company. There was no liquid market in the shares and permission was sought for Lady Hornby, Constance's guardian, to sell the shares on similar terms. The Chief Justice approved the sale of these shares for 1,440 taels.[9]

Farewell Mr Goodwin

On Hornby's retirement, Goodwin was appointed Acting Judge from May 22, 1876. He sat in at least one case in Shanghai as "Acting Chief Judge" soon after Hornby left. However, shortly thereafter, he returned to Yokohama, leaving Robert Mowat to act as "Deputy Chief Judge" in Shanghai. Goodwin stayed in Japan for six more months sitting as the Acting

8 Hornby, Autobiography, Introduction by Constance Drummond (nee Hornby); *North China Herald* December 8, 1886, p606 for Hornby's arrival in Shanghai and March 30, 1887, p365 for his departure. *Western Times*, June 23 1892, p4 for Hornby's involvement in local politics.

9 *North China Herald*, April 2,1902, p660.

Chief Judge. He returned to Shanghai with his family in early 1877.[10]

Before leaving Japan, Goodwin appointed H.S. Wilkinson as Acting Law Secretary of the Supreme Court with "power to dispatch all summary criminal offences, to appoint prosecutors and even exercise the Supreme Court's authority to dispense with a jury where it would ordinarily be required."[11]

Wilkinson had just returned from an attachment to the court in Shanghai where he had acted as Law Secretary from October 1876. During this time, Wilkinson was also appointed Vice-Consul at Niigata on the north side of Japan. However, as far as can be ascertained, he never physically went to Niigata, remaining in Yokohama as the Acting Law Secretary and, for a period of time, acting as Vice-Consul in Tokyo. James Troup, the consul in Niigata, reported in his 1876 Trade Report that there was "no ostensible British trade to report on. No British ships have visited the port during 1876, and no British merchants have ever settled here." There was no need for a Vice-Consul in Niigata, but appointing Wilkinson to the

Hiram Shaw Wilkinson,

HER BRITANNIC MAJESTY'S VICE CONSUL.

NIIGATA.

H.S. Wilkinson's name card as Vice Consul in Niigata.
He may never have actually gone to Niigata.

10 Short report on *Myers v Carmichael*, North China Herald, May 27, 1876, p503 with Goodwin as Acting CJ in Shanghai; *Nakajima v Mitchell*, Japan Weekly Mail, July 22, 1876 p22 for Goodwin as Acting CJ in Yokohama; North China Herald, August 19, 1876, p167 re Mowat as Deputy CJ; Japan Weekly Mail, December 23, 1876, p1,154 and London and China Telegraph, February 19, 1877, p 148 on Goodwin returning from Yokohama.

11 C. Roberts, *The British Courts and Extra-Territoriality in Japan 1859-1899*, p26 citing a letter from Goodwin to Wilkinson dated 20 December 1876, FO 656/39.

position gave him the necessary rank to try cases without using one of the busy vice-consular positions in Yokohama.[12]

During 1877, the local newspapers in China and Japan carried reports that Goodwin would be promoted to Chief Judge.[13] But by late 1877, the decision had been made that a new Chief Judge would be brought in from outside and Goodwin would be appointed to a new position as Judge for Japan. The *Japan Weekly Mail* welcomed this news, if true, saying "we trust the community may soon have the pleasure of welcoming back a gentleman whose rare attainments and social qualities won him universal regard, and whose temporary absence has been a great loss to his friends."[14]

The news was true and Goodwin was offered the appointment in Japan. It is not clear if he accepted it, in late 1877 Goodwin was struck down by a "prolonged and serious illness" and he applied for a year's sick leave.[15]

Goodwin's illness, which he bore with "perfect patience and fortitude," took a turn for the worse in early 1878 and he died on January 17. He was buried in a vaulted grave on the south side the Shanghai Cemetery (later called the Pahsienjao Cemetery). The service was conducted by the Very Rev. Dean Butcher. From the legal community, Robert Mowat and Richard Rennie acted as pall bearers along with the British Consul, A. Davenport, Capt Dupuis of the HMS *Frolic*, General Stahel, United States Vice Consul and J. Hart, the Chairman of the Municipal Council. Goodwin's grave has long disappeared - the Shanghai Cemetery is now Huaihai Park on Huaihai Road. He has not, however, been completely forgotten. In recognition of his remarkable contribution to Egyptology, a bust

12 R. Chang, *Justice of the Western Consular Courts in Nineteenth Century Japan*, p63; British Consular Trade Report for Niigata for 1876, *Japan Weekly Mail*, March 14, 1877, p209; C. Roberts, "Hiram Shaw Wilkinson (1840-1926)", *Britain and Japan Biographical Portraits*, Vol VIII, p167.

13 *North China Herald*, June 3, 1876, p531 and *Japan Weekly Mail* June 3, 1876, p486.

14 *North China Herald*, December 13, 1877, p546 and *Japan Weekly Mail*, December 22, 1877, p1153.

15 C. Roberts, The British Courts and Extra-Territoriality in Japan, 1859-1899, p53.

of Goodwin was erected in the remembrance section of the gardens of Cairo Museum.[16]

Goodwin was an extraordinary man, with extraordinary gifts. This was reflected in the emotional outpouring that occurred on Goodwin's death. Flags were flown at half-mast and the British Consulate closed for two days.[17] The American Consulate also closed for a day. There were many fond remembrances of Goodwin published in numerous obituaries in China, Japan and England. Given his numerous achievements, some of these obituaries mixed up Goodwin's greatest talents. Goodwin's brother, Reverend Harvey Goodwin, in a letter to the Athenaeum magazine in London, wished to correct an impression that Goodwin had been an Anglo Saxon and Coptic scholar. He had been, but his brother was at pains to emphasize:

> "Now, the fact is that Egyptology was my brother's earliest as it was his most persistent love. I am one of the few persons who can give testimony on this point; and my brother's childish devotion to this subject, coupled with his mature labour and success, appears to me to be quite remarkable enough to be worthy of record."[18]

The *North China Herald* published a long obituary that after reciting his many achievements said:

> "But those who enjoyed the great privilege of Mr Goodwin's acquaintance remember him with that affectionate regard which is secured by qualities not always associated with profound antiquarian scholarship; He was one of the most charming companions that it was

---

16 *North China Herald*, February 21, 1878, p 178; *Japan Weekly Mail*, February 2, 1878, p101; W. Dawson, *Charles Wycliffe Goodwin, a Pioneer in Egyptology*, p48.

17 *North China Herald*, January 24, 1878, p79.

18 Reproduced in *North China Herald*, May 18, 1878, p519.

possible to meet. His conversation was studded with recondite allusions, with 'happy expressions', and with all the evidences of learning alike accurate and profound; but it was lighted up with the most playful fancy, and enhanced by the modesty which Chaucer describes as inseparable from the true scholar.

'And gladly wolde he lerne, and gladly teche.'" [19]

The *Japan Weekly Mail* in a leading article lamented:

"The kindly smile has vanished, the pleasant tones are hushed, the conversation full of quaint illustration and curious learning will never again astonish by its wisdom or charm or by its wit."[20]

The *Mail* gushed in an obituary in the same edition that Goodwin was "a man who is mourned in his death as he was beloved in his life, and who, passed from this world, 'may look his angel in the face without a blush.'"

The *North China Herald* in Shanghai concluded its obituary:

"We may sometimes regret, in the interests of science, that a more congenial field than a Judgeship in Shanghai was not found for a man so peculiarly and richly endowed with gifts; and whose bias certainly pointed out other spheres as far more congenial to his taste and adapted to his powers; but at the same time we were fortunate for many years in having amongst us a man of rare learning, who was at the same time, an embodiment of some of the most loveable qualities, and a model of honour, simplicity, and purity of aim. Those who knew him intimately learned something fresh

19 *North China Herald*, January 24, 1878 pp81-2.
20 *Japan Weekly Mail*, February 2 1878, p101 for leading article and p98 for obituary.

from every conversation they had with him, and feel
that the loss made by his death is in many senses ir-
reparable. But far deeper is the bereavement sustained
by his family, with whom we can only express our
sincere sympathy — "

This was followed by two lines from a sonnet by the Italian poet Petrarch:

"Non Omnia Terra
Obruta: vivit amor, vivit dolor."[21]

Or, in English:

"Not everything is buried
in the earth. Love lives, grief lives on! "

The next two lines of the poem were not published, but
well-educated readers of the *Herald*, would have known they
translated into English as:

We are denied the sight of those sweet features;
but it is left for us to weep and to remember.

---

21 The sonnet was made famous by Coleridge who used it as a eulogy to Dr Middle-
ton, Bishop of Calcutta who had introduced Coleridge to William Bowles, an early poet
who heavily influenced Coleridge. Coleridge thought the bishop was dead but he was
actually still alive. The full sonnet is: Ingenium celebrare meum, calamumque solebat/
Calcar agens animo validum. Non omnia terra/Obruta; vivit amor,vivit dolor; ora nega-
tur/Dulcia conspicere; at fiere et meminisse relictum est. Translation: Who, with lavish
praises, was wont to celebrate my genius and my pen, setting a sharp spur to my spirit.
Not everything is buried in the earth. Love lives, grief lives on! We are denied the sight
of those sweet features; but it is left for us to weep and to remember. Special thanks to
Henry Wheare for research on this point.

PART THREE:

REORGANIZATION
(1878 TO 1881)

CHAPTER 13

Reorganising the Courts

THE RETIREMENT OF SIR Edmund Hornby and death of Charles Goodwin, the two founders of the British Courts in China and Japan, not surprisingly, led to major changes in the structure and staffing of the British courts in both countries. Even before Hornby had announced his retirement, changes to the Orders in Council were under consideration. With Hornby's retirement these moved ahead.

New judges

First, a new Chief Judge had to be appointed. Mr Philip Currie of the Foreign Office proposed, in order to save costs and also to follow the practice that had been introduced in Constantinople after Hornby had moved to Shanghai, that the positions of Chief Judge and Consul in Shanghai be amalgamated.

The matter fell to be decided by Sir Julian Pauncefote, now the Legal Assistant Undersecretary for Foreign Affairs. Pauncefote was well placed to consider the issue. After serving for 8 years as Attorney General in Hong Kong, Pauncefote had been Chief Justice of the Leeward Islands in the West Indies before moving back to London, first with the Colonial Office and, then, the Foreign Office. Pauncefote had also in Hong Kong acted as a judge of the Hong Kong Supreme Court while serving as Attorney General. On at least one occasion he had been forced to recuse himself as a judge from a number of cases he was hearing because, as Attorney General, he had signed the indictment.

Sir Julian Pauncefote, now at the Foreign Office in London – architect of the new British legal structure in China and Japan

Pauncefote in a memorandum dated September 1877 rejected Currie's proposal on the basis that executive and judicial positions should be kept separate.[22] There would be particular problems if the Judge was called on to decide on the legality of actions of consular officers. Clearly reflecting his own personal experience in Hong Kong, he said:

"Those who have not had experience of British Colonies and Settlements in that part of the world can hardly form an idea of jealousy with which the relations between the Executive and Judicial Authorities are watched. In Hong Kong and Singapore, the slightest appearance of interference with the Chief Justice in the way of pressure in the discharge of his functions is the signal for violent attacks by the public press, indignation meetings, petitions and demonstrations of every kind. The community look to the Chief Justice as their protector against any attempt by the Governor 'to trample on their liberties.'"

He went on with a perhaps darker warning:

---

22 FO881/3482. This was considered an important memorandum and was formally printed for the Foreign Office on February 6, 1878. Re Pauncefote's time in Hong Kong, see, Norton-Kyshe, *History of the Laws and Courts of Hong Kong*, vol 2, p172-8 and 224-225.

"In the same spirit, the British community in China and Japan, which is the most powerful and wealthy community of British subjects to be found anywhere out of her Majesty's dominions, and who represent far greater interests than are at stake in any but the largest colonies, look to the Chief Judge of Her Britannic Majesty's Supreme Court for protection against any illegal or arbitrary action on the part of Her Majesty's Diplomatic and Consular Authorities."

He added that Shanghai on the other side of the world, could not be compared to Constantinople in Turkey, which was easily in touch with London and any mistakes quickly corrected either by the Foreign Office or the Privy Council. He concluded:

"I am of the opinion it would be very impolitic and inexpedient to change the character of the Supreme Court by the appointment of a Chief Judge who should at the same time be Consul, and thus at the same time be under the immediate authority and control Her Majesty's Minister at Peking."

The idea of amalgamation did not, however, die. Currie himself moved up in the Foreign Office and later resurrected the idea of amalgamating the office of Chief Justice and Consul-General. As we shall see, Pauncefote must have been using a crystal ball with 20/20 vision when he wrote his memo. All he said would come to pass, did come to pass.[23]

Pauncefote had also been asked to consider what salary the Chief Judge should be paid. Hornby had been making £3,500 per year. This was considered excessive and Pauncefote decided the Chief Judge should be paid the same salary

23 See Chapter 22

as the Chief Justice of Hong Kong, namely, £2,500 per annum with a housing allowance of £300 per year as the cost of living in Shanghai was much higher than in Hong Kong. Pauncefote also directed that the position of Consul in Shanghai be raised to Consul-General and that the Consul–General, who would be "the Official Head of the British Community in the Settlement," would take precedence to the Chief Judge who in turn would take precedence to the Consul.

George French, the former Chief Justice of Sierra Leone, was appointed Chief Judge on these terms. French was born in Tortola in the West Indies in 1817, making him 60 at the time of his appointment. His father, Mark Dyer French, was a barrister in the West Indies who had also served at one time as Registrar of the Court of Common Pleas of the British Virgin Islands. French studied at Gonville and Caius College, Cambridge, where he obtained a B.A (jun. op.) in 1839 and an MA in 1842. His father died while he was at university and left him the relatively large sum for the time of £5,000. He was called to the Bar at Lincoln's Inn in 1844. As a barrister, French "did not have a large business in court," but he was well known in the courts as a law reporter for the *Times* and the *Law Journal* in the court of the Vice Chancellor. For a number of years he sat as a Deputy County Court Judge.[24]

In 1867 French was appointed Chief Justice of the courts of Sierra Leone. He also sat as a Judge of the Mixed Courts in Sierra Leone from 1871 to 1875. In his capacity as Chief Justice, he was also Acting Governor of Sierra Leone from December 1874 to 1875. In 1875, the Sierra Leone government faced serious financial difficulties and French was placed on a pension. When the Foreign Office was looking for a new Chief Judge for Shanghai, Julian Pauncefote had recently moved from the Colonial Office to the Foreign Office. It was likely suggested

24 Biographical History for Gonville and Caius College, 1349-1897; Navy List, corrected to March 20, 1934; *North China Herald* December 20, 1877, p574; *The Standard,* July 1, 1867, p3; The *Morning Post* February 22, 1878, p5; *French v French*, Reports of Cases Decided in the High Court of Chancery by Shadwell VC, 1840-1841 p257.

to Pauncefote by his for-
mer colleagues in the Co-
lonial Office that French
would be a good candi-
date for the position in
Shanghai.

At the same time,
Robert Mowat after nine
years as Law Secretary
at the age of 34 was pro-
moted to Assistant Judge.
Mowat thereby became
the first of the judges appointed to the court to
come from the consular
corps in China and the
first judge to have learnt
Chinese.

Robert Mowat promoted to Assistant Judge

Mowat's old position of Law Secretary as a dual administrator and prosecutor of cases was peculiar and did not exist
in any other British court in the world. In the same memorandum that rejected the amalgamation proposal, Pauncefote
directed that the position of Law Secretary be abolished and
that positions for a Registrar, to handle administrative matters and act as a magistrate, and Judge's Clerk, to assist the
judges, be created in the new Order in Council then being
drafted. Accordingly, with effect from January 1, 1879, the
position of Law Secretary was abolished and a Judge's Clerk
appointed. The Order in Council provided that the Assistant
Judge could also be the Registrar of the Court. Mowat was
made Registrar of the Court.

The Crown Advocate
Pauncefote also decided to change the way in which prosecu-

tions were handled. This was done by the creation of a new role, that of Crown Advocate, to conduct prosecutions on behalf of the Crown as well as to advise the British legations on legal issues.[25] The role was similar to that of a colonial Attorney General (which Pauncefote had himself been in Hong Kong). The Crown Advocate was a practising barrister and was allowed to also handle cases for private clients so long as they did not conflict with their duties advising the Crown. He was paid a relatively low stipend of £500 per year (compared to the annual salary of £1,200 for an assistant judge).

Nicholas Hannen was appointed to be the first Crown Advocate in October 1878, a position that became a stepping-stone for four out of six Crown Advocates to judicial appointments. Initially, the status of the Crown Advocate was not clear. Soon after his appointment, Hannen asked if the position was a civil service position. In February 1879 he wrote to George French to request that French ask the Foreign Office if the position was "an established capacity in the permanent civil service of the State" under the Superannuation Act. [26] French replied five months later to Hannen that it was not a civil service position. He said the Treasury had advised that as the appointment as Crown Advocate allowed liberty to practice privately and "as you retain your private practice, and do not give your whole time to the public, you do not come within the provisions of the Superannuation Act."[27]

For the remainder of the existence of the court, the office of Crown Advocate continued to be a part time position with the Crown Advocate also working for private clients as far as his position allowed him to. Remuneration also remained a live issue. Subsequent Crown Advocates made numerous submissions on their poor remuneration compared to the work they

---

25 FO881/3482, Pauncefote memo, p4; London and China Telegraph December 9, 1878, p1045.

26 FO656/53, letter from Hannen to French dated February 6, 1879.

27 FO656/53 letter from French to Hannen dated July 3, 1879.

had to undertake. A particularly common complaint was that when the Crown Advocate was absent from Shanghai, an acting Crown Advocate would need to be appointed. No provision was ever made for payment by the Crown to acting Crown Advocates. The Crown Advocate was left to agree a deal with the person acting for him and pay him out of his own pocket.[28]

Challenged in Japan

The situation in the British Courts in Japan still needed to fixed by the establishment of a proper court system. Throughout 1877 H.S. Wilkinson had continued in his role as Acting Law Secretary as the principal British judge in Japan. He had taken up the task with relish. A number of cases came before him which, as he put it himself in a letter home, "were of considerable international importance, involving questions of civil and criminal jurisdiction of Her Majesty's Court in those countries."[29] He, as he was to do for the rest of his life, wrote long decisions dealing with the issues. Wilkinson was justifiably proud of these early decisions and kept printed copies of them for the remainder of his life.

His first case involved the prosecution of a young British woman, Elizabeth Scarfield, who had been engaged as the servant of the master's wife on board the American barque the *Annie W. Weston*.[30] Scarfield had become pregnant and given birth. The baby appears to have been stillborn and Scarfield threw it out of a porthole in her cabin. The master's wife had seen "traces of recent delivery" and reported the matter. The American Consul-General in Yokohama then brought a prosecution against Scarfield in the British court. The question Wilkinson had to decide was: did he have jurisdiction? Scarfield was on

---

28 FO 656/101 H.P. Wilkinson letter dated May 28, 1908 to the Secretary of State for Foreign Affairs; Letter from Allan Mossop to Sir Skinner Turner dated July 20, 1925 included as an attachment to a letter on FO 656/219; FO 656/101 Letter from Duncan McNeill to FSA Bourne Acting Chief Justice dated January 14, 1903.

29 PRONI, D1292 Wilkinson Letter to Lizzie, dated January 14, 1876.

30 *R v Scarfield*, March 10 1877, PRONI, D1292/M/7.

an American ship so the British court had no jurisdiction based on the nationality of the ship. Wilkinson found from analyzing the ships logs and the evidence of Dr Edwin Wheeler, a British doctor in Yokohama, that Scarfield had given birth just after the ship had entered Tokyo Bay meaning the offence had been committed in Japanese waters. Even though not on land, given that the Japanese had by treaty given to Britain the right to try their own subjects within the jurisdiction of Japan, the presence in territorial waters was sufficient to give him jurisdiction. The next question was whether it would be more proper for the case to be tried in the US Consular Court. After analyzing the authorities he held both courts may have jurisdiction but, given the US Consul-General had himself brought the prosecution in the British court, it was clear the United States agreed to Britain exercising jurisdiction. Scarfield was sentenced to one month imprisonment.

Wilkinson in a letter home proudly noted that "the case had to be referred home as it involved a question with United States and the Law Officers of the Crown took the same view of the case as I had taken."[31]

In another shipping case, Wilkinson had to decide whether the court had jurisdiction over a British Navy Captain, Philip Colomb, after the ship he was commanding, the *Audacious*, collided with a Japanese merchant ship, the *Chiri Maru*. Wilkinson held the court did have jurisdiction. The case then proceeded to a jury trial where after six days of hearings, Wilkinson set the jury 15 questions to be answered. The jury returned saying they were deadlocked but Wilkinson sent them back again. They then returned with a verdict but after answering five of the questions that had been set, Wilkinson asked if they had reached a verdict as to damages suggesting that the answers given were not applying any logic. The foreman said that they had reached a verdict as to damages

---

31 Wilkinson Papers, PRONI, D1292 Letter to Lizzie, dated January 14, 1878.

The Japan Punch's view of the Chiri Maru case

but Wilkinson then decided to discharge the jury. The official case report provided no further comment, however, a *Japan Punch* cartoon showed this was due to one juror showing undue levity. The case was listed to be re-heard later that year, but Capt. Colomb did not appear and the case appears to have been resolved diplomatically.[32]

Wilkinson's other cases included: whether a party who

....

32 *Iwasaki Yataro v Captain P.H. Colomb*, June 28, 1877 (Wilkinson Papers) Japan Weekly Mail, June 30, 1877, p550 and July 7, 1877, p592 (trial); C. Roberts, *The British Courts and Extraterritoriality in Japan 1859-1899*, p206

had obtained a judgement from the Russian consular court could seek an order from the British court ordering a British subject to pay a debt owed to the Russian directly to the British judgment debtor (Wilkinson held that you could not); whether it was a defence to a claim by the Governor of Tokyo for rent that the Governor was in breach of the treaties by leasing land to a foreigner outside a foreign settlement (Wilkinson held that it was not a defence); and, whether a Chinese concubine was entitled claim on a promissory note for $500 given to her by her now deceased lover after she had inherited a far greater sum of $10,000 from him (Wilkinson held that she could).[33]

One other case heard by Wilkinson resulted in a clear conflict between decisions of the Japanese courts and the British courts on exactly the same factual issue. Malcolm Wilcox & Co had sued Kensuke Yokuzawa in the Japanese court to order Yokuzawa to take delivery of 300 pieces of velvet.[34] Yokuzawa had paid a deposit of $150. The Japanese court ruled that the goods did not meet the standard of the sample provided by Malcolm, Wilcox & Co and accordingly Yokuzawa did not need to take delivery. But the Japanese court had said that it did not have jurisdiction to order Malcolm, Wilcox & Co as a British company to return the deposit. Yokuzawa therefore sued in the British Court. The principal defence was that the velvet was up to standard but that Yokuzawa had come to Malcolm Wilcox & Co to say he could not pay for the order. Wilkinson accepted evidence from the Yokuzawa's expert that the goods were not up to the standard of the sample. Despite this, he found for the English Defendant. Wilkinson held that under English law where a contract was for sale by sample of

---

33 *Andrew Duncan v Nestor Nicolay Nordenstedt (Judgment Debtor) and Charles John Strome (Garnishee);* June 16,1877; *Kusumoto Masataka, Chiji of the Tokio-fu v Bridget Blockley,* August 29, 1877 (decided as Vice-Consul); *Ah Choy v John Grigor* November 15, 1877 all PRONI D1292/M/7. The decisions are all also printed in the *Japan Weekly Mail.*

34 *Yokuzawa Zensuke v Malcolm, Wilcox & Co, Japan Herald* 21 and 22 March 1877; also in PRONI D1292/M/7.

specific goods, if the buyer considered them substandard, the remedy is to take delivery and then sue for the loss caused by the poor quality. Although the velvet was not to the standard of the sample, it could have been sold at a price resulting in no loss to the Plaintiff and accordingly the deposit did not need to be returned.

Wilkinson proudly noted in the same letter home in early January 1878 that "no appeal has been prosecuted from any of my decisions."

This was not to last long. Soon after he sent this letter one case came before Wilkinson that shook the foundations of British justice in Japan. Wilkinson made a decision that showed his strong legal reasoning and independence as a judge, but at the same time most likely set back his ambitions for a full time judicial appointment.

In late 1877, a British pharmacist in Edo, John Hartley, had tried to import opium into Japan, allegedly for medical purposes.[35] The Trade Regulations under the British-Japan Treaty of 1858 specifically prohibited the import of opium and provided that if any British ship came to Japan for trade carrying more than 3 catties (about 2.5 kilograms) of opium, the surplus quantity could be destroyed by the Japanese customs authorities. A fine of $15 per catty could also be imposed on anyone smuggling or attempting to smuggle opium.

Despite the ban in the treaties, until 1872, Japan had not sought to restrict the import of opium intended for medical purposes. In 1872, they seized a shipment of opium and, after protests, in 1873 brought in regulations seeking to restrict the import of medicinal opium by charging double the tariff. The regulations also required foreign pharmacists to report

35 This section based on *Reg (on the prosecution of the Imperial Customs) v John Hartley*, the *Japan Times*, March 2, 1878. For further details of the case, see R. Chang, *The Justice of Western Consular Courts in Nineteenth Century Japan*, Chapter 3 and J Jennings, "The Opium Empire: Japan and the East Asian Drug Trade: 1895-1945" a PhD dissertation for the University of Hawaii, 1995, p 13 onwards. Regulation II of the British-Japan Treaty prohibited the importation of opium; For Pauncefote's answer in parliament, see *London and China Telegraph*, December 23, 1878, p1085. The article also defends Wilkinson's decision.

to the Japanese authorities their dealings in opium. This was objected to by all the treaty powers other than the Americans, on the basis that the regulations infringed on foreign nationals treaty rights by making them subject to Japanese law. The Americans at the time held a view that the Japanese could enact laws binding on Americans, but that enforcement must be in the American courts.

Between 1872 to 1875 the import of powered opium as medicine had generally been allowed by the Japanese authorities. Some shipments were stopped by customs, but the majority of them were allowed to go through. From 1875 to July 1877 the Japanese then allowed foreigners to import opium freely, before again banning it.

According to Hartley, Dutch traders, but not others, were then allowed to import opium. Hartley considered it to be an infringement of his treaty rights and he decided to import opium again himself. In December 1877, Japanese Customs found 20 pounds (10 kilograms) of opium in a shipment destined for Hartley and brought a prosecution against him in the British Court. Even before this case was heard, Hartley was caught trying to smuggle another 14 catties (about 10 kilograms) of opium in early 1878. Japanese Customs brought another prosecution against Hartley.[36]

Both cases were heard in Yokohama in early 1878, by Wilkinson in his capacity as Acting Law Secretary of the Supreme Court for China and Japan. John Lowder, a former consular official (who had arrived in Japan as a student interpreter in 1862) now practicing as a British barrister in Japan, appeared for the prosecution on behalf of the Japanese Government. Hartley represented himself. In the first case, Hartley claimed that the opium was for medicinal use and was therefore not prohibited.

The trial lasted six days. Hartley called evidence was that

36 *Japan Gazette,* Yokohama Semi-Centennial, p60-62 at p62.

the Japanese government also considered medicinal opium
to be a medical necessity and that in fact to meet demand
in Japan the Japanese government had allowed it to be imported. Lowder, the prosecutor, himself told the court that
the Minister of Foreign Affairs was drawing up rules to allow for the import of medicinal opium. Hartley also called
evidence from current and former Japanese customs officers
that medicinal opium had been allowed to be imported from
time to time.

Wilkinson wrote a very long judgment agreeing with
Hartley. He held that the distinction between smoking opium and medicinal opium had been clearly established. "The
only point, therefore, to be decided is, whether the regulation which speaks of opium without any express qualification was intended to apply to medicinal opium." He looked
at the evidence that showed medicinal opium had a much
higher quantity of morphia and was unsuitable for smoking.
He went on:

H.S. Wilkinson delivers judgment in the Hartley case
John Hartley is on the left, John Lowder is to the right

"It was assumed throughout that opium smoking is
a great evil, which having happily no hold over the
people of Japan, it is desirable to avert from them, even
if stringent measures should be necessary for that purpose; and it is admitted that the object of the regulation
is to avert that evil. As to medicinal opium, on the other
hand, the evidence shows it to be an inestimable bless-
ing to suffering humanity."

Wilkinson, relying on various rules of international law
and statutory interpretation, held that the tins of opium Hartley had tried to import "are not prohibited to be imported;
and the person importing them, even though he smuggled
them, is not liable to punishment either of fine or confisca-
tion under *that particular provision of the regulation*." These last
words were emphasized in Wilkinson's judgment. He said
that the import of medicinal opium may be a breach of other
regulations and ordered that the tins of opium remain in the
Customs House under the seal of the court.

In the second case, the opium was of a lower grade and
could not be used for medicinal purposes. Wilkinson convicted Hartley and imposed a fine of $165 dollars being $15 for
each catty in excess of the limit in the treaty. He ordered that
the remaining three catties should be re-exported.

The first decision upset Japanese officials and the public
very much. They considered the treaty to clearly prohibit any
import of opium. This was a fair contention. The relevant regulation in the treaty stated: "the importation of opium being
prohibited…" before setting out the three catty rule and fine.

The *Hioron*, a Japanese newspaper, commented on the decision, questioning "will the public believe the judgment to
be impartial and just? Will our government be satisfied with
that judgment or try to have it reversed? Or does it intend to

a bitter pill to swallow.

Harry Parkes forcing Opium on the Japanese. H.S. Wilkinson looks on.

appeal?"[37] The *Hioron* said that it could not agree with the decision: "the misery brought upon China by the opium trade is so notorious." This is why the Japanese government decided to prohibit it. The fact that Wilkinson had made this decision made things worse. *Hioron* was "greatly surprised by the British judge whose impartiality and uprightness are so well known, having acquitted the accused." There was no difference between "me-

37 Translation printed first in the *Japan Herald* and then reproduced in the *Hiogo Shipping List* March 18, 1878.

dicinal" and "smoking" opium. If opium smoking became a habit in Japan it would be "a great calamity."

Finally, addressing the way in which the Japanese government was handling extraterritorial cases, *Hioron* commented unfavourably on the practice of the Japanese government using foreign barristers to argue cases on its behalf in the consular courts. The reason given for this was that "Japanese are not sufficiently learned in foreign jurisprudence and not accustomed to plead in foreign courts." However, foreign barristers are "countrymen and have many feelings in common, however much each of them may want to serve his client, he may occasionally labour under impediments." Japan now had hundreds of judges, one of whom could surely act for the Japanese government, and the fact they did not, "is it not a great shame for a great Empire like Japan?"

The Japanese government was not taking the matter lying down and instructed the Japanese Minister to Great Britain, Kagenori Ueno, to file an appeal to the Privy Council.[38] They also made a formal protest to the Foreign Office, first to Sir Julian Pauncefote and then directly to the Foreign Secretary Marquis of Salisbury. They protested that the decision breached the "absolute prohibition of opium" and that the decision opened the possibility of Japan being "flooded" with opium.

Wilkinson's position was at the forefront of the attack on the decisions. First the Japanese said that the servant of one treaty party (that is, Wilkinson) could not make a decision as the interpretation of a treaty between the parties. Second, they questioned Wilkinson's right to hear the case given he was, officially, the Vice-Consul in Niigata and not assigned to Kanagawa. Third, they questioned the legality of his appointment as Acting Law Secretary of the Supreme Court for China and Japan.

----

38 The basis on which the Japanese Government could appeal to the Privy Council was questionable. Wilkinson told Lowder it could be done under the courts inherent jurisdiction. See C. Roberts, *The British Courts and Extra-Territoriality in Japan, 1859-1899*, p256.

This latter argument caused great concern to Pauncefote and the Foreign Secretary Lord Derby. They asked the government Law Officers for an opinion on the legality of the appointment of Wilkinson as Acting Law Secretary and whether he had been acting within his powers when he decided the Hartley case. The answer was, not surprisingly, a resounding "No." Hornby, the judge who had put the arrangements in place, had himself written two years before that:

The Japan Punch *comments on the Tokyo* Times *view of Wilkinson as a puppet of British Minister, Harry Parkes*

"As things at present stand, the Assistant Judge of the Supreme Court is, and has been for some years, permanently stationed at Yokohama under a kind of fiction that he has been directed by the Judge (in virtue of the powers vested in him by Section 38 of the Order of 1865) "to visit" the Provincial Court at that place and hear cases there arising and pending. This is an unsatisfactory state of things in many ways. Apart from the forced construction of the Section which gives so wide an effect to the term "visit", many and grave doubts have from time to time arise on such important points as the extent of this peculiar jurisdiction, the suppression of the authority of the Provincial Court there, the right of appeal to the Supreme Court – all of which have been resolved more as considerations of convenience or expediency dictated, than as a strict reading of the language of the Order would perhaps warrant."[39]

The Law Officers held the same opinion. They stated that the only power the Judge or Acting Judge had under the Order in Council was to appoint an Assistant Judge or the Law Secretary to hear a specific case, not cases in general.

The Japanese government's appeal to the Privy Council was a very real threat to the Foreign Office and to the legality of almost all judgments handed down in Japan by Hannen, Goodwin and Wilkinson in the last eight years. The only exceptions would be the decisions made by Goodwin when he was Acting Judge after Hornby's retirement.[40]

The Law Officers' opinion put great urgency into the need to reform the set up of the British courts in Japan. In May 1878, a decision was made to establish a British Court for Japan as part of the planned amendments to the Order in Council. The Japanese government was informed of this in August. In order to deal with the threat of an appeal, in February 1879 the Marquis of Salisbury officially told the Japanese that the British Law Officers had advised that Wilkinson's decision could not be upheld. In public, however, the British authorities maintained that the decision was a judicial decision that they could not interfere with. Pauncefote, in an answer to a question in the British parliament, said that the Foreign Office had no power to confirm or reverse the judgment. The Japanese appeared to be satisfied with the communication that the decision could not be upheld. They did not go forward with an appeal, partly so as not to cause the Foreign Office to lose

---

39 PRONI D1292/M/5 Memorandum on the draft "China and Japan Order in Council, 1876." The memorandum does not bear Hornby's name but reads very much as if it was written by Hornby.

40 R. Chang, *The Justice of Western Consular Courts in Nineteenth Century Japan* Chapter 3. For Goodwin sitting as Acting Judge see, for example, *Hughes and Anor v O.C. Thomas, Japan Gazette,* July 15, 1876. For this period, his decisions were reported as being in the Supreme Court for China and Japan and not the Provincial Court at Kanagawa.

face and further strain relations between the two countries.[41]

Hartley himself suffered greatly from the cases. His business was boycotted. He closed his offices in 1879 and returned to England. He returned to Yokohama in 1899 and stayed for four years and then moved to Shanghai.[42]

Wilkinson, unlike his earlier important international decisions, did not keep copies of the Hartley decisions amongst his personal papers. This is perhaps not surprising, because the decisions certainly cannot have helped his career, in the short term at least.

The British Court for Japan

The new Order in Council establishing the British Court for Japan removed the Supreme Court's concurrent jurisdiction to hear cases from Japan. Instead, the Court for Japan became the sole British first instance court for the Kanagawa consular area and the appellate court for appeals from all Provincial Courts in Japan. First instance cases from other consular districts could also be brought directly to the Court for Japan. Appeals were to be heard by the Chief Justice (the new title for the Chief Judge) and Judge (formerly the Assistant Judge) in Shanghai with a final appeal to the Privy Council.

The Order in Council provided for the appointment of a full time judge in Japan, the Judge for Japan, and that the British Consul in Kanagawa would *ex officio* be the Assistant Judge of the Court.

Wilkinson had hoped that his time as Acting Law Secretary would put him in prime position to receive the substantive appointment as Judge for Japan. Just before Goodwin had died he had written to a friend, Lizzie, seeking her father's assistance in applying for the acting position while Goodwin was on sick leave. (I have not been able to ascertain who Lizzie or her father were.) Wilkinson hoped to obtain the

41 R. Chang, *The Justice of Western Consular Courts in Nineteenth Century Japan*, pp61-67.
42 *Japan Gazette*, Yokohama Semi-Centennial, p60-62.

substantive appointment as Judge for Japan if Goodwin did not return. He said, "I like the judicial work and it offers an opening to something higher than consular service." He emphasized that he was happy in the consular service:

> "But the respective advantages of a Consulate and a Judgeship are indicated to some extent by the salary – the highest Consulate in Japan being £1,000 a year, and the Judgeship being £1,500 a year."[43]

Just after Goodwin's death, a note was sent on Wilkinson's behalf, presumably by Lizzie's father, to the Foreign Secretary, Earl Derby, formally applying for the position seeking the "post of Assistant Judge of the Supreme Court for Japan." The note was acknowledged with a statement that Wilkinson's application would be considered.[44]

Wilkinson knew that his chances were not necessarily good. In his letter to Lizzie he said Robert Mowat was considering applying for the job and as Wilkinson's senior by one position in the consular service and because of his time with the Supreme Court in Shanghai, Mowat had a better claim. He had also heard from Mowat that "Hannen, who acted here some years ago, and who has the influence of his brother, the judge of Probate Court, to help him, may still be seeking to get employed."

To the surprise of many, Richard Rennie, the barrister from Shanghai, was appointed as the first Judge of the Court for Japan. The *Japan Weekly Mail* reported that this was a surprise to Yokohama residents, "simply because it was always expected that Mr Hannen would have been nominated."[45]

....

43 PRONI, D1292 Letter to Lizzie, dated January 14, 1878, Wilkinson Papers.

44 PRONI D1292 Unsigned note dated February 1878 headed "Wilkinson, Hiram Shaw" and note of acknowledgement, dated Feburary 11 1878. Wilkinson Papers.

45 *Japan Herald*, October 31,1878; the appointment was notified by a telegram from the Marquis of Salisbury to Chief Justice French. Japan Weekly Mail, November 9, 1878, p1199.

Rennie, as we have seen, commenced practice in Shanghai in 1866. While in Shanghai, he had been legal adviser to the Municipal Council. In a speech given sometime later, he described the realities of a lawyer giving advice to a council run by businessmen, commenting to much laughter:

"I confess that when I first had the honour of entering upon the duties of that office, it was not carried out quite in accordance with my ideas of legal regularity. When the berth was offered to me by the then Chairman, my excellent friend Mr Cunningham said that as long as he was head cook and I was head bottle-washer, he thought there would be very little law in the affair."

He then recalled an incident, to even more laughter, when during the absence of Mr Cunningham, a notice was put up on the Garden Bridge which seemed to Rennie "to savour strongly of illegality and to be largely beyond the powers of the Council." Rennie protested to the Vice-Chairman who told him that "he didn't care a ------- if it was legal or not but he wasn't going to have the affairs of the Municipality bossed by the legal adviser!" He concluded that after that he felt it "was necessary to be a little more elastic in my ideas of law."

Then in praise of the Municipal Council he said: "But really, joking apart, gentlemen, looking back upon my experience of Municipal government in Shanghai, it is a wonderful institution. When one comes to consider how the government of this port is effected by a Council composed of all nationalities, of men of business who voluntarily give up their time for no reward, it is extraordinary how well it is done." To much applause and laughter he continued: "The only reason I can assign for it is the entire absence of officialism and red tapeism." Becoming more serious he finished:

"The fact remains that it is a model government, and

HER BRITANNIC MAJESTY'S COURT FOR JAPAN.

THE China and Japan Order in Council, 1878, having commenced and having full effect from and after this date, Her Britannic Majesty's Court for Japan has this day been opened by the undersigned, who has been appointed Judge of the said Court by Her Majesty, by warrant under Her Royal Sign Manual, bearing date the 30th day of October, 1878.

Mr. HIRAM SHAW WILKINSON has, under instructions from Her Majesty's Principal Secretary of State for Foreign Affairs, been appointed by Her Majesty's Minister in Japan to be Acting Assistant Judge of the said Court in the absence of Mr Consul ROBERTSON. Under section 6, sub-section 1, of the said Order in Council, Her Majesty's Consul for the district of the Consulate of Kanagawa has ceased to hold and form a Provincial Court, and by section 12 of the said Order in Council, all suits and proceedings, civil or criminal, instituted or taken in the district of the Consulate of Kanagawa before and pending at this date, are transferred to the jurisdiction of the said Court for Japan, and the same may be carried on and shall be tried, heard, and determined in and by the Court for Japan as nearly as may be as if the same had been instituted or taken in the district of the Consulate of Kanagawa after the commencement of the said Order.

RICHARD TEMPLE RENNIE, Judge.

Kanagawa, 2nd January, 1879.　　3in

I think all visitors to Shanghai will recognise that we are mainly indebted for our good roads, our good lighting and our good police to the absence of officialism or show of authority. The place is run quietly and well, and I am very proud to have had the honour of being its legal adviser for so long."[46]

On Rennie's appointment as Judge of the Court for Japan, Rennie resigned his post as Legal Adviser to the Municipal Council and Nicholas Hannen, now Crown Advocate, was appointed in his place.[47]

The last hearing of HBM Court of Kanagawa was before Wilkinson on December 31, 1878 in the case of *Hart v Herhausen* where an application was made that $500 paid into court be forfeited. On the same day, members of the bar also expressed their thanks to Wilkinson for how he had carried out his duties as Acting Law Secretary. The *Japan Weekly Mail* paid tribute to Wilkinson on Rennie's arrival saying, "we cannot allow Mr Wilkinson to vacate the bench which he has so long and so efficiently occupied without a word or two of thanks and sympathy. He has shown himself to be the most pains-taking and industrious judge we have ever had here." High praise indeed, particularly given the

46 *North China Herald*, April 3, 1891, P.408-9.
47 *North China Herald*, January 4, 1879, p10.

very high praise the *Mail* gave Hannen on his departure. The *Mail* concluded: "He retires into the Consular office with the good wishes of all, and when occasion next serves for his translation to the judicial bench, his decidedly strong claims are not likely to be overlooked."[48]

The British Court for Japan formally opened on January 1, 1879.[49] The Provincial Court for Kanagawa was abolished and all pending cases transferred to the Court for Japan. During January 1879 advertisements were placed in the *Japan Herald* in Rennie's name, announcing the creation of the court. The staff of the consulate who had been engaged in the work of the court were transferred to the court.[50]

When the appointment of Rennie had first been announced, the *Japan Punch* published a cartoon showing Rennie arriving in Japan and Wilkinson been packed off to Ni-

Rennie arrives in Japan with Wilkinson packed off to Niigata

48 *Japan Weekly Mail*, December 21, 1878, p1391.

49 *Japan Herald*, January 1, 1879, p2.

50 *Japan Herald*, January 3, 1879, p3. The advertisement was repeated on a number of occasions subsequently. The advertisement also announced Wilkinson's appointment. T/1/16717, Letter from Rennie to Marquis of Salisbury, dated April 18, 1879 .

igata carrying a big bag of judgments. Japanese were shown presenting him with a box of "Genuine Medicinal Opium." The clear suggestion was that his decision in the Hartley case had taken him out of the good books of the Foreign Office.

Contrary to the suggestion of the *Japan Punch*, Wilkinson remained in the Foreign Office's good books and his strong claims to being appointed to the bench were not overlooked. At the time the Court for Japan was established, the Consul in Yokohama, Russell Robertson, who was by virtue of his position, the Assistant Judge, was on leave. Wilkinson was immediately appointed Acting Consul and Acting Assistant Judge during Robertson's absence.

When Nicholas Hannen had gone to Japan in 1870 to establish the ill-fated branch of the Supreme Court, the court was initially set up in a bungalow with two rooms and a court room in the British Consular Compound in Yokohama. This was found to be very inconvenient, particularly for Hannen, because consular or Japanese officers required in the court would need to go through his private room to get to the court. In a long letter of May 10, 1873 to Hornby, sent at Hornby's invitation, Hannen complained of this and other problems and suggested his room be moved upstairs. Hannen also noted the rooms were very cold and the security was poor. In fact, the Registry of the Court had been burgled in November 1872.[51]

With the establishment of the new court, a proposal was made that the former British General Post office in Yokohama be converted into a courthouse. By this time, the Japanese had established an efficient postal service and the British postal service was about to be discontinued. The Treasury rejected this, stating that taking further property was not necessary and that it would be inexpedient to continue the lease on the Post Office.[52] The Court for Japan, therefore, continued to sit in rooms in the consular premises.

51 FO17/660.
52 T 1/17063.

Rennie, like Hannen, found the arrangements unsatisfactory. In a report on the establishment of the court to the Marquis of Salisbury he wrote:

"The Court Room and Offices in the Consular Building formerly used by the Provincial Court and now occupied by the New Court, are wholly insufficient for the latter's requirements. The Court room itself is sufficiently large and with certain moderate alterations will probably suffice for the general purposes of the new Court, but it would be very desirable that there should be a separate Police Court in which summary cases and police charges might be heard and disposed of, whilst matters of great importance are being taken in the main Court room."[53]

Besides the court room, only two other rooms had been allocated to the court. One was the Judge's Chambers which also had to double up as the jury room. The other was multi-functional, serving as the "Registry, Treasury, Clerk's Office, a waiting room for witnesses, Robing room for counsel &c &c." Not surprisingly, Rennie complained that it was "small and ill suited for its purposes."

The first reported case for the Court for Japan was in *H. Ahrens & Co v Ellies, master of the British ship Zingra* on January 4, 1879 where an application was made to Rennie for increased security for costs. Montague Kirkwood appeared for the plaintiffs and John Lowder appeared for the Defendant. The application was refused as being premature.[54] This case came on for trial at lightning speed, six days later, on January 10. The Plaintiff alleged that the Defendant had failed to deliver gunpowder shipped aboard the ship *Zingra*. The defence was that due to an emergency, certain parts of the cargo had

---

53 T/1/16717, Letter from Rennie to Marquis of Salisbury, dated April 18, 1879.

54 *H Ahrens & Co v Ellies, Japan Herald* January 4, 1879, p 2.

A trial before Richard Rennie in the Court for Japan

had to be thrown overboard. Under English maritime law, when this occurs, under the principle of "general average" all those who have shipped products on board are expected to share in the loss. Rennie found that a general average had occurred and found in favour of the Defendant.

On January 6, 1879, Wilkinson as Acting Assistant Judge and Rennie as Judge both had cases before them. In the case before Wilkinson, John Lowder apologized for not being in court at the hearing on December 31, 1878 when Henry Lichtfield had expressed sentiments of regard for how Wilkinson had carried out duties of Law Secretary. Lowder "asked his Honor to accept the assurance of his very high sense of the manner in which his Honor had discharged his difficult duties as acting law secretary."[55]

In the case before Rennie, Rennie deported a seaman, Daniel Robinson alias "Ice Cream Bob", who had entered Japan in breach of a previous deportation order. Ice Cream Bob's

---

55 *Japan Herald* January 6, 1879. Lichtfield's sentiments were reported in North China Herald of January 24, 1879, p74 citing the *Japan Mail*.

defence was that he had joined a ship as a sailor and did not know it would be coming to Japan. Rennie simply ordered Ice Cream Bob be deported again but warned him that if he came to Japan again he would face a fine or imprisonment. Ice Cream Bob was back in court two days later for assaulting a turnkey, or guard, at the Consular Gaol and was sentenced to one month imprisonment after which he was to be deported.[56]

Wilkinson goes to Shanghai

Wilkinson also went, at Rennie's request, to try a jury case in Kobe. When Russell Robertson was due to return from leave in April 1879 an even better opportunity arose. Around the same time Robert Mowat was due to depart Shanghai on long leave. At Chief Justice George French's request, Wilkinson was offered the position of acting Assistant Judge of the Supreme Court in Shanghai during Mowat's absence. French had obviously heard good things about Wilkinson. He wrote to Harry Parkes, the British Minister in Japan, "there is no Consular Officer in China who could take [Mowat's] place as judge of appeal and the remuneration which would be paid to Mr Mowat's substitute would not be sufficient to induce any legal practitioner here to give up his practice."[57]

Not long after Wilkinson arrived in Shanghai, a case on the legality of the sale of opium in Shanghai came before him. Wilkinson again showed that he was his own man. While his decision did not cause an international incident like the Hartley case, he almost certainly ruffled some feathers on the Shanghai Municipal Council.

The import and sale of opium was legal in Shanghai. But in order to sell opium in the International Settlement, under a Municipal Council bye-law you needed a license from the Shanghai Municipal Police.

---

56 *R v Daniel Robinson, Japan Herald,* January 8, 1879, p2 (before Rennie).

57 *North China Herald* April 15, 1879, p356 and FO656/50 French to Parkes, December 12, 1878 cited in C. Roberts, *The British Courts and Extraterritoriality in Japan,* 1859 to 1899.

George Martin, "a thorough Chinese scholar", decided to open an opium and tea house on Sungkiang Road (Songjiang Road). In order to get a license, it was necessary to set up shop first and then apply to the Superintendent of Police, Charles Penfold. Martin did so. Until this, all other applicants had been granted licenses. The Council, who ran the police, told Penfold to refuse the license. Martin was not told the reasons why the license was refused.[58]

Penfold then sent a Chinese police constable to the shop who saw opium being served. Penfold brought a prosecution against Martin and appeared in court to prosecute the case himself. He must have thought he had an open-and-shut case. The bye-law prohibited selling opium without a license. Martin did not have a license but had sold opium. The case must be unanswerable. However, as one famous English judge once said:

"As everybody who has anything to do with the law well knows, the path of the law is strewn with examples of open and shut cases which, somehow, were not; of unanswerable charges which, in the event, were completely answered; of inexplicable conduct which was fully explained; of fixed and unalterable determinations that, by discussion, suffered a change."[59]

As is also well known to those who practice law, sometimes the judge can save you from the bench with a point you have not even thought of. Wilkinson did so in this case.

Martin had arranged for a lawyer, Mr Brougham Miller, to defend him. Miller objected to the form of summons. As this point was being argued, Wilkinson, said that he considered that the case may be a "malicious proceeding."

Just as Wilkinson said this, Nicholas Hannen, like a "Jack

---

58 *R (Charles Penfold) v George Martin, North China Herald,* August 26, 1879, p216.
59 Megarry J in *John v Rees* [1970] 1 Ch. 345 at 402.

in the Box" as Miller put it, arrived in court to represent the Council. This was a reversal of roles for Hannen and Wilkinson. In Yokohama in the early 1870s, Wilkinson had been the one to appear before Hannen.

Miller had also made an objection to Penfold appearing to prosecute. He said Penfold had no written authority to do so. As Hannen was the council's attorney, Miller dropped this objection. Wilkinson did say that a formal power of attorney should be prepared for Penfold or other police to prosecute in the future.

The case was re-scheduled to be heard two days later so as to allow Hannen to prepare. When it resumed, Penfold was called to give evidence. He said that two lawyers, Messrs Myburgh and Cowie, had complained to him on behalf of neighbours about Martin's shop. Myburgh and Cowie said it would cause a nuisance. The Municipal Council had then told Penfold not to issue a license. After Penfold had finished giving evidence he spoke to Hannen. Hannen then asked if he could recall Penfold to ask one more question. Wilkinson admonished Hannen as only someone who previously appeared before him could:

"You know well, Mr Hannen, that you cannot question a witness after communication with him when he has left the box."

Hannen then submitted that it was an open-and-shut case. Opium had been sold without a license; the bye-law had been contravened. Wilkinson was having none of this. He said the "prosecution is a most ill-advised one," and that he was certain that if Hannen had been consulted "it would never have been brought at all." Martin had tried to obtain a license but had been refused without reasons. It was incumbent on the Council to give Martin an opportunity to know the objections to the shop being opened and for Martin to be given an opportunity to make submissions. He dismissed the case and said that Martin could run the shop for a month while the council considered his application.

For the Council, which - as Richard Rennie described it - did not have much truck with the niceties of the law, Wilkinson's decision must have grated.

Wilkinson remained in Shanghai (still technically as Vice-Consul in Niigata) until October 1880. George French was very happy with his performance and wrote to the Foreign Secretary:

> "I have great pleasure in expressing to your Lordship, my sense as well of the care an ability with which Mr Wilkinson has discharged his own duties as of the ready and obliging manner in which he has always rendered me any assistance I may have asked of him."[60]

After completing his posting, Wilkinson took long leave, going back to Belfast where he returned to Queen's University to study for a Doctorate of Laws and spend time with his sons, Harrie and Thomas.

Wilkinson had in the Hartley case caused an international incident. He was out of Japan when the next case to cause international tensions came before the courts there.

---

60 PRONI D1292, Letter dated October 21, 1880 from French to Earl Granville. See also FO656/58, Letter to French from the Foreign Office in response to its dispatch No. 11 of October 1880 dated 3 December 1880.

Chapter 14

The Bullion Dollar Question: The Ross Case

IN WHAT WAS TO become a major diplomatic incident, very soon after the establishment of the Court for Japan, a British subject, John Ross, killed a fellow sailor on board a United States merchant ship, the *Bullion*.

The United States consular authorities prosecuted Ross in the US Consular Court for murder causing much diplomatic correspondence to pass between the Britain and the United States. The US President, Chester Arthur, even devoted three paragraphs of his State of the Union address in 1881 to explaining the United States' position.[1] The case eventually found its way to the US Supreme Court, challenging both the jurisdiction of a US consular court to try a British subject and the constitutionality of trial without jury in the American consular courts in the Far East. The decision became the leading decision on the constitutionality of trials before US consular courts.

The facts of the case were relatively simple and fairly brutal.[2] Ross, 30, who had been born in Canada, making him a British subject, had signed on to the United States Merchant Marine, joining the *Bullion*. While the *Bullion* was anchored in Yokohama Harbour, Ross had gone ashore drinking with the second mate of the ship, Robert Kelly, and the cook. Kelly

---

1 Chester A. Arthur, State of the Union Address, December 6, 1881.

2 *Japan Weekly Mail*, May 15, 1880, p640 (inquest); *United States v Ross Japan Weekly Mail*, May 15, 1880, p641 and 664; *North China Herald*, May 25, 1880, p461 (inquest).

and Ross had a heated argument and then returned drunk to
the ship around 4.00am on May 9, 1880. The cook was making
Kelly a cup of coffee in the galley when Ross came in with a
long knife and asked Kelly if he was "as good a man on board
as he pretended to be on shore." Kelly told Ross to lie down
and came part way out of the galley. Ross stabbed Kelly in
the neck, arm and face. Kelly died almost instantly. Ross was
immediately arrested by the crew and the US deputy marshal
was called to the *Bullion*.

The deputy marshal upon arrival on the ship found meat
and bread on a plate in the galley all covered in blood. He
also found bloody clothes and a bloody knife in Ross' bunk.
Ross was very drunk and noisy when the marshal arrived
and "threatened to do for someone else." Ross was shown
the body and asked "you see what your have done?" He replied "Yes, that's all right. Let me shake hands with him. I'm
friends with him now as before. He was the best friend I had."
As they left the ship, the marshal said to Ross: "There is the
man you killed." Ross replied: "Yes I killed him. I suppose
I'll swing for it, but I don't care a damn." After being taken
onshore, Ross was placed in a rickshaw to take him to the
Consular jail. Someone asked the marshal why they were taking him and the marshal said Ross had killed Kelly. Ross then
sadly interjected: "Me kill Kelly? I had no reason to kill Kelly.
He was my best friend."

John Read, the captain of the *Bullion*, filed a formal complaint against Ross with the US Consul, first describing him
as "supposed to be a citizen of the United States." This was
later amended to read that he was an "American seaman,
duly and lawfully enrolled and shipped and doing service as
such seaman on board the American ship *Bullion*."

A coronial inquest was held before the US Consul, Thomas
van Buren (the famous Civil War general), and a jury of two,
Mr C.H. Haswell and Mr E.S. Smith. The jurors found that
Ross had killed Kelly and that the killing was deliberate and

US Consul General Thomas van Buren in front of the US Consulate

malicious. Van Buren committed Ross for trial in the US Consular Court.

At his trial, Ross challenged the authority of the US Consular Court to try him by presenting an affidavit that he was a native of Prince Edward Island, and thus a British Subject. This was rejected on the basis that, as a seaman on a United States ship, he was subject to American jurisdiction. The British Acting Consul-General at the time then formally demanded that Ross, as a British subject, be released, but this request was rejected. Ross also challenged the fact that he was not being tried by a jury, as guaranteed by the United States Constitution. Van Buren rejected this argument on the basis that the statutes creating consular jurisdiction did not provide for a trial by jury.

When Ross was asked to plead he replied that he "remembered nothing about it as he was in liquor when he went on board." A plea of Not Guilty was recorded. Given the evidence, it is not surprising that van Buren and the assessors found Ross guilty of murder saying, "a more deliberate, foul and malicious murder it would be difficult to conceive." They added: "You were not drunk but had swallowed just enough of the vile compounds sold in the dens of Yokohama to fit you for the deed you contemplated." Ross was sentenced "to suffer death in such manner and at such time and place as the United States Minister in Japan may direct according to law, and may God have mercy on your soul."

Ross replied, "I do not remember the first thing about it, your Honour. If I did it I would not be ashamed to own it."

The sentence was confirmed by the American Minister, but with a recommendation that the sentence of death be converted to one of life without parole. The US President, Rutherford Hayes, pardoned Ross on the condition he agreed to be detained at Albany penitentiary in New York State for the term of his natural life.

Ross was transported to Albany via San Francisco. He was accompanied all the way by a special deputy US Marshal, Mr Latham. On arrival in San Francisco, Ross' lawyer, Mr Henderson, immediately filed a *habeas corpus* petition against Ross' detention on the basis that his conviction as a British citizen by a United States consular court was illegal and his trial without a jury was unconstitutional. The petition was withdrawn when it became clear that the case would need to go to the Supreme Court. Henderson said at the time a new petition would be filed in Washington.[3]

Ross was then taken from San Francisco to Albany. On the way, in New Mexico, in a scene straight from a Wild West movie, Ross had a chance to escape at the junction of the Southern Pacific and the Topeka and Santa Fe Railroads. This part of New Mexico was what the *New York Times* described as "probably one of the worst places in the United States ...

---

3   "A Murderer from Japan", *New York Times*, April 15, 1881 for his trip to US and detention.

there being no law or authority in the place." Latham "expected to lose his prisoner or his life, or both." At the junction, the car first filled with a group of "desparadoes" before the Sheriff and a posse arrived to arrest "Six Shooter Bill" for murder. The arrival of the posse signaled the departure of the desparadoes and the conductor signaled the departure of the train. Mr Latham pulled his revolver and threatened to shoot the first man who came near him. Ross sat through the whole event, as he had for his whole trip from Yokohama, in a "most orderly manner." Ross and Latham arrived safely in Albany and Ross was put to work in the shoe-making department at the penitentiary.

Ross' trial and conviction created a huge diplomatic incident between Britain and America.[4] Interestingly, given that it was usually the Americans who were legalistic and the British who took a practical view of extraterritoriality; in Ross' case it was the Americans who were practical and the British legalistic. The British position was that the treaties with Japan (and China) did not allow one treaty power to try nationals of another country. Extraterritorial jurisdiction was personal and the treaties only allowed the British to try British subjects and the Americans to try American subjects. The British were being consistent in this position. Five years earlier, in 1875, the Foreign Office had already taken advice from the Law Officers of the Crown as to the right to try foreign seaman on board British ships. The case had arisen from the arrest of Peter McCondville, a British subject on board an American warship the *Lackawanna*. He had been arrested by the Japanese for assaulting a Frenchman and been handed to the US authorities. The US Consul then handed him over to the British Consulate and he was tried in the Provincial Court for Kanagawa and fined a substantial sum. The American captain of the *Lackawanna* objected and the matter ended up be-

4 FO 656/31 and Foreign Relations of the United States, 1881, p372 et seq for the correspondence between the countries.

ing considered in both Washington and London.[5]

The British advice had been clear that "no treaty which we know of gives a jurisdiction to a foreign court to try and punish as criminals the subjects of another foreign country", and "accordingly the Order in Council is confined to persons who are subjects of Her Majesty." It continued that all a foreign national did by signing articles was to "submit to the discipline of the ship according to the laws of the country and that he cannot be held to have become for all purposes a subject of the country ... to which the ship may belong." They did however, add one caveat in a subsequent letter that "we have never expressed any opinion to the effect that grave offences committed by a foreign seaman on board a British ship, wherever she may be, cannot be punished by British Courts."

In the Ross case, the British Secretary of State wrote to the United States Secretary of State stating that because "Ross was a British Subject, his offence was justiceable only in the British Consular Courts and that the arrest, trial and conviction by the Consular Court of the United States were unlawful."

The United States' formal position was set out in a very long letter of June 3, 1881, from the new US Secretary of State, James G. Blaine, to the British Minister in Washington, Sir Edward Thornton. Blaine had been appointed Secretary of State on the election of James Garfield as president. The outgoing Secretary of State had, in a previous letter to Thornton, said that formal response to correspondence to date should be left to the incoming administration.

The first point Blaine made was that "if the fact of nationality is to be the test of jurisdiction, who is to decide it?" Blaine said that if the Captain of a US ship denied a seaman's nationality this would need to be decided on a preliminary basis by the US Consul who would otherwise only make an arrest on the basis of comity. Second, prisoners would seek to

---

5   D. Howland & L. White, *The State of Sovereignty: Territories, Laws, Populations*, p38.

play a nationality game – claiming to be a different nationality as it suited them - to avoid arrest and punishment. Third,
if the British Court assumed jurisdiction it would need the
assistance of the US Court to compel witnesses and detain the
ship pending trial. Blaine conceded that in "heinous" cases,
cooperation would no doubt be forthcoming but in lesser
cases there may be "differences of opinion" that would render assistance impossible. Fourth, in the case of smuggling by
crew members, the ship's owners or officers would, in fact, be
very happy to see jurisdiction transferred to make it easier to
avoid liability themselves.

Turning to the treaties, Blaine conceded that the wording of the treaties made it clear British subjects were to be
tried by British courts and Americans by American courts.
But, there was an exception that applied to seamen of the
mercantile marine. Article 9 of the US-Japan treaty of 1858
provided that the Japanese would assist in arresting any de-

*Richard Rennie holds the scales of justice while British and American
officials look on*

serters from American ships. The US had enacted legislation
to enforce this and the "position of the United States Government was that a foreign seaman duly enrolled on an American merchant vessel, is subject to the laws and entitled to the
protection of the United States to precisely the same extent
that a native born seaman would be during the period of his
service." This principle Blaine said was also maintained by
the British Government in the Merchant and Shipping Act of
1854 which declares that "all offences against property or person, committed ... afloat ... by a seaman" shall be dealt with
by British Courts in the same manner as if the seaman was
British. Blaine then cited a number of British cases where British jurisdiction had been asserted against foreign seaman and
said that US practice was in "entire conformity" with British
practice. Blaine conceded that if Ross had been a passenger or
had come on board the *Bullion* temporarily, the "question of
jurisdiction would have been very different." But, as it was,
he was "part of the crew" and subject to US jurisdiction.

Finally, Blaine pointed out that in a number of cases, the
British had not assisted where America had asked for assistance in Japan. In one case, a witness subpoena had been refused. In another case a British subject had helped to facilitate
an escape from an American jail. The British consul had told
the Americans that the alleged offender could not be punished because the jail was not British – it was only an offence
for a British subject to help an escape from a British jail. There
had also been a recent case where a sailor had fallen between
extraterritoriality's cracks. A Belgian sailor on a British ship
had attacked an American. The British had declined jurisdiction because he was Belgian and the Belgians had declined
jurisdiction because he was a British seaman; resulting in no
punishment at all. Blaine concluded his letter by stating that
going forward, the US would exercise jurisdiction over all
foreign sailors on their merchant ships and hoped that the

British Government would "recognise the advantages of the approach." As we shall see, the British did, but with a classic British bet each way.[6]

Ten years later, in 1890, Ross made a *habeas corpus* application against the superintendent of Albany Penitentiary, Mr McIntyre. The case found its way to the US Supreme Court under the name *Ross v McIntyre*. Ross alleged that McIntyre was illegally detaining him because his original conviction was unlawful on the basis that as a British subject, the United States Consular Court in Kanagawa had no jurisdiction to try him and because he was constitutionally entitled to a jury. The first objection was rejected on the basis that, having voluntarily enrolled on an American ship, he was subject to American jurisdiction. The Supreme Court reviewed the State Department correspondence, which cited numerous British cases to show that the British had also asserted jurisdiction over foreign seamen aboard British ships. The court agreed with these decisions and finished by stating that the views were "in harmony" with the long standing position that England could not claim seamen from United States ships. In a nationalistic flourish, the Supreme Court added that "its enforcement was deemed a great indignity upon this country, and a violation of our right of sovereignty; our vessels being considered as parts of our territory. It led to the war of 1812, and, although that war closed without obtaining a relinquishment of the claim, its further assertion was not attempted."[7]

With regard to the constitutionality of trial by assessors, the court took a purposive approach by saying that by the time the Constitution was enacted, consular jurisdiction already existed and thus "the framers of the constitution, who were fully aware of the necessity of having judicial authority exercised by our Consuls in non-Christian countries." When trading with these countries, the founding fathers "never could

6   See Chapter 19.
7   *Ross v McIntyre*, 140 US 453.

have supposed that all the guaranties in the administration of the law upon criminals at home were to be transferred to such Consular establishments." Such a requirement would destroy the whole purpose of having consular jurisdiction in the first place. While Americans subject to consular jurisdiction may lose some rights, on the other hand, they gained rights by being "withdrawn from the procedure of their tribunals, often arbitrary and oppressive, and some times accompanied with extreme cruelty and torture."

For the remaining half century of American extraterritorial jurisdiction in East Asia, the Supreme Court decision that there was no right to trial by jury in an American extraterritorial court stood despite a number of challenges. The decision was so important that it simply became known as the "Ross case."

The British courts in Japan had not played a role in the Ross case. In China, however, the British courts had to deal with a number of challenges from Chinese interests.

The original courthouse of the Supreme Court for China and Japan

The British Consulate in Yokohama – Home of the British Court for Japan

Originally consulates were established in Chinese or Japanese buildings like the British consulate above in Tainan. Later, western style buildings like those in Kobe and Amoy shown below were built.

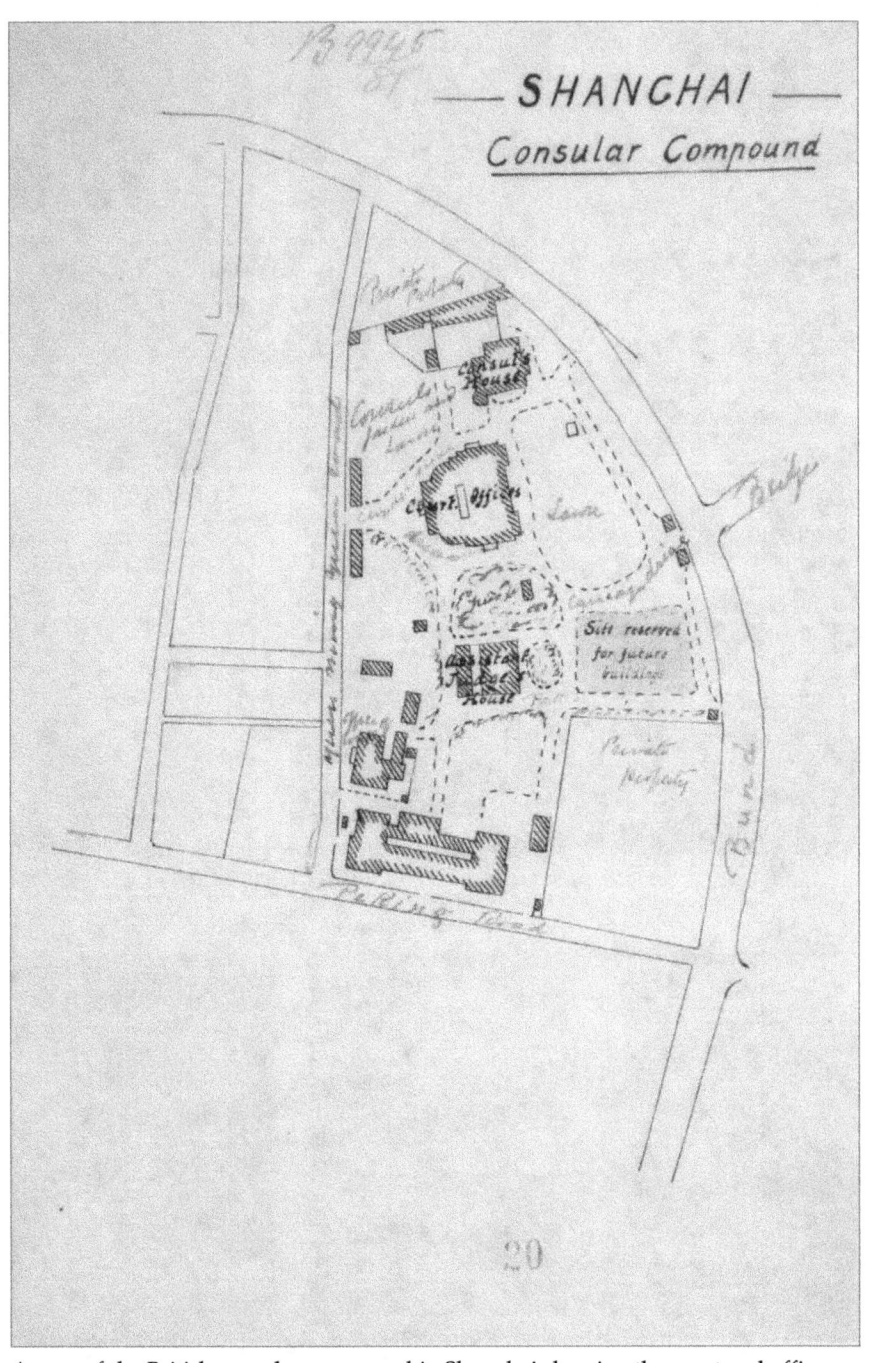

A map of the British consular compound in Shanghai showing the court and offices as well as the Consul-General's and Assistant Judge's house.

Charles Goodwin

Sir Edmund Hornby

Robert Mowat

George French

Sir Richard Rennie

Sir Nicholas Hannen

George Jamieson

HS Wilkinson

Frederick Bourne

HP Wilkinson

John Carey Hall

Russell Robertson

Robert Mansfield

Eustace Burrows

Thomas van Buren US Consul-General in Yokohama

The Capture of Chusan during the first opium war

Some of the destruction of the Yuanmingyuan looted by British and French troops in 1860 after the second opium war

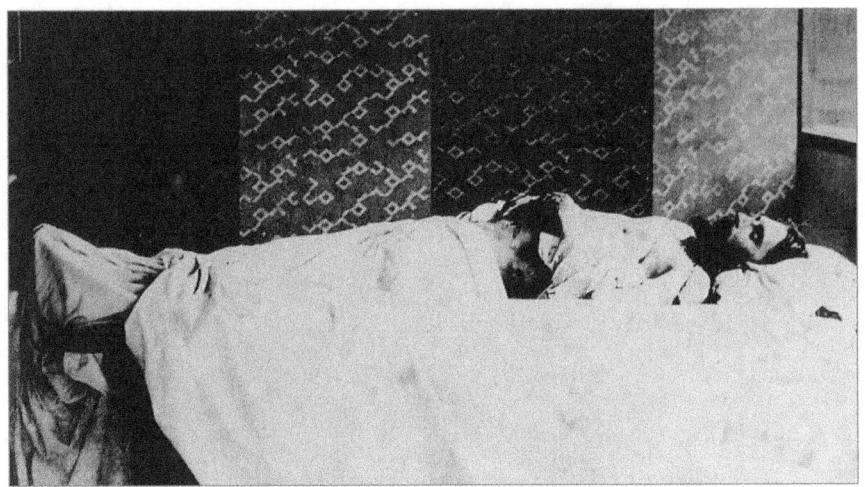

The body of Charles Richardson. His death at the hands of a samurai triggered the bombardment of Kagoshima in 1863

British, American, French and Dutch forces capture Japanese cannon at Shimonoseki in 1864

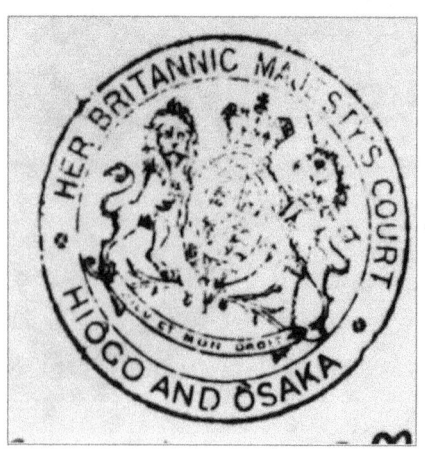

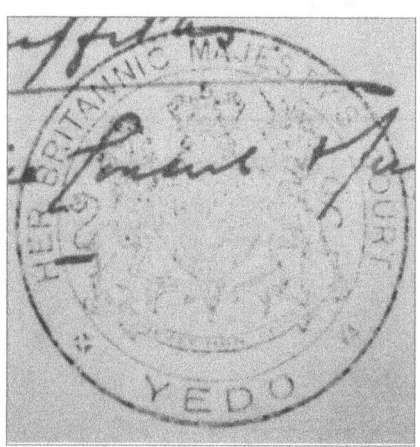

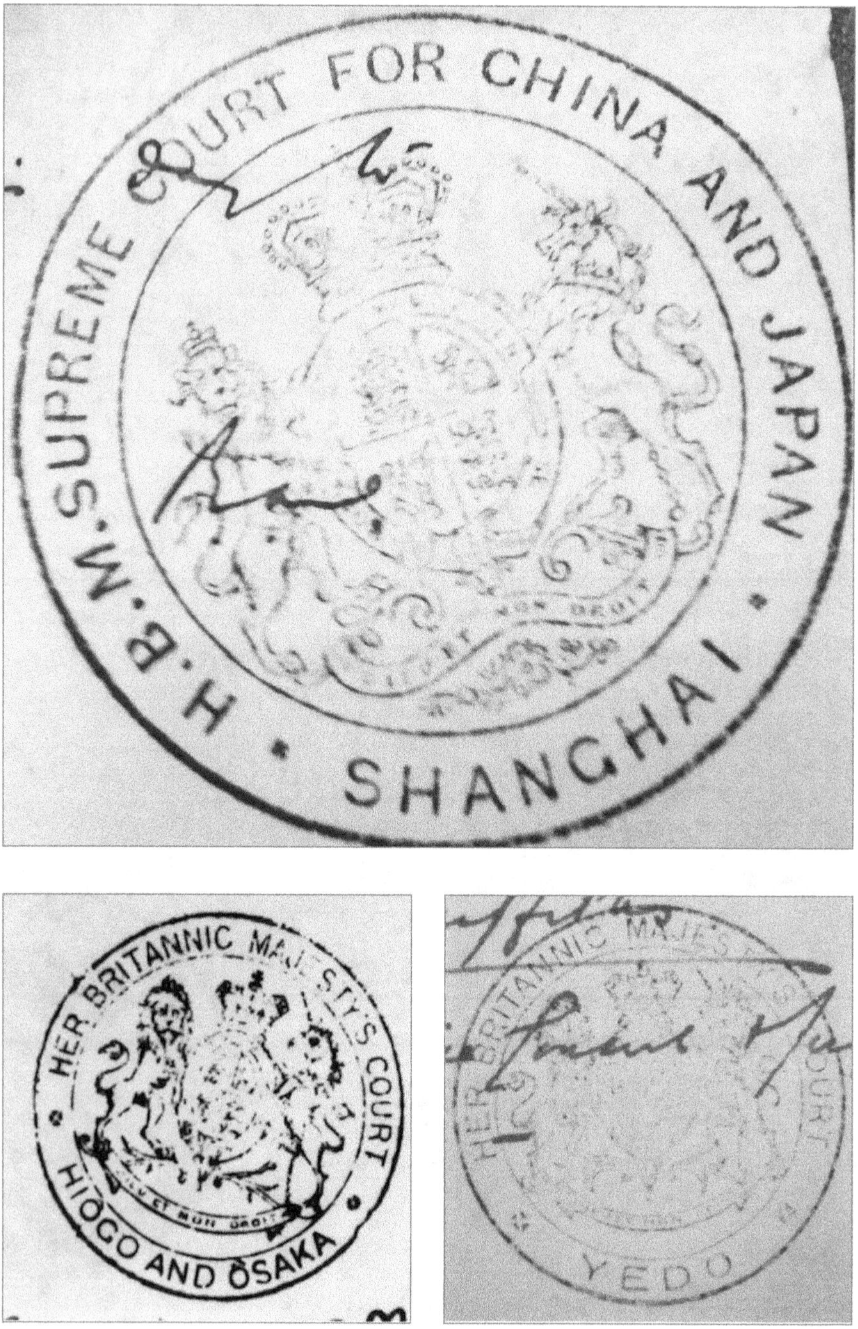
H.B.M. SUPREME COURT FOR CHINA AND JAPAN
SHANGHAI
HER BRITANNIC MAJESTY'S COURT
HIOGO AND OSAKA
HER BRITANNIC MAJESTY'S COURT
YEDO

Court Seals

Robert Hart, Inspector-General of the Imperial Maritime Customs, who challenged the authority of the British Courts a number of times.

John Richard Wolfe, Head of the Church Missionary Society in Foochow, defendant in the Wushishan case

John Lowder, prosecutor of John Hartley; Edith Carew's defence Lawyer

John Hartley, opium importer to Japan. His acquittal led to a major diplomatic incident.

Juilian Pauncefote, AG of HK, sued for false imprisonment of Chinese coolies

Philip Currie, architect of the amalgamation of consular and Judicial positions in Shanghai

Prince Kung, founder of the Tsungli Yamen

Victor Deacon who acted for the Chinese government in the Canton claims commission. His firm, Deacons, still exists today.

Agnes Hall, nee Goodwin, daughter of CW Goodwin and wife of JC Hall. Laid the foundation stone to the SCCJ.

Jessie Hannen, wife of Sir Nicholas, in a ricshaw at the British consulate, Shanghai

Sir Nicholas Hannen, as Consul-General, inspects the Shanghai Volunteer Corps in 1897

Lieutentant James Hetherington. Acquitted of killing his wife's lover, Briton Gower Robinson in 1892.

Walter Carew in the bar of the Yokohama United Club sometime before he was poisoned in 1896

The Yokohama Bund where Hetherington shot Robinson. The Yokohama United Club Hotel is the second building. The Club where Robinson died and Walter Carew worked is just after that.

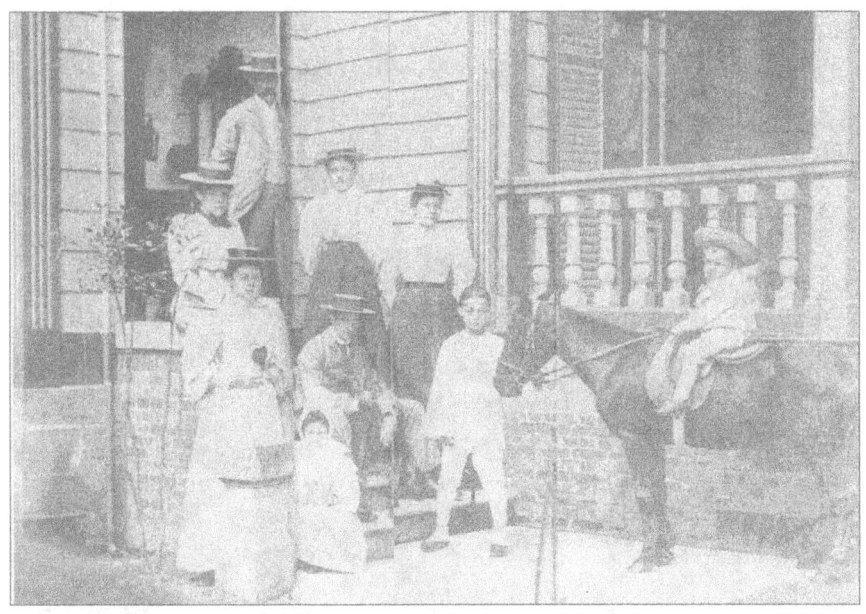

The Carew Family at their house on the Bluff. Walter is standing in the doorway, Edith is seated to his right. Mary Jacob is standing in front of Edith.

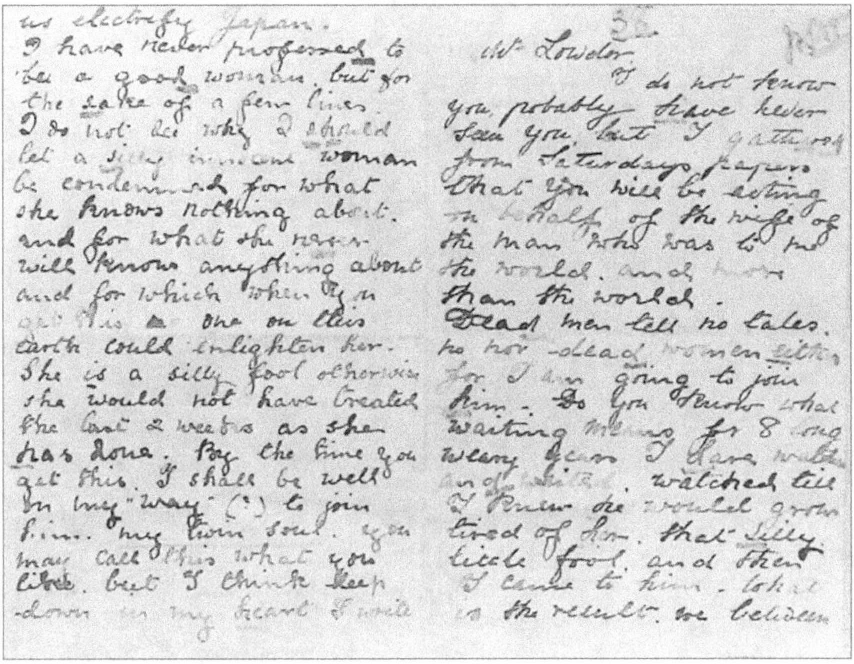

us electrify Japan.
I have never professed to
be a good woman, but for
the sake of a few lines
I do not see why I should
let a silly innocent woman
be condemned for what
she knows nothing about.
and for what she never
will know anything about
and for which when you
get this no one on this
earth could enlighten her.
She is a silly fool otherwise
she would not have treated
the last 2 weeks as she
has done. By the time you
get this. I shall be well
on my "way" (?) to join
him. my twin soul. you
may call this what you
like. but I think keep
down in my heart I write

Mr Lowder
I do not know
you probably have never
seen you, but I gathered
from Saturdays papers
that you will be acting
on behalf of the wife of
the man who was to me
the world. and more
than the world.
Dead men tell no tales.
no nor dead women either
for I am going to join
him. Do you know what
waiting means for 8 long
weary years I have waited
and waited, watched till
I knew he would grow
tired of her. that silly
little fool. and then
I came to him. what
is the result. we between

"We between us electrify Japan." Annie Luke's letter to John Lowder

Sir Nicholas Hannen's Funeral Cortege on the Maloo in April 1900. The Town Hall is in the background.

Frederick Bourne and priests look on as marines from HMS Hermione lift Hannen's coffin on to the gun carriage

Mourners gathered in the gardens of Trinity Cathedral

George French CJ's sad lonely grave in Futatabi Cemetery, Kobe

John James Enslie's grand grave in the same cemetery

"We reap our sowing, and so goodbye." Walter Carew's grave in the Yokohama Foreigners'Cemetery

Together in death: John Carey and Agnes Hall's grave also in Yokohama

CHAPTER 15

The Chinese Challenge

GEORGE FRENCH, the new British Chief Justice, had a tough time in his few years on the bench in China. For most of the time he was physically ill. His condition cannot have been helped by the two very tricky cases that came before him involving the rights of British missionaries to lease land and to what extent British employees of the Imperial Maritime Customs were subject to the jurisdiction of the court.

The position of missionaries

Foreign missionaries in China created numerous frictions and problems. Most foreigners were happy to live in treaty ports and have as little to do as possible with local Chinese. Even for trade with Chinese they relied on compradores, or Chinese middlemen, to handle the buying and selling of products. The majority of cases involving Chinese in the British and American courts were therefore criminal cases where a foreigner had killed or injured a Chinese.

Missionaries on the other hand were on a mission to convert Chinese to Christianity. They wanted to live amongst the Chinese, they learnt the language and tried to talk to Chinese and deal with them on a daily basis. The local Chinese were suspicious of these foreigners and what they were doing in China. Numerous rumours were spread, including that the missionaries ate babies they took into their orphanages. Riots broke out frequently against missionaries all over China and throughout the Qing dynasty. One of the major duties of foreign gunboats was quelling anti-missionary riots.

These disturbances could be very serious. Frederick Bourne, who later became a judge of the British Supreme Court, early in his career when he was the British Consul in Chungking (Chongqing) deep inland on the Yangtze River almost lost his life when he was attacked by a Chinese mob protesting against the activities of foreign missionaries. The riots had started due to the activities of American missionaries at the China Inland Mission. Bourne had gone to the local magistrate's Yamen to ask for assistance. For his return journey he was provided with 40 armed men to protect him, but they were no match for the mob and his chair was destroyed. His arm was badly hurt and a stick hit him on the temple. For at least half an hour he thought that he might be killed at any minute. The magistrate arrived with more armed men just in time to save his life and take him to safety.

Even after being saved by the mob, Bourne thought he would be killed and wrote a dispatch which ended: "The affair looks now as bad as it can be and I am very doubtful whether I shall write another letter." He then spent the next seven months living in various yamens, wearing Chinese clothes and eating Chinese food until the Chinese authorities thought it safe for him to publicly resume duties. Bourne blamed the affair on American missionary imprudence in building a new building that offended Chinese sensibilities.[1]

A few years before in Foochow (Fuzhou) on the coast of Fukien (Fujian) Province, riots had broken out, triggered by the construction by British missionaries of a large foreign building that by its shape and height was offensive to Chinese sensibilities. The riots were only quelled by the arrival of the Gunboat HMS *Swinger* and other men-of-war in Foochow port. After diplomatic negotiations failed, the dispute ended up being decided by French, after a special hearing in Foochow.

---

1   P.D. Coates, *The China Consuls*, p308-309.

The Church Missionary Society (CMS) had first arrived in Foochow in 1850 even before missionaries were allowed by treaty into China. Originally, the missionaries were not permitted to live inside the walls of the city but they soon signed a lease for a piece of land owned by Taou Shan Kwan (Daoguanshan) Temple on Wu Hsih Shan (Wushishan). The Mission was located in a beautiful position. The Reverend John Wolfe, the head of the mission, described the view in a letter home in 1863:

"Hill rising behind hill, in beautiful order, form the extensive plain into a natural and most magnificent amphitheatre. Looking down upon the city with its 600,000 inhabitants inside the walls, fills the mind of the spectator with thoughts and feelings which can be realised only by himself. The whole city is seen from our door, so we can never go out or come in without being reminded of the vastness of our work, and our want of strength to accomplish it. The entire beautiful valley of the Min lies spread before our eyes; the river itself, flowing noiselessly along, having its surface enlivened with crowds of boats – the various plots of ground formed by canals which pass through the whole vale – the crops of rice and wheat waving in the sun – the clumps of trees and hamlets scattered irregularly over the plain, with a grave or a mausoleum occasionally attracting the attention and reminding one that death is the same everywhere."[2]

Over the years, the CMS leased more and more land. All the agreements had to be registered with the Chinese authorities through the British Consul. In one case where the CMS effectively tried to buy land by leasing it in "perpetuity," the

2   Reproduced in E Stock, *The Story of the Fuh-Kien Mission*, 1877, p13-14.

* In the engraving, the hill in the left foreground is Black-Stone Hill. About the left centre of the picture, on this hill, will be observed a white wall; behind it a house with a slightly gabled roof looking as if it were on the highest point of the hill; and behind that, the top of a small pagoda. This wall surrounds the C.M.S. Mission compound; and the house is the old mission-house, now burnt down, but replaced by a new one built by the late Rev. J. E. Mahood. To the right, but lower down, and almost exactly in the centre of the picture, is another English-looking house, which is now used as a girls' school, and as the residence of the Native Pastor, the Rev. Wong Kiu-taik. Between the two houses, and a little behind, is the temple of the "Pearly Emperor Supreme Ruler," the great idol whose title (Shangti) is the term used by most of our missionaries to express "God." Another hill, crowded with buildings, will be seen in the background, with a famous pagoda half-way up it. Just beneath this pagoda, between the two hills, a building stands up from the mass of houses: this is the city gate, the lower ground to the right being the suburbs.

A view of Wushishan and the CMS compound

lease was rejected because under Chinese law it was not possible to enter into a lease in perpetuity.

The CMS had a very difficult relationship with the local Chinese. The local gentry did not want them in the city at all. Complaints were made about their encroaching on land not leased to them or building buildings larger than those allowed for in the lease. In 1869, the mission chapel was attacked, allegedly by Chinese soldiers, and its furniture destroyed. Serious damage was also inflicted on the building.

In 1878, the Society leased more land from the Temple

and started to build a new theological college. They planned to build a three-storey building that would lie against the side of the hill. Because of this, the second storey was larger than the first and the third larger than the second. The building was planned to have 48 small rooms for study and a large dining room and lecture room. The local Chinese gentry complained to the local Chinese authorities about the construction of such a large building of "foreign design" and the officials passed on the complaint to the British Consul. The Chinese officials offered to relocate the mission to an old telegraph building, but the Society refused and continued the construction work.[3]

In the heat of summer, in late August 1878, a Chinese mob took matters into their own hands and, while local Chinese officials and British consular officials looked on, burnt the new building down. The riot appears to have been, as far as riots can be, a relatively civilized affair. Nobody's life appears to have been threatened and none were lost. The local Chinese gentry were reported to have looked on while smoking their water-pipes.

There were rumours that two weeks later, the "mob, elated by their previous success, have determined to burn down the whole of the buildings belonging to the Church Missionary Society on September 11, 1878." Two days before this planned attack, the HMS *Swinger* arrived in port and over the next 10 days another three British and one American men-of-war arrived to deliver the clear message that destruction of the mission would lead to the destruction of Foochow.

Under pressure from the Tsungli Yamen and the British, the local authorities punished some locals for their role in the riots. The local authorities, however, wanted to get the mis-

....

3 Background to the case: *North China Herald*, October 31,1878, p420; September 14, 1878, pp 269-270; September 21, 1878, p285; E. Carlson, *The Foochow Missionaries 1847-1880*, Chapter VIII and James E Kirby, "The Foocow Anti Missionary Riot" August 30, 1878, The Journal of Asian Studies, Vol. 25, No. 4 (Aug., 1966), pp. 665-679 provide full details of the case.

sion out. Having no other option, they decided to take action in the British courts. They instructed a senior lawyer from Hong Kong, Thomas Hayllar QC, to act for them. In October 1878, the Foochow Office of Foreign Trade sent an eviction notice drafted by Hayllar to the Society. Later in early March 1879 they formally filed a petition in the British Consular Court in Fuzhou seeking eviction of the Society.

Sir Thomas Wade, the British Minister in Peking took a personal interest in the case. He arrived in Hong Kong on March 10, 1879 on his way back to Peking from long leave and decided to first go to Foochow to try to reach a settlement. He negotiated directly with the new Chinese Governor General of Fukien, Ting Jih Chang, and Reverend John Wolfe, the head of the mission, but failed. Despite generous offers from the Chinese and British authorities to provide new premises in the old telegraph office that had been offered before, Wolfe refused to leave.

The only way to solve the problem was for the case to continue in British courts. However, given the issues at stake, the case was transferred to the Supreme Court. Chief Justice George French came from Shanghai in early April 1879 for the trial.

The small court in the British consulate was not large enough to fit all the good and the great as well as the local foreigners and Chinese who wanted to attend. So that everyone could be accommodated, a house owned by the China Mercantile Bank was leased to serve as the courthouse.[4]

The British Minister, Sir Thomas Wade and Governor General Ting both attended the hearings sitting near the bench. A number of other senior Chinese officials including the local magistrate and the President of the Foreign Trade Board and the Judicial Commissioner also attended.

4   Report of the Case of *Chow Chang Kung, Lin King Chun, Loo King Fah, Sat Keok Min, Directors of the Taou Shan Kwan Temple at Wu Shih Shan, Foochow, versus, Rev John R Wolfe, of the Church of England Missionary Society,* Reprinted from the *Hong Kong Daily Press,* 1879, also at *North China Herald,* May 27, 1897, p527.

Hayllar represented the temple at trial. The mission also called in a big gun, getting Nicholas Hannen, who at the time was the Crown Advocate in Shanghai to represent them. Hayllar needed to be admitted to the bar of the Supreme Court for China for the purposes of the case. Hannen made an application for this to be done requesting that, "as Mr Hayllar was so well-known to the court, the usual affidavit be dispensed with." French agreed to this and Hayllar was admitted.[5]

The case itself, as almost all landlord and tenant cases are, was as dull as watching paint dry. The temple alleged that the lease agreements with the Church Mission Society were void or that the Society was in breach of the agreements. The trial lasted eight days from April 30, 1879 to May 9, 1879. Numerous witnesses were called on behalf of the temple to show the breaches of agreement. Two Chinese officials also testified on the requirements of Chinese tenancy law. Reverend Wolfe, the actual Defendant in the case, also gave evidence regarding the signing of the tenancy agreements. He was adamant that the Society had not breached the agreements. At the end of the hearing, Chief Justice French said that given the importance of the case he would reserve his judgment and arrange for it to be read later in Foochow.

Two months later the judgment was read out in courtroom of the consulate in Foochow. French had spent his time writing a masterful judgment that gave something to everyone and could allow both sides to claim to be winners.

The first issue French had to decide was whether to apply English or Chinese law to the contract. Hannen had insisted during the trial that English law should be applied in particular because there was no pleading of Chinese law. French dealt with this quickly. He simply stated that the general principle of English law was that the "law of the place where the land, the subject of the contract, is situate, governs its con-

---

5   A brief CV of Hayllar can be found in the *North China Herald* January 31,1882, p 129.

struction," and accordingly, "the law of China applicable to the contract in question must govern its construction."

French then found that the evidence did not show any breach of contract by the Church Missionary Society in rebuilding its buildings. French added, however, that he could not, sitting in a British court in China, decide the boundaries of the land, as this would affect other neighbours not before the court.

He then came to his formal decision. Before doing so, he sounded a warning to all involved that they should not be hoping for too much from a court judgment:

> "I may here observe that the case is an anomalous one, and not likely to be of value as a precedent. Nor is the value of the interests involved in it of much moment. But other circumstances have drawn to it a factitious degree of attention which neither the value of the interests involved nor the importance of the points raised justify."

He dismissed the temple's claims – a victory for the missionaries. But, and this was a big but, he found that the lease agreement could be terminated by the temple on three months notice if they genuinely needed the land for use of the temple. This was a very big victory for the Chinese.

French also ordered that each side bear their own costs.

The decision was very diplomatic. It effectively gave the Chinese an easy way to terminate the tenancy if they wanted to but also the Society the face of not having been found in breach of the agreement. By not ordering either party to pay the others costs, he also did not establish who the real winner or loser was. And perhaps in this case, the real winner was justice. The decision was a fair one that defused a difficult situation. Following the decision, the temple immediately terminated the tenancy on the basis that it needed the land. The

Chinese authorities showed great flexibility and, after some further negotiations, offered the Society the telegraph office that the Society had previously turned down as a site for their new mission. The Society initially said that they would appeal to the Privy Council, but cooler heads prevailed and they agreed to move. All that remains of their mission in Wushishan today is a stone marker in Chinese recording the site as the "Former Location of the Wushishan Church Case."

Servants of the Chinese Empire

A year and a half later, in March 1881, French had to deal with an even trickier case over the rights and duties of foreigners employed by the Chinese Emperor. The case was particularly difficult because it involved the Imperial Maritime Customs, a Chinese government body run by foreigners. As a foreigner, the Scottish Inspector General of the Customs, Robert Hart, was much more willing to challenge the powers of the foreign courts in China. He did everything in his power to obtain a decision that would find that foreign officers employed by Customs were not subject to the jurisdiction of the foreign courts for acts done in their position as employees of the Chinese Emperor.

Edward Page, a watcher in the Maritime Chinese Customs, was charged with the murder of two Chinese smugglers, Li Amai and one unknown person. He had killed the two in the course of trying to catch them smuggling opium.

The case caused Hart "much worry." When he first heard of the

Sir Robert Hart, British Inspector-General of Chinese Customs who was willing to challenge the authority of the British courts (The Chinese characters are reversed in the original)

Edward O'Malley, Attorney General of Hong Kong, who was instructed by Chinese Customs to defend Page

case, he contacted the British Minister, Thomas Wade, to ask him to intervene. However, Wade told him that he could not interfere if the consul in Canton "was proceeding *judicially*," and thus the case had gone ahead. [6]

Hart fully supported Page in defending the charges. He engaged two of the leading British lawyers in Hong Kong, Thomas Hayllar QC, and the Attorney General of Hong Kong, Mr (later Sir) Edward O'Malley, as defence counsel.[7] The case therefore pitted the Queen's most senior lawyer in China, the Crown Advocate, against her most senior legal representative in Hong Kong, the Attorney General. Nicholas Hannen did not himself appear for the Crown. He was on leave at the time of the trial. He had gone to England the year before and was staying on with his wife for the birth of their first son. John Francis, a senior barrister from Hong Kong, who later became a Queen's Counsel, acted as Crown Advocate in Hannen's place.

In addition to defending Page, Hart went on the attack. He instructed Hayllar and O'Malley to bring a civil claim for false imprisonment against the British Consul in Canton, A.R. Hewlett, for arresting Page. This was scheduled to be heard after the prosecution of Page.

Before Page's criminal trial started, Hayllar and O'Malley filed a demurrer, or objection, to the charge. They argued that because Page was employed by the Emperor of China with the consent of the British Government, the British courts in China could not have jurisdiction over him for acts done in

---

6   *The I. G. in Peking: Letters of Robert Hart, Chinese Maritime Customs,* 1868-1907, p367.

7   O'Malley later went on to be Chief Justice of the Straits Settlements and Chief Judge of the British Supreme Court in Constantinople. Mr E. McKean was also instructed for the defence. As they were from Hong Kong, they were instructed by a firm of solicitors, Brereton and Wotton.

the course of that employment. Two cases where British employees of the government of Chile and Portugal were found not to be subject to British jurisdiction were cited to support this argument. French dismissed the demurrer on the basis that under the terms of the Treaty of Tientsin, the Emperor of China did not have jurisdiction to try British subjects. If the argument of the Defendant were correct, no one would have jurisdiction to try them. The Chilean and Portuguese cases could be distinguished because in those cases the governments of those countries had not given up their rights to try British subjects.[8]

Page was asked to plea to the charges. He pleaded not guilty and was put on trial before a five man jury. The Acting Crown Advocate, Francis, commenced by telling the jury that the jurisdiction the court had over Page was purely personal. Some of the witnesses in the court would not be British subjects and the court had no coercive power over these witnesses to force them to give evidence.[9]

Francis then set out the case for the prosecution. One of Page's colleagues, a Mr Davis, had received information that smugglers would be attempting to bring opium into China aboard the steamer *Tung Ting*. Davis was too unwell to try to catch the smugglers so he passed the information on to Page. If Customs officers were successful in interdicting opium they were paid a considerable percentage of its value as a reward. Page sought permission to try to catch the smugglers. Customs' rules prohibited the use of firearms without the specific consent of a superior. Customs' rules also provided that firearms should only be used in self-defence. Page, however, took a rifle given to him by Davis on his expedition.

Rather than directly trying to stop the *Tung Ting* in a

---

8   *R v Page* (demurrer), *North China Herald*, March 8, 1881, p239. The cases cited were *Dobree v Napier* Seven Bingham's N.C. 781 (Re Portugal); *Regina v Lesley* 29 L.H. M.C. 97

9   *R v Page* (jury trial) *North China Herald*, March 15, 1881, pp264 to 268. The jury members were C.A. de Britto, W.E. Mitchell, J.D. Munro, A. Roberts and G.D. Fearon.

Customs boat, which most likely would have resulted in the opium being thrown overboard, Page boarded an ordinary Chinese boat dressed in Chinese clothing. The Chinese boat fired across the bow of the *Tung Ting* to try to force it to stop. Captain Homes of the *Tung Ting* testified that he then saw a sampan being rowed from his ship towards the shore of the river. He said he also saw a man dressed in Chinese clothing in the bow of the Chinese boat standing and shooting at the sampan and that one of the men in the sampan fell. The Chinese boat then went alongside the sampan. Captain Holmes said that that was all he could see.

Page returned to Canton and told Davis what had happened. Davis then took him to the Customs Office where he reported to Mr Eldridge, the principal tide-surveyor and Mr Parkhill, chief tide-surveyor. Subsequently, he also reported to Mr McKean the Commissioner of Customs in Canton. The dead man in the sampan was brought to Customs jetty where Dr Carrow examined him and determined that he had been killed instantly by a bullet that went through his heart and lungs.

Parkhill, McKean, Eldridge and Dr Carrow were all called as witnesses to testify as to what Page had told them or, in the case of Dr Carrow, what he had found in his examination of the victim. Robert Hart officially ordered them all not to give evidence. In court, they all refused to testify on the basis that the information was the property of the Chinese government. They wished to serve the Chinese government honourably and it would be a dishonor to disclose the information. Dr Carrow and Eldridge were both American citizens. The court had no power to make them give evidence and Francis was not able to get any statements from them.

Parkhill and McKean, however, were both British subjects. Parkhill was the first to be questioned. He was asked what Page had told him when he spoke to him after the incident. Hayllar objected to the question on the basis the answer given by Page was in obeyance to an order and not voluntarily and under English rules of evidence, therefore, not admissible. He also argued that any answer given was the property of, and a secret of, the Chinese government. Hayllar said that if the incident had occurred in England, it would be for Page's superiors to decide whether to prosecute and in this case they clearly did not want to. The argument raised some tough issues. French said he would need some time to consider the matter and would resume the trial the next day.

In the morning, French overruled the first objection on the grounds that it appeared the answers had been given voluntarily. Turning to whether the information was a secret of the Chinese government, he said that a government document could be ordered to be made public when it was in the public interest do so. French said that this was clearly the case here. Parkhill then returned to the witness box. He continued to refuse to answer any questions regarding what Page had said to him on the basis that it would be dishonesty to the Chinese government. In what must have been a very tense exchange, French ordered Parkhill to answer:

French: I have held you must do it. Now, the powers of this Court are very considerable, and if you, being a British subject and in a British Court of Law, although in China, refuse to answer the question which the court thinks you ought to answer, I need not tell you that you are subject to punishment at the hands of the Court, with a view to consider whether you expose yourself to that punishment or answer the question.
Parkhill: I consider it a very dishonest thing.
French: I don't care about that at all. You have to answer it. It is not a question for you to consider.
Parkhill: With all respect, I decline.

Francis then asked that Parkhill be found in contempt

of court and punished for refusing to obey French's order. French said that he would deal with that at the end of the day and said Parkhill could leave the witness box.

McKean was then called. His evidence lasted longer, but he also refused to answer any questions as to what Page had said to him and refused to disclose the statement that he had been taken down on the basis that he had been ordered by Robert Hart not to answer the question or disclose the document. McKean explained why he was refusing:

> "It involves a question of immense principle, I may be summoned every day of my life to this Consulate in consequence of the credulity of some Consular assistant to answer for my acts. There is nothing to prevent any one swearing an oath to bring me here to know what I do every morning. My acts are of the Chinese Government only. Of that I have been advised by the most eminent lawyers that have ever lived."

McKean refused to produce the statement. The prosecution then sought an adjournment to allow the British Consulate to serve a notice on the Chinese Superintendent of Customs (called the Hoppo), who had last had the document asking him to produce the document. This was done. But the next day, no one attended to produce the document.

Francis then sought to get evidence from Mr McKean as to what the document said. This was objected to as secondary evidence as to the contents of a document that has been refused to be produced as the property of another state. French upheld the objection and ruled that McKean could not be asked further questions on this topic. McKean was then allowed to leave the witness box.

Without the evidence of what Page had told his colleagues, Francis did not have much of a case. He, however, did the best he could relying on the undenied evidence that two people were dead and Captain Homes' testimony. French summed up for the jury and gave the following directions:

> "(1) If the Jury should be of the opinion that upon the evidence it is doubtful whether a customs flag was flying from the sampan, they would be entitled to give the prisoner the benefit of the doubt and acquit him.

> "(2) If the firing were deliberately and intentionally at the people in the dug-out, it would be murder, no matter whose hand fired the shot, if without just cause and excuse.

> "(3) If the firing was in pursuit of a lawful act, which the prevention of smuggling was, the prisoner would be entitled to an acquittal if on the facts the Jury should be satisfied the prisoner did not fire the fatal shot."

Despite the lack of evidence, the jury took a long time to consider its verdict. They returned at one time to clarify the direction given by the judge regarding the shooting. French had told them they should acquit if they "should be satisfied the prisoner did not fire the fatal shot." They asked if they could alter this to "should not be satisfied the prisoner did fire the fatal shot." French allowed this and the jury acquitted Page. While an apparently small change, the jury was effectively saying they accepted someone had fired the shot and it was likely to be Page, but could not be satisfied it was him.

When Page was acquitted applause broke out in the court. French quickly suppressed it. Francis then sought an order that Parkhill be punished for refusing to answer questions. French, whose attitude had clearly softened during the trial, said that given Parkhill had been ordered by his superiors to refuse to answer, he would not punish him. Francis argued strongly against this. He said if witnesses could refuse to answer based on a superior order it would be impossible to obtain evidence for prosecutions in the future. French, however, was not in the mood to punish anyone. He said it was a "peculiar case" and that he did not suppose a similar case would need to be dealt with again soon, and hopefully not at all. He told Mr Parkhill that he was free to go.

With the decision, Robert Hart ordered that the false imprisonment proceedings against the Consul, Hewlett, be withdrawn, recording in a letter to a colleague, "they are wroth with McKean for refusing to give evidence and will be wroth with me if I go on with the prosecution of the Consul." He went on in a long-winded stream of consciousness that reflected the difficult position he was in as a foreigner heading a Chinese government agency:

> "Under the circumstances – after a full review of the situation, comprising a Yamen too weak to back me up, a possible defeat with an 'I told you so' to swallow afterwards, a possible victory in one court but renewed opposition elsewhere and intensified ill feeling everywhere, and an indisposition to sacrifice a mountain because tripped by a mole-hill – I have decided to take my own course, which is a) to stop Hewlett, b) to send home the report of the trial etc., for legal opinions at home, c) to give instructions to Canton specially and the Service generally (vide forthcoming circular) of a kind to 'save face' and d) by changing my tack, and remembering we are under sail and without steam, bend to the storm and save the ship. – But it is a bitter pill to swallow, all the same!"[10]

The circular he issued to "save face" read:

10 *The I. G. in Peking: Letters of Robert Hart, Chinese Maritime Customs,* 1868-1907, p367.

"If any foreign employee of the Chinese customs kills or wounds any person, he shall at once resign his place and report to the Consul of his nationality within whose jurisdiction he resides; if the Consul tries and convicts him, his resignation is to be permanent; if the Consul acquits him, or decides that there is no cause for trial, he may resume his official position with full pay during the time since his resignation."[11]

Two years later in Shanghai, in what Hart remarked was an odd coincidence, another man named Page was the Defendant in a case in Shanghai that again raised the question as Hart put it "are China official employees if foreigners obliged to answer judicial questions concerning their official knowledge?"[12]

In April 1883, Hart had issued instructions to the Customs Commissioners in each port concerning when and when not Customs employees should give evidence in consular courts. The rules were that if a Commissioner instructed any customs employee to attend any foreign court of law the employee should do so. The Commissioner was required to obtain from the Superintendent, Hart, a memorandum of what actions the employee was to take and what evidence he was permitted to give. If an employee was summonsed to court, he must go but he would be treated as being on leave without pay. Except where they had permission from the Commissioner, they were "forbidden to answer questions on subjects of which he had knowledge only by reason of, or through his position as an employee of the Chinese Government."[13]

In late August 1883, William Page, the Quartermaster on the P&O Steamer the *Ancona*, stole 163 balls of opium. They

11 Hose A Ballou Morse, *The International Relations of the Chinese Empire*, p319.

12 *The I. G. in Peking: Letters of Robert Hart, Chinese Maritime Customs*, 1868-1907, p488 for this and other quotes below.

13 S. Wright, *Hart and the Chinese Customs*, p456-457.

had been found during a search by Customs. Page offered John Roberts, an assistant examiner and diver with Customs, a bribe of one sovereign if he would let him throw the opium away. Page was prosecuted in the Police Court at Shanghai before Robert Mowat sitting as the police magistrate. Roberts was called to give evidence against Page.[14] Roberts first refused to appear in court unless he was subpoenaed. After he was subpoenaed he appeared the next day. He refused, however, to answer any questions concerning what happened on board the *Ancona*. He recited almost word for word Hart's instructions:

> "I cannot answer that question, as I am strictly forbidden to answer any questions on subjects of which I have a knowledge only by reason of my position as a servant of the Chinese Government."

He then said he had been ordered by the Commissioner of Customs in Shanghai, Mr Glover, not to answer any questions. Mowat told Roberts that the law did not allow him to refuse to answer, unless the answer would incriminate him, and said:

> "If you do not answer, I shall have, unwillingly, to commit you to prison. Will you answer?"
> "No, Sir."

Mowat explained the law again and told Roberts that if he did not answer he would send him to prison for seven days unless he answered in the meantime and added: "I hope you will be enabled to answer. I very much regret the course I have to take."

Roberts simply asked: "Will you allow me one favour – to

---

14 *R v William Page, North China Herald,* September 8, 1883, p292.

get my room locked up?"

"Oh, yes," replied Mowat.

Mr Wainewright who was in court to watch the case for the Customs service then tried to argue with Mowat that the prosecution could get the evidence it needed if they applied to the Superintendent of Customs "and it is for him to say whether he will allow them to give the evidence required."

Mowat was having none of that and said with finality: "It is for the Court to say whether he must answer."

Robert Hart was very upset by the case, not because Roberts had been locked up but because Roberts should have answered the question and Glover should not have ordered him not to. He wrote furiously: "the case is such a bad one for us – Glover having shut his mouth to keep in what should have come out in the public interest." Glover later told Hart that he had ordered Roberts not to answer because he thought Hart had wanted a test case and "the stronger the reasons for a man's speaking out, the more necessary for us [Customs] to get Government to say he may be silent!"[15]

Six days later, the case took a surprising turn when Page, who was presumably in the same consular gaol as Roberts, confessed to having been given the opium after it was stolen. Mowat convicted him of possession of stolen property and sentenced him to two months in prison. Then, because Roberts was no longer required to give evidence, Mowat ordered that he be released from prison. To add to the pain for Roberts, Hart said that he expected his pay to be docked for being absent without leave, even though he had been sent to jail for complying with a superior's order.

Mowat's decision upset the Tsungli Yamen and all serving customs officers. Hart considered taking action against Mowat for damages for false imprisonment and appealing against the Mowat's decision to the Privy Council. He re-

---

15 *The IG in Peking, Letters of Robert Hart, Chinese Maritime Customs*, 1868-1907 p498 and 503.

ceived advice from "eminent London lawyers" that the foreign courts had no jurisdiction over any "matters immediately connected with a foreigner's employment in the Customs service," and that an appeal would most likely succeed.

In the end, he determined discretion was the better part of valour. No doubt he would also have been concerned that an unfavourable decision from the Privy Council would make Customs' position even weaker.

Hart did modify his instructions concerning giving evidence in foreign courts so that he required the Commissioners to take the initiative to seek his instructions as to what evidence should be given.[16] He mused on the difficulty of drafting clear rules:

> "Rules and regulations and instructions are exceedingly difficult things to *get acted on*; they seem easy enough to draft, but once they are in the hands of those they are to guide, you find every man interpreting in his own way, and in addition finds 'between lines' motives, objects, etc., etc. of the most dissimilar and least intended descriptions. Seeing that a lawyer can drive a coach and four through Act of Parliament, I cannot expect to draft such rules as shall have only one plain interpretation, and result in only one continuous and consistent line of action."

---

16 S Wright, *Hart and the Chinese Customs*, p437.

CHAPTER 16

Some Corner of a Foreign Field: The Death of George French

THE TRIAL OF EDWARD PAGE at Canton was to be George French's swansong. Soon after the trial, French went on sick leave. He had been unwell almost from when he first arrived in China, and became gravely ill during early 1881. In May of that year, he went with his wife to Kobe in Japan to try to recuperate. Kobe, which is on the shore of Osaka Bay but with mountains immediately behind it, has one of the best climates in the East Asia. It has a small bay and is surrounded by hills. Foreigners in that era often used it as a retreat. The change in surroundings initially seemed to be decidedly beneficial but after a few months "little if any hopes were entertained for his recovery." In early July, French was placed on reduced salary and Robert Mowat formally took over as Acting Chief Justice. When French first went to Kobe, Nicholas Hannen was still on leave in England where his first son, also named Nicholas, was born. When it became apparent that French would most likely either not recover or retire, Hannen was called back to act as Chief Justice. He arrived in Shanghai in October 1881 and immediately took up the role.[1]

Around the same time that Hannen got back to Shanghai, it was reported that French was feeling slightly better. But it was

---

1 FO656/58 letter to Rennie from FO re Mowat's entitlement to allowance for acting dated March 22, 1883. Mowat took over as Acting Chief Justice formally on July 5, 1881. Hannen commenced acting as Chief Justice on October 31, 1881; *Japan Gazette*, November 24, 1881, p289.

not to be. He died two weeks later on November 13, 1881 and
was buried in Onohama Cemetery in the foreign settlement in
Kobe. His coffin was borne to the cemetery by a party of men
from the British Navy boat, HMS *Flying Fish*.[2]

The obituaries for French were mixed. The *North China Herald* regretted his passing but could not help from commenting
that his judgments were "tardily delivered." The *Japan Gazette*
said, "French was highly esteemed in Shanghai where in the
exercise of his judicial functions, he has given every satisfaction, while in private life he had many friends." The Hiogo
News was more complimentary:

> "The death of His Lordship will be severely felt in
> Shanghai, as he was ever courteous and considerate both
> to the Bar and suitors. His judgments were distinguished
> by painstaking research, felicity of language, and
> exhaustiveness, and on no occasion were the special at-
> tributes of his highly trained intellect more conspicuous
> than in the well known Page case, heard too at a time
> when His Lordship was already suffering grievously
> from the disorder which terminated his life while yet in
> complete possession of ripened faculties and abundantly
> competent to fulfill the weighty duties of his high office.
> Chief Justice French's successor whoever he may be;
> will have no light task to avoid contrasting unfavour-
> ably - in some respects at all events - with the cultivated
> courteous gentleman who met the common lot of poor
> frail humanity so far from home, but, happily, tended by
> those whose ministrations are never more grateful than
> at the supreme moment when life, buoyant with hope
> and aspirations for more light, passes tranquilly under
> the shadow of death."

....

2 *London and China Telegraph*, January 9, 1882, p.26; *North China Herald*, November 15,
1881, p506; *Hiogo News* quote is from the *North China Herald*, November 29, 1881, p567.

Nicholas Hannen, as Acting Chief Justice, delivered a fitting eulogy in court:

"On this the first occasion of taking my seat in this court I cannot refrain from saying a few words in reference to the sad death of its late Chief Justice. He presided here with dignity, courtesy and kindness; and to those who like myself practised at the Bar before him, his loss is a very real one, for he was ever considerate towards us, and patient and attentive to our arguments. Few know the labour which he bestowed upon his duties, and none can estimate how much of pain must have been added to the work by the state of his health. He has passed away and I feel sure that everyone who knew him must deeply regret his loss and bear him in affectionate remembrance."[3]

Onohama Cemetery where French was buried was located in the Foreign Concession near the port in Kobe. In the early 1950s, the Kobe City Government began relocating all foreigners' graves to a new Foreigners' Cemetery in Futatabi Park in the hills high above the city. This was completed in 1962. Kobe city employs over 10 people to maintain the cemetery. French's grave was moved to Futatabi and remains there to this day.

On a beautiful and relatively cool June's summer's day, I made arrangements with the management of the cemetery to visit French's grave. I travelled up into the mountains behind Kobe to Futatabi. I wondered what type of gravestone would mark the grave of the Chief Justice of the Court that at that time was the Supreme Court for all British subjects in China and Japan. I imagined something grand and ornate with an appropriate epitaph. James Enslie, the former British Consul in Kobe, is also buried at Futatabi beneath a grand grave of two

---

3 *North China Herald*, November 29, 1881, p586.

large stone blocks topped with a large cross.

French's grave was an approximately 800 metres walk into the cemetery. Besides Enslie's, there were many large and ornate graves. There were also some large memorials for foreign sailors lost at sea and 11 grand graves for the 11 French sailors killed in Sakai in the 1860s. The view over the tree-covered mountains of Kobe was very pretty. The birds in the many trees were singing merrily. It is certainly a beautiful last resting place.

French's grave was located against a wall with 20 other graves facing the mountains. I was very disappointed to find a small stone grave marked simply:

G. French
Died
13 Oct. 1881

The other 20 gravestones along the wall were of a similar type and were perhaps for those whose families did not build a large gravestone, or more likely, they were replacements for gravestones that had been destroyed during the bombing in World War II that leveled Kobe. The fact the date of birth is out by one month suggests it was a replacement gravestone.

If so, it was sad to see that French's time in service the British Crown was marked by such a simple gravestone. I was happy, however, to have found French's grave and to see the respect that the Kobe government shows to the foreigners who were buried in Kobe during the years since the city was opened to foreign trade. I was particularly happy to see that French, unlike those related to the court who were buried in Shanghai, was resting in peace in beautiful surroundings.

The small, sad gravestone marking the last resting place of French CJ in Kobe. R.I.P.

PART FOUR

CONSOLIDATION
(1881 TO 1891)

CHAPTER 17

Jockeying for Promotion

GEORGE FRENCH'S ILLNESS led to jockeying for the positions that would become vacant when French retired or died. Richard Rennie, as Judge for Japan, and as an experienced barrister was the clear choice for the position of Chief Justice. Already by July 1881 when Rennie left Yokohama on 18 months long leave, the English language papers in Japan did not expect his return, writing tributes to his short time on the bench there. The *Japan Herald*, while noting that the paucity of litigation or major crime had meant that he had not been overburdened with cases, praised his judgments which had "been characterized so much by brevity, sound sense, and good law, that critics have had but little opportunity to find fault even if disposed." The *Japan Mail* came to the point and said that Yokohama "was not to be a resting place for merit," and they "scarcely dare to expect that Mr Rennie will ever resume his judicial functions here," particularly if "promotion has any affinity with justice."[1]

The prize on offer was, then, the position as Judge of the Court for Japan. Nicholas Hannen, Robert Mowat and H.S. Wilkinson all had good claims for the job. Hannen and Wilkinson had both acted as a judge in Japan. Wilkinson spoke Japanese. Mowat had been Law Secretary and Assistant Judge in Shanghai for over 12 years.

Even before French's death, Wilkinson, back in Belfast completing his Doctorate of Laws, wrote to Earl Granville,

---

1 See extracts from the *Japan Herald* and *Japan Mail* in the *North China Herald*, August 12, 1881, p166.

the Foreign Secretary applying for "one the judicial posts that may become available" if French retired. He clearly knew that Hannen was also being considered for a position. He added "that if the claims of others preclude me from such an appointment at present, I would like to apply for the post of Crown Advocate if that post should be come vacant."[2]

Within two weeks, following French's death the Foreign Office replied that as a result of French's death the post of

---

Foreign Office, December 14, 1881.

THE Queen has been graciously pleased to appoint Richard Temple Rennie, Esq., now Judge of Her Majesty's Court for Japan, to be Chief Justice of Her Majesty's Supreme Court for China and Japan.

Foreign Office, December 21, 1881.

THE Queen has been graciously pleased to appoint Nicholas John Hannen, Esq., now Crown Advocate at Shanghae, to be Judge of Her Majesty's Court for Japan.

The London Gazette announce the appointment of Rennie as CJ and Hannen as Judge for Japan

---

Hiram Shaw Wilkinson,

Crown Advocate
Her Britannic Majesty's Supreme
Court for China and Japan.

SHANGHAI.

Wilkinson's new name card as Crown Advocate

2 PRONI, D1292/M/25 (Wilkinson Papers) Letter from Wilkinson to Earl Granville, November 4, 1881.

Crown Advocate was likely to become vacant and offering him the position if it did. Wilkinson would, however, have to resign from the consular service. Wilkinson replied the same day he received the letter, accepting the offer.[3]

Russell Robertson steps down as Acting Judge for Japan

Rennie was appointed Chief Justice in Shanghai and Hannen was appointed Judge for Japan.

Wilkinson's appointment as Crown Advocate was formalized in January 1882. He left Belfast for Shanghai in February, arriving in March 1882. He then faced the new challenge of starting practice as Crown Advocate and as a barrister in private practice. His old friends the Hannens welcomed him to Shanghai and he stayed with them on his arrival.[4]

Hannen stayed in Shanghai for the whole of 1882 acting as Chief Justice until Rennie returned from long leave in early 1883. There was some discussion about Hannen moving to Japan prior to Rennie's return with Mowat being appointed as Acting Chief Justice and Wilkinson as Acting Assistant Judge. Hannen, however, was not keen to leave for Yokohama immediately as he had just done up his house in Shanghai. Instead, Russell Robertson, the British Consul in Yokohama, acted as Judge of the Court for Japan for the whole time Ren-

---

3 PRONI D1292/M/25 (Wilkinson Papers) Letter from Lord Tenterdon dated December 8, 1881; letter in reply December 10, 1881.

4 PRONI D1292/C/16 (Wilkinson Papers) Correspondence from Wilkinson to Harry Parkes dated January 5 1882, January 26 1882 and April 5, 1882.

nie was away. Robertson had himself just returned from long leave where he had also qualified as a barrister and appears to have taken up the position with relish. The *Japan Punch* published a cartoon of Robertson with tears in his eyes when he was required to return to his position as Consul on Hannen's eventual arrival in Japan.[5]

As Acting Chief Justice, Hannen got into the job quickly and issued a number of judgments very speedily to catch up on French's backlog.[6] One of these was handed down, only two days after French was buried, on November 18, 1881, and even before Hannen had actually sat as Acting Chief Justice. Almost as if by serendipity, the appeal in case of *Langfeldt & Mayer v Green*, where it had been decided in Yokohama that the seal of the Kanagawa consulate could not be used as the seal of the branch of the Supreme Court in Kanagawa, had made its way to Shanghai. As we have seen in Chapter 9, Hannen and Mowat made a final decision that the ill-fated Supreme Court branch was only a consular court.[7]

Rennie returned to Asia in March 1883 and took up residence in Shanghai. His first hearing where members of the bar were present was on March 28, 1883 in the case of *Raphael v Benjamin*. Wilkinson appeared before him with Mr A.

Nicholas Hannen arrives in Japan

5   *Japan Punch*, February 1883.

6   *North China Herald* December 20, 1881, p662.

7   See Chapter 9

Robertson for the Plaintiff and Mr R.E. Wainewright and Mr Dowdall appeared for the Defendant. The application was for an account that was not contested. The lawyers were all really in court to welcome Rennie. On behalf of the Bar, Wilkinson expressed "their gratification at Sir Richard's appointment to the Chief Justiceship." In response, Rennie, commenting on his return to Shanghai, said it was "hardly necessary for him to say how gratifying it was to him to meet old friends again," adding that he "hoped that the good relations that had always existed between the Bench and members of the Bar would continue."[8]

Wilkinson was soon after this to put the noses of some of the Shanghai British community out of joint. Harry Parkes, who had served as British Minister in Japan from 1865, was appointed British Minister in Peking. Wilkinson had the privilege of going out with the British Consul-General to meet Parkes at Woosong when his boat arrived. Parkes and his daughters then stayed with Wilkinson while in Shanghai. While many rungs down the order of precedence, it was clear that Wilkinson had a very good relationship with the newly-arrived minister.[9]

Until 1891, there were no changes in the judges in any of the British Courts. Hannen went on long leave from Japan in 1888. Russell Robertson who had acted from 1881 to 1883 was due to act as Judge again. However, he died in April 1888, at the very young age of 48, soon after arriving back in Japan from Home leave where he had also just got married.[10] Wilkinson was offered the acting appointment in Japan, however, according to Mowat he declined because "the pecuniary sacrifice which would follow from his acceptance of a merely temporary appointment [would be] too great to warrant his

8 *North China Herald*, April 4, 1883, p383.
9 "Arrival of Sir Harry Parkes", *North China Herald*, September 8, 1883, p287.
10 *North China Herald*, April 13, 1888, p406.

incurring it."[11] Instead, George Jamieson, who had from 1886 been Acting Assistant Judge in Shanghai during Mowat's long leave, was appointed as Acting Judge of the Court for Japan. At the same time, in May 1888, John Carey Hall, the Vice-Consul in Yokohama, was sent from Japan to Shanghai to act as Assistant Judge while Rennie was on long leave.[12] Mowat was appointed Acting Chief Justice.

It would have been more logical to have Jamieson stay in Shanghai and Hall stay in Japan, but presumably because Jamieson now had experience acting as a judge in Shanghai it was considered more appropriate for him to be the sole judge in Japan with Hall acting under Mowat's supervision in Shanghai. There does seem to have been some politics behind the decision as well. Hall was at the time a Vice-Consul and junior to James Joseph Enslie (who had applied for Robertson's position) and other Consuls in Japan. If he had acted in Japan he would have been senior or equal to them even if only in an acting position.[13]

The appointment of Hall in Shanghai brought Charles Goodwin's daughter, Agnes, who had married Hall in 1876, back to Shanghai. Her husband was now a judge in the court her father had helped found, in a building for which she had laid the foundation stone.

Hall caused a huge scandal soon after his arrival in Shanghai. The scandal appears to have occurred, in part, because Hall who had spent his career to date in Japan, was more favourably disposed to believe the evidence of local witnesses. In June 1888, he convicted David Main an employee of the waterworks of assaulting a Chinese, Chao Yung-ch'ang, by striking him on the head with an iron water key while trying to shut

11 FO656/50 Mowat to le Poer Trench, April 16, 1888, cited in C. Roberts, *The British Courts and Extraterritoriality in Japan, 1859 to 1899*, p71.

12 *London and China Telegraph*, June 25, 1888, p562.

13 C. Roberts, *The British Courts and Extraterritoriality in Japan, 1859 to 1899*, p50.

off water inside Chao's shop.[14] Hall said that a "great principle and the interest of the public were at stake and that he should impose an exemplary penalty." He fined Main £5, the maximum penalty. One-fifth of the fine was ordered to be given to the Complainant, Chao. Hall's decision was met with surprise and derision by the British public, with the *North China Herald* commenting that "it is evident that Mr Hall has not much experience yet of the dark ways and vain tricks of the Chinese." It criticized his decision for saying that Main was trespassing inside the shop when the assault had occurred outside the shop.

A few days later, Hall made a statement in court that he had now found that the assault had occurred outside and not inside the shop. He said that this had not been mentioned by either party during the trial. As a consequence of the assault occurring outside the premises, Main had not been trespassing in Chao's shop. Therefore, the force used by Chao against Main was not justified. Hall said he should not have convicted Main and that he had arranged for the fine to be waived. The *North China Herald* greeted this public admission of a mistake with an article saluting Hall for his bravery and stating that he has "raised himself greatly in the estimation of all who can appreciate such a manly outspoken confession."

Hall and Jamiesons' times in Shanghai and Yokohama were otherwise uneventful. When Hannen returned from long leave in November 1889, both returned to their respective consular services.

Wilkinson, on the other had, started out on a very eventful career as Crown Advocate in Shanghai.

---

14 *R v David Main*, Case: *North China Herald*, June 29, 1888, p843; Hall retraction: North China Herald July 7, 1888, p21; Editorial: *North China Herald*, July 7, 1888, p7.

CHAPTER 18

Chinese Demand Justice

SOON AFTER HIS APPOINTMENT as Crown Advocate in 1882, another killing by a Customs Officer in Canton handed Wilkinson his first big case. First, he had to travel to Canton to prosecute the officer, James Logan, for murder. Then, the next year, he returned as a British Commissioner to clean up the aftermath of the killing, which had led to large-scale riots in the city. During the riots, the rioters took over the foreign settlement on Shameen Island and destroyed many foreign warehouses and properties.

Logan and a group of four or five other Customs officers had been put aboard a ship, the *Kiangping* off Macao on August 11, 1883. They had remained on board almost all day as the ship sailed upriver to Canton and searched the ship until midnight. They had not eaten all day and, after completing their search, went to Hing-Kee Tea House, in Honam where they were based. Honam was a local area well away from the Shameen settlement. They had food and beer and went back to their house where they played cards and drank until 6 o'clock in the morning. About 18 foreign Customs officers lived in the area and one of them had, on a number of occasions, insulted a Chinese woman living in the tea house. This had led to bad relations between the Customs Officers and the locals. Logan himself had also complained to the District Magistrate about the performance of a watchman. This had resulted in the watchman being flogged. Logan's son had been told by some Chinese a few day previously that they were going to take Logan and his son's heads soon.[1]

As Logan and the party of drinkers passed the tea house, a large crowd formed. Logan was fearful that they were going to be mobbed. The party went back to Logan's house where they got two revolvers. Logan said that he intended to use the revolvers to scare the mob. When the customs officers returned, up to 1,000 people were on the street and they started throwing stones. One officer was hit in the ankle and another on his body.

Logan fired his revolver. He hit a young boy as well as a woman and an old man. The crowd dispersed and the officers quickly returned to their homes. Three of them were subsequently arrested and locked up in the British consular gaol. One was Norwegian and he was taken before his Consul. The other was a Russian Finn, and having no Consul in Canton appeared before the British Consul. After further investigation, the Norwegian and Russian suspects were released.

The young boy died and so, allegedly, did the woman. To settle the matter, the District Magistrate gave the uncle of the boy $100, and the woman (who was in fact still alive) and the man $30 each. This did not satisfy the shopkeepers who put up posters demanding Logan's head.

On September 10, 1883 matters came to a head when a Portuguese watchman on board a Portuguese ship, the *Hankow*, killed a Chinese by kicking him and then throwing him in the water. A mob first burnt down the wharf where the *Hankow* was docked. The *Hankow* withdrew to the safety of the river. The mob of up to 1,000 Chinese then attacked the foreign settlement in Shameen Island at 8 o'clock in the morning looting all that could be carried away and burning down foreigners' offices and houses. The telegraph cables to Hong Kong had been cut so no gunboats could be called. Women and children were evacuated to two merchant boats the

1 Background to the case from the *North China Herald*, September 14, 1883, p321 and September 28, 1883, p377 and October 7, 1883, p443.

The rioting in Canton. 1. Chinese looting the Foreign Settlement. 2. A house in the foreign settlement being burnt. 3. Viceroy's soldiers defending Shameen.

Ningpo and the *Hankow* that were moored off Shameen. The foreign men armed themselves to fight off the mob. A small force of Chinese troops arrived at 11 o'clock in the morning but was too small to restore order. At about 1 o'clock in the afternoon a battalion of Chinese troops arrived "with the ling ki or warrant flag, which, after being held up in presence of the mob, authorizes the military to fire upon any rioters who refuse to disperse." According to the *North China Herald's* correspondent, the blowing of the mandarin's horn acted like magic, and they fled in all directions helter skelter." After the mob left, a "sad scene was presented at Shameen" with 13 houses burned down and four others looted. The newly-built icehouse and the Concordia Club were also destroyed. The US consul estimated that total losses were in the order of $200,000 of which only $10,000 was the property of US citizens. The main losses were to British properties.

After this, foreigners would be molested on the streets and whenever a foreigner passed the words "Fan-Kwei" ("barbaric ghost") would be shouted at them. The Viceroy issued a reward of $50 for the apprehension of anyone inciting violence

The docks in Shameen in 1883

against foreigners. The British Minister, Sir Harry Parkes, sent the Viceroy a telegram stating that the lives and properties of British subjects were in the Viceroy's hands and that "if any more riotous attacks take place, the consequences will be most disastrous for China." This prompted the Viceroy to arrest upwards of one hundred rioters who were dealt with in a "summary way." He subsequently issued a proclamation that anyone who so much as assaulted a foreigner would be decapitated. Gunboats were stationed in the river and a code of signals was arranged between the British Consulate and the gunboats in case of attack with landing parties at the ready to land within five minutes of the first alarm.

A month later, Logan was put on trial for murder of the boy he had shot. Rennie, as Judge, and H.S. Wilkinson, as Crown Advocate, travelled to Canton for the trial. The first day was very short because Logan had not instructed a lawyer to defend him. It appeared that he thought the customs service would provide him with counsel, but as the killing had nothing to do with Logan's official duties, Customs had not done so.

Wilkinson and Rennie went back to Hong Kong and re-turned to Canton two weeks later. Logan had instructed Mr A.G. Wise, a barrister from Hong Kong who later became a judge of the Hong Kong Supreme Court, to represent him. J.J. Francis (who had prosecuted the Edward Page case) from Hong Kong was instructed to watch the case on behalf of the Viceroy. Taotai Pang, representing the Viceroy, sat on the bench to the left of Rennie and Mr Popoff from the Russian Consulate at Foochow sat on Rennie's right. Popoff was there to represent his interests of the Russian Finn who had been involved in the shooting.[2]

The trial was conducted in a room at the British Consul-ate that was far too small to be used effectively as a court. The larger room that had been used for the Page case had been taken over by the Vice-Consul. The jurors were seques-tered in a room in the consulate for the length of the trial. The Chinese witnesses were also kept in a separate room so as to keep them from hearing what other witnesses had said. It was, however, reported that notes were passed to them of the evidence that had been given.

Wilkinson called numerous Chinese and foreign witnesses to the events that had occurred to show essentially that the boy had died; that Logan had fired a gun; and that no one else had fired a gun. Wise, in defence, emphasized that all the events that had occurred after the shooting should be put out of the jury's mind. They should only consider the evidence before the court. He said that the jury had to be certain that Logan fired the shot to convict him.

Logan was acquitted by the jury of murder but convicted of manslaughter. Rennie though it was murder: in sentencing commented that Logan "might congratulate himself he had not been convicted of the higher crime of murder." Given that

2   *R v Logan, The China Mail* September 26, 27 28 and 29, 1883. The jury members were R. Howie, K.D. Adams, N Komberg, G.D. Fearon and C.J. La Frentz.

there appeared to be no self-defence involved, Rennie sentenced him to a relatively long term of seven years imprisonment. Because there was no long-term accommodation for prisoners in Canton, Logan was sent to Hong Kong, where he had previously been a policeman, for imprisonment. The fact that he was found guilty satisfied the locals briefly, until they discovered that the penalty was not death but imprisonment. The Viceroy formally protested the verdict and requested a new trial. He also intimated that he could not be responsible for any outbreak that occurred due to the result of the case. He, however, did issue a proclamation asking for calm because he had protested the verdict and asked for a new trial.

The British took the Chinese complaints seriously. Julian Pauncefote, the former Attorney General of Hong Kong and now Permanent Under-Secretary of the Foreign Office reviewed the file personally. He thought the sentence was far too lenient and that Logan should have been sentenced to at least 20 years in prison, a view that the Law Officers in London concurred with.[3]

Long discussions subsequently went on between the foreign powers and Tsungli Yamen as to how to settle the claims for damages from the riot.[4] Originally, it was proposed that the issue be resolved by a panel of arbitrators. Discussions went quite a way forward with John Russell Young the American Minister leading the discussions on behalf of the British, Americans, French and Germans. But the Chinese side through Prince Kung then insisted:

"it having originated in murder, an investigation into
the circumstances of the riot should be the objective
point. These circumstances being correct, the guilty

3   P.D. Coates, *The China Consuls*, p170.

4   United States Foreign Correspondence 1883-84, in particular, note from John Russell Young to Mr Frelinghuysen dated January 6, 1883 and Inclosure 4, a note from Prince Kung to foreign ministers dated November 23, 1883.

parties could be punished according to their desserts."

Prince Kung, with whom it may be recalled Hornby had discussed due process and the separation of powers, was effectively demanding that Logan be re-tried and then executed.[5] It seems that, perhaps, the prince had not been listening as attentively to Hornby as Hornby imagined.

Young told the Chinese that the Logan case could not be reopened. Logan "had been tried by an English judge, before an English jury, according to English law, and there was no power, not even the power of the Queen which could put him in peril of his life a second time." Young said that the same law applied in the United States and "other civilized nations" and it was not appropriate to mix up the question of the losses suffered by foreigners and whether Logan had received his "just desserts." The Chinese would not budge. In a meeting with Young they said that because a British subject, Logan, had caused the riot by killing an innocent Chinese, it was the British who were responsible and they should pay the damages claimed by the foreigners, pointing out that China had paid an indemnity when Augustus Margary had been killed. Eventually, after further internal discussions, the Tsungli Yamen offered to return to their original position but insisted the arbitration board also consider the indemnity to be paid to the slain boy's family. The British Minister, Sir Harry Parkes, refused to allow this, although he indicated that the British would be willing to consider an act of grace payment. This was not viewed as sufficient and as a result, the proposal for an arbitration board was not taken further.

Ultimately, the British and Chinese agreed to establish a joint Commission to decide on British claims arising out of the riots to sit in Canton. Crown Adovcate H.S. Wilkinson was appointed to sit as the British Commissioner and Mr Kung Fan-

---

5 See Chapter 4 for Hornby's discussion with Prince Kung.

tai was appointed to sit as the Chinese Commissioner. The
Commission commenced hearings in August 1884. This was
a time of great tension in Canton because the French and the
Chinese were coming very close to war over rights in Tonkin,
Vietnam. The Chinese claimed suzerainty over Vietnam; the
French rejected this. One correspondent for the *North China
Herald* reported on the situation in early August 1884:

> "Of late this feeling of hatred to foreigners has been
> growing in intensity, owing to the Franco-Chinese dif-
> ficulty, and matters have looked so threatening that for-
> eigners have at length deemed it advisable to prepare a
> plan of defence in case of attack by the mob, and also a
> plan of retreat to the foreign men-of-war in the anchor-
> age in case of necessity."[6]

The correspondent also reported that the town had been
"placarded all over with inflammatory appeals to the Chinese
to rise and kill all the 'foreign devils.'" Gatling guns had been
brought on shore to defend the British and French settlements
and all foreign Customs employees were ordered to leave
Honam.

Into this cauldron of hatred and fear sailed Wilkinson
to sit with Mr Kung to decide the claims from the previous
year. The British Consul and Vice-Consul in Canton, Dr H.F.
Hance and Robert Mansfield as well as Sit Min Kook the former magistrate of the Namhoi District also sat on the bench.[7]
The Chinese government instructed Victor Deacon, as solicitor from Hong Kong, to represent them. The firm of Deacons
in Hong Kong, which still exists to this day, is named after
Victor and his nephew. Some of the claimants represented
themselves whilst others were represented by counsel. From

6   *North China Herald*, August 15, 1884, p185.

7   Reports on the hearings of the Commission are in the *North China Herald*, August 22,
1884, p220 and August 29, 1884, p248.

the reports of the cases, it appears that the claims work went relatively smoothly. The procedure was semi-judicial and semi-"market bargaining." The British claimants would make the claims detailing items lost and their value. Deacon then cross-examined the claimants as to their value. An offer of compensation would then be made by the commissioners. The claimants were free to reject this and to make a counter-offer. In one case, involving a Dr Wales who had lost his entire house and contents, including his 200-volume medical library, his total claim came to approximately $15,000. After cross-examination, Deacon put the value of the claim at about $10,000. Following an adjournment, Dr Wales' counsel said that he had been instructed to accept $12,000 but may be able to meet the commissioners half way. This resulted in a "somewhat lengthy private discussion between the commissioners and other occupants of the bench" which resulted in the offer being raised to $11,000, which was accepted. Other claims proceeded in a like manner.

One claim for damages to the ship the *Ningpo*, by its owners was rejected. Wilkinson told the owner's counsel, Mr Schroeder, that if the *Ningpo* had left immediately it would have left with no cargo. It would not have been able to claim compensation for leaving without cargo. As it was, after calm had been restored it had taken on cargo and, therefore, the claim ought not to be met. The other claim the *Ningpo* had was for $120 for provisions they had used to feed the people of Shameen. Wilkinson said "he was sure that neither the owners of the ship nor any persons concerned would wish him to ask the Chinese Government to pay $120 for feeding the Shameen community." In fact, Mr Schroeder did want to ask for this but Wilkinson cut him off when he started speaking. This brought the claims process to a close after only two days of hearings mainly, it seems, due to the close cooperation between the Chinese and British commissioners. One suspects that Wilkinson had a strong desire to be cooperative so that he could get in and out of Canton as quickly as possible without his work triggering further riots.

The French and Chinese did go to war soon after this, with the French attacking Foochow and Zhenhai Bay, occupying Keelung in Taiwan and blockading Taiwan. The Chinese agreed in April 1885, in another unequal treaty, to abandon their claim to suzerainty over Vietnam and withdraw troops they had sent there.

Compromised by the compradore

Despite the complaints of the Chinese government, Chinese businessmen, in at least two cases, were willing to seek justice in the British courts, although it appears in both cases they were looking for deep foreign pockets to cover losses caused by dealings with other Chinese. It could not be said, however, that the foreign defendants were completely blameless in either matter. In China, most foreign companies did not deal directly with local Chinese. Instead they made purchases from middlemen, or compradores, who would be responsible for handling business with local Chinese. The reasons for doing business this way were varied. Some related to language and culture - it was much easier for a compradore to deal in the Chinese language with locals. Some related to local business practices: the compradores could be members of local guilds and could use the guilds to enforce agreements. The compradores, as

A caricature of a compradore from the Eastern Sketch

Chinese, may also have other methods for collecting debts not available to foreigners. The existence of extraterritoriality where foreigners were subject to one legal jurisdiction and Chinese another almost certainly also encouraged the use of compradores. Foreigners who could be easily sued in their own courts but who had great difficulty suing in local courts almost certainly did not want to contract directly with locals. The compradores were generally required to put up substantial bonds by foreign trading houses to guarantee they would perform their contracts.

The first two major cases to consider the position of compradores involved the case of Hoo Mei Pin a compradore of the large British trading house, David Sassoon & Co.[8] Hoo operated a shop in Tientsin and had a large sign outside his shop saying "Lao-Sha-Soon" meaning Sassoon in English. He was also a compradore for a firm, Collins, and had a sign for them outside his shop as well. He also carried out a large amount of business on his own account using, as was the custom at the time, the receipts and forms of his principals, Sassoons and Collins.

Hoo went bankrupt. Two court actions were brought against the Sassoons as a result of business that had been done with Hoo. Both were for the sale to him of gold in November 1883 by a Wang Gan-ying and a Wu Yu-shan. Wang first brought action against the Sassoons in the Tientsin Provincial Court. The case was tried by the Consul, A. Davenport, with two British businessmen in Tientsin sitting as assessors. Wang's case was that receipts had been issued with the Sassoons' name on it and that the Sassoons were unable to pay him. The Sassoons' defence was that this was a deal with the compradore only; they had received no gold; that the Plaintiff had, in fact, com-

---

8   *Sassoon v Wong*, Privy Council Decision of December 12, 1885; *Wu v Sassoon, North China Herald*, May 1, 1885, p512-3 (judgment); 18 April 1885 (argument); T. Jernigan, *China in Law and Commerce*, p273 (Henderson's quotes come from this source). Motono Eiichi tells the story of these cases in detail in "A Study of the Legal Status of Compradors in the 1880s", Chinese Business Enterprises, Vol 2, R. Amplalaranan (ed).

promised their claim with the compradore by accepting some boxes of needles; and that the claim had only been made three months after the fact when it was clear the compradore could not make good his debt. Consul Davenport, against the advice of the assessors, found in favour of Wang, on the basis that the receipts were in the name of the Sassoons. Mr Henderson, who sat as one of the assessors on the trial in Tientsin, said later that it was "well known that compradores trade largely on their own account and use the seals or chops of their foreign employers for their private business chits; such chops are used also for business receipts and agreements." He added that "he never knew or heard of a compradore in foreign employ using a separate stamp or seal from that of his foreign employers, even for his own business."

The case was appealed to Richard Rennie in Shanghai who, in November 1884, after effectively re-trying the case also found in favour of Wang despite evidence from Hoo that he had entered the transaction on his own account. He held that if the principal allowed a compradore to use his chop that it was as good as a signature and the principal should be bound. The Sassoons appealed to the Privy Council.

Before that appeal could be heard, given Wang's success before Rennie, Mr Wu filed a case directly to the Supreme Court in Shanghai. The case came on for trial before Mowat in April 1885. The facts of the case were almost identical with Wang's case. Wu did not spare any expense, hiring, H.S. Wilkinson as his lawyer. R.E. Wainewright acted for the Sassoons. Wu called one witness on his behalf who claimed to have delivered the gold to a Mr Shekury of Sassoons. Mr Shekury gave evidence that he had never received the gold. Hoo, the Sassoons' compradore, also told the court that he had dealt with the gold on his own account. He said that he had settled the claims by paying one third of the value to Wang and Wu. They, however, believed that he had more money. Hoo said that he thought Wang and Wu had brought action against "the foreigners" to put pressure on him to pay. If he was jailed for owing money to Chinese he could pay security to get out of jail. If he was jailed for owing money to foreigners he may not be able to pay security to get out.

Mowat in giving judgment said that it was a very simple case of credibility. Should he believe the plaintiff who said he thought he was dealing with the defendant or should he believe the defendant who said it had had nothing to do with the transaction? Mowat said that, ultimately, and despite Wilkinson's able argument, it was absolutely clear Wu was dealing with the compradore directly. All of his actions after the compradore went bankrupt pointed to the contract being with the compradore. He did not approach the Sassoons. "His action, on the contrary, was that of a Chinese creditor dealing with a Chinese debtor — making a descent on his establishment, watching the premises to prevent goods being taken away, and laying hold of all he could get to reduce the amount of the debt." It was only after he found that a bank share that he had been given as payment was less valuable than he thought that he brought action against the Sassoons. Tellingly, in his pleadings, Wu had claimed to have delivered the gold to the Sassoons but in court his witness had said the gold had been delivered to the compradore. With regards to receipts for the gold that had been chopped with the Sassoon name, Mowat found that this was merely done to indicate receipt at the compradore's place of business. Mowat, therefore, dismissed the case.

The Privy Council also handed down a decision on the appeal to it, overturning Rennie's decision on the basis that the receipts were not sufficient evidence that the transaction was with the Sassoons and that it was "a story not very probable" that the Sassoons were unable to pay.

The next challenge for the court was to come from outside China as a new Order in Council expanded the court's jurisdiction.

CHAPTER 19

Enlarging Jurisdiction

THE MID 1880s SAW the jurisdiction of the British courts in East Asia enlarged in two ways. The first was the signing of treaties providing for extraterritorial rights in Korea. The second was an expansion of the courts' jurisdiction over certain individuals who were not Britsh subjects.

A treaty with Korea

While China and Japan had been forced to open to trade in the 1840s and 1850s, for many years the opening of Korea was not seen as a major issue for America or Great Britain and no serious efforts were made to seek trading rights until the 1880s.

The United States entered into a Treaty of Commerce with Korea in 1882 which provided for extraterritorial rights. Great Britain obtained extraterritorial rights the next year in 1883 under a Treaty of Friendship and Commerce which was signed in Hanyang on 26 November 1883. Ratifications were exchanged, also in Hanyang, on 28 April 1884. The treaties were not signed after a show of force or, even a threat of force. Korea knew it had no power to fight the foreign powers and did not even try to.

The British and American treaties granted extraterritorial rights along the lines of those already agreed with China and Japan. For the United States, consular officers in Korea conducted trials in the same way as was done in China and Japan but without any unified court structure covering the three countries.

In the case of Britain, Korea was brought under the jurisdiction of the Supreme Court at Shanghai. As in China, first instance cases could be brought directly to a provincial court in Korea with an appeal to Shanghai. Cases could also be filed directly to the Supreme Court.

In order to implement these changes, an Order in Council was enacted with effect from October 1, 1884. Under the new Order in Council the Supreme Court at Shanghai was given the same power over the provincial courts in Korea as it had over the courts in Japan and it was provided that "all powers and jurisdiction ... which can be exercised by the Supreme Court ... in relation to Japan ... shall be exercisable in relation to Corea."[1]

It soon emerged that this provision created uncertainty because it ignored the fact that the Court for Japan had been created as an intermediate court between the Provincial Courts in Japan and the Supreme Court in Shanghai. The Supreme Court at Shanghai did not have totally unfettered jurisdiction in Japan. It also raised the possibility that the Court for Japan now had jurisdiction in Korea. H.S. Wilkinson, as Crown Advocate, was asked to advise on this latter point. He answered it did not because jurisdiction had to be expressly conferred and could not be conferred by implication. The Foreign Office, however, also questioned whether the Order in Council gave the Supreme Court original jurisdiction for trial of serious cases. In order to solve these problems, a second Order in Council was issued in 1886. This provided that any powers that could be exercised by the Supreme Court in Shanghai or the Court for Japan in Yokohama in relation to Japan could be exercised by the Supreme Court in relation to Korea.[2]

---

1 Article 4(3) Japan, China and Corea, Order in Council, 1884, *London Gazette*, 1 July 1884, p2991.

2 FO 656/53 letter dated November 25, 1885; PRONI D1292/M1/10 (Wilkinson Papers) Memorandum on Jurisdiction in Corea from H.S. Wilkinson dated November 23, 1885; For the amending OIC, see, *London Gazette*, April 6, 1886, p1665.

Extended jurisdiction

The new 1884 Order In Council also expanded the jurisdiction of British courts in Asia in two important ways. First, the definition of British subject was extended to include "a British protected person" and second, jurisdiction in admiralty was extended to any act committed on board a British ship anywhere in the world, and not just within 100 miles of the coast of China, Japan or Korea. The first change was, as we shall see later, to have far-reaching effects on the rights of individuals from British protectorates or foreigners enrolled in the British army.

More immediately, however, it provided a solution to the question of who had jurisdiction over British sailors on American ships and American sailors on British ships that had arisen in the Ross case. The issue was resolved in two cases that Wilkinson prosecuted before Rennie. The first case, tried in Shanghai, related to an affray that had occurred on the *Lennie Burrill*, a British ship based out of Yarmouth, Nova Scotia.[3] At the committal hearing, the jurisdiction of the court was challenged on the basis the fight had occurred far out to sea and that some members of the crew were American. However, George Jamieson, sitting as Acting Assistant Judge while Robert Mowat was on leave, pointed out the amendment to the Order in Council had extended the court's admiralty jurisdiction to acts committed at sea anywhere. As seaman on a British ship the crew were "protected persons." He held that the court had jurisdiction.

One of the seamen charged, George Lee, was an American. He was defended by Mr Latham. Lee pleaded not guilty so that he could challenge before Rennie, the Chief Justice, the jurisdiction of the court to try him. This raised a technical procedural question. In order to decide if Lee was or was not a British subject it would be necessary to empanel a jury

3   *R v Lee*, Committal hearing: *North China Herald*, December 29, 1886, p700 and January 5, 1887, p5; Trial: *North China Herald*, January 19, 1887, p73.

to try the case and to decide if he was British or American or otherwise subject to the jurisdiction of the court. The issue was a complex one; in British courts until 1898, the defendant in a criminal case could not give evidence on their own behalf, so Lee would not be able to give evidence himself as to his citizenship. Wilkinson and Latham came up with a solution. Wilkinson offered to admit that Lee was an American citizen for the purposes of determining jurisdiction provided Latham admitted that Lee was a sailor on a British ship. This was agreed.

Rennie disposed of the argument quickly. He said that while before the new order had been enacted there was an argument as to the jurisdiction of the British Courts in China and Japan over seaman on British ships, "he was clearly of opinion that under the new Order, the prisoner came within the jurisdiction of the Court." He noted that a representative of the United States Consul-General was in court and that correspondence had been sent to the American Consulate about the case. The American Consul-General had responded, stating, "they could not interfere in the case, in which the Court had proper jurisdiction." Rennie concluded that he was certain the British Supreme Court had jurisdiction. Lee then changed his plea to one of guilty to unlawful wounding and was sentenced by Rennie to 12 months hard labour.

Two years later, Rennie and Wilkinson sailed to Amoy to try an American sailor, John Liscom, on a British ship, the *Loongwha*, for the manslaughter of a Chinese crew member, Bin-ziok. Liscom had found a number of Chinese crew members smoking opium and tried to get them to stop and go onshore by throwing acid into the room. He had ended up in a fight with Bin-Ziok who died later from his injuries. Mr W. Crowell, the United States Consul in Amoy, appeared at the hearing and said, "inasmuch as the alleged offence was committed on board a British vessel, the American authorities declined to exercise jurisdiction over him."

The trial then proceeded before a jury with Mr Crowell, who was also a lawyer, defending. A number of Chinese and foreign witnesses were called. In opening the defence case, Crowell told the jury what he understood to be the English law in relation to Liscom giving evidence:

> "He is in such a position that he cannot himself give any account of what occurred on the night of 12th June. His mouth is closed by law."

Rennie corrected him. In England a practice had arisen of allowing an accused to make an unsworn statement from the dock. Rennie said:

> "Not altogether, Mr. Crowell. Of late years it has been a practice of many judges at home to allow prisoners to make statement if they desire to do so. It is entirely in the discretion of the judge, but I have always, since the practice has arisen in England, allowed prisoners who so desire to make a statement at the conclusion of the case for the defence."

At the end of the case, Liscom did make a long statement explaining he had no intention to kill Bin-ziok and that he "did not know the man was hurt until the morning." Rennie in summing up commented on Liscom's unsworn statement:

> "I am glad to see that it is the practice in England to take the statements of prisoners for what they are worth, but it is questionable whether in the majority of cases such statements inure to the prisoner's benefit or not. Here, it would seem, that so far from it strengthening his case, it seems rather to strengthen the case for the prosecution."

In closing and summing up both Wilkinson and Rennie praised Mr Crowell's advocacy skills. Rennie, however, made it very clear to the jury that he considered Liscom was guilty of manslaughter. After retiring for 15 minutes the jury convicted Liscom of the lesser charge of unlawful wounding.[4] Rennie impose a tough sentence of two years imprisonment in Hong Kong "to act as a deterrent against men in your position acting in a similar way."

The extension of admiralty jurisdiction also brought a case a few years later before Nicholas Hannen in Japan which revealed the very real dangers faced by mariners in the days before radio communication. Captain Pyne of the seal-hunting schooner, the *Arctic,* appeared before Hannen accused of "involuntary marooning." The ship had spotted seals on Robben Island in the North Pacific and Pyne sent his chief mate and another member of crew to the island to see if the coast was clear. It was not. They were "pounced on by Russians" and carried off. The *Arctic* was then blown out to sea and Pyne concluded it was hopeless to try and recover the men. Pyne had no radio to call for help and no real way to get back to his men. Pyne had not tried to hide the event. He wrote it down in his own logbook. Hannen convicted Pyne and sentenced him to a fine of $25 or 14 days imprisonment in lieu.[5]

The Japanese had no concern with the British trying cases of this nature as it involved only British nationals. Another shipping case heard by Hannen in the 1880s, which did involve many Japanese nationals, caused a furore in Japan.

---

4   *R v John Liscom, North China Herald,* July 6, 1889, p25. The jury members were William Christy, George Greenhill, David R. Orr, George U. Price and John Graham.

5   *R v Pyne, North China Herald,* 29 November 1889, p653.

CHAPTER 20

Japan Demands Change

THROUGHOUT THE 1880s the Japanese worked hard to bring an end to extraterritoriality by reforming their legal system. In 1882 the new Penal Code came into effect and a Commercial Code was also being drafted in the 1880s. Japan continued its program of political and economic reform and by the end of the 1880s had elections for parliament, with limited suffrage, and its first Western Constitution.

The Captain did not go down with his ship
One case in 1886 involving a shipping accident became the *cause celebre* in Japan for the end of extraterritoriality. The case is still mentioned to this day in Japanese writings on extra-territoriality as one of the prime example of the evils of the system.[1]

On October 23, 1886, the *Normanton*, a British ship, set sail from Yokohama bound for Kobe. She had on board a British crew of 47 and 23 Japanese passengers. Somewhere off Ooshima the boat struck a pinnacle rock and started to take in water. The crew tried to convince the Japanese passengers to abandon ship but they refused. The captain and the crew took to the life rafts leaving a boatswain with the Japanese passengers to try to convince them to get into the remaining life rafts. They continued to refuse and the boatswain jumped

---

1   See R. Chang, *The Justice of Western Consular Courts in Nineteenth Century Japan*, Chapter 4 and C. Roberts, *The British Courts and Extraterritoriality in Japan*, 1859 to 1899, pp185 to 189 for background to this case.

off the ship just as it sank. All 23 Japanese passengers together with one British sailor and 12 British firemen died in the disaster.

A Naval Board of Enquiry to investigate into the causes of the disaster headed by the British Consul in Kobe and two mariners was formed. In what the *North China Herald*, normally a supporter of the British courts, was to later term a "farce", a "miscarriage of justice" and a "complete whitewash" the captain, John William Drake, was cleared of all responsibility. This was met with shocked disbelief by the Japanese public and the Japanese government and there were many public protests against the decision.

The Japanese government determined to seek to make Drake criminally liable for the deaths. John Lowder, a former consular officer now practicing as a barrister in Japan, was instructed by the Japanese government to bring a criminal prosecution against Captain Drake for manslaughter in the British Court for Japan. The *Japan Mail* called the prosecution absurd on the basis that the Naval Court of Enquiry had found that "the masters and the officers of the *Normanton* did everything in their power to save life." The findings of an enquiry, however, are not binding and it was perfectly proper to bring separate criminal proceedings.

The criminal trial commenced on December 7, 1886 before Hannen and a jury of five and lasted for five days. Henry

French artist Bigot shows Capt Drake demanding money from Japanese passengers

Lichtfield appeared as the Crown Prosecutor together with Lowder. Alfred Robinson, a solicitor from Shanghai, appeared for Drake. Various witnesses gave evidence as to what occurred including the Chief Officer and boatswain. Hannen in his instructions to the jury first dealt with a suggestion by Robinson that the Captain could not be found to be negligent if the Japanese passengers had been contributorily negligent in failing to get into the lifeboats. He said clearly this was not the law of England. The captain had the authority to and should have forced the Japanese into the lifeboats if necessary. Drake had also failed to arrange boat stations

Alfred Robinson, Capt. Drake's defence attorney

and drills and had given contradictory orders. The jury was left to answer the question as to whether this was negligent so that the death of the passengers could be considered manslaughter.[2]

The jury retired for an hour and a half and returned with a verdict of guilty. The foreman, W A Crane, however added:

> "But the Jury desire to record their sense of the difficulties of the position in which the captain was placed, aggravated by the fact of the engineers having left the ship in the port life-boat, thereby diminishing the means of saving life at his command, and also by the unwillingness, if not actual resistance, offered by the Japanese passengers to the efforts made to get them out of the alley-way towards the boats."

Following the verdict Hannen turned to Drake to sentence him saying: "that it can not but be a matter of deep regret, not only to us all, but also no doubt, to you now, that you did not take such steps as would have been more effectual towards the saving of life." He added in a true British dressing down:

2 *R v Drake, Japan Gazette* December 8, 1886 and *North China Herald* January 5, 1887, p16.

"We have been accustomed to expect from the merchant service of England heroism and devotion to the interests of the crew and passengers that I am afraid in this case were wanting."

He then passed sentence saying it was his "painful duty" to order Drake to serve three months imprisonment.

The relatives of the dead had also brought a civil case against Drake, which they withdrew after the conviction on the basis he had suffered enough. Drake in a letter from his counsel expressed his deep sympathy for the loss of life.[3]

Negotiations on the end of extraterritoriality

The timing of the *Normanton* case was unfortunate. In the mid-1880s, serious negotiations had begun between Japan and the treaty powers to bring an end to extraterritoriality. Count Inoyue, the Japanese Foreign Minister, led the negotiations for Japan. Sir Francis Plunkett, the British Minister in Japan led negotiations for the British. Nicholas Hannen was also appointed a delegate to the conference to advise on legal issues. Count Inoyue proposed that as soon as the Japanese Civil Code was enacted, consular jurisdiction should be abolished outside the treaty ports. Inside the treaty ports, consular courts could continue to operate for three years but should apply Japanese law. As a concession to foreign concerns, mixed courts would be established with Japanese and foreign judges on the bench. Also, as the biggest carrot, Japan was to be opened completely to foreign trade and residence with foreigners being able to own property. The British and Germans proposed that the mixed courts follow the model in Egypt where there was a majority of foreign judges and that all cases involving foreign parties would be heard by these courts.[4]

Once these proposals leaked in the Japanese press, the Japa-

---

3   *Japan Gazette* December 13, 1886 p 2.

4   F. Jones, *Extraterritoriality in Japan*, pp108-112.

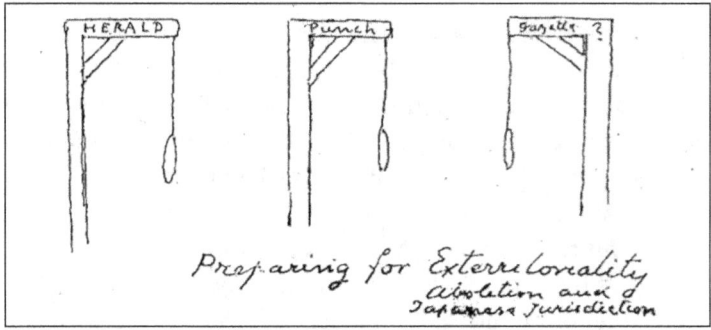

The Japan Punch's view on the end of extraterritoriality and foreign press freedom

nese public violently opposed them, particularly, with the *Normanton* case fresh in their memories. With no chance of reaching a settlement, Inoyue adjourned the negotiations in 1887.

In 1888 a new foreign minister, Count Okuma, was appointed. He decided the best way to end extraterritoriality was to negotiate with each treaty power separately. In order to create a precedent, he first entered a treaty with Mexico, who had no real interests in Japan. The treaty provided for equal treatment of subjects in each country. The same year, Japan started negotiations to end extraterritoriality in Japan with Britain, the United States and Germany.[5]

Okuma was wounded in an assassination attempt in late 1889. Viscount Aoki took over as Foreign Minister and continued the negotiations.

In order to satisfy the British that Japanese courts would be up to standard, Japan originally offered in a draft diplomatic note attached to a draft treaty to have foreign judges on their courts for at least 12 years as well as to fix a date to finalise their Criminal Code, Code of Criminal Procedure, Civil Code (including bankruptcy laws, and laws relating to shipping and bills of exchange) and Code of Civil Procedure. They also offered to translate these laws into English within

5   F. Jones, *Extraterritoriality in Japan*, pp113-117.

18 months of their being enacted.[6]

Similar terms had already been agreed with United States, Russia and Germany in unratified treaties. But the disclosure of the terms of these unratified treaties, particularly the idea of having foreign judges sitting on Japanese courts again aroused violent public opposition.

Viscount Aoki therefore proposed to the British the "withdrawal of the diplomatic notes, which would involve the renunciation of all judicial guarantees."[7] The treaties with the United States, Germany and Russia were not ratified.

The British later sent a draft treaty to the Japanese side, which still attached the two diplomatic notes providing for foreign judges and setting dates for legislation to be passed. Viscount Aoki responded with a note attaching a memorandum from the Japanese Department of Foreign Affairs setting out the reasons why it would not be possible to have foreign judges or to set dates for passing legislation. He played two trump cards which the British could not argue against: democracy and constitutionality. These were: that the new Japanese Constitution would soon come into force; there would be a democratic assembly in place and the Japanese Government could not guarantee that they would be able to have the treaty approved; and, the Japanese government could not make a stipulation as to future legislation that would interfere with "free and independent legislative functions." He added that "alienage" should not be the "chief essential qualification for office."[8]

....

6 Draft Treaty and draft diplomatic notes sent by Viscount Okabe to Marquis of Salisbury reproduced in Irish University Press, Area Studies Series, Japan Vol 3, British Parliamentary Papers, Reports, correspondence and dispatches respecting Japan 1871-1899 p296 et seq.

7 Minute of an interview with Count Aoki, the Japanese Minister of Foreign Affairs and Her Majesty's Minister on 27 December 1889. Reproduced in Irish University Press, Area Studies Series, Japan Vol 3, British Parliamentary Papers, Reports, correspondence and dispatches respecting Japan 1871-1899 p322; see also note from Marquis of Salisbury to Mr Fraser on January 16, 1890, at p321.

8 Note from Aoki dated February 28, 1890; Ministry note dated February 8, 1890. Reproduced in Irish University Press, Area Studies Series, Japan Vol 3, British Parliamen-

Aoki did, however, seek to allay British fears:

"Assuming that the amended Treaties are brought into operation within the ensuing year, a simple calculation will show that when Consular jurisdiction is finally abolished, and Japanese jurisdiction in respect of foreigners loses its facultative characteristics, the new order of things will be met by judicial organization of nearly a quarter of a century's existence; by a system of codified Criminal Laws of 16 years' standing; and finally by a Bench in the selection of which the principle of competitive examination will have exercised a controlling influence for twelve years, and the perfect independence and permanency of which will have been constitutionally guaranteed for six years."

Aoki assured the British that no case of final appeal involving foreigners would be heard except by a court the majority of which will be well grounded in the principles of Western Jurisprudence.

The British eventually accepted this but requested that while the treaty be signed as soon as possible, its coming into force be delayed five years so the operation of the new legal system could be observed. Aoki wrote to Fraser in 1890 that this could be accepted as a basis for negotiation.[9] However, soon after this a new Japanese Government was formed and Aoki and other members of the Japanese Committee for Treaty Revision retired.

It would not be for another three years until serious discussions on treaty revision recommenced. Before then, the British courts in China and Japan would see a number of chages.

....

tary Papers, Reports, correspondence and dispatches respecting Japan 1871-1899 p322; see also note from Marquis of Salisbury to Mr Fraser on January 16. 1890, at p343 to 350.

9   Reproduced in Irish University Press, Area Studies Series, Japan Vol 3, British Parliamentary Papers, Reports, correspondence and dispatches respecting Japan 1871-1899 p359.

CHAPTER 21

A New Arrival And A Fond Farewell

On November 21, 1890, a young man who had been born in Yokohama 24 years before sat in the British Supreme Court for China and Japan in Shanghai, waiting for Chief Justice Richard Rennie to deliver judgement in an admiralty case between P&O and the Shanghai Tug Boat Co relating to a collision that had occurred at night on the Huangpu River.[1]

The youngster was Hiram Parkes Wilkinson, son of Hiram Shaw Wilkinson, the Crown Advocate. The day was about to mark the start of a career of a man who was to have a deep involvement in the court and British extraterritorial justice in Asia for the next 43 years. As we have seen, H.P. Wilkinson has been born while his father was a student interpreter in Japan and had been named after Harry Parkes, the British Minister in Japan at the time. Because of this he was generally known as Harrie.

Harrie had taken a B.A. in law from Exeter College, Oxford. He had been called to the bar of the Middle Temple in 1889 and for a short period of time practiced on the Western Circuit, which covers South and South West England. He had done well at university obtaining third class honours in jurisprudence and a 100-guinea studentship in Roman law, trinity term, 1887 and a scholarship in Roman law and equity.

Just before Rennie gave judgment in the shipping case, H.S. Wilkinson, as a very proud father, applied for leave for

---

1   *The Fuhlee, North China Herald,* November 21, 1890, p693-694.

his son to be admitted to practice before the Supreme Court for China and Japan. He briefly recited Harrie's personal history, including where he had taken his degree and his practice on the Western circuit.[2] Rennie then admitted Harrie and said:

> "I am very glad to welcome Mr Hiram Parkes Wilkinson as your son and as a member of my own circuit; and I am also very glad that a gentleman who has taken such high honours in the examinations at the Bar has come to practice in this Court."

Harrie Wilkinson immediately commenced practice with his father.

A drunken German?

Harrie Wilkinson's first case in Shanghai was not in a British court, but in the German Consular Court. August Otto Schuffenhauer, had been accused of being drunk at the Lyceum Theater and assaulting a police officer, Sergeant Ross of the Shanghai Municipal Police. After being charged, Schuffenhauer brought a criminal complaint against Ross for assault and against another policeman, Inspector Reed, for assault and false imprisonment arising out of the incident. Because Ross and Reed were British, the case had to be heard in the British Police Court. Harrie appeared there as well.

The hearings in the German Consular Court lasted two days before Vice Consul-General von Loehr and two assessors, Messrs Aug Ehlers and Gustav Sierich.[3]

On the evening of Saturday December 6, Schuffenhauer was watching a play at the Lyceum Theatre on Museum Road (Huchu Road), one street back from the British Consulate. As there were no seats available, he was standing at the back of the theatre. Another patron had gotten very drunk and made

2   "H.G.M.'s Consular Court" *North China Herald*, November 21 1890, p693-694 .

3   *North China Herald*, December 12, 1890, pp732-733.

a disturbance. A Mr Holliday went outside and fetched Sergeant Ross to deal with the drunkard. In the meantime, the man had fallen asleep under some seats. Ross said later that a ticket-seller had pointed out Schuffenhauer as the drunk. Ross went up to him and, according to Ross, "tapped him on the shoulder" and asked him to be quiet. A German Inspector of the police, Obaldo Kluth, who was also at the theatre watching the performance, came up to Ross. Kluth said in court that he asked (but probably more correctly, he ordered) Ross to leave, which Ross did. Schuffenhauer was well known to Kluth who had been with the SMP for 15 years. Schuffenhauer held a high position in Shanghai society. He was a member of the Shanghai Club, a steward of the Shanghai Race Club and also sang (baritone) with the Shanghai Philharmonic Society.[4]

Schuffenhauer said that Ross had shaken him and tried to drag him out of the theatre before Inspector Kluth intervened. Schuffenhauer was very upset by this treatment. Shanghai Police were there to protect the upper crust; not push them around. He went out to the lobby, found Ross and asked him why he had assaulted him. Ross said that he had not assaulted him. Schuffenhauer then put his hand on Ross and shook him, asking him if this was an assault. Schuffenhauer then alleged that Ross hit him. Ross denied this. A number of Schuffenhauer's friends intervened and took Schuffenhauer away. They retired to the Shanghai Club, at the south end of the English Bund, where, after discussions and perhaps a few drinks, it was agreed Schuffenhauer should go to the Central Police Station to report the incident. Schuffenhauer made his

---

4   The report does not mention that Kluth was German, but Kluth was married in 1883 at the German Consulate-General, meaning that he was German (See *North China Herald*, 28 February 1883, p221); see also *R v Perry and Adler*, *North China Herald*, July 31, 1891, p160 where Kluth was referred to as "German Inspector Kluth." For Schuffenhauer's position in society, the case report mentions him retiring to the Shanghai Club after the incident. See *North China Herald*, March 20, 1891 pp344-345 for a report of his splendid baritone singing, ironically, in the Lyceum theatre; and *North China Herald*, March 1, 1889, p248 for his position as a steward of the Shanghai Race Club. He was also in 1889 a member of the committee for the Shanghai Horse Dog and Poultry Show Society, *North China Herald*, May 11, 1889, p576.

The Lyceum Theatre on Museum Road when it closed

way to the Central Police Station, which was nearby on Foochow Road (Fuzhou Road). Inspector Reed was on duty that night. Ross had arrived only a few minutes early to report the incident as well. Reed refused to take Schuffenhauer's statement "because he was drunk" and asked him to return in the morning. Schuffenhauer left. Reed, however, soon locked him up until 4am for "making a noise outside the station."

Quite a number of police officers had been on duty at the theatre that night. A large collection of foreigners, some drunken, would have been very attractive to pickpockets and petty thieves. A number of the officers, including a uniformed officer who was with Ross, a plain clothes detective, and an Indian constable all gave evidence supporting Ross that Schuffenhauer was drunk and had assaulted Ross. Inspector Kluth gave evidence that Schuffenhauer had sat down quietly after he had spoken to him. Most importantly, he made no mention of Schuffenhauer being drunk. A number of lay witnesses, including Mr Holliday the original complainant about drunken behaviour, gave evidence on behalf of Schuffenhauer saying that he was sober, but "very angry." Given Schuffenhauer's position in society and, most notably, that Inspector Kluth had not supported his fellow officers in their testimony that Schuffenhauer was drunk, it is no surprise that the German court acquitted Schuffenhauer. The Vice-Consul, in a long judgment, made a particular point of censuring Inspector Reed for his actions in locking up Schuffenhauer.

The next day, Harrie Wilkinson appeared in the British Police Court, before Robert Mowat, sitting as Magistrate, in the case of *R v Ross and Reed*, a private criminal prosecution brought by Mr Schuffenhauer.[5] Ross was charged with assault; Reed with assault and false imprisonment. Wilkinson applied for leave to withdraw the charges on the basis that the charges had been brought to clear his name; his acquittal in the German Consular Court had, in Schuffenhauer's estimation achieved this goal and he did not want "to proceed vindictively against Inspector Reed and Sergt. Ross." Schuffenhauer had, therefore, instructed Wilkinson to apply to the court for leave to withdraw the summonses. Wilkinson added that Schuffenhauer had asked him to place the facts of the case before the Municipal Council. Mr Schuffenhauer was happy for the Council to deal with the matter.

Mowat gave leave to withdraw the summons adding that: "it was in everyway desirable that, when a matter had been gone into one court and adjudicated upon, that there should be no further proceedings of the same nature in respect of it in another Court." A fair enough statement, except that Ross and Reed were not subject to the jurisdiction of the German Consular Court who could only censure them and not punish them.

Finding a bride

H.S. Wilkinson was determined that Harrie find himself a wife in Shanghai. On landing his father said him:

> "You must give a fortnight of your time during which you will call with me on every lady in the Settlement you are likely to meet again."[6]

Harrie then recalled:

---

5   *R v Ross & Reed*, *North China Herald*, December 12, 1890, p732.

6   H.P. Wilkinson Reminiscences, *North China Herald*, October 31, 1925, p200.

"From the house of Mrs Dr Burge and Mrs A.P. Wood
in Yangtzepoo to the limit of the other side of Jessefield,
we called on, as far as I can remember, 120 ladies. Of
course, every one knew every one else, and relations
between the young people of Shanghai were practi-
cally those existing between kindly disposed cousins at
home."

Harrie did marry three years later to Rosetta Mary Little
the daughter of Dr Louis Little. Harrie and Mary were hon-
oured to be married by, Nicholas Hannen, then the Consul-
General and Chief Justice at the British Consulate. This was
followed by a service in the Trinity Cathedral where both the
Archbishop and Bishop officiated. The *North China Herald* reported that there "has certainly never been a prettier or more
largely attended wedding in which the whole community felt
so personally and so heartily interested." The new tower of
the cathedral has just been completed and a "large number of
changes were rung on the new bells when the ceremony was
finished."[7]

Richard Rennie retires
Harrie Wilkinson only practiced in Rennie's court for a very
short time. Rennie retired on a pension, less than six months
after Harrie's admission on 1 April 1891. In a farewell toast, Mr
MacGregor, Chairman of the Shanghai Municipal Council said:

"Sir Richard Rennie arrived at Shanghai in 1866. He
leaves us in 1891, having completed a quarter of a
century of service in the East. During that period he has
won the warm friendship of many and he has earned
the esteem of all. (Applause) He has tilled successively

7 *North China Herald*, October 13, 1893, p563 and The *Star*, Guernsey, November 23,
1893, (Marriage Notice).

under the Crown the positions of Crown Advocate[8],
Judge in Japan, and Chief Justice of Her Majesty's
Supreme Court for China and Japan in Shanghai
(applause), the latter since 1881. His career has been
distinguished by the highest sense of honour, which he
has made the rule of his life (applause), and the duties
of his office have been fulfilled in a manner which gave
confidence to those who had occasion to resort to his
court." (Applause)

"To use the words of an able writer the other day, "he
has earned for himself and his court the same high and
immaculate character which has thrown a halo round
the English bench." (Applause.) To laymen it was
apparent that he brought to the elucidation of cases
tried by him a keen and incisive intellect, cultivated by
careful and exact study; and his wide experience often
enabled him to detect insincerity and humbug, with
which he had no sympathy whatever (applause), while
his kindness of heart prompted ready encouragement
to diffident inexperience."

On his departure from Shanghai, he was seen off by a large
crowd. In 1895 he stood as a candidate for County Council in
the Kensington Division as well as chairing the China Association Dinner held in London on February 26 of that year.[9]

In retirement he was well regarded as a whist and bridge
player and was reported to be "one of their most trustworthy
players at both games" by "the Whist Reference Book."[10]

8   The reference to Crown Advocate is a misnomer. The position was only created in
1878 the same time the 1878 Order in Council created the position of Judge for Japan.
Rennie prosecuted a number of cases but never as Crown Advocate.

9   *North China Herald*, April 11, 1895, p540 (candidate) *North China Herald* April 11, 1895,
p562 (chair).

10 Published in 1899 by the John Yorston Publishing Company, Philadelphia. A book
that described itself as being a book "wherein information is presented concerning the
noble game, in all its aspects, after the manner of a cyclopedia, dictionary, and digest all
combined in one."

In 1896, Rennie was appointed Acting Judge of the British
Court in Constantinople to hear two cases. The first related
to alleged improper conduct by the Vice-Consul, Mr Phillip
Sarell, in obtaining a loan from the Constantinople Building
Society. The second was a civil claim brought by Henry Silley,
the former chief clerk of the Supreme Consular Court, against
Sarell, Charles Tarring, the Judge of the Supreme Consular
Court, and all the other staff of the court for conspiring to
have Silley dismissed. Because the Judge of the Supreme
Consular Court was himself a defendant in one of those actions, the Foreign Office considered it advisable to appoint a
special judge to proceed to hear the cases in Constantinople.
A special Order in Council was passed so that Rennie could
handle them. In the first case, Rennie dismissed the jury after
the case broke down. The second case did not proceed.[11]

Rennie died in Sidmouth, Devon in 1905. His obituary in
the *North China Herald* read:

> "The news, which has only reached Shanghai indirect-
> ly, of the death at home of Sir Richard Temple Rennie,
> has been received with much sorrow by those who
> have been long enough resident in the East to recall the
> brilliant legal acumen and charming social personality
> of the judge who presided over the Supreme Court here
> from 1882 till 1891."

The *Japan Mail* in their obituary said:

> "He was a man of eminently high judicial abilities
> and as a friend it was impossible not to he attracted
> by his genial disposition and many charms of manner

---

11 Answer by Mr Curson in the Commons Debate of January 26. 1897 (p.501) to a question by Mr Gibson Bowles on how a problem in the Consular Court at Constantinople
was to be dealt with. Brief details of the cases are reported in the *Daily Mail*, 5 April 1897,
p5. Silley and Sarrel were back in court two years later with Silley suing Sarrell for libel.
The *Times*, April 29, 1898 (Macquarie Law School, Colonial Cases collection).

and conversation. He obeyed and improved the best
traditions of English justice; he was always foremost
in works of charity; he knew no distinction of persons;
he dispensed the widest hospitality: and whatever was
for the benefit of the community found in him an active
supporter."[12]

High words of praise, indeed. The appointment of Rennie's successor was to create an uproar in Shanghai. At the
end of his career, that successor received even higher words
of praise than this.

12 Reported in the *North China Herald*, May 5, 1905, p222.

PART FIVE

JAPAN RISES – CHINA FALLS
(1891 TO 1900)

CHAPTER 22

The Amalgamation

THE 1890s SAW the continued rise of Japan with agreements reached with all the powers for the end of extraterritoriality there. Japan also defeated China in a war weakening the Chinese government even more and increasing further the rights of foreigners.

Nicholas Hannen continued his own personal rise with Richard Rennie's retirement. He returned from Yokohama to Shanghai as Chief Justice of the Supreme Court. Robert Mowat replaced him as Judge for Japan in Yokohama.

Hannen was made an offer he could not refuse. In addition to making him Chief Justice, he was appointed Consul-General in Shanghai. Any man would find it hard to turn down the second and third most important Foreign Office appointments in China, behind only the Minister in Peking. Hannen, despite misgivings he later expressed, accepted. George Jamieson, who by now had close to three years experience as an acting judge, was appointed to the amalgamated position of Judge and Consul in Shanghai. Hannen could not speak Chinese, so it was essential to have a Chinese speaker who could deal with local Chinese officials as his consular deputy.

The appointments of Hannen as Chief Justice and Jamieson as Judge were welcomed. On the other hand, the amalgamation of their judicial and consular positions was bitterly opposed. The amalgamation was put into place by Sir Philip Currie, the new Under-Secretary for Foreign Affairs, who had replaced Sir Julian Pauncefote. Currie had origi-

Nicholas Hannen, the new Chief Justice and Consul-General
George Jamieson, the new Judge and Consul

nally proposed that the position of Chief Justice and Consul be combined in 1877. As we have seen, Pauncefote soundly Currie was rejected this in a long memorandum.[1] But with Pauncefote gone, Currie was able to push through the amalgamation of the positions as a cost saving measure. Certain other positions were also abolished, such as that of Criminal Clerk.[2] Currie was very happy with the result and regretted that money had been wasted for many years by paying salaries for two positions. He had short shrift for the idea of the British Courts in China and Japan being an example to the Chinese and Japanese of the Rule of Law. What was needed, he said, was "to promote British trade and administer consular jurisdiction, not set up caricatures of British courts of law."[3]

The amalgamation of the consular and judicial posts faced fierce criticism from the local British community. It was argued that the two posts were too important to be held by one

1 See Chapter 13

2 "The British Consular Service in China" *Times*, March 31, 1891. Hannen later wrote to the Foreign Office, pointing out that he had not been told of any cuts in positions and asking for the reinstatement of staff. Letter from Hannen to the Earl of Rosebery, dated March 30, 1893, FO17/1166.

3 P.D. Coates, *The China Consuls*, 1843-1943, pp219-220.

person. The Chief Justice was required to travel on circuit to try important cases. If the position was held by one person the Consul-General would be absent for long periods. In addition, a judge should not play an active role in the community whereas the Consul-General should be encouraged to. Further, the Consul-General needed to deal with Chinese authorities on diplomatic issues and served as a referee for the Municipal Council when grievances were brought to him. It would be difficult to have the same person serving as Chief Justice and be seen as delivering impartial justice.[4]

On March 10, 1891 a "largely attended and influential meeting of British residents" was held at the Shanghai Club to protest the changes. A petition to the Foreign Office was circulated and agreed to at the meeting that made the above points, but also emphasized the difficulties merchants faced dealing with conflicting jurisdictions:

> "Our position here is an exceptional one. We have a local Municipal Government constituted under the Land Regulations for the Foreign Settlements … while we live and have our warehouses on land held under the Chinese Government and our ships and merchandise in transit are subject to Customs regulations made by the Chinese Government, and which it claims to be enforceable by its Officials, while we are governed by British Law."

The petition stated further that in these circumstances, British subjects would have to frequently resort to Chinese courts and would often need the intervention of an independent Consul-General with long experience dealing with Chinese officials. The Chief Justice and Judge were required to have long experience as practising lawyers meaning they would not have this experience.[5]

4 *North China Herald*, January 30, 1891, pp109-110.
5 *North China Herald*, March 13, 1891, p305. The petition signed by 526 residents op-

Nevertheless, the amalgamation proposal was a *fait accompli* having already been approved. The *North China Herald* laid the blame for this directly on the Sir John Walsham, the British Minister to China. Currie had sent the amalgamation proposal to Sir John. He did not respond for one month, so the Foreign Office took it that the proposal was acceptable. The *North China Herald* was scathing in its criticism of Walsham:

"But we know for certain now another fact which has been whispered about for some time; that when the Foreign Office had decided on the new plan, it was telegraphed out to Sir John Walsham, as is customary, that he might make his objections to it, if he had any. For a whole month Sir John took absolutely no notice of the intimation, while during that time he might have let the public know what was contemplated, and there would have been plenty of time for the British community to telegraph home a protest, which we know now would have been favourably received. Action however, is not Sir John's foible. The Foreign Office, taking Sir John's, silence for consent, and having obtained the approval of the Treasury, and got the new salaries incorporated in the estimates, telegraphed to Sir John to offer the new amalgamated post to Sir Richard Rennie, and then, when it was too late, Sir John sent home his protest in a protracted telegram. So that it is really to Sir John Walsham's invincible dilatoriness that we owe the consummation of the change. Our readers may be tired of the subject, but we have thought it well to put these facts on record, now that we have them on unimpeachable authority."[6]

---

posing the amalgamation was submitted to the Consulate General for transmission to Peking on March 26, 1891 (see *North China Herald*, April 3, 1891, p386).

6 *North China Herald*, July 10, 1891, p37. This criticism of Sir John Walsham was relatively restrained. In an article of February 12, 1892 the *North China Herald* (at 157) advocating his summary dismissal described Sir John as follows: "He is simply King Log;

How the two positions of Consul-General, protecting British interests, and Chief Justice, administering impartial justice could be reconciled boggles the mind. Julian Pauncefote's memo in 1877 had made clear the many reasons why it was not appropriate. Hannen's own words in the case of David Banks, the train driver accused of manslaughter, "political expediency" should not be an issue before the court show how clearly this was an inappropriate decision.

Perhaps more importantly, the Consul General could be actively involved in the use of British force to maintain the British presence in China. Mowat, before leaving for Japan, acted as Chief Justice and Consul-General from April to October 1891. During this time he had to deal with anti-missionary riots that broke out in the Yangtze Valley. On 13 May 1891 Mowat received a telegram, which he passed on to the Vice-Admiral of the Navy:

> "Riot Wuhu, catholic premises being destroyed; send
> gun-boat immediately[7]"

And send gunboats they did. A correspondent travelled from Shanghai up the Yangtze River in December 1891. He had been given suggestions of places to visit by Hannen, whom he described as being "anxious to have some independent testimony upon a subject which engages much attention, and around which there is a great deal of heated controversy." The correspondent described 14 men-of-war laying at anchor in Shanghai, including the British despatch vessel, HMS *Alacrity*, with Sir Frederick Richards, the admiral commanding the China fleet, on board. At each port he visited, including,

---

and he takes no more notice of the despatches of his Consuls. the petitions of Chambers of Commerce, the remonstrances of the Press, than his prototype did of the reiterated *breke-kekex, koax, koax* of the frogs in the fable."

7   Correspondence Respecting Anti-foreign riots in China, presented to both Houses of Parliament by Command of Her Majesty, July 1891, p6.

Chinkiang, Wuhu, Kiukiang, Hankow and Ichang, a gunboat or man-of-war lay at anchor and foreign residents told him that if the boats were withdrawn they feared for their lives. In Hankow, he was told the foreign settlement had been saved by the presence of several gunboats in harbour at the time of the riots. In Ichang, almost all foreign properties had been destroyed and foreigners were living in ships moored on the river. The conclusion of the British Consul, Mr Gardiner, was: "So long as we have the gunboats with us we are safe." [8]

Back in Shanghai, during the riots, the Municipal Council, after consultation with the Consular Body, of which Mowat, as Acting British Consul-General, was one of the most important members, issued a notice in Chinese and English to the effect that if riots broke out, a warning bell would be rung, the volunteers would assemble and:

> "On this signal being given, all peaceable persons
> should retire to their houses as the police and volun-
> teers will have orders to disperse by force any crowd
> after such warning, and any persons remaining in
> the streets after such warning will do so at their own
> peril."[9]

The warning had the desired effect and no riots broke out in Shanghai. However, if riots had broken out and the legality of the warning had to be considered by the court, Mowat would have been severely compromised. Indeed, one missionary, George Cockburn, whose Church of Scotland Mission in Ichang had been destroyed, wrote in a letter to The Glasgow Herald that he had seen "Judge Mowat in Shanghai who is also acting for the Consul-General," to discuss his

---

8 "Through the Missions the Yangtse Yang", The *Argus*, February 9, 1892.

9 Report sent to by Mowat to Marquis of Salisbury, Secretary of State for Foreign Affairs and S J Walsham, British Minister on June 19, 1891, in Correspondence Respecting Anti-foreign riots in China, presented to both Houses of Parliament by Command of Her Majesty, July 1891 p33-34.

claim for compensation. Mowat told him to make a claim in full. This is not the sort of position a judge should be in, particularly if he later has to decide on the claim.[10]

Changing the subject, Cockburn finished his letter with the teaser: "Great revelations are expected on Monday at the Mason trial. Mason is the Customs' clerk caught smuggling arms and dynamite."

Mason - A terrorist in service of Chinese Customs?

There were indeed great revelations. Charles Mason, a mid-level employee of the Chinese Customs in Chinkiang (Zhen-jiang) on the Yangtze River, was accused of six counts of possessing dynamite. The Chinese government believed that Mason was a member of a secret triad society, the Kolao Hwei (the Society of Brothers and Elders), which was engaged in active rebellion to overthrow the Qing Dynasty. The rebellion had many thought triggered the 1891 anti-missionary riots. Mason had arranged to smuggle dynamite and other weapons from Hong Kong. The Chinese Government pushed the British Government very hard to prosecute him.[11]

The case, which illustrated the difficult position the holder of the amalgamated position of Chief Justice and Consul-General could face, commenced in the Supreme Court in September 1891. In the lead-up to the case, the British Minister in Peking telegrammed Mowat, as Acting Consul-General, directing the institution of proceedings "through the Crown Advocate against Mason, and recommending the charge should be laid under the Explosives Act if Mr Mowat thought that act applicable, and otherwise under Article 81" of the then current Order in Council. The Minister added that a charge under the latter would "have the disadvantage of involving the risk of contentious matter as to the meaning of the

10 The *Glasgow Herald*, November 11, 1891, p 9.

11 For a detailed article on the Mason case see: A Sweeten, "The Mason Gunrunning Case and the 1891 Yangtze Valley Disturbances: A Diplomatic Link."

words war, insurrection and rebellion used in that Article" being raised.[12]

Mowat, as Acting Consul-General, was deeply involved in bringing the case to trial before the Supreme Court. However, at this time Mowat was also Acting Chief Justice. The effect of this was that the Chief Justice of the Court was being instructed to bring a case to trial and to decide under which legal provisions he should do so. This was clearly inappropriate and would have been even more so if Mowat had tried the case. The court would certainly have been a "caricature" of a British court, to use Philip Currie's words. Luckily, Hannen had by the time the trial commenced arrived in Shanghai from Japan.

Mason's trial was Hannen's very first hearing as Chief Justice. The Judge (and Consul), George Jamieson, accompanied him on the bench. Before the proceedings began, H.S. Wilkinson, the Crown Advocate, offered a welcome to his old friend saying he had the "very pleasant duty to bid your Lordship in the name of the Bar a most cordial welcome to Shanghai." He added, referring to Hannen's previous period as Acting Chief Justice: "We are also glad to welcome you as a former occupant of the honourable post which you now fill and which you then honourably filled." Then, making a reference to the amalgamation, Wilkinson added "Since that time changes have taken place, the expediency of which this is neither the time nor the place to discuss; but we as members of the Bar are satisfied that we shall see in you a Chief Justice of whom we may feel that the noble traditions of the Bar are safe in your hands." [13]

Hannen responded with thanks and finished by commenting on the importance of respect being shown between the bar and the judiciary:

12 FO/656/81 p.9-16 at p9b, Memorandum from H.S. Wilkinson, Crown Advocate regarding the case, dated April 7, 1892.

13 *R v Mason, North China Herald*, October 30, 1891, p609.

"The respect which you show to me will not be personal. It is, I know, due, and you will give it, to the dignity of the office which I hold; and in the same way I trust that I shall always respect you, not only because I respect you personally, but because you represent here the two branches of that large profession which all of us honour and love so well. Gentlemen, I thank you."

The Taotai and Liu Ta-Jen the Director of the Kiangnan Arsenal were observing the case from the bench, while Mr Yu, a deputy of the Viceroy, sat at a table below the bench. What they made of this exchange of coded pleasantries, one will never know. What they will have seen was that the British Consul-General was sitting as the British Chief Justice and they cannot but have wondered about British representations as to the importance of the separation of powers.

A jury was empanelled and Mason was asked to plea. He pleaded guilty. After doing so, Mason read a statement giving an almost unbelievable explanation that the conspiracy was an invention of his and that he ultimately intended to report to both the Customs service and the British Government. Wilkinson was asked to comment on what sort of sentence should be imposed. Wilkinson said he would be very happy to leave the matter in Hannen's hands but then set out the background to the case. Following this, Hannen asked Mason if he had anything to say. Mason said that the conspiracy he was supposedly connected with had nothing to do with the recent riots in the Yangtze valley.

Hannen, noting "that confinement here in China is a much more serious punishment than it would be at home," and that this matter meant the "loss of your position and the entire ruin of your career here in China," then sentenced Mason to nine months imprisonment and to deportation upon release unless he could obtain two sureties.

This light sentence drew a vehement protest from Minister Sieh Tajien of the Chinese Legation in London directly to the British Foreign Minister, the Marquis of Salisbury.[14] Sieh expressed the "surprise and disappointment" at the light sentence and entered a "formal and emphatic protest ... on the grounds of it being incommensurate with to the gravity of the offence." Sieh went on to make the specific point that the British extraterritorial courts were administering justice in China against British subjects on behalf of the Chinese government:

> "It is the opinion of my Government, neither the Judge nor the Crown Advocate seemed to realize either the importance of the case, or to feel the responsibility imposed on them by the vicarious function devolving on the Crown, in virtue of British subjects being the objects of extra-territorial jurisdiction."

Sieh said that the evidence showed that Mason was an avowed member of the Kolao Hwei and that he recruited another 19 Europeans with plans to import weapons and dynamite to fight the Chinese government. Sieh complained that the Crown Advocate had been wrong to frame a charge as only one of possessing dynamite and that Hannen had been wrong in passing such a lenient sentence, stating in particular that "there was nothing in [the case] which called for a mitigation of the punishment: a traitor to the trust reposed in him." Sieh called the case a miscarriage of justice and requested that after Mason had finished his sentence in Shanghai he be sent to Hong Kong for trial on a more serious charge.

The Marquis of Salisbury wrote a short letter to Sieh saying he was looking into the matter. Sanderson of the Foreign

---

14 FO 656/58 – Letter from Sieh to Salisbury.

Office on behalf of the Marquis of Salisbury wrote to Hannen seeking his and Wilkinson's comments on the case. The letter principally set out the grounds of complaint from Sieh but added a clear political message:

> "Independently of any other considerations, the effect
> produced would be very bad if he were seen walking
> about free, and his treatment were contrasted with that
> of the Chinese who had been decapitated for taking
> part in the riots against the foreign missions."

Sanderson tempered this statement by adding that it appeared that nothing could be done in the specific case if Mason was able to obtain sureties.

Wilkinson was asked to prepare a report on the case. He wrote a long 18-page document setting out the full background to the case explaining why, given the lack of evidence, he had only preferred charges under the Explosives Act. He said that the Taotai had been very satisfied with the case and had wanted to give Wilkinson some Chinese scrolls in recognition of his good work.

Before the Marquis of Salisbury could reply to Minister Sieh based on Wilkinson's report, on May 14, 1892, Sieh wrote back a long letter in reply to the Marquis' first letter. This made a number of substantive comments on English law and was most likely drafted by, or on instructions of, a British employee of the Chinese Customs Service. The letter criticized the lightness of the sentence against Mason by comparing it to a sentence given to Chinese in England and pointing out that on that very date the letter was being sent, a "Chinaman will be liberated from Wandsworth Prison after having undergone an imprisonment of three months, with hard labor, for smuggling – an offence which was only one, and that the lightest, of the various offences of which it was held Mason was guilty."

The Foreign Secretary, the Marquis of Salisbury, replied to Sieh on July 2, 1892, setting out Wilkinson's report in detail. Then with regard to Hannen's position as Chief Justice, hypocritically, given Mowat's earlier role in the case, he wrote:

"As regards the sentence inflicted by the Chief Justice, I may observe that it is not in accordance with Constitutional practice in this country that a judicial officer should be called upon to render an account to the Executive Government of his action in his judicial capacity it being the essence of his office that it should be discharged with complete freedom from administrative interference."[15]

Even more hypocritically, despite this assertion, Hannen had, in fact, provided some comments to the Marquis of Salisbury and confirmed that on the evidence before him, the sentence met the justice of the case.

In his note to Sieh, Salisbury said there was only limited evidence as to Mason's involvement with Kolao Hwei. He added that it was very likely that Mason would leave China upon the expiry of his sentence and noted, while not directly linking the two issues, that "it is now a matter of public report that Mason's servants and other Chinese mentioned in the course of the enquiry concerning him have been arrested, imprisoned, and subjected to cruel torture." He concluded by commenting that a subsequent investigation of Mason's bank accounts by the Taotai with the cooperation of Mason and the British authorities had not shown any external funding of Mason's activities.

Sieh responded on August 2, 1892 in another long letter challenging Salisbury's interpretations of the law.[16] At the end, he made a clear demand for reciprocity of treatment:

15 FO656/81, p24. The quote re Hannen is at p30.
16 FO656/81, p36.

"I much regret the theory that Mason's actions were the 'outcome of a crazy imagination' should have been allowed to figure so largely in the case. It was started immediately after his arrest before the trial, and seems afterwards to have been accepted without sufficient examination. I regret it, because 'crazy imaginations' are so common, or can be so easily feigned that at some future time Mason may have his imitators; a thing that would greatly add to the difficulties of the Imperial Government. For I am afraid that, should at any time hereafter, it be sought to extenuate the burning down of a Mission station, or the perpetration of any other out-rages such as those which took place in China last year, the plea that they were the outcome of a 'crazy imagi-nation' would have little chance of being accepted, and if advances, would be little calculated to promote the harmony of our international relations."

Sieh put the matter to a close by saying even though Wilkinson had "positive proof" to do so in his hands it ap-peared Mason could not be tried for other offences. He con-cluded by expressing the "hope of the Imperial Government that it may be long before the good feeling which happily exists between the two Governments shall be troubled with such an unsatisfactory case again."

Mason did return to England after his release from prison. In August 1893, in a letter to the *Pall Mall Gazette*, he sought to explain himself:

"The truth concerning my action is then simply this: Young inexperienced, and quixotic, I threw myself and my small funds with blind ardour into what I believed, and believe, a great design for the amelioration of the

lot of a people whom I still regard as possessed of the
grandest qualities of any nation ... I have paid the price
of my quixotism in the disgrace and suffering of prison
and the most shameful of odiums, the destruction of all
hope or prospect in life, and destitution. Sacrifices that
are glorious in a poet, and for Greece, are criminal in a
clerk, for China."[17]

Gunboat *Redpole* to the rescue

Not long after the Mason case, the trial of another customs
officer meant that Harrie Wilkinson and George Jamieson required the services of a British gunboat to protect them from
threatened mob retribution if the officer was not convicted of
murder. Compared to Hornby's problems in Chefoo, better
communications made it much easier to get a gunboat to port,
warning the mob off before it formed.

A customs tide-waiter, Robert Jackson, had gone out
shooting early in the morning and had, as Harrie Wilkinson,
described it "a difference of opinion with a Chinese ferryman." Jackson's gun was loaded and "it went off, and the
Chinaman was killed."[18] Evidence from two doctors, including a Dr Lyall, was that ferryman had been shot in the back.
Jackson also told Dr Lyall that, "his foot slipped as he was
entering or leaving the boat, he fell forward and his gun went
off, the charge hitting the deceased."[19]

Jamieson went on circuit to try the case with a jury. Harrie
Wilkinson, who was assisting his father in his work as Crown
Advocate, went with Jamieson as the prosecutor. An impor-
tant Chinese official attended the trial on behalf of the Viceroy
and during the first day's hearing asked to speak to the judge.
He was told that it was better that he spoke to the prosecutor,

17 "The Mason Case", *Pall Mall Gazette*, September 4, 1893, p11.

18 Harrie Wilkinson recounted the story to the *North China Herald* on this retirement in
1925, see *North China Herald*, October 31, 1925, p200.

19 *R v Jackson*, *North China Herald*, March 17, 1893, p367.

Wilkinson and the Consul at Swatow, William Henry Wilkinson (no relation). The Chinese official told the Wilkinsons that as a Chinese had been killed, if the Defendant was not found guilty, the official "could not restrain the populace from wiping out the British Officials concerned." W.H. Wilkinson told the Mandarin that Jackson's guilt or innocence was a matter for the jury to decide, and refused to pass the message on to Jamieson.

W.H. Wilkinson, did, however, immediately cable Hong Kong for a gunboat to be sent. He also told the Mandarin that if what he said would come to pass did, in fact, come to pass, it would be "very inconvenient"[20] for the Mandarin as a gunboat was expected. Harrie Wilkinson recalled much later that the accused was "found not guilty of murder, the gunboat arrived and the incident blew over."

Jackson was, in fact, found guilty of manslaughter and sentenced to six months imprisonment, a sentence that according to the *Hong Kong Daily News* was "considered light" and "caused great dissatisfaction among the natives" and "as a precautionary measure against a possible outbreak of feeling against foreigners HMS *Redpole*, in response to a request by Mr Wilkinson, Consul at Swatow, for a gunboat to held in readiness, was despatched yesterday morning." The *Daily News* felt sure that "upon the arrival of the *Redpole*, the popular feeling, if it has not quite abated by this time, will doubtless subside."[21]

The Jackson case showed just how far apart Japan and China had grown. The days that foreign gunboats had been needed to protect foreign officals were long past. In the 1890s Japan was ready to assert itself.

---

20 W.H. Wilkinson presumably spoke to the consul in Chinese using the words "bu fangbian" to mean "inconvenient." These words have a much broader meaning in Chinese than in English and would clearly, in the context of the discussions, have conveyed the meaning that the "inconvenience" would be "extremely prejudicial" to the Mandarin's continuation in his position and even to his own life.

21 Reprinted in the *North China Herald*, March 24, 1893, p408.

CHAPTER 23

Japan Asserts Itself

IN THE EARLY 1890s, Japan was ready to join the "family of nations." It pushed for an agreement with foreign powers to end extraterritoriality in Japan. As part of their negotiation tactics they started enforcing the terms of the existing treaties strictly.

After Nicholas Hannen's returned to Shanghai in 1891, Robert Mowat moved to Yokohama to take up his well-deserved promotion as Judge for Japan. He settled in Negishi, an area outside the foreign settlement but where foreigners had been living for some years. H.S. Wilkinson visited Yokohama in the summer 1892 on the way to Vancouver and stayed with the Mowats for a night. He wrote in letter to his son, Harrie:

"He has fallen in love with Japan and I don't wonder at it. He has got a house within half an hours' jinricsha drive of the Court overlooking Negishi (Mississippi Bay) most prettily situated and commanding one of the loveliest views in Japan. He has a very modest amount of work and is his own master. Under these circumstances there is no great inducement to retire. He could not get a pleasanter house, and he could scarcely expect the conditions of life to be better than they are for him at present."[1]

---

1 PRONI, D1292, Letter from H.S. Wilkinson to Harrie Wilkinson July 18, 1892.

Mowat's love affair with Japan was bad news for H.S. Wilkinson. He had now served for ten successful years as Crown Advocate in Shanghai. Despite (or perhaps because of) this, he still longed for an appointment as a judge. Hannen had been appointed Judge for Japan in 1881. The amalgamation and appointment of Hannen as Chief Justice had required the appointment of a Chinese speaker as Consul/Judge so George Jamieson had been appointed. In any event, Wilkinson may well have by then considered that after ten years as Crown Advocate a position as an assistant judge was below him.

His only hope for a judicial appointment was that Mowat would retire early. When staying in Yokohama in 1892, he had a long talk to Mowat about his plans. The good news for Wilkinson was that Mowat intended to take long leave in 1894. Wilkinson with his experience in Japan could expect to get the acting appointment in Mowat's absence. H.S. Wilkinson told Harrie in a letter that he expected to come to Japan to act for Mowat and then return to Shanghai as Crown Advocate. He cautioned, however, "this is all a long way ahead … Like all other schemes of mice and men this one may be upset by what unforeseen events we cannot guess."[2]

A dark spot did appear on Mowat's horizon that year. This was the possibility that he may have to give up his fine residence in Negishi. As part of negotiations to bring an end to extraterritoriality, the Japanese government had re-introduced a policy of enforcing the treaties strictly. This resulted in a threat to all foreigners that they would be removed from Negishi because residing there was in breach of the treaties. One conservative Japanese newspaper, the *Nippon*, had specifically targetted Mowat by sending a reporter, on the pretext of discussing English law, to find Mowat in the international settlement. When he could not be found in the settlement the reporter had followed Mowat in a ricsha and "he could

2   PRONI, D1292, Letter from H.S. Wilkinson to Harrie Wilkinson July 18, 1892.

not believe his senses, because the house was outside limits prescribed for the residence of foreigners." Ultimately, an arrangement was reached with the Japanese authorities allowing for foreigners to stay in Negishi.[3]

Despite Mowat's brush with tough Japanese attitudes towards extraterritoriality, when revision of the Rules of Court were being considered in 1892, he suggested a change to rules that were affecting Japanese creditors collecting debts from British fraudsters. The rules required Japanese claimants to pay the costs of the debtor being imprisoned when non-Japanese were not required to make such payments. This meant that the British fraudsters would often go unpunished. Mowat considered this unacceptable. Mowat also suggested that changes be made to the way in which Japanese witnesses gave evidence in the British courts, commenting that "the whole system of swearing Japanese or Chinese witnesses in provincial courts in Japan is irregular and inharmonious. In fact there is no swearing at all, the form generally adopted being that which is called 'cautioning' and the caution sometimes consists of the simple admonition to 'tell the truth' not a word more or less." Mowat's suggestion was that the witnesses be required to make an affirmation.[4]

The sinking of the *Chishima*

The same year, Mowat had to deal with a difficult case brought by the Japanese Government. On 30 November 1892, the *Chishima Kan*, a Japanese war ship, and P&O steamship the *Ravenna* collided in the Inland Sea of Japan in the Gogoshima straits between the islands of Musuki and Gogo, less than three miles offshore from the island of Shikoku. The Japanese Government

....

3   "The Nippon and Judge Mowat", *Japan Weekly Mail*, October 7, 1893, p413 *North China Herald*, May 20, 1892, p662.

4   FO 798/17, p76 (fraudsters) and p79-80 (witnesses). Draft letter in the records of the Court for Japan, Robert Mowat, dated June 2, 1892 attaching a memorandum in response to a request for alterations to the China and Japan Orders in Council. The draft letter does not state who made the request, but it was presumably Nicholas Hannen.

in the name of the Emperor or Japan sued P&O for damages. P&O sought to counterclaim against the Japanese Government in the British Court for Japan for damages to the *Ravenna*. Mowat said the issue to be resolved was whether the point of the collision was in Japanese waters or in international waters. If the ship was in Japanese waters, the Court for Japan, as an extraterritorial court, did not have jurisdiction to allow a counterclaim unless the Emperor consented. If the collision was in international waters, the Court for Japan was sitting as a British Admiralty Court and had jurisdiction to allow a counterclaim. Mowat held that the collision was in Japanese waters as it occurred within three miles of the Japanese shore. Therefore, the counterclaim was not allowed.[5]

P&O appealed to Shanghai. Both sides brought in big guns to argue the case. P&O instructed J.J. Francis, now a Queen's Counsel from Hong Kong together with John Lowder from Yokohama and Mr A.P. Master of the law firm Johnson Stokes and Master. The Japanese Government instructed H.S. Wilkinson who appeared with Montague Kirkwood from Yokohama and his son, Harrie Wilkinson.

Hannen and Jamieson agreed with Mowat that the issue to be decided was whether the ship was in international waters but disagreed with Mowat as to whether it had been. They held that locations within three miles of shore could be international waters when they were used for international shipping. Hannen went further and held that the waters were part of the "highway of nations." Both Hannen and Jamieson held that the court, sitting in admiralty, had jurisdiction to allow a counterclaim to be made against the Japanese Government.[6]

The Japanese government could not accept this and sought leave to appeal to the Privy Council, which was granted. Re-

---

5 Imperial Japanese Government v Peninsular and Oriental Steam Navigation Company, *Japan Weekly Mail*, July 1, 1893, p24 See also C. Roberts, The British Courts and Extra-Territoriality in Japan 1859-1899, Chapter Seven and R. Chang, The Justice of Western Consular Courts in Nineteenth Century Japan, Chapter 5 for more details of this case.

6 *P&O v The Imperial Japanese Government, North China Herald*, October 27, 1893, p675.

flecting the importance of the case, the appeal was heard by seven law lords; two Queen's Counsel appeared for each side and both the Attorney-General and Solicitor-General held watching briefs.[7] The Privy Council stated in the first paragraph of their decision that the appeal "raised a question of considerable importance in regard to jurisdiction possessed by British Consular Courts in China and Japan." The Privy Council reversed the judgment of Hannen and Jamieson and restored Mowat's decision, ruling that on a proper reading of the treaties that granted extraterritorial rights, the Court for Japan (and the Supreme Court for China and Japan) did not have jurisdiction to allow counterclaims in any actions, including admiralty actions.

They rejected an argument that had been made that by choosing to sue in a British court, Japanese nationals had to take the consequences of that election on the simple ground that there was really no election. The treaty required a Japanese national to sue British subjects in the British Court for Japan. He "has no choice," but to do so. It was therefore a violation of the treaty and an excess of jurisdiction to allow a counterclaim. Perhaps more importantly, the Privy Council added that if British courts allowed a counterclaim against Japanese or Chinese subjects in British courts, the Japanese or Chinese courts would be able to allow a counterclaim when a British subject sued in those courts, destroying the whole foundation of extraterritoriality.[8]

The case produced further litigation and another Privy Council decision when the families of the 62 Japanese crew who lost their lives in the accident sued P&O in the Court for Japan, bringing one consolidated action. Mowat decided that the action could not be brought in this way but instead each plaintiff would have to bring their own action. On appeal,

---

7   The *London and China Telegraph*, May 27, 1895, p451.

8   *The Imperial Japanese Government v Peninsular and Oriental Steam Navigation*, [1895] A.C. 644.

Hannen and Jamieson decided a consolidated action could be brought. In doing so, they relied on an English Court of Appeal decision which had allowed consolidated actions. The Japanese Plaintiffs appealed to the Privy Council. By the time the Privy Council heard the appeal, the House of Lords had reversed the English Court of Appeal decision Hannen and Jamieson had relied upon. The Privy Council therefore reversed the Supreme Court's decision and held that each Japanese plaintiff was required to file an individual case.[9]

Following the Privy Council decision, the Japanese Government's claim against P&O was re-listed for hearing in the Court for Japan in October 1895 more than two years after it had been filed. The *Eastern World* noted sardonically, "when it is ended the lawyers in the case will probably own the Japanese navy and the P&O Company."[10] Perhaps for this reason, P&O decided soon after to settle the case by paying the Japanese government £10,000. Sir Thomas Sutherland, the Chairman of P&O, told shareholders at the company's 1895 shareholders meeting that before the Privy Council hearing, their advisers had confidently told them the result would be a "walk over" for P&O, instead of which it was a "legal and legitimate triumph for the Japanese Government." The Japanese had claimed £100,000; P&O's experience was that courts "blame both ships" and that P&O had "with the exception of one case, never gone to Admiralty Court without being held partly to blame. P&O was therefore potentially liable for upwards of £27,000 and to settle for £10,000 was a wise decision of the directors."[11]

Wilkinson acting in Japan

Soon after the Supreme Court decision in the *Chishima* case,

---

9 *Peninsular and Oriental Steam Shipping Company Ltd v Tsune Kijima & Ors* [1895] A.C. 661. Also Reported in *North China Herald*, August 2, 1895, p179.

10 Reprinted in *North China Herald*, August 2, 1895, p179.

11 *North China Herald*, January 24, 1896, p116.

Mowat went on long leave. As planned, Wilkinson was appointed Acting Judge in Japan. W. Vernon Drummond, the senior member of the bar in Shanghai, was appointed Acting Crown Advocate in Wilkinson's absence. Drummond regularly represented the Chinese government and other Chinese bodies in the court and on other matters including acting for the Chinese government in a dispute with Japan over Chinese extraterritorial rights in Nagasaki. He was perceived in the British community, for this reason, as being pro-Chinese. Drummond's appointment was, therefore, strongly opposed by the China Association – a newly formed merchants' association representing the interests of British businesses in China and Japan - on the basis that his appointment would "prejudice the interests of British subjects in China." Han-

Vernon Drummond, pro-Chinese lawyer who was briefly appointed Acting Crown Advocate

nen, as Consul-General, was asked to pass on a telegram to the British Minister opposing the appointment.[12] Hannen did so. In a clear slight to Drummond, Hannen's letter to the Minister was published in the *North China Herald*. Nevertheless, Drummond was appointed Acting Crown Advocate in February 1894. Due to continued opposition, he resigned eight months later. Harrie Wilkinson, who himself had only just recovered from an illness, at the tender age of 28 was appointed Acting Crown Advocate for the rest of his father's absence.

Harrie, just before his appointment, had been convalescing in Chefoo when he had heard cries from Mr J.J. Hatch who was in trouble far out to sea. Harrie plunged into the water and swum out to save him. The next year, a ceremony was

---

12 *North China Herald*, January 26, 1894, p132.

arranged to recognise Wilkinson's bravery at the Supreme Court in Shanghai. Hannen was on long leave in England, where he was knighted at Windsor castle. George Jamieson, as Acting Chief Justice, after a brief speech presented Harrie a Royal Humane Society's bronze medal and certificate for gallantry. Harrie was self-effacing in response saying that "it was not a question of bravery but of common-sense. There was no one handy to get him out, and I suppose I went and did it." [13]

His father's time in Japan was less eventful. No major cases came before H.S. Wilkinson while he was Acting Judge in Japan but he clearly endeared himself again to the British community. On his departure at the end of May 1895, a party was held which most of the leading British residents of Japan attended. The *Japan Weekly Mail* was glowing in it praise:

> "It would have been impossible for any official to win greater popularity in this Settlement than Mr Wilkinson has won during the year of his residence. He possessed, it is true a wide circle of friends before he re-visited Japan to preside over the Court at Kanagawa, but even without such antecedents, his open-handed hospitality and genial kindliness must have opened every heart to him. Of his capacity as a judge it is unnecessary to say much. Thorough research, conscientious accuracy, and sound insight have always been characteristic of him, and he displayed these high qualities during the year of his Judgeship in a manner that commanded universal respect and confidence. His departure from Japan is a matter of genuine regret." [14]

Agreement to end extraterritoriality in Japan

During the time Wilkinson was in Japan, the British and Japanese governments were able through negotiations in London

13 "Presentation to Mr Wilkinson", *North China Herald*, March 29, 1895, p484.

14 *Japan Weekly Mail*, June 1, 1895, p613.

to reach an agreement to terminate extraterritoriality in Japan by the end of the 19th century. Ironically, at the same time in 1895 under the Treaty of Shimonoseki, Japan was to extract from China greater extraterritorial rights than any power had to date.

As we have seen, Japan had by 1890 almost reached agreement ending extraterritoriality but a new government had been formed and the Japanese committee negotiating the end of extraterritoriality disbanded. Two years later a new committee was formed. The Japanese, however, postponed the enactment of their new legal codes, resulting in a delay in when negotiations could re-commence. The Japanese Foreign Minister gave a speech in the Japanese Upper House on May 26, 1892 saying that while "Japanese public opinion was unanimously in favour of immediate revision of the treaties," the only method to achieve this was to enact a "Code of Laws fit to be accepted by the civilized nations of the world." [15]

He added that one should not look back and criticize those who signed the original treaties:

Foreigners fear being subject to Japanese law

15 Irish University Press, Area Studies Series, Japan Vol 3, British Parliamentary Papers, Reports, correspondence and dispatches respecting Japan 1871-1899 p365.

"The Treaty Powers could not have been induced to subject their precious lives and property of their subjects to the laws of Japan, and that for the very good reason that there were at the time no laws fit to enforced in a civilized society, to whose protection their lives and property could have been committed."

Japan was at this time, planning to negotiate treaties with other countries that would provide for extraterritoriality for Japanese subjects. The Foreign Minister therefore needed to be able to justify why Japan would ask for extraterritoriality from other countries while at the same time they were seeking to rid Japan of extraterritoriality.

By late 1893, the question of treaty revision had become a political hot potato. The democratic representatives in the Japanese parliament, the Diet, opposed any treaty that gave foreigners any residual rights. Others were opposed to the idea of allowing foreigners freedom to travel anywhere in Japan. Hirobumi Ito was now Prime Minister of Japan again and determined that strong measures needed to be taken to get the treaties signed. In order to silence criticism, he recommended to the Emperor that the Diet be dissolved. The government also prohibited several political societies and certain newspapers.[16]

Negotiations went forward relatively quickly and an agreement reached in mid-1894. On July 16, 1894, Earl Kimberly and Viscount Aoki on behalf of Great Britain and Japan signed a Treaty of Commerce and Navigation in London. The treaty completely ended the treaty port system in Japan. The foreign settlements were to be returned to Japan and foreigners were allowed to freely travel and reside anywhere in

16 Translation of report from the *Japan Mail* of Speech by the Premier (Count Ito) to the Diet on May 16, 1894, Irish University Press, Area Studies Series, Japan Vol 3, British Parliamentary Papers, Reports, correspondence and dispatches respecting Japan 1871-1899 p434.

Japan. The British treaty provided that Japanese could also travel and reside anywhere in Britain, even though this was a right that they already had.

With regards to extraterritoriality and the Court for Japan, Article 20 of the treaty provided that from the date the treaty came into force that all previous treaties shall cease to be binding and:

> "in consequence, the jurisdiction then exercised by British Courts in Japan, and all exceptional privileges, exemptions, and immunities then enjoyed by British subjects as a part of or appurtenant to such jurisdiction, shall absolutely and without notice cease and determine, and thereafter all such jurisdiction shall be assumed and exercised by Japanese Courts."

It was agreed that the treaty would not come into effect for at least five years after its signature. The Japanese government was required to give one year's notice that it wished to activate the treaty. The earliest date the treaties could come into force, therefore, was July 17, 1899.

The United States quickly agreed to sign a treaty on very similar terms to the British with a treaty being concluded on November 22, 1894.[17] This needed to be ratified by the Senate. War had already broken out between China and Japan that year and just before the Senate vote, there were news reports that the Japanese had massacred Chinese soldiers at Port Arthur, leading the Senate to amend the treaty in a way unacceptable to Japan. After further negotiations, and assurances from Japan that there had been no massacre, the Senate agreed to a form of wording acceptable to all and the treaty was ratified in February 1895. Under the treaty, US extraterritorial rights were set to expire at the same time as British rights.

---

17 F. Jones, *Extraterritoriality in Japan*, p157-158.

Over the next year, Japan continued to negotiate with the other treaty powers, obtaining agreements from all for the end of extraterritoriality on July 17, 1899. The only exception was France where it was agreed extraterritoriality would come to an end on August 4, 1899.

Sino –Japanese War

Just as Japan agreed to abolish extraterritoriality, the Sino-Japanese war of 1894-1895 ended with Japan imposing an "unequal treaty" on the Chinese.

The war had broken out over control of Korea over which China had for centuries claimed rights of suzerainty. The newly-strong Japan did not wish China to occupy too strong a position in the country, so, they invaded Korea and subsequently China, occupying large parts of Manchuria and Shantung Province.

When the war broke out, Hannen and Jamieson, as Consul-General and Consul, were again involved in diplomacy. They sought undertakings from the Japanese not to attack Shanghai and its surrounding area so that the Chinese would not block the port by sinking a line of junks in the Wusong River.[18] Hannen (with other consuls) also took steps to prevent ships leaving Shanghai with war supplies for the Chinese even though "strictly speaking, we are all stretching our powers beyond what we are legally entitled to do."[19] Very interesting words coming from the Chief Justice who, would arguably, have had to decide if his actions were legal, if they were challenged in his court.

Li Hongzhang had been put in charge of defending China but his supposedly modern army and navy proved far too

18 British Documents on Foreign Affairs: Reports and Papers from the Foreign Office Confidential Print, Series E, Volume 13, pp1-5. Correspondence from Hannen to Mr Trench, September 15, 1894. See also speech by George Jamieson reported in North China Herald January 31, 1896, p170.

19 British Documents on Foreign Affairs: Reports and Papers from the Foreign Office Confidential Print, Series E, Volume 13, pp12 - Correspondence between Hannen and Earl of Kimberly, July 1894.

weak - many say because funds had been syphoned off by corrupt officials - leading to a series of quick Japanese victories. In order to end the war, Li led a Chinese delegation to Shimonoseki, in Western Japan, to negotiate peace.

The Japanese delegation was led by Hirobumi Ito, the Prime Minister. The Japanese had purposefully chosen Shimonoseki as the place for the negotiations. The site overlooked the Kanmon Straits between Kyushu and Honshu, which was heavily trafficked by Japanese warships making their way to China or Korea, thus sending a clear message every day during the negotiations as to Japan's military strength.

The building in which the negotiations were conducted was destroyed by Allied bombing during World War II, but a small museum stands nearby and holds the relatively small table that was used for the negotiations. Most striking is a photograph of the negotiators. The Japanese are all dressed in Western formal wear, having cast off their traditional clothing. The Chinese are all in traditional Chinese clothing with queues. From the small hill you can see clearly across the relatively narrow Kanmon Straits and imagine them full of Japanese warships. The Japanese clearly had the upper hand.

The only trouble to arise in the negotiations for the Japanese was that a Japanese nationalist tried to assassinate Li during the course of the negotiations. Li was shot and wounded. The loss of face to the Japanese of having a peace envoy injured while in their care caused them to agree to a ceasefire while negotiations were ongoing.

The Japanese presented a first draft of a treaty to Li. Li provided some responses, to which the Japanese responded with a final draft of the treaty. Li provided some further comments, which prompted Ito to send a final note to Li, with a clear message that the Japanese had learnt very well the lessons of gunboat diplomacy:

"It only seems necessary for me to say in response

to Your Excellency's note that the demands which I handed to your Excellency on the 10th Instant, being final, are no longer open to discussion.

"Demands arising as a result of war are not proposals in the ordinary sense of that word and the Japanese Plenipotentiaries by permitting the demands of the Imperial Government to be made the subject of discussion, went to the extreme limit of concession in the interest of peace, and if their spirit of conciliation has been misunderstood they have the right to disclaim all responsibility for the consequences."[20]

Put simply: "This is not a negotiation. We made you an offer you can't refuse."

The key terms of the treaty were that China and Japan agreed that Korea was an independent nation and China would no longer seek tribute; the Liaotung (Liaodong) Peninsular in Manchuria, Formosa (Taiwan) and the Pescadores Islands were ceded to Japan; Japan was accorded Most Favoured Nation status with other territorial powers; China agreed that Japanese (and hence under Most Favoured Nation clauses, all foreigners) could manufacture in China and import manufacturing equipment; and, a number of other cities were opened to foreign trade. China agreed to pay an indemnity of 200 million taels and Japan was also allowed to keep troops in Weihaiwei, Shantung Province, until the indemnity had been paid in full. The treaty gave Japanese citizens full extraterritorial rights in China and took away Chinese citizens' extraterritorial rights in Japan.

The granting of manufacturing rights was to change the face of China. Such rights had long been sought by foreign companies and had been opposed by China. In 1893, Hannen, as Consul-General, had sought advice from H.S. Wilkinson,

---

20 Final Note from Ito to Li dated April 13, 1895, reproduced in the *Japan Weekly Mail*, June 1, 1895, p624.

as to whether a Hong Kong company, Major Brothers Limited which had been making matches and soap in China, could obtain favourable tax treatment from the Tsungli Yamen for goods they had manufactured in Shanghai. The advice was that the British Government should certainly not seek to obtain any favourable treatment for them and would most likely "cause amongst the Chinese genuine alarm at the danger of allowing foreigners to manufacture at all" and would furnish them "an argument against allowing manufacturing by foreigners to continue."[21]

In negotiating with the Japanese, Li had strenuously opposed the granting of manufacturing rights on the basis that the Diplomatic Corps in Peking had agreed it not be sought. Li emphasized that if foreigners could manufacture in China it would "tend to destroy the livelihood of Chinese and work a serious injury to native industry."[22] Nevertheless, as we have seen, Li had no choice but to agree and foreigners quickly established manufacturing facilities in China, particularly in Shanghai. This brought the industrial revolution to China.

The colonial land grab

The Russians, who had their own territorial ambitions in China were strongly opposed to the cessation of Liaotung Peninsula to Japan. Together with the Germans and French, the Russians staged a "tri-partite intervention" where they warned the Japanese that taking the Liaotung Peninsular was not acceptable. Under pressure from all three countries, Japan agreed to retrocede the peninsula and asked for an increase in the indemnity to be paid from 200 million taels to 250 million taels. The Russians negotiated the additional payment down to 30 million taels and offered a loan to China to pay

21 FO658/81 pp74-77 Letter to Hannen dated March 21, 1893. The letter is unsigned and does not indicate who it came from but it was most likely H.S. Wilkinson, the Crown Advocate.

22 Note from Li Hongzhang to Japanese negotiators dated April 5, 1895, reproduced in the *Japan Weekly Mail*, June 1, 1895, p624.

the amount.[23]

The Japanese considered this intervention by Russia to be humiliating, particularly as Russia was expanding its own interests in Manchuria. The Japanese set about building their own army and navy so as to be in stronger position in future. In 1896, Ernest Satow who, after serving in postings in Uruguay, Morocco and Siam, had been appointed British Minister in Tokyo the previous year, sent a note to the Marquis of Salisbury reporting on a conversation with the Japanese Minister of Foreign Affairs. Japan was building a large army and navy that would be seen as a threat to her neighbours. The Japanese Foreign Minister, Count Okuma, was unapologetic about this, telling Satow:

> "as every nation these days was arming to the teeth, it behoved Japan to follow suit. If she had no such neighbours as China and Corea these extensive armaments would not be required; but in case of serious complications such as a civil war in either country, the Japanese people would be unable to look on unmoved, and it was necessary to have an army large enough to admit of troops being dispatched to the mainland. Besides, the downfall of China could not long be delayed, and Japan must be prepared to play her part in the events that would follow."[24]

And, indeed, the late 1890s did see an unseemly scramble for concessions in China. In 1897 the Germans took a lease on Kiaochow Bay (Jiaozhou Bay) around the Tsingtao (Qingdao) area; the Russians took a lease on Port Arthur and obtained concessions to build railways in Manchuria. The French

---

23 I. Hsu, *The Rise of Modern China* (4th Ed), p346.
24 British Documents on Foreign Affairs: Reports and Papers from the Foreign Office Confidential Print, Series E, Volume 13, pp38. Correspondence from Satow to Salisbury, November 5, 1896

took a lease over Kwangchow Bay (now called Zhanjiang) in Guangdong Province. The British as a foil to the Russians, in 1898, took a lease over Weihaiwei after the Japanese armed forced evacuated it and extracted a promise that no rights would be granted to other powers in the Yangtze River Valley. They also obtained a 99-year lease over the New Territories in Hong Kong.[25]

Such high politics was not a matter for the British or American courts in China or Japan. They did, however, continued to deal with the, often scandalous, legal affairs of their nationals.

---

25 I. Hsu, *The Rise of Modern China* (4th Ed), p348-349. See also, Robert Bickers, *The Scramble for China*

CHAPTER 24

Infidelity and Murder in Yokohama

WHILE THE FOREIGN powers were scrambling for China, in 1890s, a number of foreigners in Yokohama were scrambling under their bedsheets with people other than their spouses. This infidelity led to two murder cases that made international headlines. In both cases the dead were Englishmen: the first George Gower Robinson, who was described as a "popular young man," "dude" and "professional seducer" at the hand of an enraged Lieutenant Hetherington of the United States Navy; the second, the philandering Walter Carew, poisoned by his equally unfaithful and richer wife, Edith.

A professional seducer gets his dues?

In his short story, "Mr Know-All", Somerset Maugham tells the story of travelling in a ship's cabin bound for Japan together with Mr Kelada, a pearl merchant. Over dinner one night, Mr Kelada spots a fine pearl necklace on the neck of the wife of the American consul in Kobe which he values at US$30,000. The consul says this is rubbish; his wife bought it for $18 at a department store. The consul bets Mr Kelada $100 they are fake. After seeing the "wide and terrified eyes" of the consul's wife, Mr Kelada admits he was wrong and pays over the bet. The next morning an envelope containing $100 was anonymously slipped under Mr Kelada's cabin door. Maugham's narrator asked Mr Kelada if the pearls were real.

"If I had a pretty little wife I shouldn't let her spend a year in New York while I stayed at Kobe," Kelada answered grimly.

In the case of US Navy Lieutenant J.H. Hetherington and his wife, it was Lieutenant Hetherington who should not have let his pretty little wife spend three months in Yokohama while he remained at sea. The Hetheringtons had married shortly before he had been assigned to Yokohama. They had intended to travel together to Yokohama but he had been ordered to spend extra time at sea. Mrs Hetherington went on herself with their infant daughter and soon threw herself into the social life there, meeting Gower Robinson, a young and handsome "man about town."

It seems they fell in love, or at least Robinson fell in love with Mrs Hetherington. He wrote a letter to her declaring his love, which Lieutenant Hetherington found. Hetherington confronted Robinson who agreed to go away to Kobe. From Kobe, Robinson wrote to Hetherington that he intended to return to England. Hetherington said that Robinson could return to Yokohama and arranged to meet him on Yokohama Bund. On Saturday afternoon February 13, 1892, Robinson approached in a cart from the direction of the Bluff with a good friend, Mr Pors. Hetherington ran alongside the cart and shouted to Robinson "Stop, you blackguard." He then shot at Robinson three times. The third shot hit him in the hip and lodged in his stomach. Robinson was carried to the United Club Building on the Bund where "he lingered until 11 o'clock Sunday night" when he died. Before his death he dictated a dying note to American Admiral Bellknap giving his pardon to Hetherington and requesting that Hetherington should be treated with the greatest leniency. Robinson was buried on February 23 at a funeral attended by most leading residents of Yokohama.[1]

The case made news worldwide. Hetherington's father in an interview said he approved of his son's conduct. If his suspicions were correct: "His honour demanded that he should

---

1 *New York Times*, March 15, 1892.

kill Robinson or himself, and he would not be tolerated in the Navy if he had done neither."

Extraterritoriality meant that two inquests were held into Robinson's death. The first was in the British Court for Japan to determine his cause of death, the second in the US Consular Court to determine if Hetherington should be prosecuted for murder.

The inquest in the British court was held before James Troup, Consul, in a packed court. Captain Bartlett of Hetherington's ship was in attendance to represent him.[2] Dr Edwin Wheeler gave evidence of treating Robinson. He said that Robinson was perfectly conscious until 6pm on Sunday night. Robinson had said that Hetherington had fired two or three shots and had been "running alongside the wheel on the left side of the trap." Dr Wheeler confirmed the bullet was the cause of death. Pors and the Japanese policeman who had arrested Hetherington also gave evidence. Not surprisingly "to profound silence" in the court, the jury concluded that Robinson had been murdered by Hetherington. The British court, however, had no jurisdiction over Hetherington and the matter fell to be decided by the American courts.[3]

Consul-General W.D. Tilotson and a jury of two held an inquest. It found that Hetherington had willfully killed Robinson and he was charged with murder. Tilotson then tried Hetherington with four assessors, Mr N.F. Smith, Eugene S. Booth, Samuel Sondheim and J.R. Simon.[4] Henry Lichtfield, the British Crown Prosecutor, prosecuted the case and Alexander Tison, a Professor of Law at the Imperial University in Tokyo, defended with Captain Bartlett from Hetherington's ship also sitting at the defence table.

Tison had two preliminary challenges. First, he objected

---

2 British Inquest, reported in *Japan Weekly Mail*, February 20, 1892, p259.

3 The *Japan Weekly Mail* was highly critical of this verdict. See "The Coroner's Jury on the Recent Shooting Affair", February 27, 1892, p278 and reply by juror on p287.

4 *Japan Weekly Mail*, April 2, 1892, p455 and April 9,1892, p489 and April 16,1892, p530.

W.D. Tilotson, US Consul-General in Yokohama who tried Hetherington

to the jurisdiction of the consular court to try Hetherington, presumably on the ground he was serving on a Navy ship. Second he sought to challenge extraterritoriality itself, arguing that the offence was an offence against Japanese law, not American law. Tilotson overruled both motions without argument, so it is not possible to know the exact reasons Tison wanted to put forward. Lichtfield then called various witnesses to prove that Hetherington had shot Robinson.

Tison opened the defence with a histrionic speech, declaring that he would do what he had to do to defend his client. Murders bring out the worst in a small community with all the local gossip being dredged up. Tison said, "It is not my intention to disturb the grim and ghastly family skeletons which abide in Yokohama, and those who possess these things in their private closets may be reassured that the spectres there kept will not be danced before the public to fright the town out of its propriety." But, he said, his ear had "been turned into a common sewer through which all the muddy sediments of this town for the last 25 years has been poured."

Numerous witnesses were called for the prosecution, to prove the killing, and for defence to show the close relationship between Robinson and Mrs Hetherington. The main and only important witness was Hetherington himself.

Hetherington said that when he arrived in Yokohama, he went to the Grand Hotel where his wife was staying and immediately realized something had changed. "I found my wife estranged and cold." Robinson dined with them on a number of occasions. Hetherington recalled that on one occasion his wife had gone upstairs and lost her veil. She had also "refused me the privileges of a husband." He wrote to Robinson asking him not to see his wife. Robinson wrote back that he was in love with her but that he "wished to assure me nothing wrong had occurred." Hetherington, in the best Victorian tradition, said he objected to this "because it had never occurred to me that anything wrong need be suspected." Robinson promised not to see Mrs Hetherington. When Hetherington's ship then went out for target practice, Hetherington engaged detectives from the Japanese police to keep an eye on Robinson. They reported that Robinson "had not kept his word," and had tried to see his wife, but she had refused him. He later found a letter from Robinson to his wife addressed, "my dear pet" and declaring his undying love. He also found a later letter addressed more formally to "Mrs Hetherington" which Hetherington took to be a scheme for Mrs Hetherington and her child to flee with Robinson.

Turning to the fateful evening in question, Hetherington said that he knew Robinson was back in Yokohama and had gone to the Bund to meet him. He saw a trap coming.

"As it got nearer, however, I saw Robinson was in a trap with a friend. They were about 30 yards from me at this time. When the horse's head was up to me I turned, drew my revolver, and said, 'You damned scoundrel, you have come back, have you?' I carried a revolver about me for the purposes of protection, and also with the intention of bringing him to – holding him up ... I then said 'stop.' The men never said anything and did not attempt to pull up, or stop, and I fired into the air."

When Robinson did not stop, he fired again, claiming "I did not fire at him but into the air, just as we in the navy fire across the bows of a ship when we wish to haul it up." He said it was his intention to make Robinson stop so he could horsewhip him.

Lichtfield decided not to cross-examine Hetherington. He did not really need to. He had his confession. Hetherington admitted firing the gun. He had not given any evidence to justify this as self-defence. Robinson's actions, no matter how despicable, did not amount to provocation in law. Hetherington, by firing a gun recklessly and killing a man, was clearly guilty of murder or, at the very least, manslaughter. Cross-examination may have only brought out further evidence that would weaken the case.

Tison then closed with a long speech. His argument was effectively that it was an honour killing: "The law excuses and applauds self-defence, and in defending my property from another, I may indeed take life in doing so. Shall a man then not be permitted to defend his wife and baby?"

Lichtfield tried to keep it simple and said that Hetherington clearly "took his gun to go into the fray armed and reckless of human life, and a fatal deed was done." Murder, plain and simple.

Consul-General Tilotson and the assessors retired for a few hours before giving judgment. Lichtfield was not in court when the judgment was due to be given. In a good sign for Hetherington, the Consul-General said he would give his judgment anyway. He started by making what in modern American courts would be considered a startling statement: that the goal of the law was not to punish wrongdoers but to protect the living. He said:

"I desire in connection with this branch of the subject to point out the fact that the object of the law is to prevent, not to punish crime, and if a man has done only what an average man would do if placed in the same circumstances, it would be persecution to punish, him, and instead of protecting society would injure it. The law does not punish to avenge the dead, but to protect the living."[5]

Tilotson said there were a long train of circumstances leading up to the killing. Hetherington had had his suspicions about his wife and Robinson. He had warned Robinson off but Robinson had continued to pursue the wife "relentlessly, almost fiendishly." Then, early in December, Hetherington had learned "positively that his former vague and misty suspicions of Robinson being the cause in the change of his wife's conduct were well founded." Then on 2 February his wife confessed. "She tells him of a wild midnight ride to Robinson's house, Oct. 23, 1891. She tells him everything of his threats and pursuits." Tilotson added, coyly, "whether all or more than this actually took place is not for the Court to decide."

Hetherington arranged to meet Robinson on the Bund that fateful day.

"He undoubtedly intended to inflict, some chastisement, but, when he found Robinson was getting away, he lost his self-control, and I believe, he did not exactly know what he was trying to do, or wanted to do, or how to do it."

Tilotson held that he was satisfied that Hetherington was only trying to protect his wife and his family and that: "there was such provocation that under the pressure of grievances his mind had been strained to such an extent that he was not responsible for his actions at the moment the fatal shot was

5 *Japan Weekly Mail*, April 16, 1892, p532. See also *London and China Telegraph* May 16, 1892, p382.

fired, and, therefore, I find him not guilty."

The acquittal was greeted in court with a "vociferous cheer" and much celebration by the Americans in Yokohama. Overseas press reports suggested the British community was not happy with the acquittal at all. This, however, seems to have been exaggerated - one presumes that Robinson had not limited his attentions to American women only. The *North China Herald* reported that 260 Englishmen put Hetherington on a carriage to take him to his hotel after the acquittal.[6] Hetherington and his wife left Yokohama soon after this. The US Navy considered court-martialing him but decided not to.[7]

Poisoning in Yokohama

Four years later, in the British Court for Japan, an even greater scandal played out when the young and beautiful Edith Carew was prosecuted for murder for poisoning her husband, Walter Carew.

Walter was the secretary and manager of the Yokohama United Club on the Bund (where Robinson had been

Walter Carew

Edith Carew

6   *North China Herald*, April 29, 1892, p549.

7   The *Times*, Trenton N.J., June 6, 1892.

taken after being shot). He and his wife, Edith, who was 15 years younger than him, lived in Yokohama. They had moved there a few years before from Singapore at the invitation of British barrister John Lowder, a good friend of Walter's and one time Chairman of the United Club. The Carews had married against the wishes of Edith's parents. She came from a well off family in Glastonbury in England, where her father had at one time served as mayor. Edith had an income from her family of about $2,000 per year. Walter liked to party. His salary from the club was not enough to keep the family, meaning that they had to draw on Edith's income. Edith had a financial incentive to be rid of Walter. They both also had extra-marital relationships.

On October 15, 1896, Mr Carew had become sick with what appeared to be a liver complaint. Against his wishes, Edith called his doctor, Dr Edwin Wheeler, who treated him but to no avail. A week later Dr Wheeler met a Mrs Dunlop at a funeral who told him that the Carews' children's nurse had been in great distress. The nurse had said that she needed to tell Dr Wheeler about the poison or Mr Carew would die. Dr Wheeler immediately made arrangements to move Walter to hospital but he died soon after from acute vomiting and diarrhea. On the day of his death, Mrs Carew told Dr Wheeler that her husband had asked her to get some arsenic, then still used as a medicine to treat a number of ailments. Dr Wheeler refused to sign the death certificate and a coroner's inquest was opened on October 24 before John Carey Hall, now British Consul in Yokohama.

The Coroner's jury returned a verdict that Mr Carew had died by arsenic poisoning but did not identify who had administered the poison. Five days later, Edith Carew was charged with murder and committal proceedings were brought before the Assistant Judge, James Troup. Troup committed her for trial before Robert Mowat in the British Court for Japan.

Corona Advocata Japonica

A caricature of Henry Lichtfield on his appointment as Crown Prosecutor in Japan

Judge Robert Mowat was most concerned that Henry Lichtfield, the Crown Prosecutor in Japan, was not up to the case. He wanted H.S. Wilkinson, the Crown Advocate in Shanghai, to be brought over to prosecute. In a particularly unjudicial move, he wrote a note to the British Minister, Ernest Satow, asking: "Will you of your own motion retain Wilkinson to appear with Litchfield on behalf of the Crown? Or shall I write officially to you and request you to do so?" Mowat added, "If you are clear it should be done – just as you thought it right to instruct Litchfield to appear before the Magistrate then I wouldn't trouble to write."[8]

Satow shared Mowat's view that "the crown should be represented by senior counsel," and that Wilkinson was the best man for the job. He had, in fact, already written to Wilkinson three weeks earlier seeking to retain him. He wrote to Wilkinson that: "Mr Carew the Secretary of the Club has died suddenly under very suspicious circumstances" and attached newspaper reports on the case. Satow told Wilkinson he expected John Lowder to defend with assistance from Mr Walford.[9] Noting that Wilkinson would most likely need permission from Peking, he asked: "If we send you a retainer can you come over and conduct the prosecution leading Litchfield?" Wilkinson was not going to miss a chance like this. He responded by telegraph on November 4, 1896: "Affirmative answer in reply to

8   PRO 30/3/6/5.
9   PRO 30/33/6/6 p2. Note dated October 27, 1896 from Satow to Wilkinson.

your private letter of 27 October. Wilkinson"[10]

Satow wrote an unofficial note to Francis Bertie, Head of the Asiatic Section of the Foreign Office, on November 24, 1896 explaining why had had retained Wilkinson to lead the prosecution:

"Litchfield is as deaf as a post, and quite unable to conduct a cross-examination or to hear the speeches of Counsel. Moreover, he is exceedingly dull & slow. But I could not ever put this in a despatch. The second point is that Mowat wrote privately to me urging that Wilkinson should be retained, and offered to address me officially on the subject. But as I think the judge ought not to appear officially except on the bench, I have not accepted his offer, the more so because I feel that Wilkinson's being entrusted with the case is absolutely necessary."[11]

Wilkinson brought his son, Harrie, with him to assist with the prosecution.

The trial itself was a sensation in Japan, China and, indeed, the rest of the world. It was still being written about more than 50 years later in America and even a hundred years later it was the subject of two books, one in Japanese, *An Occurrence in Yokohama*; and, one in English, *Murder on the Bluff*.[12] Of the thousands of cases that were tried by all extraterritorial courts in China and Japan, Mrs Carew's was and remains the highest profile.

10 PRO 30/33/6/6 p4.

11 I. Ruxton (ed), *The Semi-official Letters of British Envoy Sir Ernest Satow from Japan and China (1895-1906)*, Ruxton, Ian (ed), p 57.

12 Much of the commentary in this section is taken from *Murder on the Bluff* as well as the trial transcripts. A full transcript of the trial was published in the *Japan Weekly Mail* in a Supplement dated January 9th 1897 (sic). The *North China Herald* also carried an extract transcript on January 15, 1897, p75; January 22, 1897, p122; January 29, 1897, p176; 5 February 1897, p207; 12 February 1897, p253. The *Japan Gazette* published a full transcript of the coronial inquest, committal and trial. This is available on the Harvard University Library Page Delivery Service.

And for good reason. It had all the right ingredients for a sensation: a philandering husband; a beautiful, much younger wife who also had a secret lover; a mystery woman who wrote letters claiming responsibility for the murder; disappearing evidence; and, the private prosecution of one of the main prosecution witnesses for the same crime. All of this was played out in a strange oriental land in a packed British courtroom before a bewigged British judge and a row of bewigged British barristers with Mrs Carew's fate in the hands of a British jury.[13]

Poisoning cases are notoriously hard to prove and in the late 19th century they were even harder to prove than today. The administration of the poison will either have occurred secretly or only in the presence of the accused and deceased. Further complicating this case, was the fact that arsenic was used as a medicine. As was coyly brought out at the trial, it was principally used to treat sexually transmitted diseases. Mr Carew had been in the habit of taking arsenic, in the form of Fowler's solution. The fact he had taken arsenic could not in itself prove his wife had poisoned him. He could have overdosed himself or could have been suicidal.

Wilkinson and Lichtfield as prosecutors faced an uphill battle to prove the case beyond a reasonable doubt, particularly when a beautiful young lady such as Mrs Carew was in the dock. Their job was all the more hard because Mrs Carew was a wily defendant who had done her best to sow seeds of doubt about who the real killer was. In Lowder, she had an experienced defence attorney, an old friend of her husband, who passionately believed in her innocence, and who would use every seed of doubt sown by Mrs Carew to seek to have her acquitted.

Even before Walter had fallen ill Edith had written a note to

13 The jury of five was made up of A.H.C Watson, R.C.K. Johnson, D. Maclaren, J. Patterson and J. Davieson. J. Walter, A. Owston, C.B. Bernard and G.K. Dinsdale all did not appear in response to the jury summons and were fined $50 each.

him on October 10 that a "woman in black" had come to visit him at home and left a calling card with the initials "A.L." and the year "1888." Walter had had an intimate relationship with an Annie Luke back in England in the 1880s. He apparently blanched considerably when he saw his wife's note. Edith later told Walter that the lady was dressed entirely in black and was wearing a black veil. Two days later Edith sent Walter another note saying that the lady in black had visited again and left the same card. Walter hurried home but could not find the lady. A few days later he received a letter saying:

> "I must see you. Why have you done nothing since you got my two cards? Or perhaps your wife never let you get them. I cannot meet her again. She makes me mad, when I think of what our life together might have been. I cannot give you my address. I am living wherever I can find shelter; but you can find me and help me if you will, as I know you will for the sake of old times. Annie"

None of this made any sense. If Annie really wanted to see Walter, why not just go to the club? Why contact his wife? Further, no strange Englishwoman had been seen in Yokohama. Still, Walter tried to contact Annie writing to her care of the post office and arranging to meet on the Bund at 5.30pm. Walter was not able to make it because he was struck down by illness overnight. Not that it would have mattered; the letter lay uncollected at the post office. Walter did not to recover from the illness and died.

During the coronial inquest further letters were written to Mrs Carew, Mr Lowder and the coroner, John Carey Hall. The letter to Mrs Carew was short and to the point, reading:

> "I have done what I can for you, true, I have made you suffer, but I have written to Mr Hall and to Mr. Lowder,

The Carew Case: Sketches made during the hearing
Judge Mowat, Edith's lover, Harry Dickinson,
A friend of Miss Jacob, Dr Wheeler, H.S. Wilkinson

Yokohama will be troubled no more by A. L."

Annie Luke's letter to Lowder, whoever wrote it, was clearly the product of a tortured, if not demented mind. She started: "Dead men tell no tales: no nor dead women either, for I am going to join him." Then in apparent self-pity, added "Do you know what waiting means for eight long weary years? I have watched and waited, watched till I knew he would grow tired of her, that silly little fool, and then I came to him." She and Walter had met and:

"We, between us, electrify Japan."

Hot stuff, if it was true. Truly demented, if it was written by Edith.

Annie Luke then confessed: "I do not see why I should let a silly innocent woman be condemned for what she knows nothing about, and for which, when you get this, no one on this earth could enlighten her."

To finish, she added that by the time Lowder received this "I shall be well on my way to join him; my twin soul."

Her letter to the coroner repeated the confession and her intention to join her "twin soul."

Lowder was desperate to find Annie Luke and on November 7 he advertised in the papers for anyone who had seen her. No one came forward. On November 11 he received another letter from "A. L." showing she was very much alive and still as demented as before:

"Mr. Lowder,

"It never occurred to you did it that 'my way' to join him might be by the French mail, it never occurred to you did it that I can disguise myself as well as my name, it never occurred to you did it that you never could and never would find me. Who am I and what is my name eh? Is it A L or M J or was I during my stay in Yokohama passing under some other name eh

A. L. ! !"

M J were the initials for the Carew's governess, Mary Jacob.

The trial began on January 4, 1897 before Mowat and a jury of five men. There was no real contest at the trial that arsenic poisoning had killed Mr Carew. The prosecution called medical evidence that Mr Carew had been killed by arsenic. Later, the defence called doctors who said that he may not have died due to the arsenic dosing. They were, however, not willing to say he had not been killed by arsenic. The prosecution medical evidence took up close to four days. The fifth day, Saturday, January 9, 1897 consisted principally of John Carey Hall, the Consul, reading into evidence the transcript of the coroner's inquest. Perhaps it was no surprise that there

were numerous spare seats in the courtroom for members of
the public.

Wilkinson expected to finish Hall's evidence on Monday
setting the stage for the real battle to begin. The remainder
of the prosecution evidence Wilkinson planned to call would
aim to prove that Mrs Carew had obtained more arsenic than
was necessary to treat her husband; that she had a motive
to kill her husband; and that her behaviour before and after the poisoning would lead to the conclusion that she had
killed her husband. The Annie Luke letters also had to be addressed. They could raise a reasonable doubt as to whether
Mrs Carew was the killer. The prosecution needed to show
that either Mrs Carew wrote the letters or, at least, that Annie
Luke never existed. From day six onwards things were going
to get interesting.

Monday, January 11, 1897, day six, started with a bombshell.

The court was packed, not for the prosecution of Mrs
Carew for the murder of Mr Carew, but for the committal of
Mary Jacob, the Carew's governess, for the murder of Walter
Carew. The charges had been brought by John Lowder, Mrs
Carew's lawyer. James Troup, the Assistant Judge, heard the
case. Mr Lowder appeared "in person, not professionally, but
simply as a member of this community who considers it to be
his duty to prefer this charge." Lowder alleged that Jacob was
the author of the Annie Luke letters. The letters were a confession to the killing. Jacob had written them and she must
therefore be the killer.

On Sunday, January 10, Lowder had filed a private complaint against Jacob to the British Consulate who had issued
a warrant for Jacob's arrest. This was executed that afternoon
at the house of Mrs Brittan where Jacob was now working as
a governess. Brittan was American, so the US Marshal was
also in attendance with a document from the US Consul-
General empowering the British official to make an arrest on
the premises. Mary's rooms were searched and certain letters

she had written seized. Sensationally, Lowder was allowed to keep these letters overnight to review them.

The arrest and prosecution of Mary Jacob was a very brave move by Lowder. By bringing a prosecution alleging Walter Carew had been killed, he was effectively admitting that he had been. Of course, by this stage, the prosecution's medical evidence had been heard and it was clear that Walter's death was no accident. Lowder, perhaps, then thought that the only way to save his client was to raise doubt in the jury's mind as to who the killer was. The best way to raise this doubt was to charge someone else with the crime.

He may, however, have had a further, trickier, motive. Under the law of England at the time, Mrs Carew could not give evidence on her own behalf at her trial, the theory being that the accused was bound to lie anyway, so the evidence would serve no purpose.[14] She could, however, give sworn evidence in the committal hearing of Miss Jacob. In a small place like Yokohama, the jury would have no way to avoid finding out what that evidence was.

This was, however, highly risky. The arrest of Miss Jacob, a relatively poor girl with no money to defend herself, caused outrage in Yokohama. Mr George Scidmore, the US Vice-Consul, volunteered his services to defend her and a fund of $1,100 was quickly raised to cover her expenses. An application was made as quickly as possible for bail and Messrs W. W. Till and F. S. James both provided bail bonds. She was quickly granted bail to "a general tone of exultation."

Wilkinson and Satow were both so concerned about the arrest that they wished to pardon Jacob so as to stop her committal from becoming an unnecessary distraction. Satow telegraphed the Foreign Office which after consulting with the Home Office did not recommend the course. After some legal research, it was found that, in any event, the Minister only

14 The law was changed the next year by the Criminal Evidence Act of 1898.

had the power to pardon a convicted person and not someone charged with a crime.[15]

At the same time Jacob was arrested, a telegram was sent through Dalziel's agency that was circulated worldwide announcing her arrest and that she had confessed to poisoning Mr Carew and to sending the Annie Luke letters. Newspapers around the world picked this up, reporting this sensational, but untrue, development.

Jacob's committal hearing proceeded for an hour on Monday morning, Lowder first called a Miss Hutchinson and Edith's brother, Mr Porch, to confirm Edith and Mary's handwriting. The case was adjourned until 8.45 am the next day to allow for the trial of Edith Carew to proceed.

After some delay waiting for Mowat (who presumably had been speaking to Troup about the committal proceedings against Jacob), the main trial re-commenced with the monotony of Hall reading into evidence the record of the coronial inquest. Lowder, did receive one unexpected surprise, when he asked Hall if he had suspected Edith of poisoning Walter solely because Dr Wheeler had told him of his suspicions. Hall said that this was not the case and that when Walter was sick, he and his wife, Agnes, had been out walking and bumped into Edith. Hall said of Edith that "she seemed laboring under very strong mental excitement and was very much preoccupied." At the time, he put it down to Walter's illness, but after Dr Wheeler told him of his suspicions "it at once suggested an entirely different explanation to account for the singularity of Mrs Carew's behavior at the time."

The last witness of the fifth day, Monday, January 11, was a clerk from a Japanese pharmacy, Maruya, who gave very inconclusive evidence as to who had purchased arsenic. Mowat then adjourned the case until Wednesday January 13, to allow

....

15 FO46/150, Foreign Office to Home Office, 11 January 1897 cited in C. Roberts, *The British Courts and Extra-Territoriality in Japan 1859-1899*, p258; See also Whittington-Egan, *Murder on the Bluff*, p138.

the committal proceedings against Mary Jacob to proceed.

The next day at Jacob's committal hearing, Mr Hodges, the British constable and gaoler, gave evidence relating to his arrest of Mary Jacob. John Carey Hall was called, again, to give evidence relating to the coronial inquest.

Lowder then called his main witness, Edith Carew. She gave evidence about the various letters. She denied that some were written by her. She said that Mary had access to the Carew's bookshelves, including one book, the *Play Actress*, that had a chapter, the Lady in Black, as well as a book, the *Romance of Two Worlds*, which included a phrase:

"Thou shalt love and be beloved for ever by thine own Twin Soul; wherever that spirit may be now, it must join thee hereafter."

Mr Scidmore cross-examined Mrs Carew but was not finished by the end of the day. The committal proceedings were adjourned until time could be found for them to recommence.

The next day the courtroom was packed for Edith's trial. Mowat asked the counsel try to speed the case up. The witness from Maruya's was recalled for cross-examination. He did not add much.

Then, the witness everyone had been waiting for, Mr Harry Dickinson, Edith's alleged lover, was called. He and Edith had been in close correspondence on almost a daily basis. They also had a secret signal where Edith would hang a handkerchief in her window so that Dickinson would know the coast was clear and he could visit her. Dickinson was asked to read out intimate letters between himself and Mrs Carew. These included numerous phrases declaring his passion for her and saying that he was envious of Mr Carew. To great embarrassment, he was forced to read out the following declaration of love:

"Dearest, the scene of last night shall not take place
again. We cannot help now I think loving. I know it is
wrong but you are not to blame I think so much as I,
but for others' sake than our's th – grosser sin shall be
avoided."

Dickinson also said Edith had told him Walter mistreated
her and demanded money. She had told him she planned to
speak to Mr Lichtfield about getting a divorce. Dickinson said
that he now believed Edith had been lying to him and leading
him on.

Edith had sent Dickinson some telegrams. Wilkinson had
applied for copies of these through the Japanese courts but
they had not been forthcoming in providing assistance. As
the British court had no jurisdiction over the telegraph office
nothing further could be done.

Edith was clearly embarrassed about the relationship with
Dickinson. During the committal proceedings one of his letters to her had gone missing. It had been found when Martha
Hodges, the wife of the constable of the court searched her
and found the letter inside Mrs Carew's cuff. Mrs Hodges
was called to recount this incident to the jury.

Day ten was to be Wilkinson's turn to play lawyer tricks
on Lowder. First he had a big name witness; a really big name
witness. He called Sir Ernest Satow, the British Minister to Japan. Satow had received a letter from a Mr Price complaining
of the conduct of the inquest into Mr Carew's death. Wilkinson and Lichtfield had asked Satow to give evidence. Satow
had said that he needed approval from the Foreign Office.
No reply had been received by the time they wanted to call
Satow. Wilkinson wrote a note to Satow, saying that he hoped
the "lying press telegrams" about Jacob's confession had not
slowed down receiving Foreign Office approval. Their handwriting expert had told them the Price letter was a "most important link in the chain of evidence, the absence of which

will weaken the case for the Crown very materially." Licht-field and Wilkinson had therefore determined that "despite the weighty objections to calling you as a witness" they must accept the "serious responsibility" of doing so.[16] Given this build up, Satow's evidence was anti-climatic. He confirmed that he had received the letter and was not cross-examined. Wilkinson later proved that Mr Price did not exist, inviting the jury to conclude that Mrs Carew had written the letter.

Despite his protestations in his note to Satow, Wilkinson surely had a secondary goal in calling Satow. That was to impress on the jury the importance of the case: Satow, the most important British official in Japan was prepared to come to Yokohama and give evidence. This impression must have been strong. Before giving evidence, Satow sat on the bench next to Mowat, clearly spelling out his importance and seniority.

Wilkinson then called his handwriting witness, Mr William Mason, a Scot who had worked in the English and Japanese post offices for 23 years in total. Wilkinson had used his love of photography to arrange large-scale enlargements of the letters that were printed on rubber backing for the jury. Mason said that Mrs Carew had, in fact, written the "Annie Luke letters."

Lowder challenged Mason's expertise, in the way only a lawyer in a small town could do. Mason had for many years been the Chess Editor for the *Japan Mail*. One correspondent who sent correct solutions for a whole year went by the pen name "Scacchi." Mason had suspected this was Lowder. Lowder asked him why. Mason said it was because the handwriting of the solution was that of "an Englishman and a lawyer." Lowder then asked if Mason ever found out who Scacchi was. He had. It turned out he was half right. Scacchi was a lawyer, but he was a Scotsman and none other than "His

Lordship on the bench," Mowat.

Lowder in cross-examination got himself into the biggest trouble you can in a jury trial - getting the judge to disagree with you. He asked Mason about one letter:

> Lowder: I should like witness to take Exhibit O and the letter signed "Edith" and addressed to the deceased at the boat-house. It begins: "Dearest Walter, A mysterious lady came here." The h is not looped, is it?
> Mason: I beg your pardon, it is distinctly looped.
> Mowat: I think it is looped, look at it again, Mr. Lowder.
> Lowder: I have looked at it with the glasses and should consider it is not. Perhaps my eyesight is defective.

Lowder then opened the defence. He spent two days reminding the jury that they could only find the defendant guilty if they were satisfied of her guilt beyond reasonable doubt. There was medical evidence that Mr Carew's death may not have been caused by the arsenic doses; a number of witnesses to testify to Mr Carew's taking of arsenic to treat illnesses; as well as some of the Carew's staff. Lowder closed his case reminding the jury again that if they had any reasonable doubt they should acquit.

Wilkinson, in reply, went through the evidence emphasizing that after considering all the testimony, there could be only one verdict, that of guilty.

It was now Mowat's turn to address the jury. On the final day, February 1, 1897, he gave a detailed and very fair summing up. He told the jury the medical evidence pointed strongly to Mr Carew having been poisoned. It could only be suicide or murder. There was no suggestion of a motive for suicide. The evidence of Mr Carew's arsenic use was not recent. He pointed out strongly that Mrs Carew's failure to tell Dr Wheeler about the arsenic earlier was highly suspicious.

With regard to the Annie Luke letters, Mr Mason's testimony that they had been written by Mrs Carew appeared to be strong. The jury should also consider why no one had come forward who had seen or heard of Annie Luke. He suggested the Price letter to Ernest Satow was not of great importance. The evidence of Mr Dickinson, Edith's lover, did not necessarily give a motive, but, in any event, they were not required to identify a motive to find the Defendant guilty.

He then charged the jury, who retired at 2.23pm and returned at 3.03pm after deliberating for less than 40 minutes.[17] Mr Moss, the Chief Clerk, asked, his voice quivering with emotion, the foreman, Mr Paterson, if they had agreed upon a verdict. Paterson replied that they had. He was then asked if their verdict was guilty or not guilty. Mr Paterson replied a deep Scots accent:

"Guilty."

The court was completely silent. Mowat then asked Carew if she had anything to say as to why sentence should not be passed on her. Carew stood "with blanched cheeks and a quivering mouth" and in a "voice whose husky dullness contrasted painfully with her wonted tones" responded through "trembling lips" with a faint:

"No."

Mowat addressing Lowder said that the sentence that he was about to pass could not be carried into effect without the approval of the British Minister, Ernest Satow. Satow would review the evidence and proceedings and then give instructions as to whether the penalty should be inflicted.

Mowat was obviously moved by the case and the verdict

17 This section on the verdict and sentencing is sourced from the *London Gazette* of March 8, 1897 p195 and *North China Herald* February 12, 1897, p268.

he was now forced to deliver. He perhaps also remembered witnessing the execution of Robert George all those years ago in Shanghai. The correspondent of the *Japan Mail*, in tortured prose, described the scene:

> "Then amid even more painful silence he assumed the three-cornered black cap, and, in a voice broken and trembling, uttered the words of doom:
>
> > 'The sentence of the Court upon you, Edith May Hallowell Carew, is, that you be forthwith taken from the place where you now stand to the British Consular Jail at Yokohama, and there remain interned until after a convenient time, when, on a subsequent day appointed by the proper authority, you shall be led out to the place of your execution within the precincts of the Consular Jail, and there be hanged by the neck until you are dead, and your body shall then be taken down and be buried within the precincts of the jail.'"

Mowat, visibly trembling, in a voice that was "scarcely audible," forced the final sentence from his throat:

> "May God have mercy on your soul."

> "Thus," concluded the *Japan Mail's* correspondent, "Edith May Hallowell Carew, the bright attractive, refined lady, whom so many in this small community have known intimately, and so many have been happy to call their friend passed from the pale of society that she once graced – stepped down, a condemned felon."

The file then went to Satow to approve the sentence. Satow was not squeamish about death. He had been with the British troops in Kagoshima and Shimonoseki. He had refused entreaties from the Japanese to spare a former samurai who had killed a Briton. He had then watched and recorded in detail the former samurai performing harakiri.

But this was different. Satow now held the power of life or death in his own hands. He felt Mowat's pain and obviously did not want to be the man responsible for Carew's execution. He wrote later, "you can imagine what it must be for a man for the first time in his life to pronounce a sentence of death: Just say the words out loud and see how you feel them. It was horrible. For me I had the comfort of never having seen her before trial, and him I had seen only twice."[18]

Satow reflected further, "and for the whole community who know both the poisoned and the poisoner, and dined, played, walked, bicycled, danced with one or the other. The cases we read in papers are no more to us than a story out of a book, but here is someone out of their own daily life."

Satow had an awesome responsibility now on his shoulders. He had appointed Wilkinson to prosecute. He had given evidence for the Crown at her trial. He had done all he could to get a verdict of guilty. He now had to make a decision: Life or Death?

He blinked.

The formal announcement read:

"In view of the Imperial Proclamation of His Majesty the Emperor dated the 31st of January, granting to all Japanese subjects under sentence on that day a remission of punishment, it appears proper that a similar measure of grace should be extended to the criminal in this case whose trial ... was about to be brought to a

---

18 This and following quotes from Satow regarding commuting Carew's sentence are from Sir Ernest Satow's Private Letters to WG Aston and FV Dickins (Ian Ruxton, Ed), p220 (from PRO 30/33 11/6).

conclusion at the time of His Majesty's Proclamation."[19]

Satow commuted the sentence to imprisonment for life with hard labour.

Even this was a fudge. The remission granted by the Japanese Emperor came into effect on the Emperor's birthday on January 31. Carew had been convicted on February 1. Satow acknowledged this, writing "it was a great relief that a way could be found out of issuing a warrant for execution." Mowat was, perhaps, even happier writing to Satow on February 4, "I was pleased that you saw your way to commutation, and relieved at not having had to express any opinion."[20]

As to where she should serve her sentence, Mowat wrote to Satow suggesting Hong Kong. Carew was transferred to Hong Kong in October where she was detained in Victoria Prison for some months. In great secrecy she was then and put on a ship to England to serve the remainder of her sentence in Aylesbury Women's Prison in Buckinghamshire.[21]

Following Edith Carew's conviction, Lowder withdrew the case against Mary Jacob and apologized in a public letter to her for bringing the charges. He then dropped a bombshell that was hidden in obscure legalese. In a letter to Mr Scidmore, Jacob's lawyer, he wrote:

"The publication of the letter I addressed to Miss Jacob on the 13th inst. has resulted in a communication to me of facts which indicate the existence of the duplicity and deceit which is to my mind unimaginable, inconceivable; of which I among others, have been the unconscious dupe, and Miss Jacob the victim; and which would go far to reconcile the most advanced modern

---

19 *North China Herald*, February 12, 1897, p247.

20 PRO 30/33/6/6.

21 S.79 of the Order in Council allowed for the transfer of prisoners. Re Carew leaving Hong Kong: *China Mail*, December 20, 1897.

thought with the answers of the Judges to the questions propounded to them by the House of Lords in 1843, arising out the decision of M'Naghten's case. Words fail me to express the regret which hearing of the story has filled me; for I feel that an act of injustice has been committed for which, had it been intentional on my part, no reparation in my power could be adequate.

"You will be able to explain to your client that a lawyer, even under the developed circumstances of this case, may not be at liberty to make public all he knows, and may be prevented from adducing evidence which Miss Jacobs might justly demand without opening open to any accusations of inquisitiveness; but short of the revelation of a professional confidence I shall be glad of any suggestion from her or yourself as to what farther action you would wish me to take for the more complete vindication of her character."[22]

For a layman this is almost meaningless. But there are two clear clues in here. First, M'Naghten's case is a famous decision of the House of Lords to determine the criminal liability of the insane. Second, English lawyers are prohibited from revealing what their client has told them about a crime they have committed.

Put the two together, and Lowder's message is completely clear:

"Mrs Carew is crazy. She has now told me she killed him. She set Mary Jacob up. I was tricked just as much as you. I am truly sorry."

Despite this, the case had one more twist in it. It seems that Jacob had herself, in England, been convicted of theft and had

---

22 *Nagasaki Shipping List*, February 24, 1897, p2. See also the *Nagasaki Shipping List* of February 18, 1897, p2 for Lowder's letter to Jacob.

written fake letters to explain away her crimes.[23]

An application was made to the Privy Council for leave to appeal Carew's conviction on the basis that she had only had a trial before a jury of five instead of 12 jurors. This was rejected.[24]

Her family made numerous applications for early release, all of which were refused. In particular, the false accusations against Mary Jacob appear to have weighed against her. She was released in November 1910 from Aylesbury Prison.[25] She lived for a further 40 years with her daughter, without remarrying, in Wales.

Edith Carew on her release from prison, on the other side of the world from where she committed her crime, became probably the last person imprisoned by an extraterritorial court in Japan to be set free. This brought to a close, for Japan, the bizarre system of extraterritoriality.

Some minor traces of the system that can still be found in Japan. Chief Justice George French is buried in Kobe. Four of the main characters in the Carew case, Walter Carew, John Lowder, the coroner, John Carey Hall and the doctor, Edwin Wheeler, are all buried in the Yokohama Foreigners' Cemetery on the Bluff.

Walter's grave is at the top of the cemetery in a beautiful location overlooking Yokohama Harbour. The gravestone reads: "In Loving memory of my husband."[26] Four lines from Tennyson's poem "Crossing the Bar"[27] are enscribed:

---

23 For more on the aftermath of the case, see Molly Whittington-Egan's *Murder on the Bluff*.

24 *London and China Telegraph*, July 19, 1897, p597.

25 *North China Herald*, November 4, 1910, p257.

26 Walter's gravestone lies on the path of a tour that is given on most Saturdays but can also be seen from outside the cemetery. It is the fourth grave in from the far Western edge on the top of the bluff. The gravestone is placed almost horizontally on the ground.

27 One wonders if this poem was chosen purposefully by Mrs Carew given her trickery. The full poem is: Sunset and evening star,/ And one clear call for me!/ And may there be no moaning of the bar,/ When I put out to sea,/ But such a tide as moving seems asleep,/ Too full for sound and foam,/ When that which drew from out the boundless deep/ Turns again home.

"Twilight and evening star,
and one clear call for me:
and may there be no moaning of the Bar
when I put out to sea."

This is followed the last two lines of a poem by George Du Marier. Given that Edith Carew was convicted of murdering her husband and sentenced to death, the words are spine chilling:

"A little trust that when we die,
we reap our sowing, and so goodbye."[28]

Twilight and evening bell,/And after that the dark!/And may there be no sadness of farewell,/When I embark;/For tho' from out our bourne of Time and Place/The flood may bear me far,/I hope to see my Pilot face to face/When I have crost the bar.

28 The full words are: A little work, a little play/To keep us going – and so good-day!/A little warmth, a little light/Of love's bestowing – and so, good-night/A little fun, to match the sorrow/Of each day's growing – and so, good-morrow!/A little trust that when we die/We reap our sowing – and so – good-bye!

CHAPTER 25

Endings and New Beginnings

Mowat retires hurt

SOON AFTER PASSING sentence against Edith Carew, Robert Mowat went to Nagasaki to deal with a lunacy case, but instead had a complete nervous breakdown himself. The *Nagasaki Shipping List* reported "that Judge Mowat has contracted a severe illness since his arrival here about a week ago, and his physicians have ordered him a season of perfect rest and change, and attributed this to the very heavy strain of the Carew case."[1]

Chief Justice Nicholas Hannen wrote to the Foreign Office from Shanghai in early March 1897 recommending that Mowat be allowed to retire "as this beastly Carew case has completely broken him up." This was followed in mid-March, by a note from Ernest Satow, the British Minister in Tokyo, to Francis Bertie, Head of the Asiatic Section of the Foreign Office, saying he had heard from Shanghai, where Mowat had gone for his "perfect rest and change," that Mowat had written to the Secretary of State applying to retire on grounds of ill-health. Satow added, "I have not seen him for some time, but before the Carew trial he was in a very nervous condition, and he seems to have completely broken down. So I suppose the Treasury will not oppose his application."[2]

1 *Nagasaki Shipping List*, February 25, 1897, reported in the *North China Herald* of March 5, 1897.

2 Hannen to Sanderson, March 4, 1897, FO17/1324, cited in C. Roberts, *The British Courts and Extraterritoriality in Japan, 1859 to 1899*, 54n; *The Semi-official Letters of British Envoy Sir Ernest Satow from Japan and China (1895-1906)*, Edited by Ian Ruxton, 1997, p73.

Satow also telegraphed Wilkinson who had just returned to Shanghai asking him if he could travel to Nagasaki to handle the lunacy case as Acting Judge. Surprisingly, Wilkinson was reluctant. He wrote to Claude MacDonald the British Minister in China, to say that "my son has been lain up for some time with fever; and my absence in Japan for the Carew case has put me in such a position that a similar absence would entail very great inconvenience." On the other hand, Wilkinson knew he was in prime position for his long-held dream to be appointed a full-time judge and added: "But as the judicial work at Nagasaki is of such a nature that there might be some difficulty in arranging for the dispatch of it unless I go, I am prepared to devote the necessary time for the purpose."[3]

Wilkinson was not the only candidate to replace Mowat full-time. George Jamieson also made an application to Lord Salisbury for the postion of Judge for Japan. He had no particular desire to go to Japan but did want to be Chief Justice. He appreciated that if Hannen retired, "the applicant from Japan will have a better claim" for the position of Chief Justice.[4]

Wilkinson, however, had the support of the Satow who strongly recommend him to the Foreign Office for both the position as Judge for Japan, to run the two years until the treaty expired in 1899, and as Chief Justice of the Supreme Court in Shanghai, when Hannen retired two years later. He concluded his letter to Bertie by saying that Wilkinson was:

"the only available man to take Mowat's place, and would be a very efficient judge. I trust therefore that he may receive the substantive appointment on Mowat's retirement. He has been in the service one way or an-

....

3 PRONI, D1292 Letter from Wilkinson to Claude MacDonald, February 25, 1897, Wilkinson Papers.

4 FO17/1324 Letter from Jamieson to Salisbury, April 23, 1897, cited in C. Roberts, *The British Courts and Extraterritoriality in Japan, 1859 to 1899*, 48n.

other for 34 years and has done a great deal of excellent work."[5]

Satow addressed the possible concern that it may be "inexpedient to appoint him Judge for Japan when there are only 2 years more to run before the new Treaty comes into operation," but observed that "Hannen will about that time be entitled to retire, and Wilkinson would be his obvious successor at Shanghai, so that the question of pensioning Wilkinson after only 2 years at Yokohama is scarcely likely to arise."

Hannen, himself, supported Wilkinson's appointment arguing that it would be unfair on the British community in Japan not to appoint a full time judge and that Wilkinson was "the best man to fill the post. He was very good in filling the Acting Post to the detriment of his private practice here and has a kind of claim to the permanent appointment."[6]

Wilkinson was appointed Acting Judge in Japan from June 18 to November 10, 1897. On that date he was appointed Judge of the Court for Japan upon the formal retirement of Mowat.

Harrie Wilkinson, at the very young age of 31, saw his career advance very quickly when he was appointed the next month to replace his father as Crown Advocate in Shanghai. The only downside in the appointment for Harrie was that

OUR LEADING LAWYERS

No. I.—Mr. H. P. Wilkinson, Crown Advocate

Harrie Wilkinson succeeds his father as Crown Advocate

5   *The Semi-official Letters of British Envoy Sir Ernest Satow from Japan and China (1895-1906)*, Edited by Ian Ruxton, 1997, p73.

6   FO17/1324 Hannen to (private), March 4, 1897, cited in C. Roberts, *The British Courts and Extraterritoriality in Japan, 1859 to 1899*, p56.

Nicholas Hannen took away the chambers that had been assigned to the Crown Advocate in the courthouse on the basis
that having the Crown Advocate located in the courthouse
could lead to a perception of bias.[7]

Mowat moved back to England and after retirement he almost completely disappeared from sight. Unlike other former
judges, such as Rennie and Jamieson, he did not attend China
Association dinners in London, even when there were special
events such as Ernest Satow's retirement. He did attend one
function in 1902 for Hirobumi Ito, the former prime minister of Japan, when Ito visited London but other than that he
appears to have made no public appearances. Despite his ill
health when he retired, Mowat lived for another 27 years to
the ripe old age of 82. He died in 1925 in Hove.[8]

The Extraterritorial boot on the other foot

Nicholas Hannen continued to act as Chief Justice and Consul-General in Shanghai. In his capacity as Consul-General he
had to deal with one case which almost certainly he would
have been very happy to pass on to a consular official. This
was a claim made by a British company Bennertz & Co
against the Kiangnan Pay and Defence Department (PDD) in
relation to four ships that it had hired from the PDD. Bennertz claimed that the PDD had agreed to pay for repairs on
the ships that Bennertz had carried out. The PDD alleged that
Bennertz had become insolvent and had not paid its charter-
party fees. The PDD arranged for the ships to be stopped by
Chinese Customs officials and in the case of one ship applied
to the Hong Kong Supreme Court for it to be arrested. This
led to additional claims by both parties. Bennertz claimed
for lost profits because the ships had been seized. The PDD

7   C. Roberts, "Hiram Shaw Wilkinson (1840-1926)", in H. Cortazzi (ed.), *Britain and
Japan Biographical Portraits*, Vol. VIII, p173 and n50.

8   Mowat at reception for Ito: *London and China Telegraph*, January 6, 1902, p 12; Obituary, *Times*, June 9, 1925.

claimed for losses because it could not use the ships and had to hire other ships.[9]

The case was the subject of intense diplomatic negotiations. At one point the Chinese side offered to have the case arbitrated by two foreign arbitrators. Bennertz rejected this proposal, stating that he would only accept it if the Chinese first admitted they had breached the contracts and that the arbitrators should only decide how much damages should be paid.

The Chinese did not agree to this. In the end a special *ad hoc* court was established to hear the case. Tsai Chun, the President of the Bureau of Foreign Affairs at Nanking was appointed as judge by Imperial High Commissioner Liu of the Nanyang Administration and Viceroy of the Liang Kiang provinces. Pursuant to the Chefoo Convention Nicholas Hannen attended "merely … to watch the proceedings in the interests of justice." Hannen, who by this time had sat as a judge for almost 20 years, clearly chafed at being a mere observer. At the trial, Mr Tsai sat on a raised dais with his interpreter, Mr Fung Yee, to the left. Hannen also sat on the dais to Mr Tsai's right with his interpreter, Mr James Scott, the British Assessor at the Mixed Court, on his right.

Harrie Wilkinson, together with Mr E. Nelson of the law firm Johnson Stokes and Master, appeared for Bennertz. Vernon Drummond appeared for the Defendants.

The first day of the hearings was in early summer starting on 30 June 1897. The Court was held in an improvised court in a building known as the Ambassadors' Hall adjoining the Temple of Heaven in Shanghai. All of the arguments and submissions were made in English with the proceedings being interpreted into Chinese by the interpreters. The proceedings effectively took place in the open air, as most of the court was open to the sky. This was described as "a most satisfactory

9 *North China Herald,* September 4, 1897, P387. "The Judgment in the Bennertz case in Hong Kong," *North China Herald,* December 17, 1897.

arrangement under the circumstances of the weather." Towards the latter part of the proceedings, tea and cigarettes were passed around.[10]

On the first day of the hearing, Wilkinson was not able to attend, so Nelson opened the case for Bennertz. The PDD had filed a counterclaim against Bennertz. Nelson immediately raised an objection to the counterclaim on the basis that a claim against a British subject should be brought in the British Court. Drummond responded that while under the decision in the *Chishima* case this may be correct in a British court, "that decision had no binding effect upon a Chinese Court, as that now sitting was. He thought it was within the power of the Court to take all such circumstances into consideration on both sides and give judgment."

Tsai retired to consider the matter and then without making a ruling told Nelson to proceed with his case. Nelson then read out the Plaintiff's claim and the Defendant's defence and counterclaim.

While the proceedings may have started in beautiful weather, they were to go on for six weeks, dragging into midsummer. At some point they were moved to the Canton Guild Hall. Drummond was well-known for taking his time on cases. He was ably assisted by the fact that as an ad hoc court there were no rules of procedure and by the fact that Tsai was more than willing to allow the case to run on and on. Numerous witnesses were called on each side, with Drummond, in particular, taking his time over questioning them.

This lead to fireworks in the first week of August, the peak of Shanghai's unpleasantly hot summer. Drummond was cross-examining a Mr Pollack concerning the accounts of Bennertz and Co. Pollack said that he "could not speak accurately upon the accounts as he was not familiar with the details."[11]

10 Bennertz v The Kiangnan Defence and Pay Department, *North China Herald*, July 2, 1897, p39.

11 This and other quotes regarding August 4, 1897 are from the *North China Herald* of

Hannen asked Drummond if it was not a waste of time to ask questions about the accounts if the witness did not know about them. Hannen made clear what he thought, saying that if it were his court he would consider it a waste of time.

Drummond responded that he was entitled to ask any question he liked.

Hannen had had enough and the following testy exchange occurred:

Hannen: I say it is a waste of time, and I think that the length to which this enquiry has gone is a scandal. However, if the Court chooses not to take any notice of it I cannot do any more, but I would point out that in my own Court I should regard this as a waste of time. If this Court chooses to go on hearing questions which the witness cannot answer, then all I can say is I have done my best.
Drummond: I should like to know what particular matter you refer to when you speak of this being a scandal.
Hannen: This case has been going on from the 30th of June; and I say the mere length of it is a scandal.
Drummond: That is a very strong statement and a very general one to make. I should like to know whose fault it is.
Hannen: I did not direct it at anybody.

Drummond was not willing to back down and after some further discussion lay the blame for much of the delay on Hannen, saying: "All the difficulty in this I think has arisen from your own action in the matter. A good deal of time has been wasted on discussion arising out of points raised by you." Drummond then added that the case raised very intricate issues, to which Hannen responded that those issues had not even been broached.

Things then got even hotter than the weather when Drummond accused Hannen of bias:

> Drummond: Well, that is your opinion, but my opinion
> is they have been broached to a very great extent. I am
> quite aware that your opinion is entirely different. I have
> known that from the beginning; and before the case
> began.
> Hannen: That has nothing whatever to do with it; if you
> have it in any of my dispatches you have a right to say
> so.
> Mr. Drummond: I have it from your dispatches and your
> own language.
> Hannen: Anything that can be discovered from my own
> dispatches you have a right to mention. I am not aware I
> have ever expressed an opinion.
> Drummond: I am distinctly of the opinion that you have
> so committed yourself to the support of Mr. Bennertz'
> case long ago that it would be impossible to take this
> case into the English Court. That is a simple question.

Hannen then sought to dampen down the flames by bringing the question back to whether the witness should be questioned further on the accounts.

Hannen may possibly have been testy because the next day, he was due to try a case involving the alleged killing of a Chinese by the English quartermaster of the P&O mail steamer, the *Thames*.[12] No judge can enjoy trying a case where the possible penalty includes death. He may also have been concerned for Wilkinson and Nelson because they were both due to appear in the case, Wilkinson as the prosecutor and Nelson for the defence. The quartermaster, Richard Ryan,

----

12 *R v Ryan, North China Herald*, August 6, 1897, p 280. See also an editorial in the same edition at p246.

had been charged with manslaughter. He was alleged to have pushed Ko Chuan-ping, a cargo boat coolie into the river three weeks before on July 16, 1897. The prosecution case was fraught with difficulties, the most important being that no body had been found. The River Police had found two bodies near the site but they had not been identified as Ko's. The case relied solely on the evidence of Chinese witnesses, who said they had seen Ryan push Ko. The trial commenced on August 5 with Hannen sitting with the Chinese city magistrate. The case had started after Ko's brother had filed a petition with both the British Consulate and the City Magistrate. The Magistrate had conducted an enquiry, but because the accused was British he had to be tried by the British Supreme Court. A jury of five was empanelled. In a rare occurrence, it appears that the jury was not all white. A Mr J. Moosa, who was most likely of Indian descent, was a member of the panel. The other members of the jury were Messrs A. McKelvie, W.T. Phipps, G.V.T. Marshal and J.C. Grant. Four Chinese witnesses were called, including the deceased's brother and brother in law. All gave evidence that Ryan had pushed Ko into the river. They said that after Ryan had pushed Ko, they had challenged him. Ryan had got on the *Thames* and come out with two guns.

Inspector Mellows of the River Police gave evidence that in total eight bodies had been fished from the river in the past month. He added that in summer a body would normally float within 24 hours unless caught on a pontoon. In winter, the longest he had seen a body stay down was eight months.

Opening the defence, Nelson requested that verdict of not guilty be directed on the basis that no body had been found and that the case law was that, other than in exceptional circumstances, unless there was a body there could be no conviction. Wilkinson accepted that as the law for murder but not for manslaughter. Hannen ruled that a prosecution for murder or manslaughter could proceed without a body and it was a matter for the jury to decide. Four witnesses from the *Thames* gave evidence. The Captain said that Ryan was a quiet man. One witness had reported someone falling in the river. One witness said that Ryan had been standing on the pontoon with a long hook looking like he was trying to recover something.

Hannen and all those in the court would have been acutely aware of how British justice was conducted (or seen to be conducted) in this case would have a significant impact on the Bennertz case. Indeed, it is a surprise that the case was even prosecuted given there was no body and no apparent motive for the killing. Perhaps "political expediency" had come into play and pressure put on Wilkinson to prosecute a weak case. In any event, Hannen summed up as fairly as he could by saying the jury were in a "difficult position because there was no doubt that there was nothing improbable or extraordinary about the Chinese evidence until they came to the rebutting evidence. For the defence, one witness said distinctly he saw the man running, that the quartermaster did not push him, and that the man slipped on the beam and fell in. Then there were three or four other witnesses, and "if they were believed the story of the Chinese witnesses could not be true." The case clearly had not been proved beyond reasonable doubt and in other circumstances, Hannen may have been more direct with the jury. In any event, the jury retired for five minutes and returned with a verdict of "not guilty."

Hannen, Wilkinson and Nelson returned to the Guild Hall the very next day to continue the Bennertz case, which ran for another three weeks, eventually finishing on August 29. Tsai said that his decision would be announced in open court after notice was given to the parties.

Two weeks later, on September 11, 1897, Tsai issued his decision to the newspapers without a hearing. He repeated in the decision the various arguments that had been made and then found for the Chinese Defendants, dismissing Bennertz's claim in its entirety. He said that the evidence was that Bennertz and Co were in financial difficulties and the PDD had been right to have the ships seized. He added a, perhaps justified, flourish of nationalism:

"The power of detaining the said steamers, according to my opinion, rested solely on the fact that they were flying the Chinese flag, hence the steamers were amenable to the Chinese law. Moreover, China is an independent country and the Chinese authorities had a perfect right to detain their own ships. Hence, the claims of the plaintiffs are ordered by me to be refused. I find that the plaintiffs are wholly in the wrong, and that they unreasonably detained the said vessels for a whole twelve months."

He said that the Plaintiffs should compensate the Defendants but "as the latter have not given any evidence of the amount they have lost, nor have they pressed the Court to make an award, there is no necessity for dealing further on the point," adding finally that the Plaintiff should return the ships.

The true reason for not ordering the Plaintiff to compensate the Defendant was probably more political than legal. While the Chinese may have liked to assert a right to try British companies and subjects, this would have been certain to provoke a strong reaction as being a breach of the treaties granting extraterritorial rights.

The judgment as it stood produced a strong enough reaction. First, British gunboats were ordered to prevent Chinese officials from moving the ships from their moorings.[13] Second, Hannen issued a blistering protest.[14] He complained first that Tsai had ordered there be no personal communi-

---

13 *London and China Telegraph*, September 19, 1897, p780.
14 *North China Herald*, October 8, 1897, p663-664.

cation between himself and Hannen concerning the case. Hannen said this was without precedent, noting that in the Mixed Court, the Magistrates and Assessors would regularly confer privately. He then complained about the length of the proceedings and that the proceedings were "as it seemed to me, controlled entirely by the defendants' counsel whose suggestions on important or unimportant points were adopted in every instance, sometimes without hearing the plaintiffs' counsel's objections." He made some other criticisms of the procedure and then addressing Drummond's behaviour said:

> "During the course of the case, the defendants' counsel made remarks and addressed me in a manner which everybody acquainted with the ordinary rules of courtesy in courts must have felt to be unseemly; and this was done without one word of remonstrance from the presiding judge. Had such remarks been made to a Chinese magistrate sitting at the bench with me, I should have insisted on an apology and I should have known how to enforce it."

Hannen did not, however, want to be personally critical of Mr Tsai and added:

> "I desire to add that so far as Mr. Tsai himself is concerned I have experienced the greatest courtesy and consideration I make every allowance for the position in which he was placed, in conducting an important case in a novel and unfamiliar manner, and I quite see that his position was a very difficult one."

He then said that it was unfortunate that Mr Tsai would not consult with him because their views of the case had proceeded on "different planes."

Pausing for a moment, it is worth considering how Chinese officials felt in the British Courts. No doubt they were treated with the greatest courtesy and consideration. However, they were not allowed to speak to the jury nor to even address it. They must have felt very much like Hannen felt: frozen out.

Hannen in his protest then addressed the substance of the decision shortly saying that if the Defendants had a claim against the Plaintiffs under the treaty they should have made a claim to the British Consul or the British court. He finished by saying that if Tsai's comment that the steamers should be returned was an order, Tsai had no jurisdiction to make it.

The British did not let the matter end there and continued negotiations with the Chinese. Bennertz went bankrupt, perhaps due to the losses and costs of dealing with the case. The British Official Receiver took over the claim and it was subsequently reported that the case was resolved with the Chinese paying 72,000 taels of the total claim by Bennertz of 170,000 taels and the ships being returned.[15]

The Bennertz bankruptcy was handled by Hannen in the Supreme Court. One can imagine that he must have felt a tinge of guilt at not having been able to help Bennertz more in the case.[16]

Amalgamation ends

Hannen's protest in the Bennertz case was signed "Nicholas J Hannen, HBM's Consul-General." This was to be one of Hannen's last acts as Consul-General. Opposition to the amalgamation had continued since it was introduced. In 1893, Hannen had sent a note to the Foreign Office saying that reversion to the old system would please everybody. In 1896, Byron Brenan, a senior consular official, in a report on British trade in China said that the two offices had to be

15 *London and China Telegraph*, June 20, 1898, p595.
16 *North China Herald*, April 25, 1898, p729.

separated. He emphasized that the Consul-General, at times, had to be partisan and act in ways unbecoming of a high judicial office. He added that, in practice, Hannen was acting as Chief Justice and Jamieson as Consul-General. It would be better for all if the *de jure* position corresponded with the *de facto* position.

Philip Currie, the architect of amalgamation, had by this time moved to Constantinople as British Ambassador to the Ottoman Empire. With its main supporter gone, the decision was made to end amalgamation to separate the roles of Chief Justice and Consul-General.[17] The amalgamation of the two roles officially came to an end on December 8, 1897. An official notice was issued on that date stating that:

> "It has been decided on public grounds to separate the offices of Chief Justice and Consul-General at Shanghai."

Hannen continued as Chief Justice and surrendered all consular responsibilities. Jamieson, who had been made a Companion of the Order of St Michael and St George (CMG) in June that year in recognition of his services, was appointed Consul-General. Hannen retained his full salary of £2,100 and precedence as Chief Justice.[18]

Early the next year at a dinner for some British cyclists, who were cycling around the world, Mr R.W. Little, a former Chairman of the Shanghai Municipal Council, rose to toast Hannen and Jamieson. He said:

> "When the amalgamation of the Chief Justiceship with the Consul-Generalship was decided on, it was re-

---

17 P.D. Coates, *The China Consuls*, p220.

18 *London and China Telegraph*, December 16,1897, p1045; Telegram from Salisbury to Hannen, December 30, 1897, FO17/1342 p49n cited in C. Roberts, *The British Courts and Extraterritoriality in Japan, 1859 to 1899*; Jamieson CMG: *London Gazette*, July 6, 1897, p3699.

marked then objectionable as the new departure was, it was alleviated to us by the appointment as the first occupants, of the dual posts of the two best men that could have been selected, Sir Nicholas, Hannen and Mr. George Jamieson. (Cheers) Experience has amply proved the justice of the remark."[19]

Mr Little praised Hannen highly for the way in which he had handled his role as Consul-General:

"But I wish specially to say a few words on the work that Sir Nicholas has done as Consul-General. Rudyard Kipling has made it a great point in the character of Lord Roberts - and it has become a proverb -- that 'he doesn't advertise,' and I may say the same thing of Sir Nicholas. He doesn't go about with a placard oh his back, 'I'm the British Consul-General, and don't you forget it.' (Laughter) He doesn't come up to you and say 'Of course, I don't want you to say anything about it, but it was I who put that affair through.'"

Jamieson was expected to serve as Consul General for some time, but to the disappointment of the Foreign Office, retired from consular service due to ill health at the end of April 1899. After retirement, he became a director of the British and Chinese Corporation, the Chinese Central Railways and Yangtse Valley Company.

He also helped establish a "China League" due to disagreements with the policies of the China Association. After this was patched up, he served as the president of the China Association from 1914 to 1917. In 1916, on the nomination of the China Association, he was appointed a governor of the School of Oriental Studies, now the School of Oriental and

19 *North China Herald*, January 7, 1898, p21.

African Studies (SOAS), in London. He died in London on December 30, 1920.[20]

Before his death, Jamieson completed a book, *Chinese Family and Commercial Law*, based on translations that he had prepared many years before of sections of China's General Code of Laws. The book, which also included Jamieson's translations of various cases from the International Mixed Court, was published in 1921. Interestingly in the Frontispiece of the book, Jamieson identified himself as a "Barrister-at-Law" and "Formerly HBM Consul-General at Shanghai," but made no mention of his position as Judge of the Supreme Court for China and Japan or that he had sat as an assessor of the Mixed Court.[21]

In the introduction to the book Jamieson noted that "China is going through a period of transition and a recasting of her laws and judicial procedure is occupying the attention of her jurists. Already a criminal code has been revised and it is understood that a Civil Code is in course of preparation. The time therefore may not be inopportune to present this pioneer treatise on Civil Law as it now prevails."

He then dedicated his book:

"To the men engaged on such work and especially the young law students who will be the future pleaders and judges of the Courts in China I venture to dedicate this work."

Hannen goes to Bangkok

Hannen was held in high regard not just in Shanghai, but internationally. Just before the positions of Chief Justice and Consul-General were separated, in recognition of his high standing as a jurist and diplomat, Hannen received an appointment from the United States and Thailand to arbitrate

20 *London and China Telegraph*, January 3, 1921, p7.
21 G. Jamieson, *Chinese Family and Commercial Law*, 1921, Preface and Introduction.

a dispute between the estate of Dr M.A. Cheek, an American Citizen, and the Government of Siam.

In 1889, Cheek and the Government of Siam had entered into a ten-year agreement to exploit teak logging concessions in Northern Siam in and around Chiang Mai.[22] As part of the agreement, Cheek agreed with Prince Warawan Naokorn to borrow 600,000 ticals (about US$300,000). The loan carried an interest rate of 7.5% per year. Under the agreement Cheek had also mortgaged all teak wood and his 76 elephants as security for the loan. Cheek was required to deliver at Bangkok certain quantities of wood to pay the mortgage. In those days, logs were floated down river during the rainy season for delivery in Bangkok. In 1891, the first year of the agreement, the rains had come and Cheek had been able to get his logs to market, sell them and then pay the interest on the loan. However, in 1892 and 1893, due to the lack of rain to fill the rivers, Cheek had not been able to get any logs to market. In 1892 the Prince had agreed to roll over the interest until the next year. In 1893 after Cheek could not pay, the Prince decided to call on the mortgage. In 1894 when logs could be floated downstream, the Siamese government issued orders seizing Cheek's logs and then sold them at auction at a low price. The Siamese claimed Cheek still owed them money. Cheek claimed damages for improper seizure, arguing that it was the custom when financing logging operations that loans would be rolled over in dry years until wet years came. Sometime in the course of this, Cheek died, but his estate continued the claim.

Americans had extraterritorial rights in Siam at the time. The Siamese should have brought a claim against Cheek in the US Consular Court, but this did not happen. Instead, the Siamese just seized the logs and sold them. Cheek's claim

---

22 The background to this arbitration and all US correspondence has been reproduced in a report on the case by President Grover Cleveland sent to the Senate on March 2, 1897 reproduced in Foreign Relations of the United States.

would normally need to be heard in the Thai courts, where, of course, Cheek's estate had no chance of winning against the Crown Prince. It was therefore agreed between US and Siam that the issue should be arbitrated.

Originally, it was suggested that the arbitrator be the British Governor of the Straits Settlement, but the US Minister in Bangkok, Mr Barrett preferred to secure a "distinguished jurist, if possible." Barrett suggested Hannen's name to the Siamese foreign minister who "at once accepted" and they agreed to address a joint telegram to Hannen asking him if he would accept the appointment.

Barrett in a note to Mr Olney of the US State Department said of Hannen:

"In my opinion, if Sir Nicholas J. Hannen will consent to act, we will be assured of an able and impartial arbitrator. He ranks as one of the most capable jurists in the Far East, is an authority on extraterritoriality and international law and has a thorough knowledge of Asiatics."

Hannen agreed to act, subject to the approval of the Foreign Office. The Americans and Siamese both telegraphed to the Foreign Office for approval, which was granted. The Americans had originally proposed a neutral location for the arbitration, but the Siamese insisted that the arbitrator should sit in Bangkok. The final agreement was reached for the arbitration to proceed in June 1897. However, given the approaching summer, which could be unbearably hot in Bangkok, a date in December was agreed upon.

The only outstanding issue was Hannen's remuneration, payment of which was to be shared between the government of Siam and Cheek's estate. Hannen had been at the game for a long time and knew how to get the best deal for himself. He suggested an all-in fee, including expenses, of 10 guineas a day for the total time he was away from Shanghai. He estimated this would be 60 days, meaning a fee of 600 guineas or £630. Hannen's annual salary was £2,100 at the time, so this was not a bad deal. Hannen almost certainly intended to lessen his expenses by staying at the British Legation in Bangkok.

The US side then found that they would need to gather evidence in Chiangmai, which would require a one-month trip upriver and 15-day trip downriver, not leaving enough time for the arbitration to commence in December. The hearing was postponed to February 1, 1898. Hannen, who was susceptible to the cold, probably preferred a hearing in February because it meant that he would be out of Shanghai for both January and February, the coldest and most unpleasant months of the year in Shanghai.

In his award, Hannen found that Siam had not proved that the contracts had terms that allowed for the seizing of the logs and no default on the part of Cheek had been proved. Accordingly, he found in favor of the Cheek Estate, ordering the Siamese government to pay 700,000 ticals (about $200,000) in damages.[23]

Harrie Wilkinson as acting judge

Hannen's absence in Siam meant that someone needed to act as Chief Justice. The replacement for Jamieson as Assistant Judge was not immediately available to take up his post. Harrie Wilkinson, therefore, continued his meteoric rise and, despite having only been formally appointed Crown Advocate on December 10, 1897, was just one month later in mid-January 1898 appointed Acting Chief Justice for two months. For this period, he outranked his father, H.S. Wilkinson, who as Judge for Japan was below the Chief Justice in Shanghai. Indeed, H.S. Wilkinson, whose own appointment as Judge of

23 Award of Nicholas J. Hannen, rendered on March 21, 1898, *In the case of Dr Cheek, between Siam and the United States* reproduced in *Pasicrisie Internationale 1794-1900: Histoire Documentaire Des Arbitrages Internationaux* (edited by Henri La Fontaine), p580; *Boston Evening Transcript*, April 4, 1898, p12.

the Court for Japan had just been finalised, wrote, no doubt very proudly, to Harrie as Acting Chief Justice to inform him formally of his appointment to the Court in Japan.[24]

Later that year, in July 1898, Harrie Wilkinson was again appointed Acting Assistant Judge of the Supreme Court to conduct the first-ever trial of the British Supreme Court sitting in Korea. Wilkinson travelled to Seoul to try a case where the Legation constable, Mr O'Neil had, as Wilkinson put it, "physically reproved" the Legation head gardener who subsequently died. The case was tried before Wilkinson and a jury of five. The Governor of Seoul, Ye Chai-yen, attended throughout the trial. Mr Ottowill from the British Consulate in Seoul acted as the prosecutor. The *Seoul Independent* reported that the trial lasted until 8 o'clock at night and that "no pains were spared to get at the truth of the case" and all the witnesses were examined very carefully. The jury found O'Neill not guilty.[25]

Harrie Wilkinson later described the case in what to modern ears, appears very strange terms:

> "The defence was borne out in court by competent medical evidence that this was one of those interesting cases where an Oriental injured in his feelings will turn his face to the wall and die."

One wonders what the competent medical evidence could be to show that a man had just decided to die.

Bourne to be a Judge
With the reversal of the amalgamation decision and George

---

24 *North China Herald*, January 14, 1898, p 40; FO17/1324, Letter from Hannen to Lord Salisbury, 18 November 1897; F0656/49, Letter from H.S. Wilkinson to H.P. Wilkinson dated 20 January 1898, cited in C. Roberts, "Hiram Shaw Wilkinson (1840-1926)", *Britain and Japan Biographical Portraits*, Vol VIII, p177.

25 *R v O'Neil*, Case report *North China Herald*, July 25, 1898, the quote from Wilkinson comes from his reminiscences published in the *North China Herald*, October 31, 1925, p200-201. The jury members were Messrs Kenmure, Emberly, Hodge, Murdock and Hay.

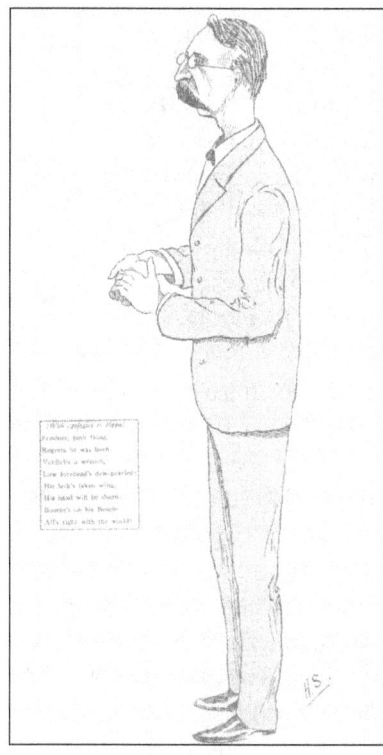

Frederick Bourne
Hannen's new Assistant Judge

Jamieson being returned to full-time consular duties, the Foreign Office needed to appoint a new Judge of the Supreme Court. Frederic Samuel Augustus Bourne, a long time consular officer in China was appointed to the position. He had at the time of appointment been in consular service for over 20 years.[26]

Bourne was born in October 1854, making him 43 at the time. He was the son of Rev. S. W. Bourne, Rector of Winfarthing, Norfolk, and Mary Caroline, daughter of late Henry Cassin, M.D. His father had died leaving "a widow and six children in reduced circumstances." At the age of 18, Bourne had found himself a job as a clerk in the War Office earning £110 per year. He had been advised that "pay and prospects were better in China" and started studying for the Foreign Office exam. He passed a competitive exam on February 14, 1876 and was appointed a student interpreter in China on March 10, 1876.

Bourne had been called to the Bar of Lincoln's Inn in 1890 during long leave at home in England. Bourne appears to have had a slightly mischievous personality. He was described as

26 Biographical information from: FO List 1917, p 209; Who's Who in the Far East (June) 1906-7; Edward Walford, *The county families of the-United-Kingdom or royal manual of the titled and untitled*, p41; *London Gazette* April 26, 1901; *London Gazette*, February 22, 1916 p 1946; P.D. Coates, The China Consuls, pp308 and 346.

being "young at heart" even on his retirement at the age of 62, as well as being a "cheerful and witty companion." In one case he used a delightful Latin phrase to describe a situation created by circular logic as a "circulus inextricabilis."[27]

Bourne had served all over China, including Chungking, Pagoda Island, Wuhu and Tamsui (near Taipei). As mentioned in Chapter 15, he was almost killed by a Chinese mob early in his career and spent nine months living and dressed as a Chinese. While in Chongqing he had gone on a six-month tour through modern-day Sichuan, Yunnan, Guangxi and Guizhou to report on the potential for trade. His report was presented to both Houses of the British Parliament in June 1888.[28]

Bourne was also a keen botanist. He collected various botanical samples when in China and has two species of plants named after him, the *Bournea sinensis* and *Bournea leiophylla*.[29]

Just before his appointment he had been consul in charge of a mission by the Blackburn Chamber of Commerce to investigate trade with China for a year from 1896 to 1897.[30] At the time, the China Consular Service was becoming top-heavy and the Foreign Office was looking for posts for senior officers. The Blackburn Commercial Mission had paid Bourne's salary for the year he was part of the mission and the Foreign Office now needed to find another position for him. Bourne's appointment as a judge appears to have come as a surprise. He had sat as a judge in the provincial courts while a consul or vice-consul - the room he used as a court and the cell to which he sent prisoners can still be seen today at the former British Consulate in Tamsui, Taiwan. But unlike all previous

---

27 *North China Herald*, November 13, 1915, p527 and *McDonald v Anderson*, *North China Herald*, February 5, 1904, p247 at 249, column 1.

28 China No. 1 (1888) Report by Mr FSA Bourne of a Journey in South-Western China. Two copies are kept in the Xujiahui Branch of the Shanghai Library.

29 http://www.genera-gesneriaceae.at/genera/bournea.htm.

30 Bourne published his section of the report in 1898. Report of the Mission to China of the Blackburn Chamber of Commerce. There is a photo of Bourne in the report.

and later appointments, Bourne had not acted as a judge of any higher court.

Perhaps for this reason, there are very few cases reported of Bourne sitting in the British Supreme Court before the turn of the century.[31] He was given a number of other positions. He was appointed consul in charge of the land office and also appointed to be an assessor at the Mixed Court. It seems that he was not expected to be a full time judge and quite possibly, given the paucity of cases Hannen assigned to him, Hannen did not value his legal skills. Bourne's Chinese language skills were, however, valued in the Mixed Court. In at least one case, Bourne translated the decision of the Chinese Magistrate, Mr Cheng, into English.[32]

Bourne was relieved of one duty that assistant judges had had to carry out until his appointment. He became the last Judge to also be the Registrar of the Court. Soon after his appointment as Judge, in October 1898, a new Order in Council was issued under which the Judge ceased to be the Registrar.[33] The Order in Council provided that the Registrar should henceforth be a barrister or solicitor admitted in England, Scotland or Ireland. No minimum period of practice was prescribed. The Registrar was empowered to hear summary criminal cases, making him effectively also the Police Magistrate. The Chief Clerk of the Court, Eustace Hubert Burrows, son of Major General Burrows of the British Army and cousin of Lord Jellicoe, was appointed as the Registrar of the Court.

Bourne as Judge of the Supreme Court for China and Japan was the last British judge appointed in China with appellate jurisdiction over Japan. This role, also, soon came to an end.

31 He did cause consternation to Sikh parties soon after his appointment by ordering that the court would no longer pay for interpreters and that the parties would need to pay for an interpreter themselves. *North China Herald*, October 17, 1898, p711.

32 *McElroy v The China Merchants Steam Navigation Company* (Mixed Court), *North China Herald*, December 24, 1898, p1214. Harrie Wilkinson also appeared in this case for the Plaintiff.

33 The China and Japan Order in Council 1898; *London Gazette*, December 2, 1898, p7816 for Burrows' appointment.

CHAPTER 26

A Time for Rejoicing Not Revenge

On July 17, 1899, the British and American treaties ending extraterritoriality in Japan were due to come into effect.

The end of the treaties was very much welcomed in Japan. A local Japanese newspaper, the *Mainichi Shimbun* called July 17, 1899 "a day of festival unprecedented in the twenty five-centuries of Japan's national existence." Japan was the first Oriental State to obtain admission to the comity of Occidental Powers. The *Mainichi Shimbun's* explanation was that Japan had, unlike other Asian countries, not hesitated to adopt the best of Occidental civilization. Another Japanese newspaper, the *Chuo Shimbun*, equally rejoiced but emphasized that the end of extraterritoriality was only the beginning of the task of achieving equality.[1] Numerous celebrations were held throughout Japan, including in all the treaty ports.

A ball was held at the Imperial Hotel in Tokyo in August organized by the Economical Society, and attended by Prince Kanin and other Japanese notables as well as members of the diplomatic corps. Baron Osaki, the President of the Society was effervescent:

"As subjects of His Imperial Majesty, we can not but rejoice over the revision of the treaties, which has become an accomplished fact, as an epoch making event in the history of this country's foreign intercourse. From the

1 *Japan Weekly Mail*, July 22, 1899, p79.

moment the revised treaties come into operation, we enter into new relations with all the countries of the world, nay, are admitted into the comity of civilized nations."

Osaki commented on the position of foreigners under the old treaties:

"Heretofore foreign residents in Japan were like drops of oil in a glass of water. There may have been a mechanical intermixture, but there was no chemical combination. Heretofore though our foreign friends lived in the same land as us they were standing, as it were, outside the walls of our residence."

Then in a spirit of goodwill and welcoming he said:

"But now we throw open our gates, and invite them to come in to the inner most part of our residence and feel themselves at home. Come friends, come!"[2]

A cartoon published in the *Mainichi Shimbun* emphasized this welcome, showing foreigners, who had previously been on the outside looking in at Japanese society, as new members of Japanese society.

Viscount Aoki, the Minister for Foreign Affairs, speaking in English, added that Japan had now entered a new era in which it was opened fully to foreign intercourse and that all foreigners could live safely in Japan. He then thanked all those from various countries who had been involved in the negotiations, including on the British side, the Earl of Kimberly, Mr Fraser and Mr Gubbins.[3]

The Japanese Government wanted the Japanese people to

2　*Japan Weekly Mail*, August 12, 1899, p161.
3　*Japan Weekly Mail*, August 12, 1899, p162.

understand that the end of extraterritoriality was a time for rejoicing, not for revenge. On July 1, 1899 just before the treaties came into force, an Imperial Rescript which was countersigned by all members of cabinet together with a separate Cabinet Instruction concerning the operation of the new treaties were issued.[4] The Imperial Rescript recited the "joy and glory" of the Imperial heart brought about by the end of the treaties. The Emperor then directed:

Foreigners' worst fear of the end of extraterritoriality

4   Both printed in full in the *Kobe Weekly Chronicle*, July 5, 1899, p540.

"We wish Our loyal and public spirited subjects, acting
under strict observance of Our desire, to behave in
strict conformity with the national policy of opening
the Empire, and with one accord to let their intercourse
with aliens be on the best of terms, maintaining the
high character of the nation, and making it their utmost
endeavor to manifest the glory of the Empire."

The Cabinet Instruction was more direct, saying that if:

"the methods by which the new Treaties are brought
into operation are erroneous, its object will not only be
defeated, but it will exhibit a breach of faith with the
Treaty Powers and dim the glories of Empire."

Both the Imperial Rescript and the Cabinet Instruction
emphasized that it was the responsibility of all Japanese officials to ensure subordinates and the people did not cause
harm to foreigners who were now able to freely travel and
live anywhere in the country.

Tales of two American murderers
The Japanese judiciary did not have to wait long to show how
they would enforce their new powers over foreigners. One
American was in a great hurry to test out the new Japanese
legal system. Within hours of the US-Japan treaty coming into
effect, before the sun had even risen on July 17, 1899, Robert
Miller, an American sailor, killed two Japanese women and an
American man, Nelson Ward, in a Yokohama saloon called,
ironically, the Rising Sun.[5]

Miller used a claw hammer and a straight razor to kill his
victims. The case was tried in the Yokohama District Court

5   "True Foreign Crime", *Japan Times Online*, November 4, 2003.

Robert Miller and his victims

before four judges on August 20, 1899. Four Japanese lawyers and a British barrister appearing by special permission represented Miller. Miller was convicted and was sentenced to death. The judges in passing verdict noted their reluctance to do so by saying:

> "It is the benevolent desire of His Imperial Majesty the Emperor that all strangers within our Empire should be treated with magnanimity . . . . It is most distressing to the judicial officials to be placed under the painful necessity of sentencing a citizen of one of the Treaty Powers to death."

Miller appealed to the Tokyo Appeal Court but his appeal was rejected. The sentence was carried out on January 17, 1900 with Miller being taken to the gallows in Ichigaya Prison in Tokyo. He was allowed a last cigarette from which he took a few contented puffs. After that, a mask was put on his head and the trap sprung. He was buried in an unmarked grave.

For another American murder, John Kelly, the end of extraterritoriality was a "get out of jail free" card. Kelly had been
sentenced to death in Nagasaki the year before, in 1898. After
a petition to the American Minister in Tokyo, his sentence had
been reduced to seven years imprisonment and he was transferred to the American Consulate jail in Yokohama. With the
impending end of extraterritoriality, other countries sent convicted prisoners out of the country. Kelly, however, was kept in
Yokohama. The American Consul-General tried to hand him
over to the Japanese authorities to serve the rest of his sentence
but the Japanese Government refused to take him. The US
Minister then instructed the Consul-General to release Kelly
because he had no power to detain a prisoner over whom he
no longer had jurisdiction. The incompetence of the American
authorities was widely criticized, with the *Kobe Weekly Chronicle* commenting they were "afraid the Japanese judicial body
will have but a very poor opinion of equity and justice of the
west when they see how it is carried out in this instance."[6]

Winding down of the Court for Japan
Despite the celebrations of the Japanese, the British Court for
Japan did not cease to exist on July 17, 1899. The 1894 treaty
did not make it clear what was to happen for cases that were
pending or for crimes or civil disputes that were committed
or which arose before July 17, 1899. Viscount Aoki, Japan's
Minister for Foreign Affairs, and Ernest Satow, the British
Minister for Japan, signed a protocol on May 3, 1899 providing that any cases before the court at the date that extraterritoriality ended were still to be handled by the Court for
Japan.[7] In a separate agreement, the jurisdiction of the court
was extended to apply to cases running up to August 4, 1899,

---

6 *Kobe Weekly Chronicle*, July 19, 1899, p38 and p43.

7 *London and China Telegraph*, July 18, 1899, p592; Drafts of the Protocol can be found
at British Documents on Foreign Affairs: Reports and Papers from the Foreign Office
Confidential Print, Series E, Volume 6, p55.

the day when French extraterritoriality ended and arguably due to the most favoured nation clause, the day when British extraterritoriality should end too.[8] This arrangement created some serious diplomatic headaches when sailors from the *Senator* were sentenced to imprisonment going past August 4, 1899 for an offence committed after July 17, 1899. The matter was resolved by getting the ship's captain to allow their release on August 4.

The British also took some time to change the name of the Supreme Court in Shanghai. It was not until March the next year, and after a letter of complaint from the Japanese Consul in Shanghai, that an Order in Council was issued formally changing the name of the court to "Her Brittanic Majesty's Supreme Court for China and Corea" and repealing "all provisions relating to the exercise of Her Majesty's power and jurisdiction in Japan."[9]

During 1899, Wilkinson wrote to Satow about the completion of pending cases on a number of occasions, seeking to put in place arrangements to deal with the winding down of the court. Wilkinson was keen to wrap things up because he expected to be acting in place of Hannen as Chief Justice in Shanghai when Hannen took leave from the middle of May the following year. Hannen in a telegram to Wilkinson described this as "leave." However, Hannen clearly intended to extend his leave so that he could retire without returning.[10]

In October 1899, with the impending closure of the Court for Japan and when Hannen had made it clear he intended to retire, Satow followed up with Bertie on his suggestion that Wilkinson be made Chief Justice:

8   British Documents on Foreign Affairs: Reports and Papers from the Foreign Office Confidential Print, Series E, Volume 6, pp112. Correspondence from Satow to Marquis of Salisbury, June 21, 1894. See p. 141 and 142 for reports on this incident. See also *Kobe Chronicle*, June 14, 1899 and July 12, 1899 p1 for an explanation of why French extraterritoriality terminated three weeks later.

9   China and Corea (Supreme Court) Order in Council, 1900, *London Gazette*, March 9, 1900, p1618.

10   PRO 30/33/6/6 Wilkinson note to Satow dated December 28, 1899, p188.

"I understand that Hannen proposes to ask for leave in May next and he probably hopes to extend his stay in England long enough to get his pension. If Wilkinson were to get the acting appointment, and to succeed Hannen when he retires, I should be very pleased. He is a thorough lawyer, and has been very helpful to me since he became Judge at Yokohama. He knows Chinese affairs well, and I do not think it would be possible to find a better man to be C.J. at Shanghai." [11]

By November 1899 there was only one case pending trial in any extraterritorial court in Japan. This was a case brought against a Mr Reynell, which had been filed on July 30, 1899 in the British Court for Japan. The Japanese Foreign Minister, Viscount Aoki, was very keen that this case not be heard as he wanted to have all remnants of foreign jurisdiction "wiped out of existence." Reynell had applied for the case to be transferred to Japanese courts and Aoki asked Satow to communicate to Wilkinson that he should not oppose this. The response was, of course, that Satow could not tell Wilkinson, as a judge, what to do. The matter was resolved by Wilkinson hearing the case as an arbitrator, rather than as a judge.[12]

In December 1899, Wilkinson proposed that the Vice-Consul in Yokohama, Henry Bonar, be appointed as Judge but said that he would endeavour to ensure that there was as little work to do as possible.[13] Much earlier that year, Satow had already flagged the possibility of the appointment of Bonar to replace Wilkinson: "If Wilkinson is able to finish all his civil and criminal cases before the end of the year, perhaps Bonar might be appointed acting judge to finish the bankruptcy case

11 I. Ruxton (ed), *The Semi-official Letters of British Envoy Sir Ernest Satow from Japan and China* (1895-1906),, 1997, p175.

12 I. Ruxton (ed) *The Correspondence of Sir Ernest Satow, British Minister in Japan, 1895-1900*, p219.

13 PRO 30/33/6/6.

mentioned in the dispatch."

In any event, Wilkinson was able to finalise all pending cases by January 31, 1900. On that date, he sat to deliver the final judgment of the British Court for Japan. The case related to a gift that James Joseph Enslie, the British Consule in Kobe, had made to his housekeeper, Kozawa Tori, out of "love and affection."[14] He had also left Miss Kozawa an annuity in his will. The question was which had precedence, the gift or the annuity. Enslie had in the past acted as Registrar and Acting Assistant Judge of the Court for Japan and as judge of the Provincial Court in Kobe.[15] Wilkinson had served in the Kobe Consulate with Enslie and knew him, and presumably Miss Kozawa, well.

Wilkinson had most likely chosen the Enslie case to be the last case of the Court for Japan. It was a case unobjectionable to Japanese public opinion. The court was ordering how a Japanese should benefit from a will. Enslie's long service in the British Japan Consular Service made it a fitting case with which to say farewell.

For the final hearing of the Court for Japan, Wilkinson delivered a lengthy judgment directing the way in which the annuity was to be paid. Wilkinson was accompanied in court by the Vice-Consul and Assistant Judge, Henry Bonar. Wilkinson's son and successor as Crown Advocate in Shanghai, Harrie Wilkinson came from Shanghai to attend the hearing. The principal members of the British bar in Japan, Henry Lichtfield, Crown Prosecutor, John Lowder, Ambrose Walford from Yokohama and H.C. Brushfield and Charles Crosse, from Kobe, appeared in court in their wigs and gowns. George Scidmore of the US Consulate also attended. Mr Idaura, a Japanese barrister who had been watching the Enslie case on behalf of Miss Kozawa, was granted a seat at the bar-

---

14 *Kobe Weekly Chronicle* January 17, 1900, p47.

15 See, for example, *R v John Bellamy, Japan Weekly Mail,* July 3, 1880 for a case where Enslie sat as Acting Assistant Judge.

risters' table out of courtesy.[16]

Lichtfield gave a farewell speech saying this was probably the last time Wilkinson would preside over the court, which had been in existence since 1879. The old order had changed in the course of evolution and change in Japan. Naturally, many who had worked with the court could not but feel regret at the change. Turning to Wilkinson as a judge, Lichtfield said that Wilkinson had given strict attention to business but that also they could feel they had a friend in him. He then hinted as to Wilkinson's next position: "if rumour was right, some of the members of the bar present would shortly practice before His Honour in another court."

Wilkinson gave a short reply in thanks. With regard to the new order:

> "he wished with others that the difficulties connected
> – and inseparably connected – with the change would
> be successfully overcome, and that over time the excel-
> lence of the court in dispensing justice may be attained
> under the new regime."

He then thanked the bar for their valuable assistance and wished them "all success and a hearty farewell."

C.D. Moss, the Clerk of the Court, then stood and brought an end to 42 years of British extraterritoriality in Japan by announcing:

> "Know all men, this court stands adjourned. God Save
> the Queen."

---

16 "The Closing of the Court for Japan", *Kobe Weekly Chronicle*, February 7, 1900, p116.

CHAPTER 27

The Full Stop in the Wrong Place: Vale Sir Nicholas

LIFE SOMETIMES WILL STRANGELY put a full stop where perhaps there should not have been one. This is certainly the case with Nicholas Hannen. On April 26, 1900, he was just two and a half weeks away from retirement to England when at the age of 58 years and after more than 25 years of service to the British Crown in Asia, he died.[1]

Hannen had been struck down by pneumonia partly caused by the long hours he had been putting in to finalise matters before he left. Upon his death all flags both afloat and onshore were flown at half-mast.[2] That Sunday, Hannen was given a funeral service with full honours, and perhaps the most international recognition ever given to an English judge.

Hannen's coffin was paraded through the streets of Shanghai from his house to Trinity Cathedral. The parade was led by the Shanghai Volunteers, which consisted of companies A and B of the Light Horse Artillery, as well as the German Companies and French Volunteers. The gunboat HMS *Hermione*, which was in port, landed a company of 125 blue jackets and 18 marines to accompany the procession. The procession

---

1   See Annual Register of World Events, Vol 142, Edmund Burke, P117.

2   Hannen Obituary, *North China Herald*, May 2, 1900, p766. The description of Hannen's funeral comes from the North China Herald of May 2, 1900, p785 -786 as well as the official notice describing the procession for Hannen's funeral, two photographs taken outside the Trinity Church and three photographs taken of the procession on the Maloo. Pippa Pettifer (nee Hannen), Nicholas Hannen's great grand daughter, was kind enough to lend me these photographs and provide me with copy of the official notice.

from Hannen's house travelled to Kiukiang Road (Jiujiang Road) and then to the Bund where a line of mourners was waiting. Once the party reached the Trinity Cathedral, the strains of Chopin's "Marche Funebre " ushered in the coffin and its attendants.

Hannen had not one but four priests in attendance. The Rev. W. Gilbert Walshe officiated but also present were the Rev C. J. F. Symons, the Rev. F. L. Hawks Pott and the Rev. Henry Dalzell, chaplain of HMS *Hermione.* Rev. Walshe delivered "an eloquent and touching address." He commenced by noting that Hannen had died during Easter:

> "During this Easter season, whilst we rejoice in the Resurrection of our Lord from the tomb, by which he demonstrated the possibility of rising superior to Death, and breaking its power; we are also reminded that 'Death' is still a word – of awful import, and death itself an experience which has not ceased to be the common lot of man."

He continued:

> "Death remains triumphant."

> "Of the fact of his continued empire over men we are painfully reminded this morning, as we meet, together around all that remains, that is mortal, of our departed friend, to render the last sad offices of respect and affection."

Then turning to Hannen as a man he said:

> "Nevertheless the sense of our own loss cannot but elicit the expression of our sincerest grief. Friends are none too numerous in this world, and we have lost a friend. What

can I say in tribute to his memory which will not be but the re-echo of that which fills the hearts of all who knew him! He was an Englishman in all that best befits the bearer of the name; one whose character for uprightness, and integrity, and loyalty to truth was above reproach — of his domestic relations, as husband and father, it is unnecessary, as it would be impertinent to speak — his virtues are the theme of all who are in the best position to appreciate and proclaim them. As a friend, I can bear testimony, from experience only 'alas' too short, to his kindly disposition and winning personality."

Following the eulogy, Lady Hannen and her daughters left to make preparations for the service at the crematorium chapel. The service continued and finished with the hymn "Abide with me." Hannen's body was then taken to the Bubbling Well Cemetery for cremation. Eight marines from the Hermione lifted Hannen's coffin and carried it down the centre aisle of the church. The four priests followed. Frederick Bourne, now Acting Chief Justice, in full dress blue consular uniform with a high Prussian collar and nine gold buttons, led the mourners to the entrance of the church where the gun carriage was waiting. Lined up on the driveway of the church were sailors in full dress uniform standing at attention. The grounds were crowded with mourners.

The marines placed Hannen's coffin on the ground at the back of the gun carriage and arranged the Union Jack on the coffin. While this was done, Bourne, lost in thought with his head bowed, standing out in front of the other mourners stared forlornly at the coffin saying a last, personal, farewell to his chief. The marines placed Hannen's coffin on the gun carriage and then arranged wreathes on the coffin and carriage. As the carriage slowly drove out of the church, the sailors on the driveway all stood smartly to attention and saluted. The mourners' carriages followed behind headed by the Bourne's carriage and then those of Naval and Military Officers. They were followed by representatives of the bar, the French Municipal Council, the Cosmopolitan Council, the Imperial Maritime Customs, the Chinese authorities and then the Consular Body.

The Shanghai Volunteers who had formed up outside the entrance to the church, headed by the band, moved off to take the head of the procession. The wail of the "Dead March" from *Saul* set the time for the slow march. The procession headed north and then turned into Maloo (Nanjing East Road).

The scene on the Maloo was very impressive. The road, which was still made of dirt, had been thoroughly cleaned before the procession. Chinese, all the men with their hair tied back in queues, lined the both sides of all the streets on either sides and filled the balconies and windows. The SVC band led the procession followed by about 250 members of the SVC marching five abreast. Sikh Policemen walked along with the procession and Chinese policemen were posted along the road. Many European families with their children marched alongside the SVC. All were dressed in their best Sunday clothes.

The gun carriage with Hannen's coffin followed. The carriage was drawn by two horses with a soldier from the SVC mounted on one. The eight pallbearers from HMS Hermione marched on either side of the gun carriage. Twelve Sikh policemen, in full dress uniform, had been assigned to march with the coffin, two marched in front and the others marched on either side and behind. While the crowd appeared well behaved, one Sikh policeman held his truncheon in his hand, ready for any trouble.

Six horse-drawn carriages carrying the chief mourners came next. The drivers were all dressed in fine gowns and wore black hats. Approximately 200 sailors from the *Hermione* and other foreign warships in port followed also marching five abreast. They were followed by a group of around

30 naval and military officers from and then by the carriages of the other mourners. The procession of carriages could be seen continuing down the Maloo for hundreds of metres. The procession continued for three miles all the way up the Maloo into Bubbling Well Road to the Bubbling Well Road Cemetery (now the site of the Jing'an Park).

At the cemetery, as many as possible entered the chapel for the final ceremony before Hannen was cremated.

The *North China Herald,* in a long obituary, was glowing in its praise:

"If it is difficult to do justice to Sir Nicholas Hannen's official record, it is still more difficult to do justice to his social qualities. We have said that he can never have made an enemy, but that is only negative praise. He was indeed kindness itself; and he made all who had the opportunity of knowing him his friends; from his first arrival in Shanghai he identified himself with the community. He was a rowing man, and to the last was always willing to serve as umpire or referee at the regattas. A charming singer, a graceful dancer, and a talented actor, be was most valuable in its early days as an active member of the Amateur Dramatic Club. He took the greatest interest in outdoor sports and was President of the Football Club, and hardly ever missed a cricket match. In his house, which was always open to his friends, he was the perfection of hospitality and courtesy, and here he was most fully assisted by Lady Hannen, his two daughters, and Shanghai's pet, his one son Beau. In fact, he had every quality which could ensure the affection and respect of all who came in contact with him."[3]

....

3   *North China Herald,* May 2, 1900, p766-767.

Farewell to the Chief

The day before Hannen's funeral, on Saturday morning, a special hearing had been convened at the Supreme Court with Frederick Bourne presiding. The *North China Herald* noted that the bench "looked strangely unfamiliar without the well-known figure of Sir Nicholas present."[4]

All members of the Shanghai bar were present.[5] Harrie Wilkinson, the Crown Advocate, and son of the incoming Chief Justice, H.S. Wilkinson, addressed the court and was overwhelming in his praise of Hannen as a judge. For Wilkinson this must have been a very emotional hearing. He had known Hannen for many years. Even more sadly, almost exactly a year before in April 1899, Wilkinson's wife, Mary, had also died of pneumonia.[6]

While Wilkinson spoke all the members of the bar stood. There was unlikely to have been a dry eye in the courtroom.

"Your Lordship, on behalf of the members of the Bar of this Court, present and absent, I pray that heartfelt sympathy be conveyed to Lady Hannen, her son and daughters, in their bereavement and sorrow. We have lost a chief; we have lost a friend; and this Court, and all Her Britannic Majesty's subjects - and indeed all those who have any business with Her Majesty's subjects have lost a wise, good, and just judge, a lawyer of sound learning, a man with a legal mind, one with a gift which amounted to intuition as to what were the rights and wrongs of a case when it was laid before him, and one whose special gift was his knowledge of the law of evidence. What must have struck your

---

4 *North China Herald*, May 2, 1900, p786. All quotes below are sourced from this report.

5 This included Mr. H. P. Wilkinson (Crown Advocate), Mr. W. V. Drummond, Mr. C Dowdall, Mr. I H Browett, Mr. H. R. Parkes, Mr. F.I. Ellis, Mr. J. C Hanson, Mr. W. A. C.Platt, Mr. D. McNeill. Mr. E. Nelson, Mr. T Morgan Phillips, Mr. J. H. Teesdale, Mr. A. S. P. White-Cooper, Mr. L E. P. Jones, and Mr. E. C. Brushfeld.

6 *London and China Telegraph*, April 24, 1899, p350 (re Wilkinson's wife).

Lordship, what has, I know, struck any of us who have practised in this Court, and who are yet here, or who have gone elsewhere, was his wonderful knowledge of business.

"The late Chief Justice was a man whom nothing escaped, who took a note of everything; and it was especially remarkable in commercial cases, how the counsel on either side in their openings and examination of witnesses were, to the outsider, explaining commercial usages, but they were only really informing the judge of what he himself knew from his long residence in the East, and from his keen interest in all that took place around him. His was a strong mind, which, secure in its ability to sift what was put before him, did not rapidly come to a decision one way or the other. His patience was infinite."

Wilkinson turned to the period where Hannen had served as both Chief Justice and Consul-General:

"There is a further part of his work which I know, to which I think it is my duty to refer because all of us who practise here have experienced his kindness in that direction, namely, while he was Consul-General as well as Chief Justice. It is not the place for me to refer to political matters, present or past, but I think the members of the Bar will agree with me in recognising the courteous but firm attitude which Sir Nicholas Hannen adopted to many important questions. The courtesy and firmness which he used I know the native authorities will appreciate and remember, for they were of the greatest service to them."

Vernon Drummond, as the oldest member of the bar and as one who had known Hannen for at least three decades, then

addressed the court. No one, including Drummond, could
have forgotten that only three years before Drummond had
publicly accused Hannen of bias in the Bennertz case and Hannen had publicly chastised Drummond in his protest. Despite
this, Drummond was eloquent in his praise; saying that Hannen "had won success both at the Bar and on the Bench, but he
did something more than that, - he deserved it." As a barrister
and as a Judge Hannen left a "bright example to all who may
hereafter either practice in or preside over this court." He finished by expressing his sympathies to Sir Nicholas' family.

Judge Bourne then addressed the court:

"Mr. Wilkinson, Mr. Drummond, and gentlemen, you
wish to put on record and I see that every practitioner
in the Court is present, your feeling of the grievous
loss we who are associated for the administration of
justice here, have suffered by the death of our Chief
Justice. Sir Nicholas Hannen was endowed by nature
with those rare intellectual qualities which go to make
a great judge; but he had something higher and nobler,
rather moral than intellectual, an impalpable tone of
mind which we Englishmen can perhaps best express
by saying that he was a high-minded English Gentleman - our national type of all-round human excellence.
Had Sir Nicholas lived to retire, as he was just about
to do, this Court might still have profited by his ripe
experience and judgment on the Judicial Committee of
the Privy Council or as adviser to H. M. Government in
the codification of our Orders in Council now going on
at home.
"All this we and the suitors in this Court have lost by
his death; but we have left to us the example of a use-
ful and blameless life and a pattern of what a judge
should be. I trust his good influence will long be felt
on the Bench and at the Bar of this Court. There will be

an order in the terms of the Crown Advocate's motion, copies of which will be sent to Lady Hannen, to each of her children, to H.M. Secretary of State, and to H.M. Ministers in China, Japan, and Corea."

Bourne expressed the feeling of all over Sir Nicholas' death finished his speech:

"Gentlemen, speaking for myself, for the officers of the Court and for you, it is with the keenest sense of personal loss of a wise and considerate chief, of a kind friend passed out of our lives, that we remember we can see and hear Sir Nicholas Hannen on this bench no more."

One can only imagine the sadness and melancholy that must have filled the court room as all those present remembered Nicholas Hannen.

Hannen's wife, Jessie, took his ashes back with her to their home at Lake Lodge in Wargrave, England. Jessie took Nicholas' death very badly. Ernest Satow visited her in Wargrave in 1903 and found her "looking very ill, and extremely sallow." In 1904 Hannen's eldest daughter, Fanny, died of cancer, adding a deeper sadness to her life. Jessie died seven years after her husband, at the age of 61, in 1907. Her funeral ceremony was conducted at Golders Green crematorium in London. George Jamieson, Hannen's Assistant Judge and Consul attended. Following this, Jessie and Nicholas Hannen's ashes were placed in the Hannen Columbarium in the churchyard of St Mary's Church in Wargrave, Hannen's hometown.[7]

---

7   E. Satow, *Peking Diary 1900-1903*, Ruxton (ed), p14. Fanny Hannen's death: *North China Herald*, January 6, 1905, p8. Jessie Hannen's death and funeral: *London and China Telegraph*, March 25, 1907. I have not been able to confirm absolutely that Nicholas or Jessie Hannen's ashes were placed in the Columbarium. One report suggests that they were. The churchyard records do not record that they were. These records are, however, of the burials in the churchyard and do not, necessarily cover the placement of ashes. Pippa Pettifer (nee Hannen), Hannen's great-great granddaughter, told me that not all

The Columbarium, which had recently been completed, had been designed by the famous English architect, Sir Edwin Lutyens, and stands to this day in Wargrave. On a beautifully sunny, but slightly chilly, autumn day in October, I visited the churchyard in Wargrave. The Columbarium, which is a very private affair, is tucked away in the left hand corner of the churchyard where a number of members of Hannen family are also buried. The Columbarium which houses the ashes of a number of other Hannens, including his son Beau, is well

St Mary's Churchyard, Wargrave, where Sir Nicholas Hannen's ashes were interred

kept. In keeping with Hannen's own personality, the Columbarium serves as an understated reminder of Sir Nicholas' long and meritorious service in East Asia.

Hannen's death at the end of the 19th Century brought a

the ashes in the Columbarium are marked. However, the Columbarium was built to house the ashes of those members of the Hannen family who were cremated and a request for planning permission in the early 1900s mentioned that two members of the family had been cremated recently. Given the Columbarium had just been completed when Jessie died, it would be very strange if Sir Nicholas and Jessie had not been placed there. The ashes of Hannen's son, Beau, and his wife, actress Athene Seyler, were placed in the Columbarium.

close to the first half of extraterritoriality's existence in East Asia. Hannen had been in East Asia for almost the entire life of the Supreme Court for China and Japan and had played a fundamental part in its development and growth. It is a great shame he did not live longer to enjoy the retirement he so richly deserved.

CONCLUSION TO VOLUME I

THE END OF THE 19th century marked the end of an era for extraterritoriality in East Asia.

At a personal level, for the British courts all the lawyers who had played an important part in building the British justice systems in China and Japan, bar one – Hiram Shaw Wilkinson, had now retired or died in office. The men who had built the system had all bravely travelled to China or Japan when both countries had just opened up to the world. Life was not easy. They faced physical threats to their safety from angry locals. The climate was not conducive to good health. Three out of seven judges, George French, Charles Goodwin and Nicholas Hannen all died in office.

Despite this they had achieved Sir Edmund Hornby's goal of building a fully functioning and respected legal system in both China and Japan that served British government interests and the interests of the British community well. Trade had been facilitated and British citizens had, from the British perspective, been protected from vagaries of the under-developed Chinese and Japanese legal systems.

No other country had established as large and effective legal system as Britain. This was one of the problems of extraterritoriality. Other countries still relied solely on consular officers trying cases which could and did in some cases lead to injustice or weak enforcement of law. One country at least, the United States, determined to address this issue early in the 20th century.

For China and Japan, the impact of extraterritoriality was far-reaching but with entirely different results in each country.

Japan after first fighting but then acquiescing to the power of the forigners, had by a concerted process of economic, political and legal reform managed to throw of extraterritoriality and become an extraterritorial power itself. Extraterritoriality had served its purpose in Japan. It had protected foreigners from an underdeveloped legal system when Japan first opened for trade. Yet at the same time, it had acted as a strong spur to the development that had driven Japan to become new economic and military power.

In China, extraterritoriality had protected foreigners, but it made a negligible contribution to the development of the Chinese legal or political system. In many ways, the presence of foreigners in the country who the Chinese government was powerless to control contributed to the political decline of the Qing Dynasty. At the turn of the century China had a weak government, a weak legal system and a weak economy.

China, therefore, entered the 20th century facing many challenges. Foreign powers (including Japan) and extraterritoriality were firmly entrenched. The world was changing fast. The industrial revolution was changing the way the world worked. Even in China, railways were now being built and large scale manufacturing starting to take off. The old ways could not last long.

How China attempted to meet the challenges of this new century, and particularly the challenges of an ever stronger Japan, is dealt with in the following volumes.

INDEX

Name

A

Admiralty, jurisdiction in (British) Vol 1: 138, 279, 282, 322-4

Alaska, law of, application in US Courts Vol 2: 85, 184, 192, 252

Alcock, Rutherford Vol 1: 39, 42, 46, 123, 125 Vol 2: 317

Allman, Norwood

  Attorney Vol 1: 102 Vol 2 : 56n, 247n

  Cases Vol 2: 353, 356 Vol 3: 19-20, 90, 92

  Internment and repatriation Vol 3: 172, 175, 180n, 199, 204

  Judges, comments on Vol 2: 117 (Thayer), 266-7 (Purdy),
  Vol 3: 80-81 (Helmick)

  Shunpao (Shenbao), owner of Vol 3: 138-9

  Student Interpreters, on Vol 1: 88

Amalgamation of British Judicial and Consular positions Vol 1:
189-91, 304-6, 379-81

American Oriental Banking Corporation Vol 3: 90-99, 97i

American-Chinese See: Nationals, dual

Anderson, Charles Graham Overbeck Vol 3: 36

Andrews, Lorrin Vol 2: 81, 86, 97-99, 104, 110-1

Aoki (Viscount) Vol 1: 287-9, 328, 392, 396, 398

Arthur, Chester Vol 1: 219

Appeals

  British Consular/Provincial Courts, from Vol 1: 46, 135-8, 207, 258,
  274, 278

  British Court for Japan, from and to Vol 1: 138-9, 207, 322

  British Supreme Court for China, from:

    • Jurisdiction Vol 1: 61, 111, 135-8, 141, 205-6 Vol 2: 59-60, 342-5

    • Full Court (Civil) Vol 2: 345 Vol 3: 21-24

- Full Court (Criminal) Vol 2: 345 Vol 3: 70, 162, 169, 171
  - Privy Council (Civil) Vol 1: 107, 275, 322-4 Vol 2: 156, 335-6 Vol 3: 66
  - Privy Council (Criminal) Vol 1: 364

Chinese Qing Dynasty Courts Vol 1: 171-2

Chinese Special District Courts, from Vol 3: 30

Hong Kong Supreme Court, from and to Vol 1: 46-7 Vol 2: 26, 174-175, 179-181

Japanese courts Vol 1: 157-8, 395

Mixed British and Chinese court (ad hoc): Vol 1: 169-72

US Consular Courts, from Vol 1: 45 Vol 2: 76

US Court for China
- Jurisdiction: Vol 2: 76, 93-5
- Criminal: Vol 2: 85, 86, 93-5, 269, 360-1 Vol 3: 98, 169, 182
- Civil: Vol 2: 238, 242, 245-6 Vol 3: 19, 83-4

Weihaiwei, High Court of, from Vol 2: 26

Archer, Charles Vol 3: 175, 180

B

Backhouse, Edmund Vol 3: 127

Ballard, James Vol 2: 17

Bank of East Asia Vol 2: 316-20

Barrett, E.I.M. Vol 2: 149-51, 195, 306-9 Vol 3: 13

Barristers

Admission of non-nationals Vol 2: 229n3, 313

Disbarment Vol 2: 228-30, 293-4

Practice in partnerships Vol 1: 73-4 Vol 2: 152-6

Bassett, Arthur Vol 2: 79, 79i, 81-2, 83-5, 88-9, 97, 107-8, 115, 141-3

Beijing See: Peking

Bennertz & Co Vol 1: 370-9

Bentwich, Norman Vol 3: 151-3

Bertie, Francis Vol 1: 347, 367-8, 397-8

Betthell, Ernest Vol 2: 121-134, 145, 153

Biddle, United States v (Biddle Case) Vol 2: 84-5, 104, 113, 114, 184, 192 Vol 3: 83

Bilibid Prison, Vol 2: 185, 245

Blaine, James Vol 1: 224-6

Boxer Indemnity Vol 2: 15, 203, 209

Boxer Rebellion Vol 2: 3, 5, 9-10, 15, 20, 60, 171 Vol 3: 223

British Court for China Vol 1: 26

British Court for Japan

  Closing Vol 1: 396-400 Vol 2: 32

  Establishment Vol 1: 15, 177, 207, 210i, 211

  Jurisdiction Vol 1: 207, 223-7, 278, 321-3, 329, 396-397

  Premises Vol 1: 212

British Court for Siam Vol 2: 37-8, 42, 49, 145, 189

British Protected Persons Vol 1: 279-280 Vol 2: 175 Vol 3: 65-7

British Supreme Court for China and Japan

  Closing Vol 3: 177, 187, 188-90, 192-3

  Establishment Vol 1: 15, 47, 59-61, 71-2, 180

  Japan branch Vol 1: 131-3, 135-40

  Jurisdiction

    • Admiralty Vol 1: 138, 279, 282, 322-4

    • British Military Vol 1: 196-7 Vol 2: 173-5 Vol 3: 161

    • British Protected Persons Vol 1: 279-82 Vol 2: 173-5 Vol 3: 63-67

    • Capital cases Vol 1: 61

    • China, in Vol 1: 60-1 Vol 2: 123 Vol 3: 177, 192

    • Conflicts of Vol 1: 195-6, 223-7, 323-3 Vol 2: 159-60, 327-8, 334
     Vol 3: 129

    • Consular/mixed courts, compared to Vol 1: 61, 169-171

    • Customs Service (Chinese), over British employees of Vol 1: 105-7,
     237-9, 247-8

    • Foreign Jurisdiction Act Vol 1: 39n, 59

    • Japan, in Vol 1: 60-1, 135-40, 207, 329, 396-7

    • Korea, in Vol 1: 277-8 396-7 Vol 2: 123, 134

    • Nationals, dual Vol 2: 297 Vol 3: 29-30

    • Nationals, non-British Vol 1: 75 Vol 2: 199, 202-3

    • Shanghai Municipal Council Vol 3: 69-71

    • Treaties, under Vol 1: 26, 173-5

    • Weihaiwei Vol 2: 26 Vol 3: 33

  Name Changes:

- "China and Corea" Vol 1: 397
- "China" Vol 2: 134

Premises Vol 1: 111-7, 121-3, 126-8 Vol 3: 205-208

Bourne, Frederick SA

Acting Chief Justice/Judge, sitting as: Vol 1: 406-9, Vol 2: 9, 16-19, 102-114, 106i, 125-130, 131-4, 132i, 135-9, 158-60

Acting Chief Justice/Judge, other mentions: Vol 1: 403-4 Vol 2: 35, 116, 145, 182

Appointment as Judge: Vol 1: 386-7, 389

Assessor, Mixed Court: Vol 1: 389

Biography Vol 1: 28, 230, 386-9, 387i

Chief Justices, relationships with: Vol 1: 389, 409 Vol 2: 36-7, 53, 147

Judge/Asst Judge, sitting as: Vol 2: 164-5,

Judge/Asst Judge, other mentions: Vol 1: 128 Vol 2: 50-1, 78, 154,195, 220, 339, 462

Knighthood Vol 1: 188-9

Land Law, on Vol 2: 161-5, 277

Retirement Vol 2: 187-8

Weihaiwei, Judge of Vol 1: 27-29, 187-8

Bourne, Kenneth Vol 2: 189 Vol 3: 106, 106i

Boxer Rebellion Vol 2: 3, 5, 9-15, 20, 33-5, 60, 171, 209

Boxer Indemnity Vol 2: 15, 203, 209

Brown, J. Warner Vol 3: 92-99, 105

Bryan, R.T. Vol 3: 25, 31, 68, 68i, 78-9, 80, 200

Burrows, Eustace Vol 1: 389 Vol 2: 47n

C

Calhourn, John Vol 1: 22

Canton (Guangzhou)

Attacks on: Vol 1: 25, 28 Vol 3: 10 (considered)

Canton Factory Vol 1: 23-4, 26, 45

Cases in Vol 1: 46, 237-43, 263-8 Vol 2: 40-41, 173-6, 316-20 Vol 3: 29, 145, 180

Claims Commission Vol 1: 269-72

Land tenure: Vol 2: 161

Riots and protests in Vol 1: 264-6, 265i Vol 2: 317

Carew, Edith, Vol 1: 337, 344-365 Vol 2: 551

Carew, Walter Vol 1: 337, 344-365

Capital punishment See: Death Penalty

Casement, Gerald Vol 3: 163-5, 182

Chalaire Walter Vol 3: 83-84

Chapman William Vol 2: 349-51

Char, Nick Vol 2: 269, 272 Vol 3: 18-9, 24-28

Cheek Arbitration (Siam) Vol 1: 382-5

Chefoo Convention Vol 1: 172-175, 371 Vol 2: 137 Vol 3: 30

Chen (Shanghai Mixed Court Magistrate) Vol 1: 154-6, 155i

Chennault, Claire (General) Vol 3: 190-191

Chiang Kai-shek Vol 2: 300 Vol 3: 9, 13, 57, 139. 149

China Association Vol 1: 325, 370, 381 Vol 2: 63, 76 Vol 3: 62

China Eastern Railway Zone Vol 3: 127-9

China Gazette Vol 2: 12, 98-9, 104-5, 111

China League Vol 1: 381

Chishima Case Vol 1: 321-4, 372

Church Missionary Society Vol 1: 231-237, 232i

Civil War (China) Vol 2: 5, 171-3, 323

Civil War (Japan) Vol 1: 10, 36, 147

Cixi, Empress Dowager Vol 2: 10, 14, 141 Vol 3: 127

Clark Kerr, Archibald Vol 3: 154-5, 162, 199-200

Colbert, John Vol 3: 99-103

Colonial Office Vol 1: 178, 189, 192-3 Vol 2: 25-26, 96, 101

Commission, Claims (Britain-China) Vol 1: 263, 269-72 Vol 2: 33-5, 66-8 Vol 3: 74

Commission, Extraterritoriality see: Extraterritoriality Commission

Commission, International (Shanghai, 1925) Vol 2: 321-3

Commissioner of Foreign Affairs (Shanghai) Vol 2: 260, 261 Vol 3: 26-7, 28

Commissioner (Chinese Customs) Vol 1: 105, 245-8

Commissioner (US Court) Vol 2: 184-7, 235-7, 280 Vol 3: 168

Commissioner (Weihaiwei) Vol 2: 24-6

Common law of the United States Vol 2: 75, 83, 85

Companies, regulation of

    American Vol 2: 211-2 Vol 3: 87-9, 138-41

    British Vol 2: 106, 108, 113, 114, 211-2, 320 Vol 3: 69

Communists (China) Vol 3: 13-4, 57, 145, 146, 196, 197-8, 200

Communists (Soviet Union) Vol 2: 211, 255-7, Vol 3: 13-4

Consular Courts

    Belgian Vol 1: 135 Vol 2: 335

    Danish Vol 1: 78

    Decisions of non-British, recognition of in British Courts Vol 2: 32

    General Vol 1: 12, 183, 286, 426

    German Vol 1: 292-5

    Italian Vol 1: 13i

    Japanese Vol 2: 312-3, 315

    Prussian Vol 1: 78

    Russian Vol 1: 198

Consular Courts (British) - Pre Establishment of SCCJ

    Hearings in Vol 1: 70

    Jurisdiction of and appeals from Vol 1: 45-7

    Problems with Vol 1: 15, 39-40, 43-44, 44i

Consular Courts (British) - Post Establishment of SCCJ

    Appeals from Vol 1: 61, 135-8, 207, 274

    Hearings in Vol 1: 140-1, 161, 223, 273 Vol 2: 124 Vol 3: 121, 125, 126

    Hornby's role in building system Vol 1: 99-102, 104-5, 109, 129, 136-8, 179-180

    Kanagawa Consular Court, premises Vol 1: 213

    Kanagawa Consular Court, abolition of Vol 1: 210i, 211

    Jurisdiction of Vol 1: 61, 196, 198, 224, 227, 278, 323, 339 Vol 3: 128

    Renaming as Provincial Courts Vol 1: 61

    Shanghai Consular Court, abolition of Vol 1: 61

    Transfer of cases to SCCJ Vol 1: 234

    Witnesses, swearing of Vol 1: 321

    Visits by SCCJ judges Vol 1: 132, 136-8, 205-6

Consular Courts (United States) – Pre-establishment of US Court for China
  Appeals from Vol 1: 45
  Cases in Vol 1: 44-5, 78-9, 140-1, 150i, 150-1 219-222
  Jurisdiction Vol 1: 39n, 44-5, 78-9, 196, 219-8
  Problems with Vol 1: 15, 39-41 Vol 2: 74
Consular Courts (United States) – Post establishment of US Court for China
  Appeals from Vol 2: 75-6
  Cases in Vol 2: 86, 205, 208 Vol 3: 190
  Concurrent jurisdiction (Shanghai) Vol 2: 184-7
  Double jeopardy Vol 2: 86
  Jurisdiction of Vol 2: 76, 86, 184-7, 237, 240-1, 254, 269, 360
  Premises Vol 2: 185
Consular jails
  Conditions in Vol 1: 40, 114n7, 388 Vol 2: 41, 129-30, 184
  Construction of Vol 1: 113-4, 118
  Escapes from Vol 1: 40, 45, 226
  Executions at Vol 1: 97, 118-9 Vol 2: 41
  Prisoners in Vol 1: 141, 215, 220, 247, 264, 360, 362, 396 Vol 2: 129-30, 240, 244, 356
  Transfers to other prisons Vol 1: 141, 268, 362 Vol 2: 129-30
Consular Regulations (US), application of in US Court Vol 3: 81, 83-4
Convention of Kanagawa Vol 1: 34
Convention of Peking Vol 1: 32
Coolidge, Calvin Vol 2: 266, 323
Coolies (Chinese) Vol 1: 138, 148-157
Corea See: Korea
Court of Consuls Vol 1: 12 Vol 3: 67, 70, 160
Covey (barrister) Vol 3: 16
Creighton, G.W. Vol 3: 124, 127
Crosse, Charles Vol 1: 399 Vol 2: 125-9
Crown Advocate
  Position and role: Vol 1 193-4, 325 Vol 2: 37, 41-2, 154, 314 Vol 3: 76,

145, 155-6, 203

Remuneration and benefits Vol 1: 194-5, 369-70 Vol 2: 58-9 Vol 3: 154

Cunningham, Edwin Vol 2: 192 Vol 3: 26, 28

Cushing, Caleb Vol 1: 21-23

Currie, Phillip Vol 1: 189-191, 303-306, 310, 380

Custodian of Enemy Property Vol 2: 200-1, 202, 332, 335 Vol 3: 203

Customs Service (China)

Authority of foreign courts, challenges to, by Vol 1: 105-7, 238-9, 240-2, 244-8

Enforcement against foreigners, by Vol 1: 305, 370

Foreign employees Vol 1: 14, 105, 270,

Offences by foreign Customs officers Vol 1: 159-65, 237-44, 263-9, 309-16, 316-7

Relatives of judges or parties Vol 1: 93 Vol 2: 498

Revenue, collection of Vol 1: 105 Vol 2: 203, 404

Structure Vol 1: 105

Customs service (Japanese) Vol 1: 143, 199-202

D

Deacon, Victor Vol 1: 270-1

Death Penalty (British and American courts)

Authority to try cases Vol 1: 45, 61, 132 (lack of), 178, 207

Commutations Vol 1: 81, 222, 361-2, 396 Vol 3: 118, 121-2, 162

Executions Vol 1: 45, 97, 118-9 Vol 2: 40-1 Vol 3: 12, 119-20 (failed)

Sentences of death Vol 1: 45, 80, 94-5, 118, 222, 360, 396 Vol 2: 40 Vol 3: 13, 33, 118, 162

Death Penalty (Japan) Vol 1: 37, 157, 395

Defence of the Realm Act (DORA), Vol 2: 197, 227

De Long, Charles Vol 1: 154

De Menil, Henry Vol 2: 88-92, 95, 137, 141, 143

Denby, Charles Vol 2: 116

Denby, Edwin Vol 2: 75-6, 116, 186

Disbarment of lawyers Vol 2: 82, 97, 229-30, 293-4, 302-4, 361

District Attorney, position and role Vol 2: 75, 81, 82

District of Columbia laws, application in US Courts Vol 2: 85, 184, 192, 252, 271 Vol 3: 81-2

Douglas, Archibald (Admiral) Vol 2: 64

Douglas, John

  Barrister Vol 2: 131, 133, 158-60, 188

  Case against former partner Vol 2: 152-156

  Death Vol 2: 196-7

  Registrar Vol 2: 27, 47, 50, 64, 145, 221

Drummond, W Vernon Vol 1: 325, 371-4, 378, 406n, 406, 407-8 Vol 2: 16, 47-8, 153

Dual Nationals See Nationals, Dual

E

Elliot, Charles Vol 1: 24-5

Ellis, Francis Vol 2: 28, 102, 103-4, 135-9, 226

Enemy Nationals Vol 1: 17 Vol 2: 200-203, 210-211 (See also Prize Cases)

Evans, R.T. Vol 3: 94-7, 94i

Extraterritoriality

  Description of Vol 1: 7-8, 12-4, 18

  Diplomatic statements on Vol 1: 21-3, 147-8, 171-2, 223-7, 312, 315 Vol 2: 20-1, 73 Vol 3: 43-47, 51-2, 114, 136-5, 147-8, 185-6

  Judges' personal views of Vol 1: 18, 59, 91, 105-6, 165, 321 Vol 2: 31, 118, 222, 336, 346-7 Vol 3: 138

  Judicial pronouncements on Vol 1: 76, 78-9, 106-7, 169-70, 323, 377 Vol 2: 129, 176, 268-9, 294, 334 Vol 3: 38

  Legacy Vol 3: 196-8

  Political statements on Vol 1: 327-8 Vol 3: 125, 136-7

  Public comments on Vol 1: 204, 320-1, 390-1 Vol 2: 74-5, 232-3, Vol 3: 106, 113-4, 125

  Treaty provision abrogating Vol 1: 329 396-7 Vol 2: 134 Vol 3: 189

  Treaty provisions establishing Vol 1: 22, 26, 29, 34-5, 277-8

Extraterritoriality Commission Vol 2: 249, 305, 323-5, 345

F

Far Eastern Bar Association 185, 238, 245, 263 Vol 3: 80

Faison, P. Vol 2: 353, 356

Feetham, Richard Vol 3: 50i, 50-1, 159

Feetham Report Vol 3: 50-1, 159

Fessenden, Stirling

    Attorney Vol 2: 80i, 81, 82-3, 157, 166, 210, 232, 233i, 234, 235, 237, 238, 280-1

    Biography Vol 3: 200

    Lobingier, Charles, defence of Vol 2: 233, 241, 247

    SMC Chairman/Director-General Vol 2: 263-4 Vol 3: 13, 61, 134-5, 135i

    Speaker/toastmaster Vol 2: 192, 246, 263-4, 266

Fischer, Oscar Vol 2: 231-2, 231i, 276, 321 Vol 3: 16, 68, 68i

Fish, Hamilton Vol 1: 154

Fleming, William

    Attack on Lobingier Vol 2: 230-47, 263

    Attorney Vol 2: 88-89, 141-143, 157, 166, 211, 284, 315, 353-6

Francis, John J. Vol 1: 238-43, 267, 322

Franklin, Cornell

    Attorney: Vol 2: 253-4, 258-264, 353-6, 359 Vol 3: 83-4, 94, 97, 200

    SMC Chairman: Vol 3: 134-5

Fraser, John Vol 1: 66i, 67-8, 73-4, 83, 90

Fraser (Foreign Office) Vol 1: 288n7, 289, 392

Foreign Affairs, Ministry of (China) (See also: Tsungli Yamen) Vol 2: 92, 207-8, 321 Vol 3: 53

Foreign Office (British)

    Amalgamation of Judicial and Consular positions, by Vol 1: 189-91, 304-6, 379-81

    Chief Justice, change in title of, by Vol 2: 46, 48, 49-50

    Colonial Office, Agreements with for sharing judges Vol 2: 27, 179, 343-5

    Consular Officers, appointment of Vol 1: 42, 83-7, 387-8 Vol 3: 37-8

    Courts, Supervision of Vol 1: 15, 104, 111-4, 189-92, 204, 206, 223, 268, 304n2, 353-4, 356 Vol 2: 40, 60 Vol 3: 121-2

    Crown Advocate, Appointment and supervision of Vol 1: 193-4,

256-7, 346-7 Vol 2: 32-3, 41-2, 58-9 Vol 3: 153-5, 187-8

Foreign Office Judicial Service Vol 2: 55, 146, 189, 218, 338

Judges, Appointment and supervision of Vol 1: 47, 51, 58, 66, 178, 212, 256-7, 303, 368, 384, 387 Vol 2: 53-5, 145-6, 147, 189, 216, 218 Vol 3: 74, 181, 187

Orders in Council, drafting: Vol 1 59, 204, 278 Vol 2: 2, 343-4, 49-50

French, George

   Biography Vol 1: 192-3

   Chief Justice Vol 1: 192, 229, 230, 234-7, 237-244 Vol 2: 53

   Sickness and Death Vol 1: 249-252, 252i, 255-6, 364, 412

   Wilkinson, H.S., praise for Vol 1: 215, 218

Fry, Marjorie Vol 3: 151-3

Full Court (Hong Kong) Vol 2: 175, 179-181

Full Court (Shanghai) Vol 2: 59-60, 216, 338, 342-345 Vol 3: 21, 162, 169-72

G

Gambling (in Shanghai) Vol 2: 56, 84-5, 269-271, 270i Vol 3: 67-72

Gaol, Ward Road Vol 3: 12, 106, 119-20, 133-4, 167, 168, 180

Gaols See also Bilibid Prison and McNeil Island Prison

Gaols, Consular: See Consular Jails

Garfield, James Vol 1: 224

Gauss, Clarence Vol 3: 141, 141i

Godfrey, C.W. Vol 2: 102, 111-3, 136

Gollan, Henry Vol 2: 322i, 322-3, 343-5, 344i Vol 3: 22

Gompertz, Henry Vol 2: 187, 198n

Goodwin, Agnes Vol 1: 64, 67, 124-5, 143, 146, 260, 354

Goodwin, Charles W

   Assistant Judge (Shanghai) Vol 1: 67-70, 73, 91, 96-7, 101, 106-7, 118, 129, 134, 138-9, 260

   Assistant Judge (Japan) Vol 1: 130-133, 142-6, 158, 179, 206, 207-8 Vol 2: 218

   Acting Chief Judge Vol 1: 118, 132, 181-2, 206

   Biography Vol 1: 16, 61-67

   Court Building (and consulate fire) Vol 1: 120, 121, 124-5

Death Vol 1: 177, 183-6, 189, 208, 412

Family members Vol 1: 64, 67, 124-5, 143, 146, 184, 260 Vol 2: 51

Judge for Japan, offer of appointment Vol 1: 183

Supreme Court and Consular Gazette Vol 1: 101

Grain, Peter

Biography Vol 2: 218-9

Assistant Judge Vol 2: 118, 276-7, 287-9, 290-3, 293-5, 337, 340, 344i

Full Court, Hong Kong Vol 2: p181n3

Full Court, Shanghai Vol 2: 343-5, 344i Vol 3: 22-3, 22i, 69-71

Jewish, purported to be Vol 2: 219

Judge Vol 2: 346 Vol 3: 12, 21-2, 22i, 61, 62-67, 70-2, 76

Magistrate Vol 2: 313

Kentwell, Lawrence, relationship with Vol 2: 291-2, 295-6, 300, 302-4

Retirement Vol 3: 73-4

Weihaiwei, Judge of Vol 2: 339 Vol 3: 32-3

Grant Jones, Penrhyn

Acting Judge, Weihaiwei Vol 3: 37

Acting Judge, Shanghai: Vol 3: 116-8, 121-2

Assessor, Mixed Court Vol 2: 394

Assistant Judge, Shanghai Vol 2: 181, 302-3 Vol 3: 67, 74, 85, 152-3, 165-6, 170, 173, 175, 187

Biography: Vol 3: 37-42, 200

Consular Officer: Vol 3: 37, 48-9

Full Court, Hong Kong: Vol 2: 181n3

Full Court, Shanghai Vol 3: 162, 171

Sikhs, view of: Vol 3: 40-2, 155

Gregson, R.E., Vol 2: 135-6

Gumpach, Baron von Vol 1: 106-7, 129

H

Habeas Corpus Vol 1: 151, 222, 227 Vol 2: 97, 361 Vol 3: 151-3, 182

Haines, Cyril

Acting Assistant Judge: Vol 3: 118n13

Biography Vol 3: 36, 200-1

Coroner Vol 3: 147-9

Registrar Vol 3: 85, 115, 120, 162, 180, 181, 187

Hall (nee Goodwin), Agnes, see Goodwin, Agnes

Hall, John Carey

Acting Assistant Judge Vol 1: 260-1

Consular Officer Vol 1: 140-1, 142n29, 146, 364

Coroner Vol 1: 345, 349-51, 354-5

Hannen, Nicholas

Biography Vol 1: 93, 134

Acting Asst Judge (Japan) Vol 1: 131-9, 142-4, 153-5, 206, 208, 212

Acting Chief Justice Vol 1: 138-9, 249-51, 257, 258

Arbitrator (Siam) Vol 1: 382-5

Barrister Vol 1: 92, 94-6, 106-7, 161-3, 167-8, 235

Crown Advocate Vol 1: 194, 208, 210, 235, 238

Chief Justice,

- administering courts Vol 1: 304n2, 367, 369, 370, 389

- other mentions Vol 1: 17, 296, 304i, 320, 321n4, 326, 397-8 Vol 2: 51, 164

- sitting as Vol 1: 310-4, 322-4, 374-6, 379 Vol 2: 164

Chief Justice and Consul General, amalgamated role Vol 1: 303-7, 310-1, 314, 330, 379-81

Consul General (Shanghai) Vol 1: 307, 321n4, 325, 330, 332-333, 371-4, 376-9, 379-80

Consul General (Shanghai), other mentions 17, 296

Death Vol 1: 401-11, 412 Vol 2: 31-2

Judge for Japan Vol 1: 255-7, 259, 261, 282, 284-6

Knighthood Vol 1: 326

Shanghai Municipal Council, advisor to Vol 1: 210, 216

Harbin Herald Vol 3: 59

Harding, Warren Vol 2: 242-3, 246

Hardoon, Liza Vol 3: 62-67, 174-5

Hardoon, Silas Vol 3: 63

Harris, M. Reader Vol 2: 313 Vol 3: 17i, 22, 69

Harris, Townsend Vol 1: 34

Hart, Robert Vol 1: 105-7, 129, 237-8, 240, 242, 244-248 Vol 2: 13i

Hayes, Rutherford Vol 1: 222

Hayllar, Francis Vol 1: 234-5, 238-41

Hays, J. Vol 2: 102, 105, 106i, 110, 226

Heath, Neil Vol 2: 352-362

Heen, M.L. Vol 2: 283-7

Helmick, Milton

  Biography Vol 3: 79-82, 202

  Extraterritoriality, views on Vol 1: 18

  Judge, sitting as Vol 3: 80, 81-84, 95-99, 99-102, 134, 139-141, 163-5, 175

  Judge, other mentions Vol 3: 87-90, 138, 179, 190

Hereira (Capt) Vol 1: 152, 155i, 155-6

Hetherington, J.H. Vol 1: 337-34

Hinckley, Frank Vol 2: 79, 104, 115, 205 Vol 3: 84

Hiogo See: Kobe

Holcomb, Chauncy Vol 2: 205-8, 237, 251, 264, 267, 268, 355 Vol 3: 78

Home, Noel Vol 2: 81, 131, 152i, 152-6, 188

Hong Kong

  Cases involving Vol 1: 151, 169-70, 189, 264-5, 309, 317 Vol 2: 328-32

  Cessation of and lease of by China Vol 1: 26, 32, 335 Vol 2: 25 Vol 3: 187

  Companies Vol 1: 104, 106, 108, 113, 114, 212 Vol 3: 192

  Executioners from: Vol 2: 41 Vol 3: 119-120

  Imprisonment in Vol 1: 81, 101-2, 268, 282, 362 Vol 2: 28 Vol 3: 134

  Rule of Law in, comment on Vol 1: 190

  Supreme Court See: Supreme Court, Hong Kong

Hong Kong Chinese See: Nationals, dual

Hornby, Edmund G

  Appointment as Chief Judge Vol 1: 47, 51, 58, 59-60, 66i, 67-71

  Biography Vol 1: 51-8, 93

  Chief Judge Vol 1: 7, 14, 16, 52i, , 56-7, 73, 75-81, 91, 94-7, 106-7, 120, 159-163, 191

  Consular (provincial) courts, supervision of Vol 1: 43-44, 99, 100, 104-105, 129-30, 141-142

  Court Buildings, construction of Vol 1: 111-114, 121-5, 212

  Coolies, on Vol 1: 148-153

  Hart, Robert, on Vol 1: 105-6

  Japan, Reform of British Court system in Vol 1: 129-132, 137-8,

170-1, 177-8, 205-6
Judicial abilities, comments on Vol 1: 55-8, 108-110, 163-4, 179-80
Mixed courts, on Vol 1: 95, 169-172
Paranormal experience Vol 1: 102-4, 178
Shanghai Volunteer Corps Vol 1: 70, 83n1
Supreme Court and Consular Gazette Vol 1: 99-102
Retirement (including discussions of) Vol 1: 108-110, 177-181
Wives Vol 1: 54, 179, 181
Hough, Frank Vol 3: 92, 95-6
Hsu, Showin Wetzen Vol 3: 31, 31i
Hull, Cordell Vol 3: 88-9, 136, 185-6
Hulme, John Vol 1: 46
Husar, Leonard Vol 2: 251-3, 260-1, 266, 269-271, 350i, 351-62,
Vol 3: 169

I

Idzumo HIJMS Vol 3: 131-2, 176
Ingenohl, Carl von Vol 2: 328-336
Ingenohl, Frederich von Vol 2: 330
Ito Hirobumi Vol 1: 36, 328, 331-1, 370 Vol 2: 121-3
Iwakura Mission Vol 1: 147-8, 157
Iwakura Tomomi Vol 1: 147

J

Jacob, Mary Vol 1: 351-6, 362-4
Jails, Chinese Vol 1: 40, 275
Jails, Consular See: Consular jails
Jails, Japanese Vol 1: 141, 395
Jamieson, George
  Acting Asssistant Judge Vol 1: 260, 279
  Acting Judge for Japan Vol 1: 260-1
  Assistant Judge Vol 1: 304i, 310, 316-7, 320, 322-4, 326
  Judge for Japan, application for position Vol 1: 368
  Biography Vol 1: 84, 86-7
  Consul (Shanghai) Vol 1: 304i, 320, 330, 380-1

Consul General (Shanghai) Vol 1: 380, 387

Consular Officer Vol 1: 90

Retirement Vol 1: 370, 381-2, 409

Student Interpreter Vol 1: 87

Jernigan, Thomas Vol 2: 81, 117-8, 166

Johnson, Bertrand Vol 3: 190-2, 210

Johnson, Finley Vol 2: 322i, 322-3

Johnson, Nelson Vol 3: 54, 88-9

Johnson Stokes & Master Vol 1: 322, 371

Jones, Loftus Vol 1: 406n5, Vol 2: 32, 195, 197n

Judd, William Vol 3: 105-116

Judges (British)

   Remuneration Vol 1: 192, 194, 215, 249, 380, 384-5 Vol 2: 59

   Qualifications required Vol 1: 61 Vol 2: 26, 180-1, 343-5

Judges (US)

   Remuneration Vol 3: 78

   Special Vol 2: 184 Vol 3: 168, 190-2

Jury trials (British courts)

   Abolition, proposed Vol 1: 177-8

   Coroner's jury Vol 1: 339, 345

   Criticism of Vol 1: 163, 269, 139-41, 469-70

   Hong Kong, in Vol 1: 45, 151 Vol 2: 174

   Japan, in Vol 1: 138, 182, 196-7, 215

   Jurors, number of Vol 1: 95-6, 364 Vol 2: 135

   Jury duty Vol 2: 58

   Trials, criminal Vol 1: 79-81, 94-5, 104, 118-9, 159-63, 239-43, 267-8, 281-2, 284-5, 316-7, 348-59, 375-6, 386 Vol 2: 16-8, 40-1, 102-14, 135-39, 197, 284-7, 313-5 Vol 3: 12, 105-12, 116-8, 161-2, 170

   Trials, civil: Vol 1: 107, 129, 196-7, 197i Vol 2: 43-4, 131-4, 305-6 Vol 3: 71-2

   Weihaiwei Vol 2: 28 Vol 3: 32-3

Jury trials (United States Courts)

   Coroner's jury Vol 1: 220, 339

   Expressions of desire for Vol 1: 16 Vol 2: 232-3, 264 Vol 3: 95, 100, 102

   Trial without, legality of Vol 1: 16, 219, 221, 227-8 Vol 2: 3, 75-6, 78

Vol 3: 94-5, 98-9, 182

K

Kagoshima Vol 1: 8, 35-6, 361 Vol 3: 148

Kanagawa See: Yokohama

Kearny, Lawrence Vol 2: 251-262, 357, 358

Kellog, Frank Vol 2: 323

Kemp, Joseph Vol 2: 343n7 Vol 3: 70

Kentwell, Lawrence

  Biography Vol 2: 273-6, Vol 3: 201-2

  Civil Actions, personal involvement in Vol 2: 280-1, 277-81, 290-3

  Disbarment 293-5, 302-3

  Grain, Peter, relationship with Vol 2: 291-2, 295-6, 300, 302-4

  Legal Practice Vol 2: 276-7, 287-9, 301

  Imprisonment Vol 3: 201-2

  Nationality Vol 2: 275, 297-9, 300, 355 Vol 3: 201-2

  Opium smuggling, possible involvement Vol 2: 354-5

  Prosecution of Vol 2: 281-7, 296-300 Vol 3: 201-2

Killings, Inter-racial

  British and Americans, of, by Japanese Vol 1: 35-36, 37 Vol 3: 127 (speculation), 146-9

  British, of, by Chinese Vol 1: 31-2, 172-3

  Chinese, of, by British Vol 1:79-81, 91, 94-97, 104, 159-165, 165-168, 237-244, 263-269, 316-7, 374-6 Vol 2: 135-141, 321-323 Vol 3: 105-116, 165-6

  Chinese, of, by Americans Vol 1: 280-2 Vol 2: 88-95, 141-3

  Japanese, of, by British and Americans Vol 1: 283-6, 394-5 Vol 3: 123-5

  Korean, of, by British Vol 1: 386

King, Gilbert W

  Biography Vol 2: 35, 35i, 219-222

  Clerk of Court Vol 2: 35, 35i

  OBE, awarded Vol 2: 337-8

  Registrar Vol 2: 145, 195-6, 201, 220i, 278, 283, 297, 306-11

  Assistant Judge Vol 2: 346, 346i Vol 3: 22, 35-6

King, Harold Vol 2: 35, 221
King, Wunsz Vol 3: 26
Kirkwood, Montague Vol 1: 213, 322
Knatchbull-Hugessen, Hughe Vol 3: 118, 133
Kobe
  Cases in Vol 1: 215, 284
  French, George, death and burial in Vol 1: 249-52, 364
  Hiogo, established in place of Vol 1: 34
  Incidents involving: Vol 1: 37, 140-2, 283-4, 338, 399 Vol 2: 36
Kong Sing Vol 2: 135, 141-3
Korea
  Cases involving Vol 1: 386 Vol 2: 9, 123-34
  Extraterritoriality in Vol 1: 14, 15, 22, 277-8 Vol 2: 3, 76, 134
  Japanese claims to Vol 1: 10, 330, 332 Vol 2: 4, 60-1, 121, 126-7, 134
Kung (Prince) Vol 1: 60, 268-70
Kuomintang (see Nationalist Party)

L

Lampson, Miles Vol 3: 44-5, 47, 53-4, 53i, 118
Land Law Vol 1: 235-236 Vol 2: 29, 160-167, 276-7
Land Regulations (Shameen) Vol 2: 317, 320
Land Regulations (Shanghai) Vol 1: 76-78 Vol 2: 165, 268-9
Law Officers of the Crown Vol 1: 54, 171, 196, 205-6, 223, 268 Vol 2: 37n13
League of Nations Vol 2: 209-10 Vol 3: 57-8, 62
Legal System (Japan)
  Traditional Vol 1: 14
  Reform of Vol 1: 37, 71-2, 147-8, 157, 283, 286-7, 327
Legal System (China)
  Qing Dynasty Vol 1: 14, 171-2 Vol 2: 20-1
  Republican Vol 2: 324 Vol 3: 14-5, 30, 137, 140, 198
  Reform of Vol 1: 71-2 Vol 2: 20-3, 141, 208, 324 Vol 3: 30-1, 43-5, 48
Levinson, William Vol 2: 225-30 Vol 3: 75
Li (Shanghai Magistrate) Vol 2: 88, 92, 137, 139-40, 143
Li Hongzhang Vol 1: 173, 330-3 Vol 2: 11, 14

Lichtfield, Henry Vol 1: 214, 284-5, 339-42, 346i, 348, 356, 399-400

Lin Zexu, Vol 1: 24-5, 27i Vol 3: 224

Lindsell, Roger Vol 2: 343n7

Lipson Ward, H. Vol 2: 293n, 297-8 Vol 3: 75

Lobingier, Charles

  Allegations against Vol 2: 230, 232-3, 236-8, 241-2

  Biography Vol 2: 182-3

  Chinese Government Decoration Vol 2: 246

  Far Eastern Bar Association Vol 2: 238, 245, 264

  Investigation of Vol 2: 242-4

  Judge, sitting as Vol 2: 205-7, 210-2, 234, 244-5, 237-40, 246-7, 252-62, 268, 280-1

  Judge, other mentions Vol 2: 191-2, 241, 244, 245-6 Vol 3: 79

  Reform of US Court for China Vol 2: 4, 183-7

  Retirement: Vol 2: 263-5

Lowder, John Vol 1: 143, 200-1, 204n, 213, 214, 284, 322, 345-64, 399

Lurton, Nelson Vol 3: 168-9, 202

Lu Chiang Hsiang Vol 2: 207

Luna Park Vol 3: 67-72

M

MacDonald, Claude Vol 1: 368

MacGregor, Atholl Vol 2: 343n7 Vol 3: 162, 171-2, 171i, 199, 202-3, 204

MacKellar, Patrick Vol 3: 161n4, 169-72, 536

MacLeod, R.N. Vol 2: 43-5, 284, 313, 313i, 315, 333-6 Vol 3: 17i

MacMurray, John Vol 3: 27

Macnaghten, Ernest Vol 3: 69-71

Maitland, E.T Vol 2: 297, 298i, 301, 309-10, 321n18 Vol 3: 15-6, 16i

Manchuria/Manchukuo

  Extraterritoriality in Vol 3: 58-60, 127-9, 155

  Japanese occupation Vol 1: 330, 332 Vol 2: 5, 61-4, 200 Vol 3: 48-9, 52, 57-8, 88, 123, 127-9

  Russian occupation Vol 1: 334 Vol 2: 15, 23, 60-1

Mandate Abrogating System of Consular Jurisdiction (Chinese)

Vol 3: 45-8

Mansfield, Robert Vol 1: 270

Maria Luz Vol 1: 137-8, 148-57

Martin, A.J. Vol 2: 284 Vol 3: 36

Master, A.P. Vol 1: 322

Master, R.F.C. Vol 2: 313

Mau Te-piau Vol 3: 106-13

McCord, United States v (McCord case) Vol 2: 82-6, 104, 107, 109, 111-2, 114

McDonald, Ranald Vol 2: 280 Vol 3: 22, 40-1, 108-15

McNeil Island Prison Vol 2: 350-1, 359-60, 361 Vol 3: 98-9, 165, 167, 169, 182

McNeill, Duncan Vol 1: 406n, Vol 2: 33, 42-6, 43i, 48, 148, 333, 339-40 Vol 3: 157

McNeill, John
  Barrister Vol 2: 340 Vol 3: 106, 109, 115, 148
  Biography Vol 3: 156-7, 203
  Crown Advocate Vol 2: 33 Vol 3: 156, 159, 160n2, 161, 170, 187-8

Mei, Hua-chuen Vol 2: 205-7, 280-1, 321n18 Vol 3: 80

Meiji Restoration Vol 1: 36

Miller, Robert Vol 1: 394-5, 395i

Missionaries Vol 1: 4, 14, 28, 42, 86, 89, 229-236, 309 Vol 2: 33, 204, 359

Mixed court (ad hoc) Vol 1: 166, 169-171

Mixed Court (French) Vol 2: 327

Mixed Court (International)
  Assessors Vol 1: 174, 371, 378, 382, 389 Vol 2: 65i, 67i, 247n Vol 3: 199
  Cases in Vol 1: 382, 389 Vol 2: 38n15, 65-6, 67i, 166-7, 231, 250, 276, 278-9, 284-6, 312-6, 321, 327 Vol 3: 37-9
  Constitution Vol 1: 173-5 Vol 2: 177, 322-3
  Disputes with foreign powers Vol 2: 64-68, 322-3
  Magistrates Vol 1: 97, 154-5, 155i, 378 Vol 2: 66, 67i
  Mock up of Vol 3: 223
  Municipal Council (Shanghai), and Vol 2: 65-6, 177, 322-3
  Rendition Vol 2: 299, 300, 323 Vol 3: 14i, 15-6, 27, 30

Morris, Idwal Vol 3: 36, 187
Mossop, Allan
  Barrister Vol 2: 188, 196-7
  Biography Vol 2: 188, 341-2 Vol 3: 203-4
  Crown Advocate (China) Vol 2: 293, 303, 341-2, 343 Vol 3: 12, 76
  Crown Advocate (China), acting Vol 2: 214-6, 225, 280
  Crown Advocate (Weihaiwei) Vol 2: 188 Vol 3: 32
  Custodian of Enemy Property Vol 2: 201
  Executor of HP Wilkinson's will Vol 3: 85
  Full Court, Hong Kong Vol 2: 181n3
  Full Court, Shanghai Vol 3: 70, 162, 171
  Judge, sitting as Vol 3: 81, 84-5, 105-114, 144, 152, 161-2, 173-4
  Judge, other mentions Vol 3: 35, 74-6, 121n19, 126-7, 129, 159, 173,
  181, 187
  Legal Counselor to British Embassy Vol 3: 203-4, 205
  Priestwood, Victor, relationship with Vol 3: 32, 75, 154
  Report on Japanese take over of court Vol 3: 177, 180
  Retirement: Vol 3: 203-4
Mowat, Robert
  Acting Assistant Judge (Japan), not considered suitable Vol 1: 131
  Acting Chief Justice Vol 1: 249, 257, 260, 307
  Acting Consul General (Shanghai) Vol 1: 307-10, 314
  Assistant Judge (Shanghai) Vol 1: 138, 193, 193i, 215, 258, 274-5
  Biography Vol 1: 83-4, 86, 87-8, 357-8
  Bourne, Frederick, views on appointment as Chief Justice Vol 2:
  53
  Deputy Chief Judge Vol 1: 181
  Japan, strict enforcement of treaties against Vol 1: 320-1
  Judge for Japan Vol 1: 208, 255, 303, 319-321, 321-3, 325, 345-62
  Law Secretary Vol 1: 90-91, 92, 94, 97, 118, 124-5, 161, 183
  Police Magistrate Vol 1: 166-8, 246-8, 295
  Retirement and death Vol 1: 367-70, Vol 2: 343
  Student Interpreter Vol 1: 87-8
Myburgh (Alexander or Philip) Vol 1: 217
Myburgh, Philip, Vol 1: 73, 80

N

Nagasaki
Dutch Factory Vol 1: 32-3
Incidents involving Vol 1: 70-1, 325, 367-8, 396
Nanking (Nanjing) Vol 1: 25-7 Vol 2: 171 Vol 3: 10, 47, 54, 57n1,
74, 133, 136
Nationalist Party (Kuomingtang)
Republican Revolution Vol 2: 171-3, 276
Canton, governments in Vol 2: 5, 173, 249, 296, 316, 318
Divisions Vol 3: 52-3, 149
Government, National Vol 2: 5 Vol 3: 14, 24, 43, 49, 51, 57, 60-1,
136, 140, 145, 151, 176n17
Northern Expedition Vol 2: 358 Vol 3: 9-11, 13, 61, 74
Recognition in British and American courts Vol 3: 17-21, 21-24
Nationals, Dual
• British Vol 3: 29-30, 84-5
• American Vol 3: 24-29, 84-5
Nationals, Enemy see Enemy Nationals
Nationality of corporations Vol 2: 318-20
Nelson, E. Vol 1: 371
Nelson, H.G. Vol 3: 164-5
Newman, K.E. Vol 2: 285 Vol 3: 162
Ninth Circuit, United States Court of Appeals See Appeals, US
Court for China, from
Niigata Vol 1: 182, 204, 211, 218
Normanton case Vol 1: 283-6

O

O'Malley, Edward Vol 1: 238
O'Shea, Henry Vol 2: 12-13, 15-20, 98-99, 101-114, 106i, 135, 139, 145
Obama, Barack Vol 2: 274
Oe Taku Vol 1: 154-6
Okuma (Count) Vol 1: 287, 334
Oppe, Henry Vol 2: 153, 197n4
Order in Council, 1865 Vol 1: 60-1, 95, 106, 132, 136

Order in Council, 1878 Vol 1: 193, 207
Order in Council, 1884 Vol 1: 277-9
Order in Council, 1904 Vol 2: 46, 59-60, 135, 155, 159-60, 174, 215
Order in Council, 1907 (Bethell Clause) Vol 2: 123-4, 128
Order in Council, 1919 (Management of British Companies) Vol 2: 212 Vol 3: 138
Order in Council, 1920 (Publication of seditious materials) Vol 2: 305
Order in Council, 1925 Vol 2: 342-3

P

Page, Edward Vol 1: 237-244
Page, William Vol 1: 245-7
Parkes, Harry
   British Minister in China Vol 1: 259, 266, 269
   British Minister in Japan Vol 1: 37, 89-90, 142, 143, 147, 158, 178, 203i, 205i, 215, 291
   Consular officer Vol 1: 28, 31-2, 42
Pauncefote, Julian
   Attorney-General of Hong Kong Vol 1: 151, 178
   Foreign Office Vol 1: 189-194, 190i, 204-6, 268, 303-4, 307
Peking (Beijing)
   Attacks on Vol 1: 8, 25, 30-2 Vol 2: 9-14, 33 Vol 3: 123
   British Ministers quarters: Vol 2: 42
   Cases in Vol 3: 123-7
Peking Post Vol 2: 203-8
Penfold, Frederick Vol 2: 39-41
Penniston, John Vol 3: 77-8
Perjury, by British in foreign courts Vol 2: 157-160
Perry, Matthew Vol 1: 8, 33i, 33-4
Peterel H.M.S. Vol 3: 176
Peters, Ernest Vol 3: 105-26
Phillips, Herbert Vol 3: 153-5
Piggott, Francis Vol 2: 179, 181
Piper, Kenneth Vol 3: 141-4

Platt, W.C. Vol 1: 406n, Vol 2: 33-4, 47-8, 59, 182

Potter, Eldon Vol 2: 318-320, 320i Vol 3: 65

Pottinger, Henry Vol 1: 8, 25, 27i, 42

Practitioners, Legal (British)(See also: Barristers, Solicitors)

 Attendance at ceremonies Vol 1: 143, 399, 406n5 Vol 2: 50, 196

 War Memorial to Vol 2: 197

Priestwood, Gwen Vol 3: 75, 156, 199, 204

Priestwood, John Vol 2: 226 Vol 3: 75

Priestwood, Victor

 Barrister Vol 2: 318 Vol 3: 32, 85

 Biography Vol 3: 75, 204

 Crown Advocate Vol 3: 85, 106, 109-11, 115, 116, 124, 145

 Termination Vol 3: 153-6

Prison, Bilibid Vol 2: 185, 245

Prison, McNeil Island Vol 2: 350-1, 359-60, 361 Vol 3: 98-9, 165, 167, 169, 182

Prisons See: Jails, Consular and Gaol, Ward Road

Privy Council

 Appeals to, civil (from China) Vol 1: 74, 107, 274-5, 322-4 Vol 2: 295, 335-6 Vol 3: 23

 Appeals to, criminal (from China) Vol 1: 237, 247-8 Vol 2: 156

 Appeals to, criminal (from Hong Kong) Vol 1: 151n Vol 2: 174-5

 Appeals to, civil (from Japan) Vol 1: 204-7

 Appeals to, criminal (from Japan) Vol 1: 364

 Decisions of, relied upon Vol 2: 164-5, 293-4 Vol 3: 66

 Jurisdiction Vol 1: 135-7, 191, Vol 2: 26, 59-60, 179, 322-4

Prize cases, WWI Vol 2: 198-200

Protests, formal

 Chinese, by Vol 1: 268, 312 Vol 2: 92-3, 141, 143 Vol 3: 113 (lack of), 151

 Japanese, by Vol 1: 204

 British, by Vol 1: 377-9, 408 Vol 3: 17 (lack of), 29 (not made), 59, 128

Provincial Courts (see Consular Courts, British)

Provisional Court (Shanghai) Vol 3: 15-17, 16i, 25-6, 28, 30-1, 68

Pu, Keng-lung Vol 2: 88-91
Purdy, Milton
    Biography Vol 2: 265-6
    Cases, criminal Vol 2: 268-70, 349-51, 352-62
    Cases, civil Vol 2: 211, 268 Vol 3: 19, 20, 77-8, 82-3
    Judge Vol 2: 265-71, 350i Vol 3: 24, 76-7, 78-9
    Lobingier, Charles, on Vol 2: 265
Plunkett, Francis Vol 1: 286

Q
Qingdao – See Tsingtao

R
Raven, Frank Vol 2: 211-2 Vol 3: 90-99, 105, 113
Rees-Davies, William Vol 2: 175, 181, 198n, 199, 331-2, 335-6 Vol 3: 210
Reeks, Hugh Vol 3: 108-112, 115, 116-20, 151, 170
Reid, Gilbert Vol 2: 203-208, 280
Reinsch, Paul Vol 2: 191, 204-7
Rennie, Richard
    Biography Vol 1: 92-3, 208-9
    Barrister Vol 1: 92, 94-6, 106, 167-8, 183
    Chief Justice Vol 1: 255, 256i, 257, 258-60, 266-8, 274-5, 279-82, 291-
    2 Vol 2: 51, 215
    Judge for Japan Vol 1: 208, 210-5, 225i,
    Retirement and death Vol 1: 296-299
    Shanghai Municipal Council, advisor to Vol 1: 208-210, 218
Republican Revolution (China) Vol 2: 171-7, 260 Vol 3: 197
Rights of Audience, lawyers
    In non-national court Vol 1: 399-400 Vol 2: 80, 302, 313 Vol 3: 16, 17i
    Solicitors, in British courts Vol 1: 73-4 Vol 2: 154-5
Riots, anti-foreign
    Canton Vol 1: 46, 263-9, 265i Vol 2: 318
    Chungking Vol 1: 230
    Foochow Vol 1: 230, 233,
    Missionary, anti Vol 1: 230, 233, 307-8, 313

Shanghai Vol 2: 64-8, 321-3 Vol 3: 15
  Yangtse Valley Vol 1: 307-8, 313
Robertson, Russell Vol 1: 89, 142, 143, 212, 215, 257, 257i, 258-9
Robinson, Alfred Vol 2: 284-5, 285i
Robinson, F. Alan Vol 2: 586
Robinson, Gower Vol 1: 337-44
Rockhill, W.W. Vol 2: 92-5, 94i
Rodger, Hewitt Douglas (H.D.) Vol 2: 234-9, 247 Vol 3: 18-20,
24-5, 88-9
Roosevelt, Franklin D Vol 3: 77, 103, 168, 528, 191
Roosevelt, Theodore Vol 2: 63, 73, 76, 97, 114-6, 117, 192, 275
Ross, John Vol 1: 45, 219-228
Ross, United States v and Ross v McIntyre (Ross Case) Vol 1:
219-228, 279 Vol 2: 3, 254, 360 Vol 3: 94, 98, 182
Russo-Japanese War Vol 2: 60-4, 61i

S
Samuel, H.B. Vol 3: 64i, 65
Sassoon, David, & Co Vol 1: 273-5 Vol 3: 63
Satow, Ernest
  Student interpreter Vol 1: 89
  Consular Officer in Japan Vol 1: 37, 43, 142
  British Minister in Japan Vol 1: 334, 346-7, 353, 356-7, 359, 361-2,
  367-9, 396-8
  British Minister in China Vol 1: 409 Vol 2: 14, 37i, 41, 59, 64n15,
  68-70
  Japanese common law wife Vol 1: 90n16
  Retirement Vol 1: 370 Vol 2: 51-2
  Wilkinson, H.P., relationship with Vol 2: 32-3, 37-8, 53, 338
  Wilkinson, H.S., relationship with Vol 1: 346-7, 353, 356-7, 368-9,
  397-8 Vol 2: 32-3, 35-8, 42, 51-2, 53
Sausmarez, Havilland de
  Biography Vol 2: 53-9, 54i, 191-3
  Judge Vol 2: 56i, 58-60, 145, 148-52, 150i, 152-6, 174, 191, 196-8,
  201-3, 220

Hong Kong Full Court Vol 2: 181

Retirement (actual and possible) Vol 2: 146-8, 213-5

Extraterritoriality, views on Vol 2: 222

Schuffenhauer, August Vol 1: 293-5

Schul, Ferno Vol 2: 235-7, 236i, 247, 280 Vol 3: 68, 68i

Scidmore, George Vol 2: 353-5, 399

Secretary of State (US) Vol 1: 22, 154, 224-7 Vol 2: 73-4, 86, 93, 97-8, 191, 323 Vol 3: 26-8, 88, 185-6

Secretary of State for Foreign Affairs (UK) Vol 1: 158, 224, 308n9, 367 Vol 2: 50, 60, 130 Vol 3: 49-54, 60, 62, 136-7, 177, 185-7

Sedition Vol 2: 5, 9, 123-9, 204-7, 305, 306-10 Vol 3: 11

Sellett, Thomas

    Biography Vol 2: 352

    Attorney: Vol 3 92-7

    District Attorney: Vol 2: 353-359 Vol 3: 26, 28, 80, 81

Seward, George Vol 1: 44-5, 78-9, 171

Seymour, Horace Vol 3: 188

Shanghai International Settlement

    Bye-laws, application outside Vol 3: 70, 107-8, 141-2

    Constitution of Vol 1: 76-9

    Laws, application within Vol 2: 215, 268-9, 308 Vol 3: 25-9, 29, 51

    Military threats to

        • Chinese Vol 1: 10-11, Vol 3: 9-11, 13, 61-2, 131-5, 132i

        • Japanese Vol 1: 128 Vol 3: 61-2, 131-5, 132i, 135i, 160, 175-9

Shanghai Mercury Vol 2: 17, 32n3, 89-90, 107

Shanghai Municipal Council

    Chairmen, statements by or actions of Vol 1: 183, 296-7, 380-1 Vol 2: 45-6, 263-4 Vol 3: 13, 134-5

    Extraterritoriality, Feetham Report on Vol 3: 50-1

    International Settlement, management of: Vol 1: 76-9, 108, 114n, 208-10, 215-7, 305, 308 Vol 2: 47 Vol 3: 134-5, 159-60

    Mixed Court Vol 2: 65-6, 177, 322-3

    Jury duty, obligations for members of Vol 2: 58

    Legal actions, against Vol 1: 12 Vol 3: 67-72, 159-60

    Legal actions, by Vol 1: 76-9, 76n7, 215-8 Vol 2: 298-300 Vol 3: 16-7

Special District Court, and Vol 3: 30-1

Supervision of Municipal Police Vol 1: 295 Vol 2: 65, 315 Vol 3: 30, 134

Shanghai Municipal Police

Arrests by Vol 2: 281, 297, 307 Vol 3: 25-6

Evidence in court by officers Vol 1: 217 Vol 2: 142, 285, 307, 355 Vol 3: 105-16, 117

Legal actions by Vol 1: 215-7, 292-5 Vol 3: 16-7, 134

Legal actions against officers Vol 1: 292, 295 Vol 3: 105-16, 116-22

Mixed Court Vol 2: 65-6

Police work Vol 1: 119, 216 Vol 3: 67-9, 133, 135-6

Riots, involvement in Vol 2: 65-66, 321-3

Sikh officers Vol 2: 148-152, 150i Vol 3: 11-3, 116-22

Shekury, Gabriel Vol 2: 157-60

Shields, Leighton Vol 3: 103, 133, 165, 168, 204

Shimonoseki Vol 1: 36, 331, 361

Siam, British Court for See: British Court for Siam

Sieh Taijen Vol 1: 312-6

Sikhs, issues with Vol 2: 148-152, 197, 306-11 Vol 3: 11-3

Simpson, Lenox Vol 3: 59-60

Singh, Atma Vol 3: 116-22, 134

Singh, Budda Vol 2: 305-6, 308 Vol 3: 11-3, 11i

Singh, Har Charan Vol 2: 305-6

Singh, Harbak Vol 2: 306-11

Singh, Harbant Vol 3: 11-2

Smale, John Vol 1: 151, 151i

Smith, Lindsey Vol 2: 145-6

Soejima, Taneomi Vol 1: 153, 154

Solicitors

Rights of audience: Vol 1: 73-4 Vol 2: 154-5

Soong, T.V. Vol 3: 21, 188, 189n9

Stark, George (Admiral) Vol 2: 252n, 255-62

State Department (US) Vol 1: 15, 151-2, 227, 384 Vol 2: 75, 77, 93, 114, 211, 233 Vol 3: 29, 76-7, 81, 88, 177, 185

Strawn, Silas Vol 2: 323

Student Interpreter Vol 1: 87-90, 140, 291, 387
Suga, Kitaro Vol 2: 322i, 322-3
Sun Yat-sen Vol 2: 171, 318, 365, 387
Supreme Court, Chinese Vol 3: 15, 30
Supreme Court, Hong Kong
    Cases in Vol 1: 151, 370 Vol 2: 174-6, 199-200, 331-2
    Judges or other staff of Vol 1: 42, 189, 267 Vol 2: 179, 181, 343n7,
    Vol 3: 118n13
    Jurisdiction of Vol 1: 45-7 Vol 2: 26-7, 174
    Full Court (Hong Kong) Vol 2: 179-81
    Full Court (Shanghai) Vol 2: 343-5
Supreme Court, United States
    Appeals to Vol 1: 227-8 Vol 2: 244-5, 332 Vol 3: 84
    Building Vol 1: 111
    Cases mentioned: Vol 1: 150 Vol 2: 240, 254
    Ross case, decision in Vol 1: 16, 222, 227-8, 279 Vol 2: 3, 254, 360
    Vol 3: 94, 98, 182
Supreme Court and Consular Gazette (including as part of
North China Herald) Vol 1: 99-102 Vol 3: 76

T

Taft, William Vol 2: 76, 86-7, 117, 143, 192, 246
Taotai (Canton) Vol 1: 267
Taotai (Foochow) Vol 1: 169
Taotai (Shanghai) Vol 1: 77, 165, 311, 313, 314 Vol 2: 88, 92, 139,
141, 162-3, 166, 167
Terashima (Count) Vol 1: 147
Thayer, Rufus
    Biography Vol 2: 117
    Judge Vol 1: 128 Vol 2: 117-8, 141-3, 157-8, 165-7, 176, 192
    Resignation 181-2
Thriftcor Bank Vol 3: 87-90
Tilotson, W.D. Vol 1: 339-434
Ting Jih Chang Vol 1: 234
Tinkler, R. Maurice Vol 2: 250, 281-2, 285, 307, 354-5, 355i Vol 3:

146-9

Tison, Alexander Vol 1: 339-342

Titlebaum, Sam Vol 3: 167-9

Treaty of Amity and Commerce (US-Japan) Vol 1: 8, 34-5, 225-6

Treaty of Amity and Commerce (Britain-Japan) Vol 1: 8, 9, 34-5, 147, 199-206

Treaty of Annexation (Japan-Korea) Vol 2: 134

Treaty of Bogue Vol 1: 26

Treaty of Commerce (US-China, 1929) Vol 3: 19

Treaty of Commerce (US-Korea) Vol 1: 277

Treaty of Commerce and Navigation (Britain-Japan) Vol 1: 328-9, 369, 396-7

Treaty of Commerce and Navigation (US-Japan) Vol 1: 329, 394

Treaty of Commercial Relations and Judicial Procedure (US-China) Vol 1: 174-5

Treaty of Friendship and Commerce (Britain-Korea) Vol 1: 277

Treaty of Nanking Vol 1: 10, 25-7 Vol 2: 222

Treaty of Shimonoseki, Vol 1: 327, 330-333 Vol 2: 60

Treaty of Tientsin (Britain/US-China) Vol 1: 29-34, 169-70, 239 Vol 2: 252, 323

Treaty of Versailles Vol 2: 208-10, 249, 303

Treaty of Wanghsia Vol 1: 21-23, 26, 29 Vol 2: 252

Treaty for the Relinquishment of Extra-Territorial Rights (Britain/US-China) Vol 3: 53-4 (drafts), 185-90

Treaty, Commercial (Britain-China) Vol 2: 21

Treaty, Peace (Russia-Japan) Vol 2: 63-4

Tri-Partite Intervention Vol 2: 333-4

Troup, James Vol 1: 182, 339, 345, 352, 354

Tsai Chun Vol 1: 371-9

Tsingtao (Qingdao) Vol 1: 334 Vol 2: 198-200 Vol 3: 144

Tsungli Yamen (Zongli Yamen) Vol 1: 28, 106, 172, 233, 244, 247, 268, 333

Turner, Skinner

　Biography Vol 2: 189-91

　Assistant Judge Vol 2: 189, 338-9

Extraterritoriality, views on: Vol 2: 346-7

Extraterritoriality Commission: Vol 2: 323, 345

Hong Kong Full Court Vol 2: 181

Judge

- Civil cases Vol 2: 279-80, 287-9, 306, 318-20, 327-36
- Criminal cases Vol 2: 284-7, 313-5
- Other mentions Vol 2: 276, 293, 311, 337-8, 339
- Special hearings Vol 2: 216-8, 225-6, 229

Shanghai Full Court: Vol 2: 343-5 Vol 3: 70

Retirement: Vol 2: 345-7

Twyman, B Vol 2: 65i, 65-6

Tyler, John Vol 1: 22

U

Ueno Kagenori Vol 1: 204

United States Court for China

Act establishing Vol 2: 75-6, 93-5 Vol 3: 192

Appeals from See: Appeals

Closing Vol 2: Vol 3: 177-9, 188-92

Establishment Vol 2: 4, 73-6, 77-8

Jurisdiction

- Companies, over Vol 2: 108, 185-7 Vol 3: 88-9, 140-1
- Consular courts, compared to Vol 2: 86, 240
- Difficulties in exercise of Vol 2: 118, 237
- Foreign nationals, right to bring action: Vol 2: 210-1 Vol 3: 140-1
- Geographic Vol 2: 121 Vol 3: 33
- Individuals, over Vol 2: 166-7, 360 Vol 3: 24-9, 169
- Treaties, enforcement of Vol 2: 253-5

Premises Vol 2: 116, 185, 436

V

Vincent, Arthur Vol 1: 117i Vol 2: 145-6

W

Wade, Thomas

  British Minister Vol 1: 159, 163-4, 166, 172-4, 234, 237-8

  Chinese Linguist Vol 1: 42, 87-8

Wainewright, R.E. Vol 1: 169, 248, 259, 274

Wake, U.S.S. Vol 3: 176

Wallis, Frank Vol 2: 317-20

Walsham, John Vol 1: 306

Wang, C.T. Vol 3: 43-4, 44i, 46-7, 53-4

Wang, Ch'ung-hui, Vol 2: 32

Wang Ching-wei Vol 3: 52, 149

Ward, John Vol 1: 30-1

Ward Road Gaol Vol 3: 12, 105, 119-20 133-4, 167, 168, 180

Warren, Pelham Vol 2: 17-8, 116, 136n, 141, 147

Washington Conference Vol 2: 249

Watson, Felthan Vol 3: 81, 92-7, 99-101, 103

Wei, Tao-ming Vol 3: 188

Weihaiwei Vol 1: 332, 335; Vol 2: 23-5, 24i, 64, 198-9 Vol 3: 31-3

Weihaiwei, High Court of, Vol 2: 23-9, 145, 187-8, 199, 216, 338, 339, 346 Vol 3: 32-4, 37

Werner, Pamela Vol 3: 126-7

Wheeler, Edwin Vol 1: 196, 339, 345, 350i, 354, 359, 364

Wilfley, Lebbeus

  Allegations against: Vol 2: 97, 98-9

  Biography: Vol 2: 77, 79i, 116

  Defamation action against Henry O'Shea Vol 2: 101-114, 102i, 106i, 135

  Examination for attorneys Vol 2: 79-82, 80i

  Judge, sitting as Vol 2: 78-86, 88-92, 115

  Judge, other mentions Vol 2: 76-8, 115-6, 192 (lack of)

  Illustrations of Vol 2: 79i, 80i, 87i, 101i, 102i

  Investigation of Vol 2: 99-101, 101i

  Washington, support from Vol 2: 86-88, 97-8, 114-5 (lack of)

Wilkinson, Hiram P (Harrie)

  Acting Chief Justice Vol 1: 385-6

Acting Assistant Judge (Shanghai) Vol 1: 386

Acting Assistant Judge (Siam) Vol 1 37-8, 49, 189

Barrister Vol 1: 292-5, 316-7, 322, 347, 371-2, 374-6, 389n32 Vol 2:
59-60, 195, 318-9 Vol 3: 64i, 64-7

Biography Vol 1: 89-90, 291-2, 295-6

Bravery award Vol 1: 325-6

Chief Judge, desire for promotion to Vol 2: 53, 146-7, 213, 215-6
Vol 3: 74

Claims Commissioner Vol 2: 33-5, 66-8

Crown Advocate (China)

 - Advising as Vol 2: 154, 200-1, 220

 - Appearance in court as (general applications) Vol 1: 406-7 Vol 2:
 196-7, 213, 288-9

 - Appointment as Vol 1: 325 (acting), 369-70 Vol 2: 33

 - Organisation of practice Vol 2: 188, 431

 - Prosecuting as Vol 2: 58-9, 102-114, 106i, 125-8, 135-9, 158-60, 273,
 281-7, 313-5

Crown Advocate (Weihaiwei) Vol 1: 27-8

Judge, Weihaiwei Vol 1: 187 (acting), 188

King's Counsel Vol 2: 220

Marriages Vol 1: 296, 406 Vol 2: 147, 195

Pidgin English, mastery of Vol 2: 138

Retirement and death Vol 2: 338-9 Vol 3: 85-6

Wilkinson, Hiram S, relationship with Vol 1: 295-6, 319-20, 385,
399 Vol 2: 32-3, 37-8, 41-2, 51, 53, 105, 146-7, 314

Wilkinson, Hiram S

 Acting Law Secretary Vol 1: 182, 195-207, 201i, 203i, 205i, 208, 210,
 211i

 Acting Assistant Judge (Japan) Vol 1: 212, 214

 Acting Assistant Judge (China) Vol 1: 215-8

 Barrister Vol 1: 258-9, 274-5, 292-3, 322

 Biography Vol 1: 83-6

 Claims Commissioner (Canton) Vol 1: 269-72

 Crown Advocate Vol 1: 256-7, 263, 266-7, 278, 279-82, 310-5, 332-3,
 346-61

Chief Justice Vol 1: 406 Vol 2: 4, 31-52

Consular Officer Vol 1: 90, 140-2, 143, 157-8, 178, 182, 211

Judge for Japan Vol 1: 324-6 (acting), 369, 385, 397-400

Judicial appointments, desire for Vol 1: 208, 255-6, 259, 319-20, 368

Knighthood Vol 2: 136

Parkes, Harry, relationship with Vol 1: 157-8, 178, 259

Retirement and death Vol 2: 41-2, 46-9, 51, 339, 343-4

Satow, Ernest, relationship with Vol 1: 347, 353-4, 357, 368-9, 398
Vol 2: 35-7, 42, 52

Student Interpreter Vol 1: 88-90

Wilkinson, Hiram P, relationship with Vol 1: 295-6, 385 Vol 2: 32-3,
37-8, 41-2, 51, 53, 105, 146-7, 314

Wilkinson, W.H. Vol 1: 87, 317

Wilson, Woodrow Vol 2: 204-6, 209

Wing, Tyco Vol 2: 288, 293-5

Wolfe, John Vol 1: 231-5

Wood, John Vol 2: 343n7 Vol 3: 118n13

Woodward, Tracy Vol 2: 351-360

Woosong Railway case Vol 1: 166-8

Wright, G.H. Vol 2: 85, 148, 421

Wushishan Case Vol 1: 231-237

Y

Yang Ki-Tak Vol 2: 127-8, 132

Yokohama

Cases in Vol 1: 142, 145, 148-57, 219-22, 337-44, 344-60, 394-5

Courts, location of principal British Vol 1: 129-33, 137-8, 143-4, 181,
205-6, 207 Vol 2: 32

Kanagawa, established in place of Vol 1: 34

Incidents involving: Vol 1: 35-6, 283 Vol 2: 241, 244

Mowat, Robert, life in Vol 1: 319-21

Young, John Russell Vol 1: 268-9

Yuan Shikai Vol 2: 11, 18, 68-70, 69i, 171-3, 172i, 200, 276

Z

Ziar, Y.S. Vol 2: 313 Vol 3: 15-7, 15i
Zongli Yamen See: Tsungli Yamen
Zung Zu-fung Vol 2: 135-141